This book brings together a selection of chapters from Volume 5 of *The Cambridge History of Japan*. Japan underwent momentous changes during the middle decades of the nineteenth century. Feudal divisions under military rulers that had characterized Japan for many centuries were replaced by a central government headed by the traditional monarch, and long-standing social and political divisions were abandoned in order to build a modern nation state. These chapters chronicle the crop failures and famine of the Tempō era in the 1830s, the crisis of values and confidence that popular culture displayed in the last half century of Tokugawa rule, and the political process that finally brought down the Tokugawa regime and ended centuries of warrior rule. They go on to discuss the peasant and samurai rebellions against the Meiji government, and the broader movement of the 1880s called "Freedom and People's Rights" that helped to push the government toward a grant of representative government with the Meiji Constitution of 1889. The significance of Japan's Meiji transformation for the rest of the world is the subject of the final chapter, in which Professor Akira Iriye discusses Japan's drive to great-power status. "Constitutional rule at home, imperialism abroad" became linked as goals for early twentieth-century Japan.

The emergence of Meiji Japan

THE EMERGENCE OF MEIJI JAPAN

Edited by
MARIUS B. JANSEN
Princeton University

PUBLISHED BY THE PRESS SYNDICATE OF THE UNIVERSITY OF CAMBRIDGE
The Pitt Building, Trumpington Street, Cambridge CB2 1RP, United Kingdom

CAMBRIDGE UNIVERSITY PRESS
The Edinburgh Building, Cambridge CB2 2RU, United Kingdom
40 West 20th Street, New York, NY 10011-4211, USA
10 Stamford Road, Oakleigh, Melbourne 3166, Australia

First published 1995
Reprinted 1997

Printed in the United States of America

Typeset in Plantin

A catalogue record for this book is available from the British Library

Library of Congress Cataloguing-in-Publication Data is available

ISBN 0-521-48238-0 hardback
ISBN 0-521-48405-7 paperback

CONTENTS

PREFACE

In the middle decades of the nineteenth century Japan was obliged to abandon institutions it had adopted in the early seventeenth century for the regulation of society, politics, and foreign policy. Where once a hereditary samurai class had ruled, supported by stipends provided by feudal lords subordinate to the Tokugawa shogun, a new government headed by the traditional monarchy evened out, and then abandoned, those social divisions. Several hundred mini-states ruled by the daimyo gave way to fifty prefectures governed from the center by state-appointed governors. Contacts with other countries once limited almost entirely to traders at Nagasaki were broadened, initially to a few treaty ports, and then everywhere, as Japan took part in the international order.

These were momentous changes. When they began Japan was a remote and inaccessible island state on the edge of Asia. After they were completed Japan had won membership in the circle of powers and joined its recent oppressors as an imperialist state in Asia. Domestic institutional changes, first begun as defensive moves to maintain national sovereignty, led inexorably to other steps that ended by transforming first Japan and then the Asian and world systems.

The chapters that follow, excerpted from Volume 5 of *The Cambridge History of Japan,* discuss some of these changes to show the nature of Japan's transformation and to show that these changes had their origins in earlier Japanese society. The Tokugawa society that Commodore Perry encountered had undergone very great changes since the establishment of the shogunate in the early seventeenth century. Two and one-half centuries of peace had built a sense of autonomy and national consciousness among samurai retainers in many of the great domains ruled by "outside" (tozama) lords that the Tokugawa founders had left in place. The system of alternate attendance (*sankin-kōtai*) duty at Edo (modern Tokyo) that the Tokugawa bakufu had imposed on all its vassal lords had transformed the upper reaches of samurai society and made it an urban aristocracy. Intermarriage and adoption now linked many of the daimyo, and ceremonial duties, education, and artistic and intellectual pursuits had pacified and demilitarized them. Their retainers had become accustomed to service in bureaucratic governments. Patterns of internal trade and commerce that had developed in response to the needs of the great metropolis of Edo, which was probably the world's most populous city with upwards of a million inhabitants, had the effect of making economic zones out of what began as discrete feudal principalities. A lively popular culture of print and theater gave evidence of the spread of literacy throughout society. The early decades of the nineteenth century saw a particular flowering of popular fiction, which ranged from sober romances that owed much to Chinese models to scabrous tales popular among the denizens of the cities' crowded alleys.

The disjuncture between this kaleidoscopic urban scene of profits, coins, and goods and the complaisant countryside, with its natural economy of food and taxes in kind with which the regime began, was so striking that many writers struggled to explain it. Political moralists of the seventeenth century extolled the virtues of submission and cooperation. Their successors in the eighteenth century struggled to reconcile that idealized past with the complexity of the society they knew, and wondered what had gone wrong. The remedies they proposed ranged widely: returning the samurai to the land in order to escape the evils of merchant greed, returning to a natural economy, adulterating the coinage, and limiting or banning all further exports of silver and of copper to the Chinese and the Dutch.

In most cases writers took for granted that there was a fixed total to Japan's production as an island country and that the problem was one of the shares of distribution. If merchants were getting more, as they clearly were, it had to be at cost to samurai well-being. Since most who wrote were themselves samurai, it was natural that they thought so; their own incomes, whether in land ratables or in bales of rice secured as stipends from the warehouses, were fixed according to their ancestors' merit, and pride and provisions of rank prevented them from becoming productive. When Tanuma Okitsugu, a late eighteenth-century shogunal leader, thought in terms of raising productivity and was even suspected of planning to deal in foreign trade, many of his contemporaries credited his unconventional proposals to personal profligacy and intellectual aberrance, confusing intellectual innovation with systemic corruption.[1]

1 See John W. Hall, *Tanuma Okitsugu (1719–1788), Forerunner of Modern Japan* (Cambridge, Mass.: Harvard University Press, 1955.)

There were three major attempts to deal with these deep-seated economic ills during the Tokugawa years. Each of them was prompted by hardships that were caused by crop failures for which the closed economy had no answer; each also followed a period of urban growth accompanied by remarkable cultural developments. The efflorescence of the decades before and after 1700[2] was followed by the famine and reforms of the eighth shogun, Tokugawa Yoshimune, in the Kyōhō era (1716–36). He and his ministers attempted to remilitarize society and make it more responsive to genuine need by vigorous efforts to tighten up the administrative structure: providing supplementary salaries for official service, easing retainers' economic distress through official grants, establishing reclamation projects, promoting production and cultivation of commodities imported at Nagasaki, and instituting currency reforms. All such efforts dealt more with the results than with the root causes of economic distress, however, and few outlived the incumbency of those who sponsored them.

A second period of reforms, this time featuring austerity and discipline, followed the exuberance of the years of Tanuma Okitsugu and became known as the reforms of the Kansei (1789–1801) era. The first minister of the Tokugawa bakufu, Matsudaira Sadanobu, was a grandson of Yoshimune and tried to emulate his reforms. By his time the proliferation of domain schools had resulted in a wide variety of philosophical positions. The bakufu now pronounced the Confucian interpretations of the Sung dynasty Chinese savant Chu Hsi as orthodox, and tried to establish intellectual uniformity in instruction and administration. Literacy and educational training became more important for Tokugawa administrators, and bakufu officials were measured against new standards of Confucian integrity.

The Kansei reforms incorporated many measures that gave evidence of the centrality of urban life and problems for the Tokugawa bakufu in its last half century. Popular literature was censored with a new vigor, and in some well-publicized cases publishers paid with their equipment and authors with their freedom for literature viewed as salacious or disrespectful. Administrative spending was curbed by the imposition of new limits. Immigration into Edo was curbed, and efforts were made to lessen the city's dependence on the provinces of western Japan. The Edo town office grew in size as social services and official vigilance increased. New bureaus were charged with aid and

2 The Genroku era is treated by many authors. Howard Hibbett, *The Floating World in Japanese Fiction* (London: Oxford University Press, 1959), provides translations and commentary on popular literature.

relief for the urban poor, and granaries were set up to provide emergency famine relief. Samurai loans contracted prior to 1794 were declared void in an effort to ease retainers' hardships. Restrictions on foreign trade at Nagasaki, which were already severe, were tightened further.

The intensity of official rectitude at the center in the Kansei years was mirrored in measures adopted by many of the domains. The pace of the establishment of domain schools for future samurai administrators showed a dramatic increase. Between 1781 and 1803 fifty-nine such schools were set up, but in the next forty years, seventy-two new schools were established. This should be understood as an administrative response to the growing maturity and complexity of Japanese society. It found echo in an equally rapid increase in the number of private academies and parish schools for commoners.

Many of Matsudaira Sadanobu's reforms had a lasting impact on later Tokugawa society. His own tenure in office, however, was of short duration. He fell afoul of the eleventh shogun, Tokugawa Ienari, whose fifty years in office set a record for the Edo bakufu. After his minister's resignation in 1793 the shogun set an example of self-indulgence that seemed to set the tone for the early decades of the nineteenth century, which were some of the most colorful and prosperous in Tokugawa history.

The third and last period of Tokugawa reform, orchestrated by the bakufu minister Mizuno Tadakuni after the demise of Tokugawa Ienari, followed crop failures and famine in the 1830s. The Tempō era is the subject of the first chapter in this collection by Harold Bolitho. An index of the hardships of the era, one that was true of each of the reform periods, was the number and severity of protests and agrarian rebellions. The most spectacular revolt of the Tempō era came in Osaka, Japan's second city and economic heartland, in 1837. This was organized by a Tokugawa samurai official. Many of the domains had warehouses from which they merchandised their surplus tax rice in Osaka, and the news of this rebellion spread to every corner of Japan as rapidly as the fires that burned much of the city. Professor Bolitho's essay shows that the reforms that the bakufu mounted proved unsuccessful and decidedly unpopular. During the same years, however, several major domains launched reform programs of their own that fared better, leaving them in a relatively stronger position than the Tokugawa overlord. A large, integrated domain could control its borders and manage its economy more easily than the bakufu, whose lands were spread throughout much of Japan.

But the crisis Japan now entered was more than economic, and its roots led deeper than the Tempō or even the Kansei eras. Professor Harootunian's essay on late Tokugawa culture and thought deals with the crisis of values and confidence that popular culture displayed in the last half century of Tokugawa rule. His discussion embraces themes that were popular in the urban culture of the commoners, and goes on to deal with the nature of new religions and nativist teaching that spread throughout the countryside. Of particular interest and importance in late Tokugawa thought was a school of nativist and nationalist teaching that developed in the Tokugawa domain of Mito. Mito learning, as it was known, emphasized the moral responsibility of the shogun to protect and bolster the national cult that centered on the imperial house. It was to play an important role in the thought of activists and idealists who espoused the cause of the emperor and deplored the coming of the "barbarians" in the last decades of Tokugawa rule.[3]

Each of the periods of reform was affected by problems of foreign relations. Yoshimune's Kyōhō program included the substitution of Japanese for imported products. In Kansei times fears of the Russian advance from the north led to defensive measures and subsidization of and controls on materials about Western technology and problems of coastal defense. By the Tempō era there was a new awareness of danger from the south, where English naval power was beginning to threaten China at Canton. By this time books brought to Nagasaki by the Dutch and Chinese had alerted growing numbers of Japanese to the possibility of an impending crisis. The bakufu had established a translation bureau in 1811 and co-opted many scholars of Dutch to work in it. By the 1830s discussions became less theoretical and more political; by the end of the decade they intersected with factional rivalry to result in charges of disloyalty against scholars of Western learning. News of China's defeat by England in the Opium War in 1842 spread quickly in Edo and the castle towns, but in an increasingly stagnant political setting there was no response until Perry's arrival in 1853 forced the issue.

Once faced, the problem would not rest. The bakufu was overthrown a decade after Townsend Harris negotiated the first commer-

3 Professor Harootunian has elaborated on these trends in *Toward Restoration: The Growth of Political Consciousness in Tokugawa Japan* (Berkeley: University of California Press, 1970) and treats nativism in *Things Seen and Unseen: Discourse and Ideology in Tokugawa Nativism* (Chicago: University of Chicago Press, 1988). The thrust of Mito learning is the subject of Bob Tadashi Wakabayashi, *Anti-Foreignism and Western Learning in Early-Modern Japan: The New Theses of 1825* (Cambridge, Mass.: Harvard University Press, 1986).

cial treaty in 1858. Two decades after Perry's arrival a large part of Japan's new reformist government was abroad on a world tour that extended for over a year and a half. A turnaround so extraordinary could clearly not have been "caused" by the mere appearance of foreigners in Japanese waters. Rather, it was the response to long-felt dissatisfaction with a system that had grown moribund and seemed incapable of creative change. Nevertheless it was crystallized and brought to focus by the problem of trying to accommodate the Tokugawa system to the modern world, something that proved impossible.[4] The political process that brought down the Tokugawa regime and ended centuries of warrior rule is described in Marius Jansen's chapter on the Meiji Restoration. As a watershed in Japanese history the Restoration has attracted the attention of many historians, and all judgments of Japan's modern society begin with estimates of its nature and significance.[5] Left-wing analysts often argued that twentieth-century Japanese militarism was the result of the "incomplete" nature of the restoration, while post–World War II commentators professed to see Japan's progress toward democracy as a continuation of trends that began with the young Meiji emperor's promise in the Charter Oath of 1868 that "deliberative councils" would be established so that "all matters" could be decided by "public discussion."

The central feature of the Meiji turnover was the development of centralized institutions in a land that had known the particularism of 260 feudal domains. In 1869 domain administration was evened out, and two years later the domains were abolished. Loyalties directed to local feudal lords would now center on the young Meiji Emperor, and a grid of administrative, school, and police districts transformed the baku-han system of Tokugawa into one of the world's most centralized states. Yet while Western example was important at each step, it was selective and invariably adjusted to Japanese predispositions and needs.[6]

Changes so sweeping affected the samurai class first of all; their

4 The Tokugawa foreign policy crisis can best be followed in the introductory discussion of W. G. Beasley, *Select Documents on Japanese Foreign Policy, 1853–1868* (London: Oxford University Press, 1955).

5 In English, the standard summary is that of W. G. Beasley, *The Meiji Restoration* (Stanford, Calif.: Stanford University Press, 1972); the events of the Tokugawa fall are analyzed from the winner's side in Albert M. Craig, *Chōshū in the Meiji Restoration* (Cambridge, Mass.: Harvard University Press, 1961) and from the loser's in Conrad Totman, *The Collapse of the Tokugawa Bakufu, 1862–1868* (Honolulu: University of Hawaii Press, 1980).

6 D. Eleanor Westney, *Imitation and Innovation: The Transfer of Western Organizational Patterns to Meiji Japan* (Cambridge, Mass.: Harvard University Press, 1987) and Marius B. Jansen and Gilbert Rozman, eds., *Japan in Transition from Tokugawa to Meiji* (Princeton, N.J.: Princeton University Press, 1986).

income and, indeed, identity had been premised on their special status as fief holders and warriors. The development of a conscript army and the distribution of land titles to farmers as the basis for a new and national tax system now made samurai expensive and outmoded relics of the past. Small wonder that the new regime found itself facing protest and rebellion from former samurai, especially those from domains that had led in the Restoration struggles and had particularly high expectations of reward. They resented the inadequacy of their pensions and felt themselves betrayed. Stephen Vlastos's chapter, "Opposition Movements in Early Meiji, 1868–1885," considers rural protests and the samurai rebellions, a series that peaked with the great Satsuma Rebellion of 1877, and goes on to discuss the movement calling for "Freedom and People's Rights" of the 1880s. This began with the agitation of former samurai who saw themselves outmaneuvered by their former peers, but quickly became a widely based national demand for constitutional government as an answer to authoritarianism and favoritism. In response to this the Meiji government implemented its 1868 promise of "deliberative councils," but did this as a gift from the ruler, freely given, and not worked out in response to suggestions from below. Once again study missions traveled to the West to select what seemed appropriate. The examples found in Germany, which had itself been united only a decade earlier, seemed preferable to those of Western Europe and America, and German advisors worked closely with their Meiji employers to blend tradition with modernity.

The Meiji Constitution that was promulgated in 1889 was worked out in secret. Its preamble portrayed it as a modern version of imperial benevolence of earlier times. It was designed "to promote the welfare of, and give development to, the moral and intellectual faculties of Our beloved subjects, the very same that have been honoured with the benevolent care and affectionate vigilance of Our Ancestors." Japan was the first non-Western country to inaugurate constitutional government, and although the constitution's removal of military control from elective hands proved fatal in the 1930s, its other provisions were sufficiently flexible to permit steady growth in political party power.[7]

The significance Japan's Meiji transformation was to have for world history is the subject of the last chapter, in which Professor Akira Iriye discusses "Japan's Drive to Great-Power Status." His discussion takes

7 See Carol Gluck, *Japan's Modern Myths: Ideology in the Late Meiji Period* (Princeton, N.J.: Princeton University Press, 1985).

the story from the consolidation of domestic and foreign affairs in the early Meiji period to the victories over China (1895) and Russia (1905) that signaled the arrival of a new imperial state. With colonies in Taiwan and Korea and a foothold on the continent in the Liaotung Peninsula, Japan was poised to take a full share in world politics. Inevitably its self-image changed; imperialism and militarism came to be associated with modernity. By the time the Meiji Emperor died in 1912 his words and image had become surrounded with cultic solemnity. An indemnity from China had been devoted to launching a steel industry, and Japan's future navies would be built in domestic yards instead of being purchased in Europe.

"Constitutional rule at home, imperialism abroad," in the words of Ukita Kazutami, a popular journalist, became new goals for a generation.[8] The Restoration generation passed from the scene around the time of World War I. It had presided over immense changes at the center. Local application and individual appropriation in village, school, factory, and barrack would be the task for twentieth-century Japan.

8 Marius B. Jansen, "Japanese Imperialism: Late Meiji Perspectives," in Ramon H. Myers and Mark R. Peattie, eds., *The Japanese Colonial Empire, 1895–1945* (Princeton, N.J.: Princeton University Press, 1984), pp. 73–4.

CHAPTER 1

THE TEMPŌ CRISIS

On the sixteenth day of the twelfth month of the year 1830, Japan entered a new era. By coincidence, that same afternoon, in a cottage not far from Shibuya, Matsuzaki Kōdō, a Confucian scholar, observed a flock of white cranes, "skimming over the hill" (as he wrote in his diary)[1] from the direction of Aoyama. He recorded their appearance the following morning, too, "wheeling northwards in the sunlight," his unmistakable delight suggesting just how reassuring it was that these stately and auspicious birds should show themselves at such a time. No era could have had so propitious an opening. Matsuzaki was equally happy with the new era name itself – "Tempō," or Heavenly Protection. It was well known that selecting era names was a delicate business, for the least carelessness – the use of Chinese characters already encumbered with unhappy associations, or those inviting ominous paranomasia – could well prejudice the prosperity of the entire nation. In this case, there seemed nothing to fear. The two characters for Tempō, as the elderly scholar construed them, paid tribute to two previous eras, the first being the Tenna era (1681–83) and the second, the Kyōhō era (1716–35). Matsuzaki did not need to remind himself that for scholars at least, both periods carried favorable overtones, suggestive of new hope, of depravity reformed, and of righteousness restored. This, too, augured well for the future.

Unhappily, in the course of the next fourteen years, these expectations were to miscarry. True, the Tempō era is remembered as one of Japan's great periods of reform. In the central government, the Tokugawa bakufu, it ranks with Kyōhō and Kansei as one of the "three great reforms," and equally significant, all around the nation, the provincial rulers, or daimyo, were also swept along on a wave of regenerative enthusiasm. Culturally, as well, the Tempō era saw one of Japan's great flowerings. This, after all, was the time of Hokusai's *Thirty-Six Views of Mount Fuji*, his *Eight Views of Ōmi*, and his famous

1 Matsuzaki Kōdō, *Kōdō nichireki*, 6 vols. (Tokyo: Heibonsha, 1970–83).

waterfall series; when Hiroshige (whose *Fifty-three Stages of the Tōkaidō* began to appear in 1832), Kuniyoshi, Eisen, and Kunisada were at their peak. Some of Japan's most notable painters, too, men like Tanomura Chikuden, Tani Bunchō, and Watanabe Kazan, were active in the 1830s. The famous *Edo meishozue* appeared in the Tempō era, as did large sections of two of Tokugawa Japan's runaway literary successes – Takizawa Bakin's *Nansō Satomi hakkenden* and Ryūtei Tanehiko's *Nise Murasaki inaka Genji;* so did the complete version of a third, Tamenaga Shunsui's *Shunshoku umegoyomi*, which was published in 1832. Add to this the activities of thinkers as diverse as Hirata Atsutane, Ninomiya Sontoku, and Aizawa Seishisai, and we have a cultural profile as varied and distinguished as any part of the Tokugawa period can present.

Nevertheless, despite its auspicious opening, its reforms, and its cultural achievements, the Tempō era was to prove calamitous for both the common people of Japan and those who ruled over them. In terms of human misery and social dislocation, only the Temmei era (1781–88) caused more havoc, whereas for damage inflicted on Tokugawa Japan's system of government, the Tempō era had no peer. Indeed, Matsuzaki Kōdō quickly came to have his doubts. Just a few hours after his cranes had wheeled off toward Aoyama, he found himself speculating on two extraordinary phenomena: first, there had been earth tremors in Kyoto, a city in which they were virtually unknown, and second, the cherry trees had come into flower with uncanny disregard for the season. He was both puzzled and afraid at these portents: "Our ruler is virtuous, and our habits upright," he wrote, "so there should be no reason for any disasters. . . . All we can do is pray for the Heavenly Protection of yesterday's new era name." Two days later he was still uneasy, filling his diary with notes on previous earthquakes.

THE TEMPŌ FAMINE

In fact, his unease was premature, for real tragedy did not strike Japan until 1833, the fourth year of the Tempō era, and when it came, it proved to have nothing to do with earthquakes. The problem was the weather. It was unusually cold during the spring planting of 1833, exceptionally so during the summer growing season (to such a degree that in some areas farmers were obliged to bring out their padded winter clothing), and the autumn saw abnormally early snowfalls. Whereas the spring had been dry, itself an ominous sign, the summer was, unfortunately, wet, with high water covering the young rice plants for as much as four or five days at a time. The result was a general crop failure, in which rice, particularly sensitive to any but optimal conditions, was the chief victim but in which other staples like wheat, barley, and even bamboo shoots were also severely damaged as well.[2]

As was always the case, the worst effects were felt in the northeastern part of Japan, the Tōhoku. The cool climate there accommodated agriculture only grudgingly, and rice growing, needing an average temperature of twenty degrees centigrade during the crucial months of July and August, had always been particularly hazardous. In 1833, the Tōhoku yielded only 35 percent of its normal crop, and in some specific areas – Sendai, for example – it was much less than that. Farther to the south and west, in places like Hiroshima, the harvest was also poor.[3]

By itself, one bad season was an irritation rather than a tragedy. No doubt many would have reacted initially like the Sendai farmer at the beginning of 1834, writing laconically in his journal, "No New Year celebration; no *sake*."[4] Temporary suffering could always be alleviated by the distribution of food and seed. But tragically, 1833 was to be just the first in a run of bad harvests. The next two years were only marginally better, and the harvest of 1836 was infinitely worse. Even in Edo that year, as Matsuzaki Kōdō's diary shows, it rained almost incessantly throughout the summer. It was cold, into the bargain; on July 13 and 14 (5/30 and 6/1 by the lunar calendar), Matsuzaki was obliged to wear his winter cape, and on the night of August 25 (7/13 by the lunar calendar), one of his friends saw city roof tiles encrusted with frost. Once again the effects of this extraordinary weather were felt chiefly in the Tōhoku, where the harvest was estimated to be only 28 percent of normal, but this time they were spread over a far wider area. At Mito, 75 percent of the rice crop and 50 percent of the wheat and barley crop were lost, whereas at Tottori, over on the Japan Sea, only 40 percent of the harvest was salvaged. Indeed, there were complaints of crop damage as far afield as Hiroshima and even Kokura, in Kyushu.

There was a grim parallel to be drawn here, as contemporaries knew. Matsuzaki Kōdō certainly did: "The weather this year is almost exactly the same as it was in 1786," he noted in his diary, and so did

2 See, for example, Saitō Shōichi, *Ōyama-chō shi* (Tsuruoka: Ōyama-chō shi kankō iinkai, 1969), p. 101; *Miyagi-chō shi, shiryō-hen* (Sendai: Miyagi-ken Miyagi-chō, 1967), p. 700.

3 *Rekishi kōron* (Tokyo, 1976), vol. 9, pp. 33–4.

4 *Miyagi-chō, shiryō-hen*, p. 802.

Ninomiya Sontoku, observing what he called "the worst harvest in fifty years."[5] Just fifty years earlier, in 1786, a similar spell of weather had brought on the Temmei famine, with its legacy of deserted villages, unburied corpses, and tales of cannibalism. This time the season was almost as bad. Indeed, in some respects it was worse, for the bad weather was more widespread and affected some areas left largely untouched by the earlier catastrophe, like Tottori, for example, where officials estimated what happened in 1836 to be "worse than the fearful Temmei famine."[6]

As Susan Hanley and Kozo Yamamura have pointed out,[7] it is not easy to estimate how many died in the famines of the Tokugawa period. In 1836, we are told, over 100,000 starved to death in the Tōhoku, and in Echizen the following year the death rate was three times the normal figure. In Tottori, officials were claiming that of a total of 50,000 people in distress, 20,000 died. The difficulty is, of course, that these figures were all too often thrown together on the basis of hasty and confused impressions, as there was little real opportunity for counting heads. Officials, moreover, safe in the knowledge that no one would ever check, could afford to exaggerate the distress in areas under their care; in fact they could hardly afford not to, as aid would go only where the need seemed greatest.[8]

Nevertheless, there is ample evidence to suggest, if not prove or quantify, that the famine that reached its height in 1836–7 was a crisis of no ordinary proportions. The reports of people eating leaves and weeds, or even straw raincoats, carry a certain conviction; so do the instructions circulated in some areas to bury corpses found by the roadside as quickly as possible, without waiting for official permission. Nor is there any reason to disbelieve reports of mass movements out of the countryside, with people descending on towns and cities "like a mist," to be greeted by gruel kitchens if they were lucky or otherwise by doors hurriedly barred with bamboo staves by nervous householders. There is, too, the evidence of some reliable figures. In 1833, at the very beginning of the famine, the Tokugawa bakufu had received 1.25 million *koku* of tax rice from its widely dispersed holdings; in 1836, when the harvest was universally bad, that amount had dwindled to 1.03 million *koku*, an indication of something out of the

5 Kodama Kōta, ed., *Ninomiya Sontoku*, vol. 26 of *Nihon no meicho* (Tokyo: Chūō kōronsha, 1970), p. 452. 6 *Tottori-han shi* (Tottori: Tottori kenritsu toshokan, 1971), p. 610.

7 Susan B. Hanley and Kozo Yamamura, *Economic and Demographic Change in Preindustrial Japan, 1600–1868* (Princeton, N.J.: Princeton University Press, 1971), p. 147.

8 *Rekishi kōron op. cit*; *Tottori-han shi*, pp. 615, 621.

ordinary. The price of rice is also suggestive. In Osaka, during the summer of 1837, it was fetching three times its 1833 price; in Echigo the cost had risen fivefold. In Edo, a little later, it was more expensive than it had ever been.[9]

The effects of the Tempō famine were felt everywhere. They were felt first in the countryside, where those whose crops had failed were forced to compete for dwindling supplies with such little cash as they could muster. The cities were the next to suffer, as prices rocketed upwards. "What shall I do?" a despairing Matsuzaki Kōdō asked in his diary as rice suddenly grew more expensive, "What shall I do?" Nor were the samurai unscathed. All around Japan domain governments, anticipating lower revenues and higher costs, tightened their belts, reducing samurai salaries in the process. There was, too, a more general problem connected with the famine. "A sickness is spreading," wrote the Sendai farmer nervously in 1834, all thoughts of *sake* forgotten, and spread it did, right through the 1830s, in a variety of forms – pestilence, smallpox, measles, influenza – among those too weak to resist.[10]

CIVIL DISORDER

Not surprisingly, the people who suffered most from the hunger of the 1830s quickly made their unhappiness known. Popular unrest had always mushroomed during famines, and the 1830s proved to be no exception. What was now exceptional was the depth of the resentment displayed, for in the frequency, scale, and violence of its popular protests, the Tempō era came to surpass any previous period in Japanese history. The people were unusually fretful in the 1830s, and their behavior showed it. Indeed, even before the famine there were symptoms of abnormal ferment. As early as 1830, for example, there had been an extraordinary outbreak of *okagemairi*, the peculiar form of mass hysteria during which vast numbers of people, young farmers for the most part, spontaneously set off on a pilgrimage to the Grand Shrine at Ise. This in itself was not so unusual. *Okagemairi* had been erupting, at roughly sixty-year intervals, for a long time; the last one had taken place in 1771. By 1830, therefore, the sexagenary cycle having run its full course, Japan was due for another, so there was no

9 Imaizumi Takujirō, ed., *Essa sōsho* (Sanjō: Yashima shuppan, 1975), vol. 2, p. 311; Ōguchi Yūjirō, "Tempō-ki no seikaku," in *Iwanami kōza Nihon rekishi* (Tokyo: Iwanami shoten, 1976), vol. 12, p. 329.
10 Fujikawa Yū, *Nihon shippei shi* (Tokyo: Heibonsha, 1969), pp. 62–3, 110–11.

surprise when it came. Nor was there surprise at concurrent reports of such miracles as shrine amulets floating down from the sky. Rumors of *prodigia* like this, spreading from village to village, were the customary call to pilgrimage. Rather, it was the scale of the 1830 outbreak that was so extraordinary. In 1771, two million had visited Ise; now within the space of four months, there were five million, jostling, singing, shouting, begging (or occasionally stealing), and all fighting their way into the shrine precincts.[11]

The authorities naturally were nervous. They were never comfortable when unruly bands of people strayed about the countryside, disrupting the placid agricultural round. But although they were not to know it, worse was to come. The 1830 *okagemairi* was soon to be dwarfed by developments that, if far less spectacular, were infinitely more threatening. From 1831 onwards, and particularly in 1836, Japan was struck by a wave of unprecedented popular protest. Opinions differ on just how much there was, but Aoki Kōji, whose research on the subject is by far the most detailed, has credited the Tempō era with a total of 465 rural disputes, 445 peasant uprisings, and 101 urban riots, the two latter categories reaching their peak, like the Tempō famine, in 1836.[12] There is general agreement that no matter how many incidents there were or how they are classified, Japan had never before seen such civil commotion.

Mere numbers alone, however, do not explain why the disorder of the Tempō era was so remarkable. To understand this, it is necessary to look at certain aspects of the incidents themselves, for they displayed features that were both new and alarming. The rural uprisings, for example, seemed to be of a new kind. Before, such protests had followed a fairly predictable pattern, with a delegation (normally composed of traditional village leaders), representing a fairly limited area (a few villages, at most), presenting local authorities with a list of demands – usually for tax relief, for freedom to sell their produce at the highest price, or for the replacement of officials seen to be dishonest or unsympathetic. After a ritual show of solidarity, these demands would be put politely, in the expectation of at least some concession. Elements of this tradition persisted into the Tempō era, but they were overshadowed by unmistakable signs of something quite new.[13]

First, the scale was different. Now, instead of a few villages, whole

11 Fujitani Toshio, "*Okagemairi*" *to* "*eejanaika*" (Tokyo: Iwanami shoten, shinsho ed., 1968), pp. 32, 78–9.
12 Aoki Kōji, *Hyakushō ikki sōgō nempyō* (Tokyo: San'ichi shobō, 1971), app. pp. 31–2.
13 Miyamoto Mataji, ed., *Han shakai no kenkyū* (Kyoto: Minerva shobō, 1972), p. 535.

regions were caught up; in 1831, in Chōshū, for example, a routine demonstration against the domain's cotton monopoly suddenly spilled over into fourteen similar incidents, in which more than 100,000 people terrorized the entire area.[14] In 1836, too, during the famine, the Gunnai region north of Mt. Fuji saw an incident involving an estimated 30,000 angry, hungry protestors – an event without parallel, according to one contemporary observer, "even in old military histories and chronicles." Just a month later, another 10,000 demonstrators plunged the province of Mikawa into uproar, while in 1838 almost the entire island of Sado – some 250 villages in all – rose in anger.[15]

Such numbers made it inevitable that the control wielded by traditional village leaders over the direction of protest would crumble. Uprisings on this scale simply would not respond to direction, as one of the initiators of the Mikawa rising found to his dismay when rioters included his house on the list of those to be burned down. Further, because almost all the participants were poor and often desperate, they were not nearly so amenable to the wishes of their richer fellows. At Gunnai, indeed, where the unrest was initiated by an elderly farmer (one of the poorest in his village) and a peripatetic mathematics teacher, the poor provided leaders as well as followers, and that was not all. One of the features of that incident was the enthusiastic participation of people from outside the area, "not just the poor," it was remarked, "but gamblers, vagabonds, and those posing as *rōnin*."[16] The new scale of rural protests may to some extent have reflected difficulties peculiar to the Tempō crisis, but their changing composition spoke eloquently of the social polarization through which many country districts had been split irrevocably into rich and poor. So, too, did the violence, for these incidents, no longer directed by gentleman farmers, were anything but gentlemanly. In fact, as often as not, the gentleman farmer class was the object of mob hatred. It was their houses, stores, granaries, breweries, and pawnshops that were ransacked and burned during the Tempō unrest. This was so in Chōshū, in Mikawa, and in Gunnai (where more than five hundred buildings were treated in this way); even on Sado Island 130 gentleman farmers felt the force of local discontent.[17]

Sooner or later, all these incidents subsided or were put down, leaving the authorities free to step in and make a few examples –

14 Aoki, *Hyakushō ikki sōgō nempyō*, pp. 225, 277–84. 15 Ibid., p. 242.

16 Aoki Michio, *Tempō sōdōki* (Tokyo: Sanseidō, 1979), pp. 194, 197.

17 Thomas C. Smith, *The Agrarian Origins of Modern Japan* (Stanford, Calif.: Stanford University Press, 1959), pp. 180–200.

torturing some, crucifying others, or imposing sentences of banishment or punitive tatooing. But all were concerned by the new kind of rural protest. "If we have another bad harvest," warned Tokugawa Nariaki, daimyo of Mito, in 1837, "I think there will be trouble."[18] They were to find urban unrest no less disconcerting. Tokugawa Japan had three of the world's largest cities – Edo, with over a million people, and Osaka and Kyoto, with something less than half a million each – as well as a further fifty or so substantial provincial centers, all with at least ten thousand inhabitants. Such concentrations of people, most of them highly vulnerable to food shortages and price fluctuations, had proved volatile before, during the Temmei famine. In the hunger of the 1830s they were to prove so again, with an unprecedented succession of riots, or *uchikowashi,* from the autumn of 1833 onwards. The Osaka authorities had to cope with eleven such incidents, whereas even in Edo, despite its intimidating preponderance of samurai, the common people rioted on three occasions. Elsewhere, too, there was unrest – in Kyoto, Sendai, Hiroshima, Nagasaki, and Kanazawa (where, in 1836, a mob of three hundred irate women broke into Zeniya Gohei's store demanding rice and money). Once again estimates vary, but Kitajima Masamoto claims no fewer than seventy-four urban riots for the Tempō era, a totally disproportionate 20 percent of all such incidents during the Tokugawa period.[19]

This was bad enough, but in 1837 Osaka saw planned – and very nearly executed – the most menacing urban disorder of all, on a scale unseen since the great conspiracy of 1651. The instigator was Ōshio Heihachirō, a former government official, then in his forty-fifth year. Some years earlier, allegedly disappointed at the corruption of his fellow officials in Osaka, he had surrendered his career as a police inspector to devote himself to reading, writing, teaching, and, apparently, collecting weapons. Then, early in 1837, at the height of the famine, he circulated copies of an angry document entitled *Gekibun* (A call to arms) to villagers around Osaka, summoning the common people to an attack on the city.[20] He carefully disclaimed any general challenge to the government, but the implications were obvious. "We must first punish the officials, who torment the people so cruelly," he wrote, "then we must execute the haughty and rich Osaka merchants.

18 Quoted in Kitajima Masamoto, *Mizuno Tadakuni* (Tokyo: Yoshikawa kōbunkan, 1969), p. 208.

19 Kitajima Masamoto, *Bakuhan-sei no kumon,* vol. 18 of *Nihon no rekishi* (Tokyo: Chūō kōronsha, 1967), p. 418.

20 I have used the version contained in *Koga-shi shi: shiryō kinseihen* (*hansei*) (Koga: 1979), pp. 695–7.

Then we must distribute the gold, silver, and copper stored in their cellars, and the bales of rice hidden in their storehouses." These sentiments, coming from one of Ōshio's former rank and current reputation, were disturbing. So, too, was the subsequent rising, in which Ōshio and three hundred supporters tried to take over the city. It was suppressed readily enough, within twelve hours, and succeeded in changing the condition of the poor only insofar as it burnt down 3,300 of their houses and destroyed an estimated forty to fifty thousand *koku* of rice.[21] Nevertheless it provoked a widespread sensation. Its reverberations were to be felt throughout Japan, in the "growing unease" noted by Fujita Tōko among the official class and in a general undercurrent of excitement among the common people, where it was fed by rumors and copies of Ōshio's *Gekibun*, surreptitiously distributed. It also found its emulators in smaller risings at Onomichi, Mihara, Nose, and, three months later, at Kashiwazaki, on the west coast of Honshū, where a group of insurgents, again led by a scholar from the samurai class, attacked government offices.[22]

THE FOREIGN THREAT

In the midst of this mounting unrest, Japan had to confront yet another difficulty, a threat from abroad. The policy of national isolation, imposed early in the seventeenth century, had remained intact for two hundred years, but by the beginning of the Tempō era there seemed reason to believe that it might not do so for much longer. The West was drawing nearer, as the ever-more frequent sightings of foreign vessels in Japanese waters attested. Already, to counter it, the Tokugawa bakufu had issued instructions in 1825 that all such ships were to be driven off at sight, but this was often more readily said than done. The Tempō era had hardly begun when Matsuzaki Kōdō wrote in his journal of reports of an armed clash in Ezo between local residents and foreign sailors.

The first really serious shock, however, came in the summer of 1837, while the authorities were still digesting the Ōshio rebellion. In August that year a privately owned American vessel, the *Morrison*, left Macao for Japan. On board were Charles King, an American businessman, whose idea the voyage was, and his fellow countryman, Samuel

21 Ōguchi, "Tempō-ki no seikaku," in *Iwanami kōza Nihon rekishi*, vol. 12, p. 336; *Koga-shi shi*, p. 698.

22 Okamoto Ryōichi, "Tempō kaikaku," in *Iwanami kōza Nihon rekishi* (Tokyo: Iwanami shoten, 1963), vol. 13, p. 218.

Wells Williams, a missionary; these representatives of God and Mammon were accompanied by seven Japanese castaways. Some days later, at a rendezvous in the Bonin Islands, the ship was joined by Dr. Charles Gutzlaff, a German missionary who had entered British employ at Canton as an interpreter. Ostensibly, the *Morrison*'s mission was to repatriate the castaways, but the trinity of God, Mammon, and Whitehall perhaps had other aspirations as well. Whatever they were, there was to be no opportunity to convey them – or the castaways either, for that matter – to the Japanese. On August 29, the *Morrison* anchored in Edo Bay, on the Tokugawa bakufu's very doorstep. The next morning, without any warning, it was driven off by gunfire from the shore batteries, a welcome that was repeated at Kagoshima a few days later.[23]

In itself, the *Morrison* incident, although unsettling to the Japanese, was of no great significance. Admittedly, they were taken aback to learn, the following year, that in repelling an unauthorized foreign vessel they had also, albeit unwittingly, condemned seven compatriots to permanent exile. This could never be construed as an act of Confucian benevolence, and the guilt was later to return, in grossly distorted form, to haunt them. Still, the memory of the *Morrison* was soon blotted out by more ominous developments. Later that same year it was rumored that Great Britain, already known as the reputed possessor of vast wealth, an extensive empire, and a limitless capacity for violence, was about to annex the Bonin Islands, some six hundred miles to the south. The report, as so often the case, proved exaggerated. British businessmen and officials had discussed the possibility in a desultory fashion for some years, but a survey in 1837 simply served to confirm what they all suspected: that annexation was pointless.[24] Nevertheless, to the Japanese, aware of the survey but not of its outcome, it was undeniably disquieting.

In 1840, when officials in Nagasaki received the first accounts of an armed conflict between China and Great Britain, the disquiet blossomed into panic. This time the rumors were not exaggerated, for the skirmishing between the British and Chinese at Canton the previous year had developed into a full-fledged war. The British proceeded to win it with a dispatch that, reported faithfully in Edo, left the Japanese in no doubt that their great and powerful neighbor faced a humiliating defeat. In the autumn of 1843, reports of the Treaty of Nanking confirmed their worst fears. Great Britain had come to the Far East to

23 W. G. Beasley, *Great Britain and the Opening of Japan, 1834–1858* (London: Luzac, 1951), pp. 21–6. 24 Ibid., pp. 16–20.

stay, and Japan, committed to a policy of national isolation and now saddled with a reputation for barbarism (for who but a barbarous country would fire on its own returning castaways and those befriending them?), could expect to come under foreign pressure as never before. Indeed, the Dutch in Nagasaki had been telling them as much for some time. Whether or not British policy toward Japan warranted such fears (and W. G. Beasley argues persuasively that it did not),[25] the very fact of an armed British presence a mere five hundred miles from their shores reminded the Japanese of something they had tended to forget – just how small and isolated they were.

CRITICS AND CRITICISM

The Tempō era had produced two major problems: on the one hand, an unsettled populace whose dissatisfactions (not least among them hunger) goaded them to unprecedented violence; on the other, a diplomatic situation more complex and threatening than at any time since the early seventeenth century. Alone, either of these would have been enough to dismay Japan's rulers. In combination, they brought on a crisis without parallel in Tokugawa history, shaking society to its very foundations.

Inevitably, that crisis was felt most keenly among the country's approximately half a million samurai. As bureaucrats, working either for the Tokugawa bakufu or for any one of the 264 daimyo governments, the peace and prosperity of the common people were in their hands.[26] The famine and the disorder had already raised questions about their stewardship. Equally, as Japan's standing army, it was their duty to spring to their nation's defense. As the diplomatic clouds gathered, however, their military capability, too, became an object of concern. It was a situation of some embarrassment. For more than two centuries they had laid claim to status, stipends, and privileges on the assumption that their innate wisdom and bravery entitled – indeed obliged – them to guide and protect the common people. Now, in the crisis of the Tempō era, they found themselves unable to do either. The samurai class was at a very low ebb indeed.

First, they had seen no blow struck in anger since the Shimabara Rebellion of 1637, so they were far from battle hardened. They were, into the bargain, undertrained and poorly equipped, simply because both training and equipment cost money, and nobody had any money

25 Ibid.
26 *Daibukan* (Tokyo: Meicho kankōkai, 1965), vol. 3, pp. 798–808, lists 264 daimyo in 1833.

to spare. Almost to a man, the samurai of the Tempō era were poorer than their ancestors had been.[27] They had their stipends, but inflation and rising expectations had combined to make a mockery of them. At best, the samurai's stipends had remained unchanged since the beginning of the Tokugawa period; all too often they had actually been reduced, whether on a temporary or semipermanent basis, by daimyo trying to cope with some particular emergency. For most samurai – perhaps all – only the moneylenders offered any respite, and even that was temporary, as debts (unless canceled unilaterally by government fiat) always had to be repaid. By the Tempō era, therefore, the samurai, although they had increased in bureaucratic skills, were a ragged remnant of what they had once been: poor, unwarlike, addicted to gambling, and so demoralized that it was not uncommon for them to report drunk for duty.

Those they served, whether the shogun or one of the 264 daimyo, faced similar problems and for similar reasons: the inroads of inflation combined with a more opulent life-style. More significantly, however, their incomes had shrunk. In part this was due to the damage inflicted regularly by fire, flood, and earthquake, and, of course, famines. But other factors, less obvious but even more detrimental, were also at work. The shogun and his daimyo were no longer milking the resources of their domains as effectively as they had once done, for taxation had failed to keep pace with either the speed or the direction of agricultural change. Throughout central Japan, in particular, the stable (and eminently taxable) population of subsistence farmers had long since begun to disappear, taking with it its absolute commitment to rice growing. In its place was a new kind of agricultural community, divided into wealthy landowners, at one extreme, and their tenants and laborers, at the other. Rather than producing for their own needs, farmers now grew commercial crops – cotton, tobacco, rapeseed, and indigo, among others – for sale. Some grew rich by it, and others did not; a fact that, as we have seen, helped transform the nature of civil disorder. But rich or poor, all were much more difficult to tax than their seventeenth-century forebears had been.[28]

Japan's daimyo rulers, in consequence, met the Tempō crisis in circumstances of chronic overspending and perennial indebtedness. Examples of this abound, each more bizarre than the last. The shogun's government in Edo went through the 1830s spending, each year, over half a million gold pieces more than it earned. In Tosa, over the

27 Kozo Yamamura, *A Study of Samurai Income and Entrepreneurship* (Cambridge, Mass.: Harvard University Press, 1974), pp. 26–69. 28 Smith, *Agrarian Origins*, p. 160.

same period, domain revenues never met more than 75 percent of its running costs, and few other domains would have been significantly better off. Almost inevitably, they all found their way to moneylenders. Chōshū, for example, amassed debts equal to twenty years' worth of domain income, and one-third of Kaga's revenue each year went to repay loans. These were not the conditions in which Japan's samurai would have chosen to meet the Tempō crisis, and they knew it all too well. "It is hard enough for us to keep going even under normal circumstances," acknowledged one daimyo morosely, "let alone in an emergency."[29] Unfortunately, an emergency was precisely what they now faced.

The general predicament was not new. Daimyo debts had been common in the eighteenth century, and so had bakufu penury; so, for that matter, had signs of decay among the samurai. Back in the seventeenth century, when most samurai had already left the countryside for the castle towns, there had been complaints of the corrosive impact of city life, with its unaccustomed pressures, expenses, and temptations. Their isolation certainly made the samurai less effective administrators; no less certainly their new life-style made them less effective warriors. During the Russian scare at the turn of the century, Sugita Gempaku noted the decline: "Today's samurai have lived in luxury for nearly two hundred years," he wrote, " . . . and have seen no fighting for five or six generations. Their military skills have disappeared, . . . and seven or eight out of ten are as weak as, women."[30]

The situation was far worse by the Tempō era, for the Russian threat had receded too quickly to make any lasting impact on Japan's defenses, which therefore remained as inadequate as ever: some ancient cannon (many unused for decades) at a few points along the coast, and a scattering of tumbledown towers, still known by the anachronistic title *Karabune bansho*, or watchtowers for Chinese ships. Japan's ships, cannon, and small arms, too, all were substantially as they had been for the previous two hundred years. They could still pretend to be efficient bureaucrats and even put on plausible military displays on ceremonial occasions, but they could not transform themselves so readily into an effective fighting force. Before they could be confident of repelling foreign invaders or even of suppressing domestic rioters, the samurai class needed reorganization, a fresh sense of purpose, new weapons, and appropriate training. This all would cost

29 Quoted in Miyamoto, *Han shakai no kenkyū*, p. 548.
30 Numata Jirō, et al., eds., *Yōgaku (I)*, vol. 64 of *Nihon shisō taikei* (Tokyo: Iwanami shoten, 1976), p. 296.

extra money, and money was precisely what the samurai, en masse and individually, did not have.

Nobody knew this better than the samurai themselves. They had greater access to information than anyone else did and, thanks to their education, a greater sense of historical perspective, so they could sense the dimensions of the problems facing them. As they knew all too well, the responsibility for doing something about it was theirs, so, in the Tempō era, they gave voice to their anxiety with an insistence, and to an extent, unique in Tokugawa history. Ironically enough, this criticism itself in its volume, scope, and variety added yet another element of uncertainty to an already unstable situation.

In one sense, the criticism was remarkably diverse. After all, it came from people of disparate status and experience. Daimyo of the eminence of Tokugawa Nariaki, ruler of the Mito domain, had much to say, but so too did humbler people: Hirose Tansō, a country schoolmaster, Takashima Shūhan, a provincial magistrate, and Ōshio Heihachirō, the retired Osaka policeman. Watanabe Kazan the artist, too, added his criticism, as did Takano Chōei the physiologist, Satō Nobuhiro the wandering scholar, and Sakuma Shōzan the gunner.[31] Naturally, too, all perceived the crisis in different ways. To Ōshio, the major problem was the Tempō famine and the extent to which it had been mishandled by callous bureaucrats. Watanabe Kazan, on the other hand, gave his undivided attention to Japan's diplomatic situation, compared luridly with that of "a hunk of meat left by the roadside" while Western predators prowled around it. Sakuma Shōzan, too, concerned with the same issue, was afraid that his country might have to fight a war without "the least hope of winning." For Tokugawa Nariaki – as for his adviser, Aizawa Seishisai, whose *Shinron* (New theses), written in 1825, circulated widely during the Tempō era – the crisis combined both foreign and domestic elements. "As you know," Nariaki warned in a memorial of 1838, "history shows us that internal disorder invites external difficulties, while external problems provoke internal unrest." Similarly, the criticisms took different forms. Ōshio's *Gekibun* was a public appeal, passed from village to village. The observations of Hirose Tansō and Satō Nobuhiro, on the other hand, circulated in manuscript, whereas Watanabe Kazan's

31 Material in this section is drawn from the following: "Satō Nobuhiro," vol. 45, and "Watanabe Kazan" and "Sakuma Shōzan," vol. 55 of *Nihon shisō taikei* (Tokyo: Iwanami shoten, 1974 and 1977); *Koga-shi shi*, pp. 695–7; Arima Seiho, *Takashima Shūhan* (Tokyo: Yoshikawa kōbunkan, 1958); Konishi Shigenao, *Hirose Tansō* (Tokyo: Bunkyō shoin, 1943); Nakajima Ichisaburō, *Hirose Tansō no kenkyū* (Tokyo: Dai-ichi shuppan kyōkai, 1943).

were kept secret until uncovered in a police raid in 1839. Other criticism assumed the guise of formal memorials, offered to daimyo (as in the case of Sakuma Shōzan), specific officials (as with Takashima Shūhan), or the shogun himself (as with Tokugawa Nariaki). The tone, too, varied with the form. Ōshio's *Gekibun* was as strident and inflammatory as one would expect a call to arms to be. The scholarly analyses and memorials, on the other hand, were suitably clad in their respective camouflages of academic decorum and deferential concern.

Yet differences notwithstanding, there were some common threads running through the Tempō criticism, and one was dissatisfaction with the government. Ōshio Heihachirō, observing that "when the nation is governed by unworthy men, disasters come one upon the other," was more outspoken than others, but the view was nevertheless commonly held. Others also shared his conviction that government officials "accept bribes unashamedly"; both Watanabe Kazan, in his confidential *Shinkiron* (A timely warning), and Tokugawa Nariaki, in his 1838 memorial, said much the same thing. The latter, indeed, considered that "what we must first do is stamp out corruption, for unless this is done we shall succeed in nothing." Hirose Tansō, in his *Ugen* (Circumlocutions), written in 1840, extended his criticism to the daimyo and the entire samurai class, drawing attention to their besetting sins of arrogance and ignorance. Some, like Watanabe Kazan and Takano Chōei, condemned Japan's policy of national isolation as too provocative for the nation's own good. Takashima Shūhan and Sakuma Shōzan, on the other hand, endorsed it and drew attention instead to the lamentable state of national defense.

Governments do not usually accept criticism readily, and the Tokugawa bakufu was no exception. Adverse comment had been forcibly discouraged since the early seventeenth century, with considerable success, so the Tempō authorities were simply unprepared for what now poured in on them from all sides. They reacted in the conventional way. Watanabe Kazan and Takano Chōei, together with some of their associates, were arrested during a purge of amateurs of Western learning. Takano was subsequently jailed, as, on a different occasion, was Takashima Shūhan. Satō Nobuhiro was ordered to stay away from Edo. Watanabe was exiled from Edo to his domain, a fate he shared with Satō Nobuhiro and even Tokugawa Nariaki, rusticated to his domain in 1841. Ōshio Heihachirō, of course, had signed his own death warrant by launching a rebellion. He evaded capture for six months and, when he could do so no longer, took his own life.

Still, the criticism itself persisted. The fears and the complaints that the Tempō crisis had awakened remained, to be passed from hand to hand and mouth to mouth. So, too, did suggestions for reform which, despite their heterogeneity, were all equally dramatic, revealing a general conviction that only desperate remedies could cure a nation so desperately ill. Here Ōshio, demanding punitive carnage, was on his own; Japan was not quite ready for that. Yet other calls for change were in their own way just as radical. Several critics – Hirose Tansō, Sakuma Shōzan, and Tokugawa Nariaki among them – urged that samurai be sent away from the cities back to the countryside, to lead a national defense effort in which the common people, too, would participate. In effect, this proposal struck at the very foundations of the Tokugawa social order. The diplomatic order, too, was threatened by the demands of those like Watanabe and Takano, who urged that the country be thrown open to the world.

Other proposals were to attack the Tokugawa political order, calling into question the entire *bakuhan taisei*. Under this system, political authority was delegated by the emperor (whether he liked it or not) to the shogun, the head of the Tokugawa house. The shogun in turn, while commanding an establishment of his own to coordinate certain national functions like foreign affairs and defense, delegated much of the responsibility for local administration to 264 local rulers. These daimyo (or their bureaucracies) governed their own domains, collected their own taxes, and maintained their own armies. As vassals of the shogun, they were obliged to give him whatever assistance he might require, no matter what the cost to themselves, and so should they prove negligent or miscreant, their lands and rank were to be forfeited. At least, this was how it worked in theory. By the Tempō era, however, two hundred years of inactivity had seen the authority of the shogun and his government decline and the de facto independence of the daimyo grow. Few were ever called upon to do anything for the general good, and fewer still felt the sting of bakufu displeasure. For the most part the system worked well enough, as Japan's placid history for most of the Tokugawa period shows. On the other hand, it lacked the coordination needed to cope with a national emergency. The Tempō crisis, with its famine and its massive popular unrest, displayed once more the deficiencies of a system that fragmented local authority into 265 separate jurisdictions.

Much more significantly, however, the crisis drew attention to another and particularly serious inadequacy. Tokugawa Japan could not protect itself against invasion – not merely because the samurai class as a whole had grown indigent and flabby but, rather, because the system itself did not permit it. The Tokugawa bakufu had long ago decided that it could maintain itself in power and keep the country from civil war only by limiting the military capacity of the daimyo. In the early seventeenth century it had therefore imposed several restrictions on them. The *sankin kōtai* system of alternate attendance at Edo was one, aimed at limiting their opportunities for rebellion by keeping them in Edo one year in every two. There was also the hostage system, designed to secure their good behavior by threatening their wives and heirs. More relevant to the present context, however, they were forbidden to fortify their domains or to build vessels of warship dimensions.

All these restrictions served Tokugawa Japan well. Without them, it is quite certain that its history would not have been nearly so tranquil. Yet, in the Tempō crisis, people came to realize that in restraining each other from civil war, they had also left themselves defenseless. To many critics, therefore, it seemed obvious that the system would have to change; indeed, Aizawa Yasushi's *Shinron* (written in 1825, but – wisely – not published until 1857) had already suggested this, demanding that domains be allowed to fortify themselves, acquire better weapons, and build larger ships. Tokugawa Nariaki, Aizawa's patron, spent much of the next twenty years saying the same thing. To Sakuma Shōzan, too, it appeared time for the old restrictions to be relaxed. The prohibition against building large ships, he wrote, had been drawn up in the belief that it "would keep the nation peaceful in the future," but with circumstances so dramatically changed that "we need not hesitate to revise, for the common good, a law introduced for the common good."Behind all such suggestions lay the implicit assertion that Tokugawa Japan was far too centralized for safety. Aizawa had denounced Japan's defense system for "emphasizing the center and ignoring the periphery," and Sakuma Shōzan, too, suggested that the bakufu should "lighten the burdens it imposes on the nation's daimyo, so that their domain finances may be made easier and they may devote themselves to defense."

Yet there was an alternative to the decentralization they demanded, and this was to be found in the works of Satō Nobuhiro. His *Suitō hiroku*[32] and its subsequent elaborations and glosses suggested not that domains be set free to see to their own defense but the opposite. What Satō advocated was the creation of a state far more centralized than Japan had ever seen (or, indeed, was to see until the new Meiji order

32 A title that defies an elegant, or even an inelegant, translation. Perhaps "A secret treatise on bequeathing an enhanced patrimony to posterity" suggests its purport. The most readily accessible version is found in "Satō Nobuhiro," vol. 45 of *Nihon shisō taikei*, pp. 488–517.

thirty years later), a state in which every aspect of national life, including defense, would be made totally subject to unified central control.

Each of the critics, in his own way, was calling on Japan to reform itself before it was too late – to bring about more honest government, to return to old habits of frugality, to try new kinds of diplomacy or social organization, and to acquire new and better kinds of weapons. The call did not go unheard, as the reforms of the Tempō era were to show, but it had unforeseen results, nowhere more so than for the issue of state organization. This particular issue, underlying all the others, was to prove the most intractable and, ultimately, the most divisive.

DOMAIN REFORMS

Traditionally, in Tokugawa Japan, crisis was followed by reform, and there was no reason that the Tempō crisis, for all its unaccustomed features, should have been any different. Reform, expressed variously as *kaikaku, kaishin,* or *chūkō,* was the conventional response, reassuringly optimistic and comfortably vague. After all, who could possibly resist a program centered on (as such programs always were) economy, frugality, and the promotion of "men of talent"? It could not fail to appeal to domains in financial turmoil, as they all were to a greater or lesser degree, and unable to lay the blame anywhere but on human failings. In any case, economy and frugality were the most elastic of abstractions, able to be stretched in any number of directions, whereas the use of the term "men of talent" was nothing if not subjective; in practice most people tended to reserve it for themselves and their friends.

Indeed, the concept of reform was vague enough to accommodate a variety of responses – progressive or reactionary, utopian or pragmatic, self-seeking or altruistic – or even no response at all, provided that it was decently cloaked in the appropriate rhetoric. Just how flexible it was can be seen in the wide range of reactions to the events of the Tempō era, for though none remained untouched by them, Japan's 264 daimyo domains did not react alike. Nor was there any reason to expect them to do so. They were scattered over a country of considerable economic, climatic, and topographical diversity, so the crisis impinged on them in different ways and to different degrees. In central Japan, for example, the problems of rural unrest were quite unlike those in regions where commerce had developed more slowly. Then, too, the famine and its problems loomed larger in the northeast, which had seen so much more devastation than elsewhere; the south-western domains, on the other hand, had much more reason to be concerned about foreign ships and the threat of invasion. Coastal domains, too, no matter what their location, tended to be more alert to defense issues than to those at a safer distance from the sea. One must also not forget that just as each domain had its individual problems, so too did it have its own range of options, and, to choose among them, its own administrators, with their individual preferences.

For all these reasons, the Tempō reforms, as they unfolded in the daimyo domains, could hardly have been more diverse.[33] To some domains, as to some critics, it appeared that the kernel of the problem lay in the failings of the samurai class. So at Tawara, for example, Watanabe Kazan's reforms emphasized education, in the hope that the samurai might learn once again their traditional morality, with its virtues of loyalty and filial piety. Elsewhere, similar demands were accompanied by warnings against the insidious temptations of city life. "Each one of you must be frugal in all things," the Okayama authorities told their samurai in 1833, "avoid wasteful expenditures, and set your behavior to rights."

In matters of economic policy, too, many domain reformers looked no farther than the traditional remedies. Programs of stringent economy were common enough, and as usual, one of the most convenient places to begin seemed to be the samurai stipends. These had always been the easiest of game, as there was so little risk of protest. Samurai morality, even though it condoned opposition to a daimyo under some circumstances, would never have done so over anything so contemptible as money. Domains like Echizen, therefore, could begin their reforms confidently enough by halving all stipends for a three-year period. Still, even this avenue to financial health was not without its risks. For one thing, it was a two-edged weapon, as those samurai with less money would be less effective in a crisis. At Tawara, too, it was found that salary cuts simply goaded the samurai into absconding; all they had to lose, after all, was their status, apparently not worth much, and their salary remnants, now worth even less. No less traditionally, daimyo saddled with crippling debts could choose the option of repudiating them. This was sanctioned, at least in theory, by the

33 The term "Tempō reforms" is customarily used rather loosely, including not only those of the Tempō era (1830–44) but also those initiated slightly before or after. The information appearing here is drawn from a variety of sources, of which the most important are Miyamoto, *Han shakai no kenkyū*; Ōkubo Toshiaki, ed., *Meiji ishin to Kyūshū* (Tokyo: Heibonsha, 1968); Inui Hiromi and Inoue Katsuo, "Chōshū han to Mito han," in *Iwanami kōza Nihon rekishi* (Tokyo: Iwanami shoten, 1976), vol. 12.

wide gulf in status between the merchant who did the lending and the daimyo who did the borrowing; the former could have no possible recourse against the latter, should he be determined to default. Domains like Chōshū and Fukuoka, therefore, readily used this expedient, and Satsuma and Saga came exceedingly close, the former with an announcement that although its debts (amounting to five million gold pieces) would ultimately be repaid, the process might take some time – 250 years, in fact. In the case of Saga, the domain authorities magnanimously offered to settle with one of their Edo creditors, provided he was willing to accept just 20 percent of the principal. Yet this too, like slashing the samurai's stipends, had its dangers, for in practice the right to repudiate debts had to be exercised with discretion. Few daimyo could risk alienating the business community on whose expertise, goodwill, and cooperation the economic life of their domains had all too often come to depend.

In many parts of Japan the Tempō crisis seemed a signal to turn back the economic clock, with a reaffirmation of the agrarian roots of the *bakuhan taisei*. This, so reformers argued, could be done by restricting the private commercial developments that had polarized so many farming villages and, incidentally, cut deeply into domain tax revenues. Elements of such a policy are to found in areas as geographically, economically, and socially diverse as Mito, Satsuma, Chōshū, and Saga. In some domains, too – Saga and Kokura, for example – the emphasis was on land reclamation, the most traditional of all methods of augmenting income. There was, however, one other traditional step to financial health that the domains chose to ignore. They could have increased the land tax or else extended it so that it fell as heavily on undertaxed dry fields as on rice paddies. After all, in most parts of Japan, taxes had not been readjusted for more than a hundred years. But not even the Tempō crisis could tempt the domains to take such a dangerous step. It was discussed here and there but in the end was rejected. For one thing, the aftermath of the Tempō famine was obviously not the most opportune moment. For another, everybody knew that more taxation would be interpreted in the villages as either a break with tradition or a breach of faith and vigorously – even violently – resisted.

Together with these elements of conservatism in many of the domain reforms, there were several new initiatives that suggest how seriously the Tempō crisis was viewed. Of course, a wholehearted swing to innovation was rare. Much more usual was a blend, sometimes even a contradictory blend, of the novel with the traditional, but nevertheless the new elements were unmistakable. There were, first, signs of a new approach to the chronic problems of domain finances, which, thanks to the Tempō crisis, had been moved from the category of irritatingly inconvenient to that of downright dangerous. At its most basic, this was revealed in a change of attitude, in which commercial development – under the proper auspices and for the proper purposes, of course – came to be encouraged. The pivotal influence of castle towns on the domain economy, for example, was to be recognized in many parts of Japan. At Fukuoka, it was judged important enough to justify an extraordinary *volte-face*. Elsewhere, the authorities were urging (and often compelling) their samurai to be frugal, but in Fukuoka, in an effort to develop the town center, they were encouraged to patronize local theaters and wrestling matches and to buy lottery tickets. Similarly, at Kurume calls for frugality were perfunctory in the extreme and appeared as an afterthought at the very end of the domain reforms.

The attitude of some domains toward the business community, too, seemed to be changing. On occasion this took an unusually peremptory form, in which domain officials, rather than wheedle loans from individual mechants, were prepared to force money from them, either as "loans," or – in the case of Echizen, Kokura, and Funai, among others – as "gifts." Increasingly, though, and far more significantly, it took the form of cooperation, often symbolized by offers of samurai status to members of the business community in return for expert advice and assistance. Business expertise was at a premium in those domains already engaged in, or about to begin, enterprises of their own, like domain monopolies. Ever since the seventeenth century, a few daimyo had managed to monopolize certain key items produced within their domains, forbidding their sale to anyone but authorized buyers or at anything but the authorized price, kept artificially low. Not infrequently, indeed, producers were paid in the domain's own currency, printed as needed and largely worthless in any other part of Japan. The produce was then sold at Osaka or Edo, and the profits brought back into the domain reserves of hard currency that it would otherwise not have had. Sendai rice, Awa indigo, Tottori wax, and paper from Tsuwano and Karatsu all earned substantial sums and helped cushion their domains from the general financial malaise. At Awa, indeed, where the indigo monopoly brought a profit of one million gold pieces in 1830, it was the major element in domain finances.

Understandably, the older such monopolies, the more successful they were. Imposed later, on producers jealous of their profits and unaccustomed to interference, they often provoked resistance, most notably in the Chōshū riots of 1831. The Tempō reform program in some domains in fact saw these monopolies relaxed in an attempt to pacify the farmers: Chōshū, Utsuki, and Funai all were obliged to do exactly that. Nevertheless, the prospect of controlling the domain's commercial produce was too strong for many daimyo to resist, and so the Tempō era produced a number of monopolies. Usually these were confined to products already well established – like cotton, wax, and seed oil – but not infrequently the daimyo were dazzled enough by the prospect to encourage experimentation with new products. At Mito, for example, it was hoped to add some new enterprises to the paper, tobacco, and *konnyaku* that the domain already produced, and steps were taken to begin making pottery and lacquer and growing tea. Satsuma, too, while intensifying its sugar monopoly (to such an extent, incidentally, that profit doubled during the Tempō era) also tried to introduce the production of silk, paper, indigo, saffron, sulfur, and medical herbs.

There was also fresh activity as domains looked long and hard at their defenses. Few had reason to be pleased with what they saw: soldiers armed with the weapons – swords, pikes, muskets, decrepit cannon – of their seventeenth-century ancestors and with ideas on strategy and tactics to match. Clearly, some drastic changes had to be made. Some domains contented themselves with reintroducing maneuvers or, as Utsunomiya did in 1842, with reviving target practice after an interval of twenty-six years (during which it had been considered too expensive).[34] Others, feeling more exposed, took stronger measures, streamlining their chain of command, regrouping to give greater prominence to musketeer units, or even moving samurai out of the towns into garrisons along the coast and forming peasant militia units, as the Tempō critics had urged. Mito, where Aizawa Yasushi had been calling for just such measures, was one of the first domains to do so in the 1830s. Some felt, with Takashima Shūhan and Sakuma Shōzan, that Japan needed new skills and new equipment to cope with the crisis, and this was particularly noticeable among the domains of the southwest. After its brush with the *Morrison* in Kagoshima Bay in 1837, Satsuma began to buy imported arms from Nagasaki dealers, to try making its own mortars, howitzers, and field guns, and to send men to be trained in Western gunnery at Takashima Shūhan's school. Fukuoka, Chōshū, and Kumamoto were doing the same, and so was Saga, where the main

34 Tokuda Kōjun, ed., *Shiryō Utsunomiya han shi* (Tokyo: Kashiwa shobō, 1971), p. 172.

thrust of domain reforms was toward self-defense. Saga began research into alternative artillery techniques in 1832 and, from 1835 onwards, produced a large number of high-quality homemade cannon.

The diversity of the domains' responses to the Tempō crisis, then, is clear enough. There were, however, two other elements in these local reforms so common as to be almost universal. One was the extent to which the reform programs, despite all the reassuring overtones of the concept itself, aroused bitter disagreement, particularly when they meant abandoning long-established practice and when they involved innovation. Inevitably, given the atmosphere of general crisis, each domain had its skeptics, sometimes passive, sometimes not, and all needing to be persuaded or bullied into silence. Invariably the operation demanded a high degree of daimyo support, so that in Chōshū and Fukui, for example, their Tempō reforms could not begin until the daimyo had been replaced by one either more committed or more malleable. It was this factor that delayed the "Tempō" reforms of domains like Hiroshima and Tottori until the Tempō era had come to an end.[35] Elsewhere, as in Saga, reform had to wait until the new daimyo had found his feet. In many cases, too, reinforcing the impression of energy and unconventionality, the actual planning of the reforms was entrusted to a new man, often of comparatively humble status, brought in as part of a larger administrative reorganization. For example, the key figure at Fukuoka was a physician, at Mito a scholar, at Tawara a painter, at Nakatsu and Satsuma tea ceremony attendants – even, at Tosa, a convert to Shingaku. To add to the ferment, technocrats like Ōhara Yūgaku and Ninomiya Sontoku could be brought in from outside. Understandably, factions would form, and feelings would run high. Reformers naturally saw themselves as the "men of talent" known to appear whenever a reform was begun; they customarily considered their opponents thoughtless at best or, at worst, stupid and corrupt. To their critics, on the other hand, the self-styled reformers, if radical, seemed power drunk and doctrinaire, or, if conservative, sycophantic and self-seeking. Politics was a superheated business during the Tempō crisis, as many, given time to ponder their mistakes in jail cells, came to understand. Not even the daimyo always escaped unscathed, and Tokugawa Nariaki of Mito was one who came perilously close to being repudiated by a domain unable to countenance either his personality or his politics.

The other common element in these local reforms was this. The

35 Yamanaka Hisao, "Bakumatsu hansei kaikaku no hikaku hanseishiteki kenkyū," *Chihōshi kenkyū* 14 (1954): 2–3.

Tempō crisis had shown the domains some unpalatable truths: their tenuous control over the common people, their bankruptcy, their vulnerability to outside attack. It had also made them aware that if they were ever to cope with this new and dangerous situation, it would have to be by their own efforts. Nobody else could help them, certainly not the bakufu, which had far greater problems of its own. The domains would have to husband their own resources, make their own money, and take care of their own defenses. No doubt it was a salutary lesson; rather, it might have been, had Japan some other form of government. As it was, it had the gravest consequences for the *bakuhan taisei*, that system of decentralized feudalism in which the Tokugawa bakufu and the daimyo domains joined to govern the country. The Tempō crisis forced domains onto their own resources as never before and obliged them to turn their attention inwards, to themselves and their own needs. The result was a surge of *sauve qui peut* domain nationalism. It surfaced during the famine, in the refusal of some domains to let food leave their borders, no matter how desperate were conditions elsewhere.[36] It surfaced as the domains began to use their monopolies to drive up prices and profits, competing with one another and with the bakufu, and, in the process, helping destroy the orderly commercial habits of two hundred years.[37] It surfaced, too, in an arms race, begun during the Tempō era, in which domains scrambled pell-mell for new weapons and new techniques, shattering the fragile balance of power that had kept Japan at peace since 1615. This attitude, potentially more damaging than the crisis that produced it, outlived both the Tempō era and the *bakuhan taisei* itself.

BAKUFU REFORMS

Neither the Tempō crisis nor the domains' reactions to it were to go unmarked in Edo. The shogun, who lived there, and his administration, which was based there, faced all the common provincial problems – famine, civil disorder, inadequate defenses, and an army undermanned, underpaid, and ill equipped. In this respect the shogun was a daimyo like any other.

But there was one crucial difference: The shogun administered, through his government, a far greater area than any other daimyo – almost six times as much as the largest provincial domain – and to that extent his responsibilities, in terms of taxes to collect, mouths to feed,

36 *Tottori han shi*, vol. 6, pp. 610, 613.
37 Osaka-shi sanjikai, ed., *Ōsaka-shi shi* (Osaka: Seibundō, 1965), vol. 5, pp. 640 ff.

area to police, and shores to protect, were that much more onerous. The resources of the shogun's domain were also much more difficult to coordinate – administratively, financially, and militarily – for where most daimyo domains were well-defined geographical units, Tokugawa land was scattered throughout forty-seven of Japan's sixty-eight provinces. Tax loss, therefore, and famine relief (whether in the form of reduced taxes in the villages or free gruel in the cities) bit heavily into bakufu finances, as depleted in 1836 as they had been for over a hundred years.[38] Civil unrest, too, had hit hardest at areas under bakufu control, in Gunnai in 1836; Osaka, Edo, and Kashiwazaki in 1837; and Sado in 1838.

The crisis in foreign affairs also was uniquely the shogun's concern. His very title, supreme commander of the pacification of barbarians (*sei-i tai shōgun*), made it impossible for that particular responsibility to go to anyone else. The port of Nagasaki, Tokugawa Japan's solitary link with the world outside, was part of his domain, and all decisions on national diplomacy were taken within the bakufu, his own personal administration. So, too, were those decisions concerning the deployment and coordination of all samurai, whether Tokugawa vassals or rear vassals. Therefore, as the foreign nations closed in during the 1830s and the prospect of invoking powers unused for two hundred years became imminent, so did the burden of this responsibility grow heavier.

The shogun's government, then, was caught up in the Tempō crisis to a far greater extent than was any single daimyo domain. Yet paradoxically, its reaction to that crisis seemed at first to lack a certain urgency. This is not to say that it remained passive in the face of mass starvation, civil disturbance, depleted resources, foreign penetration, and inadequate protection. No government could. The bakufu reacted, but precisely as it had always done, by reducing taxes in the famine areas, securing food supplies for its cities, distributing rations to its needy, quelling its riots, debasing its currency, and despatching fact-finding missions to its coastal fortifications. These were the tried and true responses to familiar emergencies, but in a situation that seemed to call for an entirely new approach, they were undeniably anachronistic. Elsewhere, as we have seen, in the daimyo domains, the crisis of the 1830s inspired a number of new initiatives, but whereas some domains defied tradition by entering the market place, and oth-

38 Furushima Toshio, "Bakufu zaisei shūnyū no kōkō to nōmin shūdatsu no kakki," in Furushima Toshio, ed., *Nihon keizaishi taikei* (Tokyo: Tokyo daigaku shuppankai, 1973), vol. 4, pp. 28–31.

ers by arming their peasants, the Tokugawa bakufu seemed to cling tenaciously to the status quo. Only in the middle of 1841, when three-quarters of the Tempō era had already passed, did the bakufu begin a reform program of its own.

On the face of it, the delay seems inexplicable. There is no reason to imagine, for example, that bakufu officials were ignorant of the problems confronting them. Individual ministers could hardly be unaware of popular unrest, and they were by no means insensitive to developments overseas. Nor, for that matter, could they turn a blind eye to the sorry state of bakufu finances, now so anemic that only regular transfusions from currency debasement could provide relief. In any case, the Tempō critics, from Ōshio Heihachirō to Tokugawa Nariaki, had been all too ready to alert the government to its shortcomings.

In fact, many bakufu officials had recognized them and had already given thought to their solution. But before anything could be done, they had to wait for an opportunity, and in 1841 that opportunity came. As so often, it came with a change in government. Where reform in domains like Chōshū and Fukui had waited for the accession of a new ruler, in the bakufu it followed the death of an old one – the extraordinary Tokugawa Ienari, the eleventh shogun, who had long dominated the Tokugawa political world. No other head of the Tokugawa house had reigned for anything like his total of fifty years. None of them had lived nearly as long, either, for Ienari was in his seventy-ninth year when he died. Nor, apparently, did any live quite so fully; that is, at least, if numbers of concubines (estimated at forty) and children (fifty-five) indicate a full life.[39] At a tender age, Tokugawa Ienari had come under the influence of Matsudaira Sadanobu, but he had resisted all his sanctimonious mentor's attempts to mold his character. Instead, for the next fifty years Ienari, with the help of members of his personal household, had done much as he wished. Even after his retirement in 1837, his political grip did not slacken, but at the beginning of 1841 Ienari fell seriously ill with severe abdominal cramps, and within three weeks, despite prayers offered at Nikkō and Zōjōji, he died, leaving behind him a number of grieving concubines and a government suddenly reinvested with authority and initiative. For a time, there was little outward sign of change. As at all shogunal deaths, music was forbidden within the palace; officials had their heads shaved; and an obligatory period of mourning was announced. But then, within three months, came the first portents of something

39 Kitajima, *Bakuhansei no kumon*, p. 295.

new. Three of Ienari's favorite officials, popularly known as the "three sycophants," were suddenly dismissed. Kawaji Toshiakira, writing in his journal[40] that "although I was not particularly friendly with these men, I am still astonished," reflected the general surprise and unease. Over the next few weeks scores of officials were dismissed or resigned under various pretexts, and all were replaced by fresh appointees. There was a sudden convulsion, too, at the very highest official level. Of five senior ministers holding office at the beginning of 1841, only two remained by the end of the year. Their three colleagues had resigned, pleading ill health. This was a fairly common, and occasionally legitimate excuse, and in this instance one of those in question proved his good faith by dying a week later. The other two, however, did not, for one, Ii Naoaki lived until 1850, and the other, Ōta Suketomo, was hale enough to find his way back to office some seventeen years later, apparently little the worse for wear.

Contemporaries, noting the haste of these changes ("since Ienari's death," observed one,[41] "it is as if everyone's eyebrows had been set alight"), had little difficulty in deciphering their meaning. This was a purge, and on such a scale as to foreshadow some correspondingly dramatic change in policy. It soon came. On 5/15/1841, just two days after Ii Naoaki's departure, the government made a curiously unemphatic announcement. It urged its officials to adhere to traditional principles and, in particular, "not to deviate from the policies of the Kyōhō and Kansei eras."[42] Only the reference to those two previous reform periods – the one under the eighth shogun, Tokugawa Yoshimune, early in the eighteenth century, the other more than fifty years later – under Matsudaira Sadanobu – intimated the onset of yet another paroxysm of reform. But there was no hint that this time the bakufu would be led into waters far deeper than earlier, more conventional, reforms had ever contemplated.

This, however, lay more than a year away. As the bakufu began its Tempō reforms in the summer of 1841, despite the magnitude and urgency of its problems, it seemed anxious first of all to address itself to the perennial and abiding concerns of all Confucian states. In this

40 Kawaji Toshiakira, *Shimane no susami* (Tokyo: Heibonsha, 1973), p. 327.

41 Quoted in Kitajima, *Mizuno Tadakuni*, p. 302.

42 The following account of the bakufu's Tempō reforms derives largely, although by no means exclusively, from the following: Kuroita Katsumi, ed., *Zoku Tokugawa jikki* (Tokyo: Yoshikawa kōbunkan, 1966), vol. 49; Naitō Chisō, *Tokugawa jūgodaishi* (Tokyo: Shin jimbutsu ōraisha, 1969), vol. 6; Hōseishi gakkai, eds., *Tokugawa kinreikō*, 11 vols. (Tokyo: Sōbunsha, 1958–61); Kitajima, *Mizuno Tadakuni;* Okamoto, "Tempō kaikaku"; Tsuda Hideo, "Tempō kaikaku no keizaishiteki igi," in Furushima Toshio, ed., *Nihon keizaishi taikei* (Tokyo: Tokyo daigaku shuppankai, 1965), vol. 4.

respect, much of the legislation that now issued from the Tokugawa bureaucracy might just as well have been written fifty or a hundred years earlier. Indeed some of it was, judging from the insistent references to, and, in many cases, direct repetition of, laws handed down in the Kyōhō and Kansei eras.

The bakufu appeared, for example, most concerned with the moral health of those over whom it ruled. Urban life held many temptations – drink, gambling, prostitution, pornography, and frivolity of all kinds – and these were nowhere more evident than in Edo, the nation's largest city and the center of the bakufu's domain. No reforming government could ignore them, and one of the strongest strands in the Tempō reform program, and also the earliest to develop, was its effort – in a manner that Tokugawa Yoshimune and Matsudaira Sadanobu would have recognized and applauded – to control them. "If we use this opportunity for reform and cleansing," wrote Mizuno Tadakuni, the chief minister, "and restore dignity to our way of life, . . . we will succeed in setting things to rights."[43]

Prostitution was a case in point. The Tokugawa bakufu had long since recognized this unruly industry as inevitable and, to minimize its impact on society, had segregated it, first in the Yoshiwara and then later in the Shin-Yoshiwara, on the northeastern fringe of the city, under the control of a group of officially recognized whoremasters. As with so much of Tokugawa Japan, however, by the Tempō era this tidy system had broken down. Edo's urban sprawl to the west and the south had gradually placed the official brothel quarter beyond the walking capacity of all but the most amorous. It was no more than natural, therefore, that people should seek consolation nearer home and that the forces of free enterprise, as irrepressible in this field as in any other, should mobilize to provide it. Consequently the Tempō government had to deal with irregular and unlicensed prostitution, scattered throughout the city in teahouses and restaurants where waitresses were known to behave "in a lewd fashion." These were ordered to close in 1842, and any premises used for such purposes declared liable to confiscation. It also tried to restrict other avenues by which women could make themselves available, denying them access to a number of professions, from itinerant hairdresser, music teacher, archery range attendant, and physician to cabaret artist (in which profession women were known to get up on stage "quite shamelessly, and sing most unseemly . . . Gidayū ballads" to customers not conspic-

43 *Tokugawa jūgodaishi*, vol. 6, pp. 2869–70.

uous for their musical interests).[44] Mixed bathing, too, was outlawed in an effort to bring cleanliness and godliness back together.

Equally, there were other perils for the city dweller, and the bakufu, as it had always done, warned against them. Gambling was prohibited yet again, particularly among the samurai, as were lotteries. So, too, was the practice of decorative tatooing, an important element in the gambling life-style. The publishing industry also invited bakufu intervention. Certain publications – the novelettes known as *ninjōbon,* for example, believed to have "a bad effect on morals," or erotica (even worse), or works on unorthodox religion, or ephemeral works on contemporary mores – were banned, and others were required to obtain prior approval and to carry the names of both author and publisher. Prints of a kind depicting either actors or prostitutes, too, were prohibited. Nor did the bakufu overlook the entertainment industry, particularly the large number of music halls, often unlicensed, in which diversions of an emphatically unimproving kind were offered. These were restricted in number, and their programs were to be confined to inspiring talks on religious and historical subjects. Nor did the legitimate theater (in itself a concept that Tokugawa Japan would not have recognized) escape attention. In 1842 appeared a nationwide instruction that itinerant actors, known for "ruining morals wherever they go," were to be reported to the authorities, while six months earlier the major Edo theaters had been forcibly removed from the downtown area. Their new home was to be at Asakusa, near the licensed quarter, where the two great hazards associated with them – fires and the contamination of decent folk – would be of less consequence.

Together with its attack on frivolity and immorality, the bakufu continued its constant war on other aspects of indecorum and in particular on an ever-present source of unease: the fact that people were living and spending in a manner inappropriate to their station. The traditional status system had long since been reduced to tatters, but it nevertheless remained one of the major principles informing legislative and administrative practice, and these reforms showed it. There was a torrent of sumptuary instructions: some of a general kind, some directed specifically at samurai extravagance, and others aimed at the farmers, among whom the least trace of self-indulgence seemed particularly seditious. Less than a week after declaring its commitment to reform, the bakufu warned its local officials to keep farmers from

44 Saitō Gesshin, *Bukō nempyō* (Tokyo: Heibonsha, 1968), vol. 2, p. 102.

spending too much on food, clothing, or festivities of any sort, communal and private. From time to time, as it condemned extravagance in general, the government also drew attention to more specific areas – lavish decorations at the Tanabata festival, for example, elaborate hats and kites, costly children's toys, certain brands of fireworks, sumptuous clothing, gourmet specialties, and expensive houses and garden furnishings (including lanterns, basins, and trees). Linked with this, too, was the bakufu's insistence that people not only spend according to their station but that they also behave in a suitable manner – so, for example, it was judged inappropriate that ordinary townspeople should study the martial arts or wear long swords (as these were the prerogative of the samurai) or that farmers should leave their productive (and taxable) calling to become factory workers, a position that, because it was regarded as neither worthy nor productive, was not taxed.

None of this was particularly novel. The bakufu had always hoped to achieve social stability and decorum by telling its subjects, in painstaking detail, just what they should and should not do. This was particularly marked during periods of self-conscious reform, but it was no less so in more normal times as well. The 1830s, for example, had seen a steady flow of just this kind of instruction. What does identify 1841 as the beginning of a bakufu reform period is, first, the mood of urgency, in which the steady flow of the previous decade welled into a flood and, second, a willingness, rather unusual in bakufu history, to make examples of those conducting themselves in an unseemly fashion. There were instances of mass arrest – thirty-six apprehended in connection with female cabaret performances in 1841, for example, and thirty extravagantly garbed girls from Asakusa jailed for three days the following year. In others, the bakufu deliberately fixed on celebrities, in the process making examples of Kuniyoshi and Tamenaga Shunsui, both of whom were put in manacles, the latter for his "obscene novelettes" and the former for caricaturing the shogun and his chief minister. Ryūtei Tanehiko, too, author of the best-selling *Inaka Genji*, received a reprimand, and the matinee idol Ichikawa Ebizō (later the seventh Danjūrō) was exiled for a life-style rather imperfectly attuned to economy and frugality.

This all was the familiar stuff of Tokugawa reforms, a series of minutely detailed exhortations aimed at teaching people how to behave and thereby restoring the moral fabric of the nation to that pristine condition that had obtained before two hundred years of peace and self-indulgence had taken their toll. The Kyōhō and Kansei reforms had been aimed at precisely the same sorts of target. In other areas, however, the bakufu's Tempō reforms were rather more innovative, rather less directed at recreating the conditions of some legendary golden age, and rather more concerned with reaching an accommodation, however painful, with changing circumstances.

Traces of this new attitude can be seen in the question of foreign affairs. Admittedly, as far as defense issues were concerned, 1841 marked no perceptible change in bakufu policy, for any subsequent foreign threat was handled precisely as before, that is, with a brief, nervous flurry of inquiries into defense capacity and contingency plans more or less based on them, but little practical result. On the general issue of foreign affairs, however, and in particular on the question of Tokugawa Japan's formidable xenophobia, the Tempō reforms do represent a slight, but significant, change of direction. During the 1830s the government had seemed quite adamant, ushering in the decade by executing a man for giving a map of Japan to a foreigner and, at the other end, arresting a number of amateurs of European studies, Watanabe Kazan and Takano Chōei among them. Yet in 1841, just a month before the Tempō reforms were announced, the bakufu seemed suddenly to mellow. Takashima Shūhan, whose memorial had urged the government to adopt Western military technology, was granted an audience and then, a few days later, was permitted to mount a demonstration at Tokumarugahara, with twenty mortars, a howitzer, three field guns, and eighty-five men.[45] The bakufu showed its approval by rewarding him with two hundred pieces of silver, buying two of his best guns, and arranging for him to pass on his skills to some bakufu officials, one of whom, Egawa Hidetatsu, was the following year assigned the task of training one hundred musketeers along European lines.

This in itself was a change of heart, but more was to follow. In 1842, after reports that Britain had lost patience with Japan's policy of seclusion, the bakufu issued the following directive:

> In 1825 it was ordered that foreign vessels should be driven away without hesitation. However, as befits the current comprehensive reforms, in which we are recreating the policies of the Kyōhō and Kansei eras, the shogun has graciously intimated his wish that his mercy be made manifest. Therefore, in the event that foreigners, through storm-damage or shipwreck, come seeking food, fuel, or water, the shogun does not consider it a fitting response to other nations that they should be driven away indiscriminately without due knowledge of the circumstances.[46]

45 Arima, *Takashima Shūhan*, pp. 146–51. 46 *Tokugawa kinreikō*, vol. 6, document 4085.

Hereafter, foreign ships were to be supplied with whatever they needed (before being sent away, naturally), a development that must have afforded some satisfaction to those who, like Takano Chōei (now in jail at Demmachō), had been so critical over the *Morrison* incident. Such critics would have been equally pleased when, the following year, the bakufu changed its attitude to the repatriation of Japanese castaways, who could now be brought back in Dutch or Chinese vessels – an obvious response to the accusations of inhumanity circulating after the *Morrison* had been driven away. Obviously, too, the bakufu now felt that the Dutch and Chinese ghettos in Nagasaki had their uses, for in the same year questionnaires were issued to these two foreign communities asking for whatever information they could give on the size, strength, and disposition of British forces.

There were to be some significant changes of direction, too, in the bakufu's conduct of its economic affairs, although they took rather longer to appear. No government of the Tokugawa period could turn its back on tradition altogether, particularly not one assuming the dignified mantle of reform, and so to a large extent at first the Tempō government simply perpetuated the conventional policies. There were the usual fitful attempts, some of them obsessively minute, to reduce costs, including warnings to works officials and kitchen staff to watch their expenses, and requests to everyone to avoid unnecessary wear and tear on the Edo Castle tatami. There was also the customary inquiry into the reasons for the decline in bakufu income, followed up with a number of purposeful, if conventional, initiatives. It was decided, for example, that the *tenryō* – the shogun's own land – required more efficient administration. Such conclusions were a part of every reform and, in this case, given the gradual decline in tax revenues since the mid-eighteenth century, were hardly unreasonable. With the assistance of Ninomiya Sontoku, the agricultural consultant from Odawara, the bakufu elected first to reform its local administrators – to whose complacency, inefficiency, and plain dishonesty the decline in tax receipts was attributed – and during 1842 more than half of these officials in eastern Japan (including all of those in the Kantō) were transferred or dismissed. Later that year twelve of them were expressly ordered away from their comfortable Edo residences and back to their districts, with warnings that land tax revenues would have to be restored to their former level.

There was, too, the time-honored compulsion to bring more land under cultivation, to which end the bakufu had been canvasing local officials ever since the beginning of the reforms, looking for pockets of wasteland that might be cleared or drained. In fact, as they all knew, the choicest of opportunities lay close at hand: Along the lower reaches of the Tone River, forty miles northeast of Edo, ten thousand acres of potentially rich rice-growing land lay waiting to be reclaimed. The difficulty was that it also lay, most inconveniently, under three feet of water. This was the Imbanuma, the great swamp that, could it be drained, was believed capable of producing another 100,000 *koku* of rice each year – as much as the average daimyo domain. The prospect was an alluring one. Tokugawa Yoshimune, the eighth shogun, had been tempted to do something about it in 1724, and Tanuma Okitsugu, sixty years later, had also tried his hand. Both had failed, but in 1843, nothing daunted, the bakufu undertook its third and last attempt.

There were other initiatives equally conventional. For example, it had not escaped notice that falling revenues might be due as much to the decline in the number of taxpayers as to idle and corrupt officials. Large numbers of farmers had been selling their land and taking up employment as either agricultural laborers or workers in rural industries of one sort or another, thereby removing themselves from the tax register. Others were deserting their farms altogether and moving into provincial towns or, worse still, into Edo itself, where, as the government noted in 1842, "many vagrants and vagabonds are roaming the city, and not a few of them are engaged in questionable activities."[47] Rural depopulation, although common throughout much of Japan at this period, was especially severe in the area around Edo, and the bakufu, which viewed every homeless immigrant as a drain on city resources, a potential criminal, and an absconding taxpayer, was not anxious to encourage it. To halt and, if possible, reverse this drift away from productive agriculture was therefore a matter of some urgency. The bakufu tried the usual remedies, many of them from the Kansei era – prohibiting employment in rural manufacturing industry, discouraging mendicant religious sects, and ultimately driving, or tempting, people back to their native villages.

Naturally, the bakufu's economic responsibilities did not end there. It was equally committed to protecting those in charge from exploitation, whether stemming from their own folly (controllable, the government hoped, by sumptuary legislation) or the cupidity and duplicity of others. Here, too, on the whole, the Tempō administration trod a well-worn path. Confronted, for example, by an increasingly erratic market in which during the 1830s, the price of rice, despite violent fluctuations,

47 *Tokugawa jūgodaishi*, vol. 6, p. 2926.

had risen threefold, and the prices of other commodities, in their turn, were behaving more and more unpredictably, the bakufu ultimately did what its predecessors had always done – it blamed the business community. The solution, it was believed, lay in more intensive policing of the commercial world, including lowering the prices of some commodities and freezing those of others – foodstuffs, of course, but also bathhouse fees, fuel, and even horses (not to be sold for more than thirty gold pieces, and only then if they were of top quality). Similarly, it was forbidden to speculate in rice futures or to corner the market, and limits were imposed on interest rates, pawnbroking charges, the gold–silver exchange rate, and the level of shop rents. To make sure that these were observed, special squads of inspectors were to patrol the streets and shops of Edo and Osaka.

None of this activity was particularly new, deriving to a large extent from standard bakufu policy both in its tone (which often simply echoed that of the Kansei era) and its general thrust, which was toward making the system work as its founders had intended. Yet there were some distinct changes of emphasis. Currency debasement, for example, anathema to earlier reformers, had now become far too important to be jettisoned altogether; indeed, during the 1830s it had provided the bakufu with a third of its revenue. So although no new mintings were proposed during the period of the Tempō reforms, there was never any suggestion of currency reform along Kyōhō or Kansei lines. There had been a similar modification too in the way that the bakufu had come to regard the business community. It was still seen as a nuisance, but no longer quite so unmitigated as before, as the bakufu, like some daimyo, had discovered it to be a source of revenue. Despite the unorthodoxy of such a practice, therefore, it was decided in 1843 that "to assist in Bakufu reforms," thirty-seven businessmen from Osaka, and several more from towns adjacent to it, would be obliged to "contribute" well over a million gold pieces to the treasury. Equally unorthodox, to help its samurai (acknowledged to be, as usual, "in difficulties, having borrowed money over many generations") the government refrained from a general repudiation of samurai debts. The Kansei reformers had taken this way out, with no lasting results, other than one that was neither anticipated nor welcomed: severe financial embarrassment for the *fudasashi,* the rice brokers. The entire samurai stipend system depended on the services of these men, and the government knew it, and so this time it largely left them alone and, instead, itself entered the moneylending business. From an office at Saruya-chō, samurai were to be able to borrow, at 7 percent interest (less than half the normal *fudasashi* rate) and could consider their debts discharged after twenty-five years of interest payments.

Undoubtedly, however, the most abrupt departures from traditional economic practice were in the field of price control. In the past, wherever possible, the bakufu had tried to regulate commercial activities through a system in which craft guilds, business associations, and the professions (including, as we have seen, the oldest) were guaranteed government protection in return for an annual fee. The fee itself was never particularly great, but that had never been too important: The value of the system was that it provided an avenue for government regulation. By the Tempō era, however, the emergence of independent, and more or less surreptitious, trade networks in the provinces had reduced the effectiveness of such semiofficial monopolies, whereas the current unease about prices made even a reforming government ready to question two hundred years of tradition.

In 1841, therefore, the bakufu was responsive to a complaint from Tokugawa Nariaki, by then the nation's chief complainer, attacking one of the most influential of these monopoly associations, the *tokumi-donya,* a syndicate shipping such commodities as cloth, medicines, paper, and foodstuffs from Osaka, the commercial capital, to Edo, the consumer capital. As was his habit, Nariaki put his case in the most disinterested terms: "Would there not be some effect on rising prices," he suggested, "if they [the *tonya*] were totally abolished and all goods could be transported to Edo from anywhere in the land and sold freely?"[48] It was quite disingenuous, of course, for his hostility was not toward monopolies in general but only toward those that stood in the way of his own. Whether or not the bakufu was aware of this, it fell in with his suggestion, accusing the *tonya* of unspecified dishonesty and stripping them of their privileges. "There are to be no more associations calling themselves *tonya, nakama,* or *kumiai,*" read the announcement, "and ordinary people may therefore trade freely in any of those goods shipped in the past, or indeed in any merchandise from anywhere in the land." The precise details were spelled out the following year in two notices, the second of which, observing in its preamble that "prices have increased of late, and the people are much distressed thereby" and predicting in its final sentence that goods would become cheaper, specifically linked the dissolution with the government's price policies.

The need to stabilize prices also lay behind another related, and no

48 *Mito-han shiryō* (Tokyo: Yoshikawa kōbunkan, 1970), app. vol. 1, p. 140.

less controversial, measure. During his twenty months as Osaka magistrate, a senior government official called Abe Masakura had investigated the whole subject of commodity prices and emerged with an answer. Prices were unstable, he said, because Osaka, once the distribution center for every kind of commercial product, was so no longer. Goods were going elsewhere, and Abe isolated two kinds of culprit. The first was the independent rural entrepreneur, thousands of whom were buying and selling, manufacturing and processing, with no reference to the traditional Osaka-based market system. The second was the daimyo, alert now as never before to the profits to be won from commerce, and doing much the same sort of thing. "The commercial produce hitherto sent to Osaka wholesalers by farmers and merchants," went Abe's report, "has of recent years been bought up by daimyo . . . [who have also] been buying up produce from other domains, claiming it to be from their own, and probably in not a few cases sending it off to wherever they please; . . . truly what they are trying to do is unbecoming to warriors."[49]

Back in Edo, the government had already precluded the first of these implicit recommendations. Whereas Abe wanted the government-sponsored monopoly system to be intensified, the bakufu, acting before his report was finished, abolished it. On the other hand, the second made an impression. At the end of 1842, a year after dismantling the merchant monopolies, the government turned on those operated by the daimyo. "Of late," its order read, echoing Abe's findings,

> daimyo of Kinai, Chūgoku, Saigoku, and Shikoku have been, by various methods, buying up the products not only of their own domains, but of other domains also; . . . sending them to their warehouses, and then selling them when the market price is high. . . . Consequently they are using their authority as daimyo to cause much mischief to commerce. . . . This is most irregular, particularly bearing in mind our frequent instructions to reduce prices.

Any daimyo continuing his monopolies was therefore to be reported and, presumably, made to regret it.[50]

It is perhaps not immediately apparent just how unusual this instruction was. No doubt any government as committed to price controls as this one might have been expected to turn its attention sooner or later to domain monopolies. For that matter, few Tokugawa governments derived any joy from the sight of samurai buying and selling, particularly not during periods of reform, when all aspects of commerce

49 Quoted in Harold Bolitho, *Treasures Among Men* (New Haven, Conn.: Yale University Press, 1974), p. 26. 50 *Tokugawa jūgodaishi*, vol. 6, p. 2924.

tended to come under censorious scrutiny. Nevertheless, in the context of the Tempō era, this particular prohibition was quite extraordinary. Monopolies were vitally important to the financial health, and therefore the security, of many domains; to others, they represented a hope – perhaps the only hope – for a stable future. The bakufu, itself administered by daimyo, can hardly have been ignorant of this. The prohibition of domain monopolies, therefore, carried implications far beyond any immediate issue of price controls. It implied, first, a certain disregard for regional needs and aspirations. More importantly, however, it implied a certain reappraisal of the relationship between the bakufu and the daimyo domains.

In 1642 there would have been nothing untoward about such interference in domain affairs, but in 1842, after two hundred years of peaceful coexistence, the daimyo could have been pardoned for believing that a strong central government was a thing of the past. Just a year earlier, in fact, the bakufu had been obliged to admit as much, publicly and humiliatingly: It had ordered three daimyo to exchange their domains and then suddenly retracted the order in the face of strong protests from daimyo all over Japan. "This was the first time such a thing had happened," noted the compiler of the *Tokugawa jūgodaishi*, "and from it one can see that bakufu authority was no longer what it had once been."

Nonetheless, expected or not, anachronistic or not, by forbidding access to commercial profit, the bakufu had reasserted its right to control the daimyo domains. During the next six months, from late 1842 to mid-1843, it was to do much more, challenging domain independence in one measure after another as it had not been challenged for generations. Not only monopolies but also domain currency, the very token of economic independence, was soon to be threatened. Before the year was out, money changers had been instructed not to handle any copper cash minted in the domains, and an investigation had been ordered into *hansatsu*, the local paper currency used so effectively in underpinning domain monopolies.

The onslaught assumed a slightly different form when in the spring of 1843, Ieyoshi, the twelfth Tokugawa shogun, left his castle for a period of eight days to worship at the tombs of his great predecessors: Tokugawa Ieyasu, who had founded the dynasty, and Tokugawa Iemitsu, who had consolidated it. This official progress to Nikkō, ninety miles away, may seem to have been no more than filial piety of the most praiseworthy sort. Its implications, however, were very different. First, it placed heavy demands on a number of daimyo. Three of them, at Iwatsuki, Koga, and Utsunomiya, were obliged to house the shogun and his retinue, both on the way to Nikkō and on the way back. The Utsunomiya domain records, which speak of "indescribable turmoil and confusion," suggest that this was no easy matter.[51] Other daimyo had to provide the shogun with an escort, amounting to some 150,000 men, and still others were given ceremonial duties, some guarding Edo Castle in the shogun's absence, or manning the Kantō's key strategic points – Usui Pass, Uraga, the Ōi River, and Hakone (where the daimyo of Sendai sent six thousand men). Because they cost money that none could afford, such movements provided a headache for those domains directly involved and a matter of concern for others that, if not called on this time, might well be so in the future. Beyond the immediate financial problem, however, loomed something less tangible but, in its way, far more ominous. The shogunal progress to Nikkō had once been an important, if intermittent, part of Tokugawa ceremonial life. Whether in its ostensible objective – an act of homage to the architects of Tokugawa supremacy – or in the manner in which large numbers of men from the daimyo domains were placed at the shogun's disposal, it was a symbolic celebration of Tokugawa rule and an affirmation of Tokugawa authority. That this costly and wasteful ritual should be revived now, after a lapse of nearly seventy years, by a government otherwise dedicated to economizing and frugality, was yet another tribute to the severity of the Tempō crisis and the extent to which it had goaded the bakufu into action.

By the middle of that year, the pattern was clear. Within the space of fourteen days, the bakufu reformers gave warning of their intention to restore not only conventional morality and economic stability but also the old early-seventeenth-century relationship between the Tokugawa shogun and his daimyo, characterized by unquestioned authority, on the one hand, and unquestioning obedience, on the other. One indication was the plan to drain the Imbanuma, for this project, designed to increase the shogun's own productive land, was to be carried out at the expense of five daimyo, who together were to share the cost of more than 200,000 gold pieces. It had been sixty years since daimyo had been forced to bear so heavy a burden for Tokugawa benefit.

Nor was that all. The Imbanuma project was announced in the middle of the most ambitious rearrangement of daimyo land for more than two hundred years. On the first day of the sixth month of 1843, a number of daimyo and *hatamoto* had received an unusual notice. The details differed, but the wording was roughly the same in each case:

51 Tokuda, *Shiryō Utsunomiya han shi*, p. 177.

A measure has now been announced by which, for administrative purposes, all land adjacent to Edo Castle is to become bakufu land. Therefore you are ordered to surrender land producing at least X *koku* from your fief in Y County, Z Province. In due course you will be given land in exchange. . . .[52]

In short, the bakufu was resuming land originally given to daimyo in fief. This first round of reappropriations affected land producing some 15,000 *koku*, but the next ten days were to see more, all in the vicinity of Edo. On the eleventh day, the scene shifted briefly to the west coast, with the appropriation of 600 *koku* of land from the Nagaoka domain – a relatively small area but a most important one, as it was the site of Niigata, the largest of the Japan Sea ports. Then, on the fifteenth day, came a further series of announcements, this time addressed to sixteen daimyo with land near Osaka Castle, requiring them to surrender a total of 100,000 *koku*.

In strategic terms, these measures, known collectively as *agechi rei*, were no more than reasonable. Obviously, if the nation were to face a foreign threat, then the land surrounding its two greatest fortresses should be under unified control, rather than, as was the case at Osaka, controlled by 165 different authorities. A similar case could have been made for joining Niigata to the other major ports – Osaka, Edo, Nagasaki, and Hakodate – under Tokugawa supervision. Nonetheless, as with the prohibition of domain monopolies, the *agechi rei* were significant in other respects. The bakufu did not hesitate to admit, for example, that it was reshuffling these fiefs to enhance its own financial situation at daimyo expense: "It is inappropriate," read the official statement, "that private domains should now have more high-yield land than the bakufu."[53] Therefore, the daimyo were to be required to give up their pockets of productive land around Edo and Osaka, taking in return some of the low-yielding land held by the bakufu in such large quantities. Once again, these measures were well within the bakufu's formal power; having originally bestowed the land on the daimyo, it could also take it away. Yet, nearly two centuries of freedom from interference had left the daimyo believing that despite formal subordination to the shogun and his government, their fiefs were inviolable, theirs to be held in perpetuity. Now they were reminded that this was not so and, ominously, informed that the bakufu contemplated extending the *agechi rei* into a large-scale rationalization of its landholdings. To any daimyo, condemned to discharging a whole range of administrative responsibilities on a dwindling income, it was a notably cheerless prospect.

52 Quoted in Kitajima, *Mizuno Tadakuni*, p. 425.

53 *Tokugawa jūgodaishi*, vol. 6, pp. 2955 ff.

Historians have often labeled the bakufu's Tempō reforms as conservative. In many respects they were. So much of the Tempō legislation was repetitious, self-consciously archaic, and irrelevant to the crisis that Japan faced. Nevertheless, certain aspects of the bakufu's reforms were extremely singular, and none more so than these efforts to reestablish its central authority over the daimyo and thereby to regain some kind of political and economic primacy. This, too, may have been conservative, as it was predicated on the revival of powers dormant since the mid-seventeenth century. Nevertheless it represents a dramatic departure from the pattern laid down by the earlier reforms, neither of which had compromised daimyo autonomy in any significant way. Here, at least, we can see the bakufu reacting appropriately to the demands of the Tempō crisis – appropriately, that is, from one point of view. With the nation fearful of civil unrest and foreign invasion, a central government – particularly one as weak as the Tokugawa bakufu – could legitimately call for more power. Unfortunately, the daimyo domains, subject to pressures equally intense, were less ready to listen than ever before. The Tempō crisis had spurred the domains into new and potentially divisive forms of behavior; it had now done no less for the Tokugawa bakufu. More than that, it had brought the domains and the bakufu face to face with each other's aspirations in a particularly peremptory fashion, and neither could be reassured by what they saw.

MIZUNO TADAKUNI

If the bakufu reforms were unusual, the man who had charge of them was more unusual still. Traditionally, in Tokugawa historiography, the reformer assumes his role at birth, displaying, with preternatural speed, every quality expected of a Man of Destiny. Tokugawa Yoshimune, initiator of the Kyōhō reforms, was tough, disciplined, and frugal; Matsudaira Sadanobu, father of the Kansei reforms, was talented, conscientious, and wise beyond his years. By contrast, Mizuno Tadakuni (1794–1851), architect of the Tempō reforms, was all too human. He was, for example, rather greedy. Conger eel, prepared in the Kyoto style, was his favorite dish, but his all-embracing absorption with food was well known, and Tokugawa Nariaki could contemplate winning his favor with boxes of salmon *sushi* and wild duck *tempura*. There were other weaknesses, too, for his appetites by no means halted at his stomach. In 1840, less than a year before launching his campaign to restore the nation to moral health, Mizuno Tadakuni was reputedly obsessed with sex. "I have been making surreptitious inquiries about [Mizuno's] tastes," reported one of Tokugawa Nariaki's agents, "but at the moment he cares for nothing but women," adding that the senior councilor was giving his servants money to make sure of a ready supply.[54]

A weakness for food and women, however unexpected in a Confucian reformer, was not unpardonable, but in this case there were other, graver, defects. Tokugawa Nariaki, though refusing to condemn Mizuno's passion for women, nevertheless considered him unfit for public office, citing the fact that "he does not care for soldierly things and prefers the ways of courtiers; his interests lie in court ceremonial and antiquarian information, rather than in weaponry. . . ." Mizuno's own avowed ambition, expressed at the beginning of his career, "to become senior councilor as quickly as possible and then relax," suggests that this judgment was not without foundation. Beyond this, however, and most serious of all, is the matter of Mizuno's demonstrable partiality to money. As a young daimyo, first at Karatsu and later at Hamamatsu, his financial situation had always been one of his chief concerns, and as he readily confessed, he undertook an official career confidently expecting to make something out of it. To some extent he was right. Office brought him a richly decorated mansion in Aoyama, surrounded by gardens full of rare plants and unusual rocks – "so splendid a residence," wrote a contemporary, "as to steal away the senses." It also brought something less welcome: a reputation for venality that most politicians, and reformers in particular, might have wished to avoid. "In the past people have asked [Mizuno] for favors," wrote one of Tokugawa Nariaki's informants in 1840, "and such is his nature that he has obliged them. He has, too, accepted bribes quite freely, although since this spring he has been wary and returned all gifts offered to him." Nevertheless, Tokugawa Nariaki considered him even more corrupt than the notorious Tanuma Okitsugu.

It is undeniably difficult to associate such a man with orthodox Confucian reforms. Hypocrisy was never too far below the surface of Tokugawa period morality, but exhortations to self-restraint must have rung more than usually hollow in the mouth of a known glutton, debaucher, dilettante, and taker of bribes. Yet it is still more difficult to associate Mizuno Tadakuni with the other, unorthodox aspect of the Tempō reforms. He was, after all, a daimyo and therefore subject to all the pressures of the Tempō crisis. More than that, his sympa-

54 Tsuji Tatsuya, "Tokugawa Nariaki to Mizuno Tadakuni," *Jimbutsu sōsho furoku*, no. 154 (Tokyo: Yoshikawa kōbunkan).

thies on this issue had never previously been in doubt. As the daimyo of first Karatsu and then Hamamatsu, he had consistently given priority to domain interests. In government, which he entered in 1815, he had endured, but not endorsed, the rule of Tokugawa Ienari. Then with Ienari dead, he proceeded to purge all those who had followed the eleventh shogun on his capricious and autocratic way. Clearly, to Mizuno, as to almost all of his predecessors in bakufu office, the best government was one in which the shogunal prerogative was curbed by senior officials who, daimyo themselves, saw the value of regional autonomy. Such was certainly the intent behind Mizuno's memorial to the twelfth shogun, in 1841, urging that he work through his daimyo ministers, and not, as his father had done, through personal cronies.[55]

This was not the kind of man suddenly to turn and savage his own class. But he did. His directives from late 1842 to mid-1843 – the abolition of guilds and domain monopolies, the shogunal progress to Nikkō, the *agechi rei*, the draining of the Imbanuma – all threatened, directly or otherwise, the regional independence that the daimyo had enjoyed since the mid-seventeenth century. Why did he change? The question is reasonable and straightforward enough, but unfortunately, it cannot be answered with any finality. Mizuno, like all but a few politicians of the Tokugawa period, has left us no substantial clues to the workings of his mind. The chronicle of events alone offers some assistance, but even that is tenuous. What there is, however, is suggestive. Mizuno had come to maturity in a society accustomed to isolation; nothing in his background or his earlier career could have prepared him for the hard diplomatic decisions, the rumors, and the atmosphere of impending catastrophe waiting for him in the Tempō era. Together with the critics – Tokugawa Nariaki, Watanabe Kazan, Takashima Shūhan, Sakuma Shōzan, and the rest – he would have shared fears of foreign invasion in 1838 and, like them, would have seen those fears, amorphous at first, take on British shape with news of the Opium War. "It is happening in a foreign country," wrote Mizuno, describing the affray in China in a letter to a subordinate, "but I believe it also contains a warning for us."[56] With responsibilities and access to information far more extensive than any of the Tempō critics, his concern would have been no less than theirs. Nor can Mizuno have been ignorant of the implications of the Chinese experience. If a great centralized state could be despatched so readily, then

55 Bolitho, *Treasures Among Men*, p. 215.
56 Quoted in Inoue Kiyoshi, *Nihon gendaishi* (Tokyo: Tōkyō daigaku shuppankai, 1967), vol. 1, p. 89.

what chance had Japan – small, weak, and fragmented as it was? The unpalatable truth about the *bakuhan taisei*, as politicians and critics were beginning to realize, was that it was inadequate to the needs of a country threatened by invasion. It was either too centralized (because the daimyo were forced to squander their resources paying court to the shogun in Edo) or not centralized enough (because the bakufu had no firm control over them).

There are indications that Mizuno, background and personal preferences notwithstanding, had come to incline to the latter view. One is to be seen in the bakufu's changing attitude toward Satō Nobuhiro. Satō was the critic who, more than any other, stood for stronger central government. It was not a position that won him many friends; on the contrary, in 1832 he had been ordered not to come within twenty miles of Edo. Ten years later, however, as the government began to digest the lessons of the Opium War, his works came to be read again by bakufu officials, Mizuno among them. At the beginning of 1843 Satō was pardoned and allowed back into the city where in 1845, at Mizuno's personal request, he compiled an abbreviated version of *Suitō hiroku*, the work in which he had provided the blueprints for a unified nation-state.

On its own, this is far from conclusive evidence of any change of heart. Yet taken in conjunction with Mizuno's policies, as they developed from late 1842 to the middle of the following year, it suggests that of the two possible lines along which the *bakuhan taisei* might have been modified – either in the direction of more regional autonomy or toward greater central control – Mizuno, for one, had made his choice. Events thirty years later vindicated his judgment, but this was far too late for Mizuno. All too soon he paid dearly for that choice at the hands of those infinitely less prescient.

THE AFTERMATH

It was one of the peculiarities of Tokugawa period reforms that they never reached a formal conclusion. How could they? They all began with a public commitment to precisely those virtues – honesty, frugality, the recognition of talent – most highly prized in conventional morality; no government could possibly confess itself no longer interested in such things. Nevertheless, all these paroxysms of reform subsided as quickly as they appeared. In the bakufu, the Kyōhō and Kansei reforms faded imperceptibly into the inertia of Gembun and Kyōwa. Domains like Tosa, proclaiming reforms in Genna, Kambun,

Tenna, Kyōhō, Temmei, and Kansei, saw them all come to a halt. It was a fact universally recognized but never openly admitted. With so much to be done before the golden age could be restored and human nature transformed, it would not have been politic to confess that reforms could ever end.

The Tempō reforms proved no exception. In the domains they all ended, some whimpering their way into oblivion, others culminating in an explosion in which the reformers were dismissed (as with Watanabe Kazan at Tawara in 1837) and sometimes thrown into prison as well (as with Mabuchi Kahei at Tosa in 1843). Whatever the end, they were ignored until their resurrection as models for fresh reforms in the 1850s and 1860s.

In the Tokugawa bakufu, the climax was more spectacular. Toward the end of 1843, just two years after Mizuno had declared his reformist intentions, one year after he had fired his first shots against domain autonomy, and one month after the salvo of *agechi rei,* Mizuno was tumbled out of office and disgraced in a spasm of conservative revulsion. He was accused of "dishonesty," and his dismissal was said to have brought a crowd of irate citizens into the streets to pelt his house with stones. Exactly the same thing had happened to Tanuma Okitsugu, who had also tried to strengthen the bakufu at daimyo expense. Unlike Tanuma, however, Mizuno's career did not quite end there. Within nine months, in the middle of 1844, he was reinstated, the allegations of "dishonesty" and unpopularity forgotten in the confusion of yet another diplomatic crisis. The Dutch had just sent word of an important communication from their king, and Mizuno was recalled to deal with it. His rehabilitation was brief, however (just eight months), incomplete, and hampered by ill health (genuine, not assumed). Once again it terminated in humiliation, and Mizuno was obliged to resign for the second and last time. Before the year 1845 was out, he was forced into retirement, and 20,000 *koku* was stripped from his estates. Hori Chikashige, the only other senior councilor to have given him full support, was treated in much the same way, while two of Mizuno's subordinates were subsequently jailed, and a third was put to death. The bakufu's Tempō reforms, in this, the second year of the succeeding Kōka era (1844–8), were well and truly at an end. In fact, they had never really survived Mizuno's first dismissal, in the intercalary ninth month of 1843.

Did the Tempō reforms succeed or fail? This depends on one's perception of the reforms' aims and one's definition of success or failure. In their own terms, they failed. They made no lasting impact on human nature, certainly not to such an extent that the Japanese people thereafter turned again to righteousness and resumed the simple life they had once allegedly enjoyed. No reforms ever did. In Japan, as elsewhere, human nature was always ready to ignore or circumvent whatever arbitrary restrictions were imposed on certain inalienable rights (among them spending money, drinking, gambling, and pursuing sexual gratification, whether at the bathhouse, teahouse, or street corner). Incorrigible, the public continued to read frivolous and salacious books, and the publishers, after only a momentary check, continued to provide them. Printmakers, too, seemed largely to have ignored government prohibitions. In Edo, for example, there were more variety theaters than ever by 1845, and actors were no less in the public eye. Repression of this kind, whether originating in the bakufu or the domain governments, was always doomed to failure.

To the extent that the Tempō reforms aimed at restoring a measure of peace and prosperity to the Japanese people in the wake of the Tempō crisis, they enjoyed a measure of success. Most of this, however, was accidental, more a product of better seasons and increased food supplies than anything else. Government interference, wherever it took place, tended to be disastrous. In the case of the bakufu's dissolution of merchant associations, for example, insofar as these bodies ever complied with the government's order (and even this is questionable), the effect seems to have been not quite what officials had anticipated. In some areas it reduced the traditional commercial network to chaos, leaving "everybody engaged in trade much inconvenienced," as one village official complained in his diary.[57] It promoted confusion, shortages, and economic depression – even, ironically, higher prices, the very thing the bakufu had hoped to counter. On the other hand, it encouraged commercial and industrial activities of a kind even more difficult to control, whether in the hands of independent rural entrepreneurs or the daimyo domains. When this attempt failed, therefore, the bakufu promptly returned to more familiar measures, only to see those fail in their turn. It simply did not have the means to enforce its price restrictions and by early 1845 had apparently come to doubt not only the feasibility of such an enterprise but even its desirability, observing lamely that "naturally prices will rise and fall according to circumstances and according to the volume of goods available."[58] What is certain is that prices had remained high throughout Mizuno's tenure of office and were still the object of official complaint in 1845, on the eve of his final departure from the political world.

57 *Essa sōsho*, p. 312. 58 Quoted in Okamoto, "Tempō kaikaku," pp. 239–40.

Other social problems, too, remained untouched. It is debatable, for example, just what result was obtained by efforts to drive, or tempt, people out of the cities and back to their native villages. Some scholars deny any effect whatsoever; another detected a 5 percent fall in the population of Osaka between 1842 and 1843, but even this tells us little, as the measures were aimed not so much at reducing the number of city dwellers as replenishing Japan's farm population.[59] In either case, one wonders what lasting effect was likely to be achieved by measures that attacked the symptoms of rural decline while so transparently ignoring the causes. Similarly, the system of bakufu loans for samurai would seem to have fallen well short of its mark, although in this case it is not easy to judge how effective it might have been, for like so many of Mizuno's initiatives, it had been in operation barely a year before it was hastily reversed by his successors.

Insofar as the bakufu and the domains used their reforms to retrieve some sort of financial balance by reducing debts and expenses and increasing income, the judgment is a little less certain. Overall, it is difficult to escape the impression that they failed. Mito, for example, despite all its efforts at expanding and diversifying its economic base, really solved none of its problems. Echizen, too, continued to spend more than it made, prompting even the phlegmatic Yuri Kimimasa to complain that "you never see any money in Fukui," and this condition did not begin to improve until another set of reforms was instituted in the 1850s.[60]

It would appear, however, that in at least some domains, the reforms did work, and in this context, historians usually point to the great domains of the southwest, most notably Satsuma, Chōshū, Tosa, and Hizen. This is not unreasonable, in view of these domains' later economic strength and their considerable political influence; it is, however, open to question. Satsuma is perhaps the exception. The commercialization of farming and the emergence of rural entrepreneurs had never been a problem there; nor for that matter had peasant rebellions, which were virtually unknown. New crops and processing industries could therefore be introduced and closely supervised by the Satsuma government without provoking any local opposition, for their farmers apparently did not miss freedoms they had never enjoyed. Otherwise, however, there is room for doubt. Tosa had not one but

59 Compare, for example, the views of Tsuda, "Tempō kaikaku," p. 316; and Okamoto, "Tempō kaikaku," p. 222.

60 Quoted in Rekishigaku kenkyūkai, eds., *Meiji ishinshi kenkyū kōza* (Tokyo: Heibonsha, 1968), vol. 2, p. 216.

two sets of Tempō reforms, both of which ended in disgrace – the first with the resignation of the daimyo in 1843, the second with the imprisonment of Mabuchi Kahei, the domain's financial expert, a few months later. Chōshū, too, forced to abandon its plans of marketing domain products in 1843, saw Murata Seifū, its chief reformer, resign in 1844, his Thirty-seven-Year Plan in ruins. Like Echizen, Chōshū's financial rehabilitation had to await further reforms in the 1850s.

In the case of the bakufu, there can be no such doubts. Mizuno's attempts to restore bakufu finances were no more successful than was anything else he initiated. Ideas of developing and controlling the productivity of the bakufu's own domain dissolved in a storm of rural protest in which farmers, preferring to keep their agricultural surplus in their own hands, attacked government offices and destroyed their documents. Other initiatives, among them recoinage, levies on the business community, and the addition to the bakufu domain of land reclaimed from the Imbanuma, all were casualties of their author's fall from power. The final result, therefore, was a bakufu that had failed to restore itself to financial health. This was to have disastrous consequences in the future, particularly because domains like Satsuma had done so much better. For the present, its consequences were equally serious, simply because lack of money prevented the bakufu from reorganizing national defense. Had Mizuno remained in office longer, of course, the situation might well have improved. As it was, however, he spent just 2,739 gold pieces on defense, less than 3 percent of the cost of the shogun's progress to Nikkō.

There is one more measure of the success or otherwise of the Tempō reforms. The Tempō crisis, which had entangled daimyo and bakufu in civil unrest, financial malaise, and fears of impending diplomatic, and possibly military, confrontation, obliged them all to respond. Given their separate responsibilities, they could do so only from standpoints that were radically different and, ultimately, incompatible. The domains, looking to their finances and their defenses, saw the need to move outside bakufu control; the bakufu, equally preoccupied, began to reassert its right – indeed, its obligation – to control the domains as they had not been controlled for generations. Which side prevailed, then, in this most fundamental of struggles?

In one sense it was the daimyo domains. Where Mizuno's policies could be defied or circumvented, they did so – most obviously, of course, with domain monopolies, which continued everywhere, despite official prohibition. When resistance appeared no longer possible, then a concerted movement of daimyo – some inside the bakufu itself, others not – turned Mizuno out of office, crushing his policies in the process. The *agechi rei,* for example, were canceled six days before their author's dismissal; so potent a threat to domain autonomy could hardly have remained uncorrected. Work on the Imbanuma, too, was allowed to lapse ten days after Mizuno's dismissal and never resumed, although the project itself had been on the verge of completion. All that remained of the bakufu's attack on daimyo prerogatives, therefore, were the memories and the painful financial scars of the shogun's journey to Nikkō.

In Mizuno's place they ultimately installed a much more predictable successor. This was Abe Masahiro, whose qualities immediately commended themselves. He was sober, upright, conciliatory, and totally lacking in initiative. Abe made sure that once the controversial element of Mizuno's reforms had been dismantled, he would do nothing to offend anybody.[61] His government proceeded to ignore its financial problems, as it ignored matters of defense and foreign policy. Mizuno, however maladroitly, had tried to do something about them; Abe, on the other hand, conferred endlessly and did nothing. All three issues were swept out of sight, as they touched on the contentious question of the relative powers of the bakufu and the daimyo. Watanabe Shūjirō, Abe's biographer, observed that under his government, "all the daimyo were content."[62] We may be sure that they were. But on the other hand, with all the hard decisions about Japanese political organization pushed to one side, the rest of Japan paid dearly for that contentment in 1853, when it faced Commodore Perry with no central government worth the name.

There was another sense, however, in which the results of the Tempō reforms were not quite so well defined. True, the bakufu's reforms had been destroyed, and measures had been taken to see that daimyo interests would not be further threatened. But Mizuno had shown that the bakufu was not entirely without teeth, and several domains bore the marks for some time. Tokugawa Nariaki, for example, who never forgot an injury, had cause to remember this, for it was bakufu intervention that had aborted the Mito reform program. In

61 Scholarly appraisals of Abe have varied markedly and will no doubt continue to do so. W. G. Beasley, in his *Select Documents on Foreign Policy, 1853–1868* (London: Oxford University Press, 1955), p. 21, judges him "hardly the man best fitted to meet a serious crisis." By contrast, Conrad Totman, in *The Collapse of the Tokugawa Bakufu* (Honolulu: University of Hawaii Press, 1980), p. xx, impressed by his "repeated displays of political skill," considers him to have been an "astute" politician.

62 Watanabe Shūjirō, *Abe Masahiro jiseki* (Tokyo, 1910), vol. 1, p. 52.

Chōshū, too, they had learned a lesson: Murata Seifū had felt it politic to restrict the domain's commercial activities, to avoid open conflict with the bakufu. As a result, the Chōshū reforms had been ruined, and Murata himself was forced to resign. Mizuno, although he had lost, had alerted the daimyo domains to just how formidable an opponent the bakufu could still be. By raising this specter and not laying it completely, the Tempō reforms had left Japan with its fundamental dilemma still unresolved. How was the nation to be organized to meet a troubled future? This particular legacy of the Tempō crisis remained to bedevil Japan for the next thirty years. Other aspects of the crisis could be resolved, superficially at least, by the return of fine weather and good harvests, but not this one. The foreign problem, with all its attendant internal difficulties, had arrived. No amount of sunshine was likely to alter that.

THE IMPLICATIONS

The Tempō era had been one of critical importance for Japan. Even historians who agree on little else agree on this, detecting in these years of crisis the beginning of a chain of events that culminated thirty years later in the dismantling of Japan's ancien régime. Beyond this, of course, they disagree. To some historians, perhaps the majority, the Tempō era's most important contribution to Japan's future ferment was the informal alliance concluded across class barriers by the country gentry, on the one hand, and some sections of the samurai class – the so-called lower samurai – on the other, an alliance of the kind of men who, in 1868, put paid to an establishment that excluded them and installed themselves in its place.[63] Other scholars, to whom the Meiji Restoration was far more the result of political developments than social ones, contrast the failure of the bakufu's reforms with the success of those carried out in domains like Satsuma, finding the seeds of future instability in the poverty of the one and the wealth of the other.

My personal inclination is toward the latter view, yet not without some modification. Certainly the newfound affluence of the Satsuma government held serious implications for the *bakuhan taisei*. In the diplomatic crisis of the Tempō era, wealth was already equated with

63 This aspect of the Tempō reforms has been much analyzed by Japanese historians, many of whom interpret it as a development tending toward "absolutism." I refer interested readers to Ishii Takashi, *Gakusetsu hihan: Meiji ishin ron* (Tokyo: Yoshikawa kōbunkan, 1968).

the acquisition of military power: new weapons, new ships, new training. All were necessary, but because all were expensive, few could afford them. If Satsuma could and the bakufu could not, then the balance of power that had kept Japan at peace for more than two hundred years was at risk. Yet there was a far more serious and far more general threat. Satsuma's success with its Tempō reforms was exceptional. Other domains, Mito and Chōshū among them, had tried and failed, their aspirations to wealth and power blocked by a central government that, too weak to offer them any protection, was at the same time too strong to allow them to prepare for their own. It is clear that such domains chafed at their economic impotence and at the military incapacity that inevitably accompanied it. The Tempō crisis had shown them all that the traditional balance of power was no longer workable, that one way or the other it would have to be changed; it had provided them with thesis and antithesis but, with the reforms so inconclusive, had suggested no synthesis. The dilemma was a real one. Obviously Japan needed to do something about its defenses, but nobody could decide what, because the subject was surrounded by too many uncomfortable issues. Who was to pay for the ships, the cannon and the small arms that Japan so desperately needed? Who would command them? How would they be used? Was there any guarantee that such weapons in bakufu hands would not be turned on the daimyo themselves, to complete by force the process that Mizuno had begun by edict? Conversely, if the daimyo acquired such weapons, might they not once again plunge the nation into turmoil? These were serious matters for a country in which regional autonomy had always been so prized, too serious for the Tempō era to produce a solution.

In fact, Mizuno's bakufu had already made it clear that given a choice between a Japan armed to the teeth and one helpless against foreign attack, it would prefer the latter to the former, with its implicit threat to internal stability. So much was apparent in a remarkable exchange of letters between Tokugawa Nariaki and Mizuno's government in 1843. "If you allow daimyo and shipowners to build stout ships," Nariaki argued, "it will not cost you a copper," adding later that to prohibit large ships simply because they might be misused was "like forcing everyone to wear wooden swords because a madman has unsheathed his in the palace." It was a reasonable point, but so, too, was the counterargument: "If we permit everyone to build warships," read the bakufu rejoinder, "who can tell what evils may ensue? The daimyo of the west country and elsewhere may begin to conspire and build unorthodox vessels; this will have a significant impact on our administration of the law."[64]

This reply was both honest and accurate, but it was not likely to satisfy any domain preparing to defend itself against foreign invaders. Nor were the bakufu's various interdictions – its attempt to keep Takashima Shūhan from teaching his gunnery techniques to samurai from the daimyo domains, for example, or its warning to the Astronomical Bureau (where Western works were translated) that translations of "calendars, medical books, works of astronomy, and all books on practical matters . . . are not to be circulated indiscriminately."[65] Many domains reacted, therefore, with mistrust, deception, and evasion – experimenting with three-masted ships, importing foreign arms and manuals in secret through Nagasaki gunrunners, and offering shelter to fugitives with particular skills (as Uwajima did for Takano Chōei after his escape from prison, and Satsuma for Torii Heishichi, a Nagasaki-trained gunner). It was an atmosphere in which the former *tairō*, Ii Naoaki, placing a translation of a Dutch work in his library in the autumn of 1843, could write on the box, in his own hand, instructions that it "be kept secret for a long period."[66] It was also one in which rumors flourished, particularly rumors involving those already viewed with official mistrust, "the daimyo of the west country." Satsuma, for example, was rumored in 1837 to have spirited Ōshio Heihachirō away from Osaka and into hiding aboard one of its ships; six years later it was rumored to have engineered Mizuno's dismissal. The roots of the *bakumatsu* arms race, which pitted the bakufu and the domains against each other so disastrously, can be found in this climate of mutual suspicion.

New political alignments, too, had their origins in the Tempō crisis. During these years Tokugawa Nariaki, the daimyo of Mito, became a national political figure, gathering around him the men who dominated the politics of the next twenty years. Date Munenari, soon to become daimyo of Uwajima, married Nariaki's daughter in 1839. The young Matsudaira Yoshinaga, recently made daimyo of Echizen, visited Nariaki at his Koishikawa mansion in 1843 with a list of questions on domain government and corresponded with him regularly thereafter; Shimazu Nariakira was a visitor from the late 1830s, as were the daimyo of Saga and Kurobane. Abe Masahiro, the bakufu's inoffensive senior councilor, although sharing many of Nariaki's friends – particularly Shimazu Nariakira and Matsudaira Yoshinaga (whose

64 *Mito han shiryō*, pp. 173–82. 65 *Tokugawa jūgodaishi*, pp. 2855–6.
66 *Hikone-shi shi* (Hikone: Hikone shiyakusho, 1962), vol. 2, p. 673.

adopted daughter became his second wife) – took a little longer to warm to Nariaki, but the two men had nevertheless become allies by 1846. The scholars in Nariaki's employ, Aizawa Seishisai and Fujita Tōko, were also far from idle. While their master forged his faction to defend daimyo prerogatives, they supported him by laying down the ideological barrage that, known to contemporaries as Mitogaku (Mito learning), was attracting students from domains as distant as Saga and Kurume.

As the political events of the 1850s and 1860s proved, this alignment of forces had particularly fateful consequences. So, too, did the issue of the arms race. The history of Japan would have been quite different without them. Yet the Tempō crisis produced something far more fateful than either. In 1837 Ōshio Heihachirō had begun his *Gekibun* by lamenting the disappearance of the emperor from Japanese political life: "From the time of the Ashikaga," he wrote, "the emperor has been kept in seclusion and has lost the power to dispense rewards and punishments; the people have therefore nowhere to turn with their complaints." Before another decade had passed, this situation was to change dramatically, as the imperial symbol was the obvious refuge – indeed the only possible refuge – for those wishing to justify political opposition. Increasingly, during the Tempō era, they sought shelter in it, and none more persistently than Tokugawa Nariaki. Privately, he lobbied with the court in Kyoto; publicly, he displayed his boundless respect by demanding that the bakufu repair the imperial mausolea. His scholars meanwhile worked feverishly to remind the nation that a government established by imperial consent could be disestablished by the same means.

In 1846, a year after Mizuno left office, the campaign had its effect. Sixteen years earlier, Matsuzaki Kōdō, observing the cranes, had felt his heart lift at the sight. The crane, after all, was the traditional symbol of happiness and longevity. It was also, by a convention equally venerable, a symbol of the emperor. In the flowery language of the court, the emperor's palace became "the Palace of the Crane," his command, the "Missive of the Crane," his voice "the Voice of the Crane." This time, in 1846, in an event unparalleled in Tokugawa history, the Voice of the Crane made itself heard in a formal expression of imperial concern that under Tokugawa leadership the nation was in grave danger. This time it presaged no thousand years of felicity; instead, the Voice of the Crane launched Japan on twenty years of turbulence, destroying in the process the last vestige of the Tempō world.

CHAPTER 2

LATE TOKUGAWA CULTURE AND THOUGHT

THE CULTURE OF PLAY

Japanese historiography has conventionally located the beginning of the end of the Tokugawa (*bakumatsu*) in the decade of the 1830s, when the regime and the several domains embarked on a series of reforms aimed at arresting economic failure and restoring public confidence. Historians who have concentrated on making sense of the signs of financial failure point to the implementation of the Tempō reforms as recognition of a gathering crisis. Some have established the revolt of Ōshio Heihachirō in Osaka in 1837 as the turning point in Tokugawa history. But regardless of the many opinions concerning the beginning of the end, most discussions of the end of the shogunate have used economic signs, political events, or a combination of both as criteria for periodization. Yet to establish the beginning of the end in the 1830s obliges us to accept a concomitant assumption that cultural events constitute a second order of activity; one that avoids organizing the world in terms of a base–superstructure dyad but still sees culture and ideas as determined by material forces. Culture is then made to appear as a dependent variable of economic and political processes, and the observer is diverted from recognizing that the production of culture may in fact possess a logic of its own, one that seeks to resolve problems belonging to an entirely different class of events and facts.

If we regard culture as something more than a pale reflection of changes detected earlier in the material realm, we will be persuaded to propose that the special culture of late Tokugawa culture did not begin in the 1830s, or even later, but probably in the late eighteenth century or the early 1800s.[1] Sometime in the 1830s there appeared a historic conjuncture between new forms of self-understanding, which consti-

1 This is certainly the argument of Naramoto Tatsuya, *Nihon kinsei no shisō to bunka* (Tokyo: Iwanami shoten, 1978), pp. 65–214; Maruyama Masao, *Nihon seiji shisōshi kenkyū* (Tokyo: Tokyo daigaku shuppankai, 1953); and the more recent essay by Sugi Hitoshi, "Kaseiki no shakai to bunka," in Aoki Michio and Yamada Tadao, eds., *Kōza Nihon kinseishi*, vol. 6: *Tempōki no seiji to shakai* (Tokyo: Yūhikaku, 1981), pp. 17–70.

tute the content of culture, and the critical political and economic events that began to jar the viability of the *bakufu–han* system. The realization that the order was losing viability may well have been possible only after the formulation of new forms of self-understanding and the establishment of new modalities of relating things to one another.

An essay by Professor Hayashiya Tatsusaburō offers the possibility of using the *bakumatsu* as a metaphor or historical trope.[2] By constructing a model of *bakumatsu,* which draws on the common experiences of the late years of the Kamakura, Muromachi, and Tokugawa shogunates, Hayashiya has identified a number of conditions shared by the three and the cultural means whereby contemporaries sought to represent their own sense of an ending and recognized that they were living through a time of profound change. His metaphor thus tries to bring together political, social, economic, diplomatic, and cultural developments. In all three cases the dissolution of the political order was accompanied by a displacement of the authority of the military estates and wider participation in a broader arena of struggle. This explanation presupposes a theory of "crisis" that ultimately is expressed in the occurrence of a "rebellion." Hayashiya noted vast social changes in the wake of this political event that signify transformations in the structure of values and norms, swiftly followed by the development of equally important economic forces, such as shifts in patterns of landholding, the circulation of currency, and new forms of exchange and foreign and domestic trade. Finally, Hayashiya links to this the emergent cultural styles that characterize and shape the social, political, and economic transformations. These new styles were symbolized by terms like *basara* in the Kamakura period, *kabuki* in late Muromachi times, and *ki* and *i* in the Tokugawa. *Basara* referred to love of the gaudy and ornate and the self-indulgent and unauthorized behavior with which some warrior leaders set the example for their peers; *kabuki* meant "to lean" or "to tilt" and called forth the outlandish and playful, often associated with debauchery and perversity; and in late Tokugawa, *ki* invoked the strange, curious, and eccentric, whereas *i* signaled the different, uncommon, and foreign. Thus in each *bakumatsu* the prevailing attitudes were inscribed in style and conduct previously signified as different and nonnormative, even unthinkable and unimaginable.

It is important to recognize that these new styles were not reflec-

2 Hayashiya Tatsusaburō, ed., *Bakumatsu bunka no kenkyū* (Tokyo: Iwanami shoten, 1978).

tions of more basic material forces. Rather, the real function of this metaphor is to establish a different relationship between material conditions and symbolic or cultural representation. The historical trope allows us to glimpse a unified world, a universe in which discontinuous realities are somehow bonded and intertwined with one another, thereby suggesting a network of relationships among things that first seem remote. The trope manages to establish a momentary reconciliation between the material and spiritual worlds without assigning priority to one or the other and persuades us to acknowledge disparate elements as equivalents in relationships whereby each determines and is determined by the other. It is as if the interaction resembled a form of dialectical traffic that permits a transaction between the language of social change and cultural form.[3] Such an approach to late Tokugawa culture helps us read the content of the socioeconomic macrocosm, the massive substance of the "real," in terms of form and representations that appear as significations of it. *Bakumatsu* represents a rhetorical figure, a form in time, ordering a specific reality, but precisely at that moment when the most disparate facts order themselves around a model that will later offer "meaning."

In the late Tokugawa period we can note a confluence between the content of the real, transforming productive process and the production of new cultural forms that promised to make sense of what was occurring in social life. Yet the relationship between the effort to meet the consequences of newer productive forces and social relationships and the attempts to stabilize meaning between politics and culture had less to do with a simple reflection from one "base" to the "superstructure" than with the operation of mediations. The massive transformations in the social process were translated into the cultural sphere, and this placed great strains on the social image of Tokugawa Japan and its conception of cultural praxis.[4] The polity was called on to meet the contradictory demands of stabilizing conditions of private accumulation while responding to requests for social welfare. A search for

3 Frederic Jameson suggested this conception of conjuncture in his *Marxism and Form* (Princeton, N.J.: Princeton University Press, 1971), pp. 3–59.

4 The idea of a social imaginary was advanced by Corneilus Catoriadis, *L'Institution imaginaire de la société* (Paris: Seuil, 1975); and Claude Le Fort, *Les Formes de l'histoire: Essais d'anthropologie politique* (Paris: Gallimard, 1978). The concept of a social imaginary, as used by these writers, refers not to a specular image submitted to reflection but, rather, to the indeterminate ways in which society organizes the production of material goods and the reproduction of its members. The domain of the social imaginary therefore conforms not to the fact that humans must have resources to survive and reproduce but to the variety of ways in which they are able to do so, which builds on but surpasses the basic material conditions of life. It is the way that a society seeks, through forms of signification, to endow itself with an identity different from those of other societies and from chaos.

meaning and self-understanding in a changed environment was expressed in calls for benevolence and greater political participation at a time when urban expansion and cultural participation required new definitions. New forms of cultural production accompanying the expansion of cities collectively signified what we may call, from playful literature (*gesaku*), the "culture of play." By the end of the eighteenth century this had exceeded the limits of its own formal constraints to reveal in vague outline the possibility of constructing a social imagination vastly different from the one authorized by the Tokugawa. The culture of play then turned into a play of culture committed to finding stable and permanent forms that might best accommodate new demands and expectations by reconstituting the whole.

At the core of this cultural development was the search for new and different forms of knowledge and the search for ways to implement them. The explosion of new forms of knowledge in late Tokugawa Japan was increasingly difficult to assimilate to the categories of the existing political system. What occurred in the late eighteenth century was the recognition, first in the cities but soon exported to the countryside, that the opposition of ruler–ruled and external–internal had exhausted its productivity and was incapable of constructing a vision of the political that could accommodate the complexity and plurality of the social urban environment. The physical and demographic expansion of urban sites like Edo, Osaka, Kyoto, and Nagoya, not to mention lesser castle towns functioning as regional market centers, and the resulting differentiation of social and cultural life were presented as a spectacle of social surplus juxtaposed to the "rational" and organized structures of the Tokugawa "order" imagined by Confucian ideologues. According to Hayashiya this perception was proclaimed in the calls like Yoshida Shōin's for the "different" and the strange.[5] It was inscribed in countless practices associated with the new culture of play, and it called into question the suppositions of a political ideology rooted in the logic of similitude.[6] That logic neatly divided the political and hence the cultural spheres between the rulers, who possessed mental powers, and the ruled, who labored manually. The former were supposed to know, and the latter were enjoined to follow. The social identity of the ruled was fixed in a closed, hierarchic chain, resembling elements in a stable structure that reflected the order

5 The term *social surplus* is my reading, not Professor Hayashiya's, of the sociopolitical scene.

6 On the logic of similitude, see H. D. Harootunian, "Ideology As Conflict," in Tetsuo Najita and J. Victor Koschmann, eds., *Conflict in Modern Japanese History* (Princeton, N.J.: Princeton University Press, 1982), pp. 25–61.

found in nature. Yet the material expansion of Edo as the hub of a world not yet imagined made it possible to challenge these fixed identities through the proliferation of different subject positions. The multiplication of needs and the differentiation of services contributed to the city's expansion and to the concomitant blurring of fixed distinctions between ruler and ruled.[7]

At the heart of the culture of play was a system of signification that recognized that the fixed boundaries and social identities established to guide people had become increasingly uncertain as society grew larger and more complex. The new systems of meaning agreed that social space and differentiation of positions invalidated most earlier distinctions. With the observation that people who resided in the cities acquired multiple identities, the culture of play produced a threat to the social identity of society. When, for example, the Tokugawa authorities laid down the proscription of heterodoxy in the late eighteenth century, they were recognizing the threat to social identity that the new cultural forms were beginning to pose. But even Matsudaira Sadanobu, who promoted the prohibitions, acknowledged that "principle" and "reading books" fell short of grasping the "passions of the times" and equipping the ruled with proper instruments to prosecute their managerial duties.[8] What his edict disclosed was thus an acknowledgment of social surplus that seemed to elude the conventional forms of representing the social in the fixed dichotomy of ruler–ruled. His call for the promotion of men of talent and ability through the social formation still took for granted the received political divisions. Ironically, the edict contributed to the problem of surplus and difference rather than to its solution, by encouraging the development and sponsorship of new skills in science, medicine, and Japanese and Western studies that promised to supply the leadership with practical techniques to grasp the "passion of the times."

If late-eighteenth-century Japan appeared as a scene of social surplus and blurred identities, its cultural praxis expressing play sought not only to displace fixed boundaries representing the real but also to show how the real, the differentiated masses living in the cities required new modes of representation. Play (*asobi*) referred to a form of subjectivity that existed outside the "four classes" that operated within the space of the "great peace" *taihei*.[9] A sense of liberation, closely

7 See Hayashiya Tatsusaburō, *Kasei bunka no kenkyū* (Tokyo: Iwanami shoten, 1976), pp. 19–42. 8 Ibid., pp. 43–80, 343–95.

9 Hiraishi Naoaki, "Kaiho Seiryō no shisōzō," *Shisō* 677 (November 1980): 52.

resembling the nonrelated, insubordinated autonomy associated with the free cities of the late Middle Ages in Japan, demanded freedom from fixed positions as a condition for endless movement, best expressed in excursion narratives and tales of travel.[10] Yet the reference to movement evinced still another meaning associated with *asobi*, which was to authorize crossing established geographical and social boundaries. According to Kaiho Seiryō (1755–1817), the ideal of this playful subject was the "gaze that disconnects and separates" (*kirete hanaretaru moku*): Once the "spirit" was separated from the "body," it would be possible to carry on "independent play."[11] As a *rōnin* (masterless samurai), Kaiho had abandoned fixed positions of status in order to "play" within the "great peace"; as a traveler he journeyed to more than thirty provinces in his lifetime. The conception of play held by intellectuals like Kaiho was invariably related to the production of "playful literature," the deliberate decadence of "mad poetery," comic verse, and an inordinate taste for the different and exotic. This type of autonomous individual liberated from the collectivity in some sense resembled the person who buys and sells commodities as a condition of commercial capitalism, but the relationship was less causal than homologous. On numerous occasions Kaiho expressed best what many contemporaries believed and acted upon when he proclaimed that it was human nature for the self to love the body. He saw a world of universal principles dominated by substantiality, that is, things and bodies interacting with each other. In this arrangement, thing or object (*mono*) was increasingly identified with commodity (*shiromono*), and each person functioned as both buyer and seller. Rules that now constituted the social related more to calculation and self-interest than to moral imperatives of status, and they were mandated by the exchange of commodities.

Late Tokugawa cultural practice seemed to converge upon the body, making public what hitherto had remained private, whether in eating, drinking, speaking, bedding down with either a man or a woman, or relieving oneself, and often led to gargantuan indulgences coming from the joys of the flesh. Despite the variety of forms of verbal fiction that proliferated in the late eighteenth century to meet the rapid diversification of tastes, pleasures, and demands for greater "consumption," the content of playful culture invariably focused on the activities of the body. This concern for the autonomy of the body, expressed in Kaiho's "independent spirit" of movement, constituted the subject matter of

10 The argument is made by Amino Yoshihiko, *Muen, kugai, raku* (Tokyo: Heibonsha, 1978).
11 Hiraishi, "Kaiho Seiryō no shisōzō," pp. 52–3.

most of verbal fiction and woodblock illustrations. One of the distinguishing features of the culture of play was its tendency to juxtapose a part, whether limb, organ, face, or body itself, to a larger entity, not as a substitute for the whole, but, rather, as an adequate alternative to it. To dismiss the whole in this way was clearly to discount it. Centering on the body and its activities emphasized the physical and the manual; by the same token it called into question the superiority of mental over manual skills on which the older distinction between ruler–ruled, external–internal, and public–private had rested its authority. Finally, the emphasis on the body as the maker and consumer of things put daily life in the forefront and valued the things that composed it. Late-eighteenth-century Japan was a time when recalling Marx, "the frames of the old *orbis terrarum* had been broken" and "only now . . . was the earth opened up . . . ," when the search began to find ways to link real history, the daily life, to the space of the real earth.[12]

What the verbal fictions of the culture play first disclosed was a new form of time and its relationship to earthly space. This resulted in individualizing personal and everyday occasions, separating them from the time of collective life identified with the social whole, precisely at that moment when there appeared one scale for measuring the events of a personal life and another for historical events. When Hirata Atsutane sought to figure a narrative that would recount the tale of the folk collectivity, he was reacting to a culture that had already divided time into separate units and differentiated the plots of personal life – love, marriage, travel – from the occasions of history. In texts that provided the plot of "history" and the private plots of individuals, interaction between the two levels took place only at certain points – battles, the ascension or death of an emperor, transgressions – and then ended as they proceeded on their separate ways. Although political economists sought to reapprehend the relationship between the life of nature and that of humans in order to retain the category of nature, and nativists tried to naturalize culture in an effort to restore it to a place of primacy, the two were increasingly uncoupled under the new regime. Now the various events making up daily life – food, drink, copulation, birth, death – were denatured and separated from the conception of a whole and integrated life to become aspects of a personal life. Existence became compartmentalized and specialized.

Hence the life narrated in late Tokugawa fiction is presented as individual and separate sequences and personal fate. The social for-

12 This quotation is from M. M. Bakhtin, *The Dialectic Imagination*, trans. and ed. Michael Holquist and Caryl Emerson (Austin: University of Texas Press, 1981), p. 206.

mation was being differentiated into classes, groups, and specialized constituencies, each conforming to functional scales of value and each possessing its own logic of development. The activities of daily life that concentrated on bodily performance lost their link to common labor and a common social whole; instead, they became private and petty matters on which writers reported as though through a peephole.[13] Contemporaries increasingly saw that peephole as habit or custom and deportment and went to great lengths to classify its range and variety. And yet to discover and categorize it so also presumed a conception of the whole, of society itself, even though the *gesaku* writers consistently apprehended personal affairs as mere particularities that implied no conception of a larger whole or meaning.[14] The impulse to "pierce" the crust of custom necessitated paying close attention to detail. More often than not, tactility, rather than a discernible storyline, was figured as the plot of the narrative and usually told the tale that the author wished to pierce. The absence of any real story in many "narratives" in favor of continuous dialogue about the interaction of things attests less to a diminution of literary standards than to their being in contest. These literary productions of the culture of play managed to convey a sharp dissatisfaction with conventions of narrative closure. Writers seemed convinced that failure to attend to the way that things were arranged, people were dressed, and foods were presented risked losing any chance to penetrate the surface of affairs. Readers were required to recognize differing levels of meaning in order to plumb hidden intentions below the surface. By making the familiar objects that inhabited daily life seem "strange," they persuaded readers to believe that they had been living in a hole, and not the whole, a rut whose very surroundings had obscured a recognition of the way that things really were. The texts (*kokkeibon*, amusing books) of Shikitei Samba (1776–1822) and Jippensha Ikku (1765–1831) offered an endless stream of snapshots of the most mundane, familiar, and trivial activities that townsmen encountered in their daily life and on the road. But by rearranging them so that they appeared unfamiliar, by forcing readers to look at activities that they performed habitually and objects that they took for granted, writers could jar them into seeing custom in a new and different light. Laughter was recognition of the familiar made to appear strange and even alien. The

13 Nakamura Yukihiko and Nishiyama Matsunosuke, eds., *Bunka ryōran*, vol. 8 of *Nihon bungaku no rekishi* (Tokyo: Kadokawa, 1967), p. 60; see also Mizuno Tadashi, *Edo shōsetsu ronsō* (Tokyo: Chūō kōronsha, 1974), p. 17; and Nakamura Yukihiko, *Gesakuron* (Tokyo: Kadokawa, 1966), p. 137.

14 Nakamura, *Gesakuron*, p. 137.

world of Ikku's Tōkaidō travelers is peopled by characters who, when they are not about to seduce a maid or slip out of an inn without paying the bill, are preoccupied with farting, soiled loin cloths, and a round of trivial involvement. The conversations that Samba records in barbershop and bathhouse relate to the most mundane affairs in the daily life of readers who now see and hear themselves speaking. Both writers emphasize the details and particularity of life in conversation or movement, such as eating, bathing, drinking, burping, and farting, in which the readers recognized their quotidian existence. Even in the more solemn historical romances of Bakin or the books of emotion (*ninjōbon*) which were preoccupied with the trials of love, the effect was to confront the reader with the familiar in an entirely different context. Bakin's explorations into the grotesque and fantastic in the well-known *Nansō Satomi hakkenden*, for example, concern a dog who performs a meritorious act of loyalty and then demands the reward, which happens to be the daughter of his feudal lord. And Ryūtei Tanehiko's *Nise Murasaki inaka Genji monogatari* retells the Genji story in a different historical setting and projects contemporary custom and speech into the fifteenth century. At another level it still remained the world of the shogun Ienari, now identified with a familiar exemplar of corruption in the past.

Although the focus on the body as a maker and consumer of things emphasized the parts, it ultimately drew attention to the idea of a whole and a conceptualization of the social order, but in terms that were new and different from the officially sanctioned version. Bodily imagery in both verbal and illustrated texts signified a different kind of social reality with an inverted scale of priorities for the Edo townsmen. It was an order that had as its head the genitalia or anus and as its heart the stomach. Often, verbal fictions described the body, with its mouth and arms as a devouring, consuming totality; humans appeared as bodies that related to the world through their orifices rather than through public duties demanded by fixed social status and disciplined intention. Moreover, the body's needs were never satisfied and never completed; people continued to eat, drink, speak, make love, and evacuate ceaselessly without any prospect of an end. To portray the infinite details involved in partying, with its random arrangement of empty cups, vomit, and half-filled bottles the morning after, or to pay close attention to foods, eating, and the accompanying conversation – all recognizable as appropriate subjects (not objects) for representation – dramatized a world of activity and things that no longer referred to anything outside it. Tokugawa verbal fiction and woodblock illustrations enforced a new awareness of a world that people had habitually placed in the background by repositioning it in the foreground of represented experience. It also offered human alternatives to the world of public or official ideology. To the demands of the heavenly way (*tendō*), often satirized by writers, it provided space for play, laughter, and passion in anatomical representation, a veritable people's utopia, an arcadia of flesh, joy, and pain experienced by the body, a ceaseless delight that came from endless consumption and to the discharge of waste. In this regard, late Tokugawa fiction appropriated the common and customary to work on the dominant ideology in order to make it appear unfamiliar and to recast the somber requirements of official expectation within the world of play. By using immediate experience as its subject and making people aware of their daily lives and surroundings, writers were able to transform the quotidian experience into a system of knowledge that even the most common could possess and master. In this way, verbal fiction and the illustrator's art made the body into a text and reading an act of consuming knowledge.

Finally, the mass readership of late Tokugawa times was far more interested in identifying and recognizing contemporary custom than in retrieving ethical lessons from a history that, according to one authority, probably assaulted their sensibilities.[15] Early-nineteenth-century writers like Samba and Tamenaga Shunsui, for example, wrote with an eye for details and nuances of contemporary life among the different quarters of Edo. Their production of *gesaku* helped define the conception of a coherent social world signifying changing conditions propelled by the constant interaction of humans, making and consuming, even though it consistently opposed the part to the whole. The early-nineteenth-century kabuki playwright Tsuruya Namboku portrayed what he called a "world" (*sekai*) bounded by "living custom" (*kizewa*). But Tsuruya's world, often darkened by violence, bloodshed, and conflict, was still nothing more than a reminder that social life was the stage on which contemporaries acted out their encounter with custom. This increasing identification of the culture of play and the world of theater with society – life following art – was noted by contemporaries who could agree that "its plot resembles the puppet theater" and that "its world is like the kabuki."[16]

15 Sugiura Mimpei, *Ishin zenya no bungaku* (Tokyo: Iwanami shoten, 1967), pp. 3–22.
16 Quoted in Maeda Ichirō, ed., *Kōza Nihon bunkashi* (Tokyo: Misuzu shobō, 1971), vol. 6, p. 121.

THE PLAY OF CULTURE

There were contemporary moralists and thinkers like Buyō Inshi (?–?) and Shiba Kōkan (1747–1818) who alerted their contemporaries to the dangers inherent in conceptions of society grounded in play and enjoyment inspired by the world of theater. This new social criticism brought about a conceptualization of the whole, called *seken* or *seji*, that was able to accommodate the differentiation and fragmentation of life proclaimed by the culture of play. Whether such critics were openly opposed to contemporary social life (Buyō Inshi), saw in laughter a problem and not its solution (Hirata Atsutane), or envisaged a new set of arrangements conforming to the changes that had taken place since the middle of the eighteenth century (Shiba Kōkan), they believed that the culture of play had exhausted its productivity and imperiled the prospect of maintaining a stable public order. All seemed to agree on the necessity of restoring a conception of the social whole to counteract the baneful effects of the progressive particularization and privatization of life, but it was more difficult to reach a consensus on how the whole should be reconstituted. What concerned the critics most was the way that "custom" was generating new combinations of social relationships and eroding the older guarantees of solidarity. Buyō Inshi charged that the changes noted in his narrative of contemporary history (*Seji kemmonroku,* 1816) would inevitably undermine the political order by persuading people to turn away from their public duties for the private pleasures of the body.[17] Shiba Kōkan's *Shumparō hikki* (1818), a lasting testament to contemporary changes in its recording of an excursion to the south, condemned the widespread prevalence of private desire less as evidence of moral bankruptcy than of insufficient knowledge, which made unknowing people vulnerable to the temptations of self-indulgence.[18] Nobody would deny that changes in society had uncoupled the fixed relationship between culture as self-understanding and political purpose. Yet the resolution of the crisis, many believed, required a systematic effort to reconstitute society's self-understanding in such a way as to make it possible again to realign the various parts with a whole capable of instituting public order. Critics like Buyō Inshi looked to the seven-

17 Buyō Inshi, "Seji kemmonroku," in *Nihon shomin seikatsu shiryō shūsei* (Tokyo: Misuzu shobō, 1969), vol. 8, p. 656. See also Aoki Michio, *Tempō sōdōki* (Tokyo: Sanseidō, 1979), pp. 1–9, for a useful account of Buyō's jeremiad, as well as Sugiura, *Ishin zen'ya no bungaku*, pp. 23–46.

18 Shiba Kōkan, *Shumparō hikki,* in *Nihon zuihitsu hikki* (Tokyo: Yoshikawa kōbunkan, 1936), vol. 1, pp. 404ff., 435.

teenth century and to the even more remote past to find models for the present, whereas others, like Shiba, trained their sights elsewhere and began to envisage new possibilities for the eventual reunion of politics and culture.

The specific grievance that agitated many critics was that the relentless pursuit of private desire fed the process of fragmenting interests and blinded people to the necessity of collective purpose. Everywhere people seemed to be turning inward to satisfy private desires and human needs. Yet such behavior constituted a public act, for self-understanding came to mean self-indulgence. The crisis of self-identity underscored the need to find new forms of knowing and understanding that could offer meaning in the new social environment without compromising the chance for order and stability. Any reconsideration of knowledge would have to account for the vast transformations that had taken place in Japanese society since the middle of the eighteenth century, transformations that had been noisily announced by the culture of play: the discovery and valorization of daily life, the common world of things and objects, the particularity of experience, the dehistoricization of the present, the ceaseless obsession with the body, and the possibility of constituting subjects for knowledge. What ensued in the late Tokugawa period was a play of culture, which entailed finding the means to represent stable forms of identity and meaning in discourse and a coherent voice. Although social critics like Buyō Inshi and Shiba Kōkan grasped the importance of knowledge for a resolution of the crisis of identity, they differed widely over its content. Predictably, Buyō called for a return to proper moral knowledge as a sure antidote to the "bad knowledge" of townsmen, but this meant excluding commoners as knowers in order to recast them in the role of the ruled and make the present look like the past again. By contrast, from his study of Western painting, Shiba favored a concept of empirical investigation based on the plurality of perspectives in viewing an object in order to open the way for new principles of the organization of knowledge and society. Shiba's promotion of perspective offered the prospect of making knowledge accessible to any group or person.[19]

What this play of culture inspired was a broad search for new forms of knowledge adequate to explain to certain groups the spectacle of surplus and why the social image of the past no longer applied to the early nineteenth century. Once these new forms of knowledge were

19 Shiba, *Shunparō hikki*, p. 444; also Numata Jirō, Matsumura Akira, and Satō Shōsuke, eds., *Nihon shisō taikei*, vol. 64: (1) *Yōgaku* (Tokyo: Iwanami shoten, 1976), pp. 449, 484–5.

structured, they would be able to authorize the establishment of cultural constituencies and the representation of interests and claims that had hitherto not been granted entry into official discourse. Yet almost simultaneously these new configurations sought to find political forms consistent with the content of culture that they wished to designate. The play of culture differed significantly from the culture of play in just this capacity to envisage stable or permanent political forms consonant with the new cultural constituencies. This coupling of culture and politics was mandated, and even accelerated, by the apparently rapid deterioration of domestic order and the appearance everywhere of events that seemed to signify the inevitability of decline. Catastrophic events like violent and unseasonable rains throughout the Kantō area and elsewhere, earthquakes in Echigo and Dewa (1833), urban "trashings" (*uchikowashi*), and widespread peasant rebellions were taken as signs of uncontrollable and unmanageable disintegration. Prevailing political forms seemed inadequate to prevent disorder and to provide assistance, relief, tranquility, and the semblance of safety to needy peasants. It was within this framework that the foreign intrusion, which had already begun at the turn of the century, was added as one more sign confirming the generally held belief that the realm was doomed. Thus whereas groups sought to represent knowledge of themselves in the will to form discourses, the new discourses invariably sought correspondences between culture and politics. A good deal of this activity was poured into efforts to stem disorder and to provide relief, security, and assistance. Virtually all of the new discourses of the late Tokugawa period – Mitogaku (Mito learning), national learning, Western learning, and the new religions – tried to unite a conception of culture with politics. This impulse is surely reflected in the Mito identification of ceremony and polity, in nativist conceptions of *matsurigoto* (government as ceremony), the emphasis of the new religions on a community of believers free from hierarchy, and Western learning's formulations of science and morality. Moreover, when these new discourses spoke to vital issues of order and security, relief and assistance, equality and fairness, they were pressing not only a claim to represent interests constituted as knowledge but also the right to speak on questions directly affecting their constituencies. Gradually their "business," their interest, became society's business, just as their conception of culture and political organization became a substitute for the social formation as a whole. The claim of right to participate in and resolve problems of common concern, which meant survival, order, and defense, became the condition for creating a public realm in late Tokugawa society.

The new claims were often rooted in questions of productivity and security. When they were, groups were inadvertently led to challenge the authority of Tokugawa society, whether it was invested in the shogunal arrangement of power or in principles of a natural order of legitimacy. Such acts invariably resulted in defection from the center, the Tokugawa polity, at a time when authorities were finding it difficult to meet their own responsibilities and satisfy demands for "order" and "relief." Such withdrawals to the periphery were usually prompted by the conviction that if the Tokugawa structure could not live up to its obligations, then the groups would have to take care of themselves. Thus what appeared from the 1830s onwards was a progressive retreat from the center to the periphery, not as explicit acts of revolutionary sedition, but as an expression of diminishing confidence in the system's ability to fulfill its moral duties. The new cultural disciplines provided justification for groups to perform for themselves tasks that the Tokugawa polity was now unable to perform. This required the formation of voluntary associations, some of which ultimately flew in the face of a conception of a natural order that defined groups according to their natural and expected function. The occasion for this massive impulse to secede was provided by the way that contemporary history was grasped by those who acted to arm themselves with self-definition. The move to emphasize the production of wealth, the centrality of daily affairs, the importance of the communal unity for nativist thought and new religions, and the widespread concern of all groups with aid and relief, mutual assistance, equality in the distribution of resources, along with talent, ability, and utility did not so much "reflect" the conditions of *bakumatsu* as "interpret" such facts and events. Ultimately all these new cultural discourses sought to merge with power that knowledge based on principles of inclusion and exclusion of both objects and people. To appeal to new forms of knowledge that different groups could know meant talking about different conceptions of power. Each of these groups saw itself and its response to contemporary problems as a solution to the social, and imagined that the part that it represented was a substitute for the unenvisaged whole. The proper kind of knowledge, it was believed, would lead to a solution of the problems agitating society. All assumed that a decision on one part would disclose the shape of the whole. Hence Mito turned to the primacy of the autonomous domain sanctioned by the national polity (*kokutai*); *kokugaku* (national learning) concentrated on the self-sufficient village authenticated by its relation to the primal creation deities; *yōgaku* (Western learning) celebrated a crude form of the mercantilist state, propelled by virtue and science; and the new religions announced the establishment of new forms of sacred communalism in their effort to give permanence to a conception of epiphany and the liminal moment.

All of these new discourses were formulated in the early nineteenth century. All aimed to understand the world anew and lessen its problems by offering solutions. Yet they contributed as much to *bakumatsu* problems as they did to their resolution. They all were generated by a will to knowledge that masked more fundamental considerations of power. Every manifestation of how the new discourse sought to fix rules of formation and discipline disclosed an accompanying and almost obligatory concern for the foundations of knowledge and learning. Every discussion of the status of knowledge and learning inevitably raised questions concerning the identity of the knowers and what should be known.

GOOD DOCTRINE AND GOVERNANCE

The problem of defining cultural context and finding an adequate political form for it was engaged first by a generation of samurai intellectuals from the Mito domain (Fujita Yūkoku, his son Tōko, Aizawa Seishisai, Toyoda Tenkō, the daimyo Tokugawa Nariaki) and their spiritual associates, Ōhashi Totsuan, Yoshida Shōin, and Maki Izumi. As early as the late eighteenth century, Mito writers began to search systematically for ways to enunciate a program of practical discipline and education. Mito had long been the center of an ambitious historiographical project, the *Dai Nihon shi*, a lightning rod for serious-minded philosophic speculation in the Neo-Confucian mode. But there was a difference, if not a break, in intellectual continuity, between the meditations of the so-called early Mito scholars and the discourse of the latter Mito school.[20] Whereas the early Mito writers clung closely to a rather formal Neo-Confucianism, the later thinkers selected a syncretic position that mixed parts of Neo-Confucianism, nativist religious, and mythic elements to produce a comprehensive statement very different in structure and purpose from what had gone before. Politically, Mito was one of the three collateral houses of the

20 Bitō Masahide, "Mito no tokushitsu," in Imai Usaburō, Seya Yoshihiko, and Bito Masahide, eds., *Nihon shisō taikei*, vol. 53: *Mitogaku* (Tokyo: Iwanami shoten, 1973), p. 561. Hereafter cited as *Mitogaku*.

Tokugawa family and thus occupied a relatively privileged position near the center of power. But in economic terms, Mito, like so many domains in the late eighteenth and early nineteenth century, encountered problems that seemed to resist conventional solutions. Fujita Yūkoku (1774–1826), a middle-ranking retainer trained in the Mito historiographical bureau, called attention to the diminishing domainal financial resources and the consequences for people and government. His student Aizawa Seishisai (1781–1863) later specified the cause of the contemporary "crisis" when he proposed that it had stemmed from the decision to move the samurai off the land into towns and the consequent growth of the use of money and the dependence on the market. Mito writers were especially concerned with the economic impact of these changes on the ruling class, who had incurred deep indebtedness to meet daily expenses, as they adopted luxurious lifestyles inspired by the pursuit of private interests. What worried the critics was the way that these changes seemed to have affected agricultural productivity and contributed to the growing power of merchants and moneylenders who benefited from the samurai's need for cash.[21] Yet they were no less sensitive to the recurrence of famines and other natural disasters that undermined agricultural production. Both samurai and peasants suffered from the hardships caused by such events. Taxes were relatively high in Mito, Yūkoku noted in his *Kannō wakumon*, and the population had decreased steadily since the middle years of the century.

These developments were not unique or even exceptional for the times, but the Mito writers interpreted them as signs of impending disintegration. Yūkoku complained that a fondness for money and usury had already led to a number of disrupting abuses in the domain. The most serious by far in his inventory was the growing frequency of peasant rebellions. Here, he advised the leadership to take stock of its responsibilities to rule "virtuously." Instead of relying on laws and ordinances, always a sign of slackening control, it was necessary to promote a leadership skilled in the art of governance. In the context of the late eighteenth century, what this meant was a redefinition of virtue into practicality, and the training of administrators who would be able to understand the requirements of the times. Years later, Aizawa expressed grave misgivings regarding the invasion of gamblers and idlers

21 J. Victor Koschmann, "Discourse in Action: Representational Politics in the Late Tokugawa Period," Ph.D. diss., University of Chicago, 1980, p. 30. Published as *The Mito Ideology: Discourse, Reform, and Innovation in Late Tokugawa Japan, 1790–1864* (Berkeley and Los Angeles: University of California Press, 1987).

into Mito and saw their presence as a manifestation of moral decay. He concluded that such unwanted guests had been permitted to enter the domain because of administrative laxity and ignorance concerning the way that they could corrupt village morals and encourage peasants to abandon work for drink, gambling, and expensive foods. Underlying this was the belief that ordinary people naturally loved profit and were eager to pursue private interest whenever they were given the slightest opportunity. Aizawa also feared the influence of new religions like the Fuji cult (Fujikō), which had recently established itself in Mito and was beginning to recruit large numbers of followers among the peasantry.[22] But he reserved his harshest judgment for Christianity, a "cruel and unjust religion," which won over the minds of ignorant people and diverted them from the path of moral rectitude.

The Mito writers were convinced that the problems threatening domain integrity resulted from inadequate leadership. If the masses lost their way, it was because the managerial class had abdicated its responsibilities to provide moral examples.[23] Fujita Tōko (1806–55) lamented that the way of loyalty and filiality had disappeared. Order could be restored by clarifying these principles once more and redirecting the rulers to govern the realm properly. Yet, he noted, this would require an understanding of the part and the whole, between the leader and the people, the domain and the realm.

The sanction for the Mito effort to resolve the contemporary crisis lay in the reunification of learning and doctrine. Writers like Fujita Yūkoku argued the necessity of knowing how to rectify names (*seimeiron*) and straightening the arrangement of duties so that name would correspond to responsibility (*meibunron*). In the rectification of names he saw the general problem of social decay as a failure of representation in language. In this Yūkoku shared the assumptions of an eighteenth-century discourse that had already drawn attention to the problematic relation between words and the things they were supposed to denote. Because names and status no longer conformed to reality, it seemed imperative to realign name to truth.[24] A realignment along these lines made possible by language itself promised to retrieve the archetypical way of loyalty and filiality. According to Yūkoku,

> In the realm, there are lords and retainers, and there are the upper and lower orders. If the designations of lords and retainers are not corrected, the divi-

22 "Shinron," in *Mitogaku*, p. 105. *Shinron* has been translated by Bob Tadashi Wakabayashi in *Anti-Foreignism and Western Learning in Early-Modern Japan* (Cambridge, Mass.: Harvard University Press, 1986). 23 Koschmann, "Discourse in Action," p. 34.

24 "Seimeiron," in *Mitogaku*, p. 10.

sion between the aristocratic and nonaristocratic classes will blur, and distinctions between the upper and lower orders will vanish. The strong will come to despise the weak and the masses will be thrown into confusion and disorder.[25]

His son Tōkō went even further when, following the lead of contemporary nativists, he noted that even though in ancient times the Way had no name by which it was known, everybody naturally knew and understood its requirements. Although writing did not exist in that remote age, the meaning of the Way was conveyed through song and poetry (a point made earlier by Kamo Mabuchi in the *Kokuikō*), in manners, custom, deportment, education, and government. Yet when the effort was finally made to express the Way in written texts, its "true and original nature suffered."[26] Both writers believed that rescuing the Way in language in their times was the supreme duty of leadership and the first principle of education. The Mito conception of the Way differed from the more established Neo-Confucian view of the conviction that the Way could not be found in nature but only through human effort, a proposal they shared with the eighteenth-century philosopher Ogyū Sorai. Victor Koschmann has argued, in this connection, that " . . . representation . . . means precisely the objectification of the 'natural' state (the Way of heaven, unity between Heaven and Earth) through some form of 'unnatural' (linguistic, instrumental, demonstrative) action. The object to be represented through human mediation is Heaven itself, not a temporary arrangement."[27]

By calling attention to the operation of rectification and designation, the Mito writers were able to demonstrate the primacy of the domain as an adequate space for the realization of the necessary alignments. Much of their formulation was powered by a strategy that reduced the parts to an essential and original whole, to the primal origins of the realm as expressed in the term *kokutai* (national polity or body). *Kokutai* was identified as the whole for which the parts stood. For the Mito writers, the concept represented the indissoluble link between status and loyal behavior (*chūkō no michi*) and the corresponding network of designations and duties. It was their intention to show how the realignment of name and duty could again be implemented in the domain and how, in fact, the appeal to *kokutai* mandated the resuscitation of the domain along such lines. To argue in this fashion was to propose that a morally reconstituted domain serve as a substitute for the whole. This was surely the meaning of Yūkoku's enunciation, in

25 Takasu Yoshijirō, ed., *Mitogaku taikei* (Tokyo: Mitogaku taikei kankōkai, 1941), vol. 3, p. 382. 26 Koschmann, "Discourse in Action," p. 52. 27 Ibid., p. 61.

his *Seimeiron,* of the vertical ties of loyalty that stretched from the emperor down through the lower orders. But it is also evident that the lynchpin in this hierarchical chain was the domainal lord. "How can we strengthen the rectification of duties and designation," Yūkoku asked rhetorically, "How is the country of the bakufu to be governed today? . . . At the top we live under the heavenly descendants, and at the bottom we are tended by the various lords."[28]

With this strategy, the Mito writers were in a position to interpret the events they encountered in the early nineteenth century and make reality appear less problematic. They moved along a rather broad arc whose terminal points were marked by a profound distrust of the people and a moral sense of benevolence and compassion for them. Among the recurring anxieties expressed in their writings, none seemed more urgent and frightening than the prospect of imminent mass disorders in a countryside affected by foreign intrusion and, by implication, the incapacity of the Tokugawa bakufu to stem the swelling threat of mass civil disorder. The growing incidence of peasant rebellions since the late eighteenth century, they believed, related to the disabled status of the domain itself and reflected a widespread agreement that the general administrative machinery no longer functioned properly. Mito writers regularly complained that the shogunate had departed from its earlier role as the largest domain among equals to pursue policies deliberately designed to undermine the military and financial autonomy of its peers. By the end of the eighteenth century it was clear that these policies had made the domains more dependent on the bakufu. Resolving the domains' declining status required persuading the bakufu to accept a less exalted position in the arrangement of authority. But this move was prefigured by the Mito insistence on rectifying names, duties, and designations as a necessary condition for the moral realignment of the system. If the bakufu fulfilled the expectations associated with its name, it would cease acting in a self-interested manner.

Once the relationship between shogunate and domains was rectified, it would be possible to turn to the problem of the ruled. People can be governed, Aizawa announced, only when rulers rely on the Way of loyalty and filiality. This proposition was not based simply on a dim view of human nature – most members of the managerial class in Tokugawa Japan held that as an article of faith – but on a more complex conviction that because an agricultural population was neces-

28 Takasu, *Mitogaku taikei,* vol. 3, p. 388.

sary to the survival and welfare of order, it must be made to acknowledge its duty to produce as a moral trust. This was also what Fujita Yūkoku had meant when he proposed that "people are the basis of the realm. If they constitute a firm foundation, then the realm will also be stable."[29] Aizawa, who constantly referred to the people in uncomplimentary terms, believed that because they were predictably disorderly and forever prevented from acquiring the niceties of virtue, they were capable only of being led. But leading the people meant making sure they produced. "People properly should rely . . . on rules; they should not know them."[30]

Under the sanction of this conception of privilege, the Mito writers directed their rhetoric toward explaining the reasons that the people were "naturally" excluded from having knowledge and why they had to be ruled, which meant work. If the ordinary folk were left to their own devices and were not persuaded to perform their proper duties, Aizawa explained, they would act like children and pursue profit, pleasure, and personal luxury at every opportunity. The possession of knowledge entitled a few to rule and required the many to follow. Neither the exercise of coercion nor the accumulation of wealth was equivalent to knowledge as conditions for rulership. Those who "should not know" must always depend on the informed guidance of those who "know." This conception of knowing and knowers prompted the Mito writers to look harshly on all religions organized to enlist the people, because their doctrines invariably promoted forms of nonexclusionary knowledge accessible to all. Fujita Tōko declared rather excitedly in his commentary on the establishment of an academy in Mito (*Kōdōkanki jutsugi*) that heretical doctrines continue to "delude the people" and "bewilder the world." As a result, he discerned a causal relationship between the slackening of belief in the true Way and the dissolution of ties of dependence, currently reflected in the incidence of peasant uprisings. Yet he was convinced that these disturbances were only manifestations of new forms of knowledge that actually confused and confounded the people to embark on a course of disorderly conduct.

Hence, the Mito writers viewed disturbances as expressions of private interest encouraged by new opportunities for the pursuit of self-indulgence and new religious doctrines promising rewards to all. To offset such threats they recommended the establishment of a regime devoted to benevolence and compassion and advised the leadership to "love" and "revere" the people. Once love and reverence were actual-

29 Takasu, *Mitogaku taikei*, vol. 3, p. 179. 30 "Shinron," in *Mitogaku*, p. 147.

ized in concrete measures, they believed, the fears of the managerial class would diminish, and the incidence of "unhappiness" in the countryside would disappear. Despite Aizawa's scarcely concealed contempt for "mean people," he remarked that "loving the people" required hard commitments from the leadership. He believed with his teacher Yūkoku, who had earlier called for a program promoting people's welfare, in "assisting the weak and restraining the strong, fostering the old and loving the young, prohibiting laziness and idleness. . . ."[31] He sided with Tokugawa Nariaki who, upon becoming lord of Mito in 1829, announced the promise of a reform reflecting the leadership's duty to love and provide care for the people. "Virtue is the root," Nariaki declared, "commodities the branch"; a virtuous leadership cannot "avoid bestowing blessings on the people."

The issue that the Mito writers sought to resolve was how to increase productivity and exercise greater control. The "good teachings" of etiquette and civilization, which Aizawa believed only the leadership could know, were guarantees of permanent order and wealth. By equating the status ethic and its proper discrimination throughout the domain with "loving the people," the Mito thinkers could argue that if leadership "bestowed proper blessings upon the people," the realm would administer itself. Yet if the rulers abandoned "good doctrine," the people would, according to Tōko, "Avoid political laws as one avoids an enemy. Their yearning will be like that of a child for a mother's affection." When people are not under moral control, Tōko noted, recalling Ōshio's recent rebellion in Osaka in 1837, they will resemble a "product that first putrefies and then gives way to worms and maggots. People who are heretical are similar to those who are ill. Men who govern the sick will first promote their health; men who expel heresy will first cultivate the Great Way." Nariaki and later observers continued to assert that if the "peasantry bears a grudge or resents the upper class, it will not stand in awe of them." Control required providing assistance which, in this context, referred to restoring order in the Mito domain. "If we succeed in exhausting our intentions day and night to return the blessings, we will be able to sympathize with all our hearts. . . ." But control, through the blessing of conferring assistance and relief, required returning people to the land and increasing their productive labor. Earlier, Fujita Yūkoku had outlined a program for "enriching the domain" in *Kannō wakumon,* and in the late 1830s Nariaki and Tōko worked out a comprehensive

31 Takasu, *Mitogaku taikei*, vol. 3, p. 179.

land policy that included a land survey, a realignment of tax quotas, greater efforts for empathy to draw peasants and local officials more closely together, a study of new agricultural techniques, and, not least important, a recall of samurai from Edo back to Mito. This last plank, which announced the domain's intention to withdraw from the center for a reliance on its resources in the periphery, was more than enough to disturb large numbers of retainers who had become accustomed to city life.

The lord of Mito thought that the times were ripe for a "restoration of the domain" (*kokka o chūkōshi*) in the 1830s and a "renovation of custom for the unification of all." The purpose of the economic and educational reforms Nariaki announced in the late 1830s was to halt the fragmentation of social life that had spread throughout the domain. Fragmentation referred to "evil customs," and its elimination required economic and educational renovation. Aizawa had already indicated in *Shinron* (1825) that as loyalty and filiality become one, "the education of the people and the refinement of custom is accomplished without a word being spoken. Worship becomes government, and government has the effect of education. Thus, there is no essential difference between government and the indoctrination of the people."[32] This sense of unification, realized through identifying teaching and doctrine, became the special task of the academy in Mito, the Kōdōkan, whose task was to instruct samurai and commoners (through a network of village schools) in how to "refine custom" and reinstate proper morality. Tōko's commentary emphasized this sense of union in neat slogans designed to remove differences to reach the underlying similitude of all things: "the unification of Shinto and Confucianism," "the inseparability of loyalty and filiality," "*sonnō jōi*" (revering the emperor, expelling the barbarian, a term first coined in the proclamation establishing the school; it meant renovating the domestic system in order to be able to withstand external interference), "the union of military arts and civilian skills," and the "indivisibility of learning and practice." The purpose of the school was to reunify doctrine and government, which had become distinct in the course of the long peace. Duties and designation had to be reunited, and custom brought into line with morality.

Following Yūkoku and Aizawa, Nariaki used language that called attention to the basis, as against the unessential. The solution to the contemporary problem was to return to essentials. This meant reapplying the classic injunction of the "great learning": "The base of the

32 "Shinron," in *Mitogaku*, p. 56.

realm is the family; the foundation of the family is moral discipline," to the domain itself. In tightening moral relationships the domain was required to embark on far-reaching reforms in "custom" and "military preparedness." Aizawa observed in *Shinron* that a long peace had resulted in extravagant customs, indulgent lords, and the "bitterness of the poor," and Nariaki noted in his *Kokushiden* that

> with a tranquil realm we can never forget about rebellion . . . we have forgotten about the thick blessings that have been bestowed by peace today . . . and we have been concerned only with being well fed and well clad. The samurai have become effeminate and resemble a body that contracts with illness after exposure to cold, wind, or heat. They are idlers and wastrels among the four classes.[33]

In this way the Mito discourse came to see in the domainal space the only prospect for a genuine restoration. Toyoda Tenkō, in an essay composed along restorationist lines in 1833, wrote that even though the "ancients wrote that 'a restoration is always difficult to accomplish,' it must be even more difficult to do so today."[34] Yet he was convinced that the time and place were right. The ancients had linked the achievement of a restoration to the successful termination of a rebellion, but Tenkō saw the recent decline of the domain as equivalent to embarking on the difficult task. The logic for this conception of restoration had been powerfully articulated by Yūkoku in the late eighteenth century and was eloquently restated by Aizawa, who saw in the moment an opportunity that comes only once in a thousand years. Aizawa's proposals were propelled by his belief that the bakufu had willfully followed a policy of self-interest, in which the base had been strengthened at cost to the branches.[35] Aizawa charged that this represented a distortion of Ieyasu's original intention. Ieyasu had strengthened the center and weakened the periphery in order to head off rebellion and anarchy. He had done this by assembling the warriors in the cities, where their stipends were weakened, and by sheltering the people from a military presence.[36] "The military were lessened, and the masses were made into fools." But Aizawa believed that the time had now come to reverse this policy and to strengthen both the base as well as the ends by "nourishing" and "strengthening" the lords.[37] If the lords were permitted to play the role originally designated to them by the emperor, Yūkoku had asserted earlier, they could turn to the task of rectifying their own domains. Though he acknowledged the

33 "Kokushiden," in *Mitogaku*, p. 211. 34 "Chūkō shinsho," in *Mitogaku*, p. 197.
35 "Shinron," in *Mitogaku*, p. 73. 36 Ibid., pp. 73–4. 37 Ibid., p. 78.

overlordship of the Tokugawa shogun, Aizawa wrote in the *Tekii hen* that there was a reciprocal relationship between lord and subject. The vertical relationships outlined by Yūkoku thus gained new force in the context of domain reform in the formulations of Aizawa and Nariaki. The shogun should assist the court and govern the realm, just as local leaders should support the emperor and obey the bakufu's decrees in their provinces. But "the people who obey the commands of the daimyo are in effect obeying the decrees of the Bakufu."[38] Because the bakufu was limited by the court, it had not absolute authority over the Mito domain. What this meant for Mito ideologues was the elevation of the domain and the virtual reversal of the base–ends metaphor.

The intellectual sanction for this new edifice envisaged in the Mito discourse was the identification of the whole in a mystical body called *kokutai*. Elaboration of this seminal idea was provided chiefly by Aizawa in his *Shinron*. This construct was universal and absolute, but it could mobilize the rich tradition of Japanese mythohistory.

> The heavenly ancestors introduced the way of the gods and they have established doctrine; by clarifying loyalty and filial piety they began human history. These duties were ultimately transferred to the first sovereign and they have since served the great foundation of the state. The emperor joined these divine ordinances to his own body.[39]

Just as the emperor looked up to the virtue of the heavenly descendants, Aizawa continued, so the people received in their bodies the heart of their ancestors and respected and served the emperor for an eternity. When the emperor receives the will of their ancestors, there can be no change in history. Similarly, the emperor himself, worshipping his ancestor the sun goddess, has realized the principle of filial piety and reveals this obligation to the people. Because the principle of loyalty and filiality had existed without needing to be articulated, daily practice – the practice of the body – signified the inseparability of worship, ceremony, and governance.

Such an ideal had always been represented in ritual. In the first book of the *Shinron*, Aizawa discussed how ancient rulers displayed filiality by carrying out worship at ancestral tombs and in performing the solemn ceremonies and rites.[40] The most important of these rituals was the *daijōsai*, the great food-offering ritual performed by each new emperor at the time of the first harvest after his succession. The rite

38 Koschmann, "Discourse in Action," p. 171; also Masao Maruyama, *Studies in the Intellectual History of Tokugawa Japan*, trans. Mikiso Hane (Princeton, N.J.: Princeton University Press, 1974), p. 305. 39 Koschmann, "Discourse in Action," p. 79.

40 "Shinron," in *Mitogaku*, pp. 81 ff.

consisted of offering new grain to the sun goddess (Amaterasu), but the significance of the ritual was its reiteration of archetypal themes such as the divine creation of the land and the benevolence of Amaterasu toward her people. Aizawa noted that in the actual ritual, subject and sovereign experience the presence of Amaterasu and ultimately "feel like descendants of the gods." For a moment, history is frozen; past flows into present; and the great principles of loyalty and filiality – dramatized by the exchange between sovereign, who presents the divine progenitor with riches she has made possible, and her subjects, who must return the "blessings" – are represented as timeless and universal norms. By invoking the example of this great ritual, Aizawa was able to show how mere history, a record of changing circumstances, differed from timeless truths reaching back to mythical origins. The *daijōsai* annuls history; the primal moment restores to each participant presence and self-identity. The ceremony should unify sovereign, subject, and descendants and thus dissolve the division between governance and worship. "If the whole country reveres the heavenly deities, then all will know how to respect the emperor." If civilization in Japan was to withstand the erosion of history, it was important for the people to know how to express respect as represented in ritual. The present was the appointed time, a unique opportunity, Aizawa said, "to inform the people of this principle and purify the public spirit." When this great enterprise had been accomplished, "past will be united to present," sovereign to people.

In this manner the essential national body, a mystical whole signifying origins and continual presence, validated the domain's claim to restore the great principles of loyalty and filiality. For the Mito writers, the ideal of *kokutai* functioned at several levels. It represented the whole to which the parts – the domains – could relate; it also provided the sanction for the domain, pledged to reinstate the timeless principles, to act as a substitute for the whole. *Kokutai* served to remind every generation of the essential beginnings from which all things had come and to which all things are reduced. This is surely what the Mito writers meant when they advised contemporaries "not to forget about the basis" and to "return the blessing to its origins." What could be more essential than the body of the realm, however shapeless, vague, and mystical, the *karada* (body) of the *kuni* (country)? "What is this body of the country?" Aizawa asked, and he answered, "If countries do not have a body, it cannot be made by men. If a country has no body, how can it be a nation?"[41] Aizawa envisaged

41 Ibid., p. 69.

this body as a form that distinguished the idea of a unified realm from chaos. It was his purpose to link the sense of the whole to a new political space represented by the autonomous domain. His actual proposals for reform were unexceptional and echoed Yūkoku's earlier suggestions and Nariaki's later measures. Yet they confirmed the belief in the inseparability of representation and action, learning and practice.

Changes in contemporary history altered the character of the Mito discourse. This is not to say that the Mito writers changed their minds about the veracity of their vision but only to suggest the possibility of varying emphases within the discourse. Whereas in the 1840s, Mito rhetoric was pressed into service to reconstitute the domain through a series of reforms, in the 1850s and 1860s, as the area of political space widened, the reformist impulse came to address national issues and to advocate direct action. Whereas the earlier goals aimed at rebuilding the domain without necessarily affecting the bakufu, the later course of action made the destruction of the shogunate a condition for realizing domainal autonomy. The generation of samurai intellectuals who had been attracted to the Mito discourse in the Tempō period, not to mention the retainers of the domain itself, turned gradually to representing the ideals in the form of direct action calling for a restoration of imperial authority and the destruction of the bakufu. Mito retainers themselves had taken matters into their hands in 1860 when they participated in the assassination of the shogunal counselor Ii Naosuke. Four years later the domain was torn apart by civil war. Yet the theoretical justification for extending representation to include direct action was provided by thinker-activists like Yoshida Shōin, Ōhashi Totsuan, and Maki Izumi. The general outline of this Mito theory of action was propelled by the recognition that in the new political arena of the 1850s, especially after the opening of the country (1854) and the subsequent signing of commercial treaties with Western nations, the bakufu no longer possessed either the authority or the will to speak for the nation as a whole. Such authority resided with the emperor, as the Mito writers had proposed earlier in their discussion of vertical relationships, and it was he who must now lead directly in the great accomplishment of renovation.

Yoshida Shōin (1830–59), a specialist in military instruction in the Chōshū domain, saw the signing of the commercial treaties as the opportunity to dramatize the failure of the bakufu. What he demanded of the shogunate was a domestic order that could withstand foreign contact. He recognized that the bakufu had succumbed to the treaties out of indecision and fear. But the new treaties affected the nation as a whole, not simply the shogunate or the domains. "If problems arise in the territory of the shogun," he wrote at the time, "they must be handled by the shogun; if in the domain of the lord, by the lord."[42] This was fully consistent with the Mito arrangement of authority and its corresponding definition of jurisdiction. The problems facing Japan in 1856–7 were not restricted to the shogun or indeed the lord but involved both because they now related to the security of the imperial land itself. It was the emperor, not the shogun, who had the right to make authoritative decisions concerning foreign demands, because the crisis imperiled all of Japan. "This affair (the signing of the treaties) arose from within the territory of the emperor." Hence, the shogunate had shown not only weakness but had actually committed treason by committing an act of lèse-majesté.

The bakufu had acted willfully and "privately" by agreeing to treaty negotiations. Yoshida proposed that its officials be punished and the institution dismantled for ignoring an imperial decree calling for the immediate expulsion of foreigners. The bakufu had committed a crime of unprecedented magnitude: "It has abjured heaven and earth, angered all the deities . . . it has nourished a national crisis today and bequeathed national shame to future generations. . . . If the imperial decree is honored, the realm will be following the Way. To destroy a traitor is an act of loyalty." To this end Yoshida, in his last years (he was a casualty of the Ansei purge of 1859) worked out a program that would best fulfill the requirements of direct action and loyal behavior. He called for a rising of "grass-roots" heroes, appealing principally to the samurai and independent villagers, willing to leave their homes and perform what he called meritorious deeds.

> If there is no rising of independent patriots, there will be no prosperity. How will these unaffiliated men reinstate the saintly emperor and wise lords? Men who follow my aims and are of my domain must follow this rising. Through the unauthorized power of the rising, small men will be excluded, evil men will be thrown out, and correct and able lords will be able to gain their place.[43]

Yoshida's call for an organization of grass-roots patriots willing to act directly was also the subject of Ōhashi Totsuan's (1816–62) meditation concerning the contemporary situation. Ōhashi, who came from the small domain of Utsunomiya, affiliated with Mito, and was contemplating the possibility for direct action at the same time that Yoshida

42 Quoted in H. D. Harootunian, *Toward Restoration* (Berkeley and Los Angeles: University of California Press, 1970), p. 219. 43 Ibid., p. 237.

was seeking to call his own followers to arms against the bakufu. Ōhashi was more consistently committed to classic Neo-Confucian arguments concerning the importance of differentiation between civilization and the barbarism represented by the West. Yet this philosophic conservatism merely elaborated Mito ideas on expulsionism (*jōiron*). Ōhashi's thinking on restoration first favored removing incompetents from high shogunal offices. This effort to rob the bakufu of its top leadership (favored by Yoshida as well) showed the later restorationists how to dramatize the issue of able leadership and also how to paralyze the bakufu. The failure of this tactic later encouraged others to consider raising a small army for an imperial campaign against the shogunate, something that was first suggested by the Satsuma retainer Arima Shinshichi (in 1862) and tried by Maki Izumi a year later. Ōhashi's most explicit statement on restoration appears in a work he completed in 1861 called *Seiken kaifuku hisaku* (A secret policy for a restoration of political authority). The work was written in response to the bakufu's attempt of 1860 to unite court and shogunate by securing Princess Kazu no Miya as the consort of the shogun. His plan sought to extend the culturalism of his earlier writings.

> Since the coming of the foreigner and the expansion of commerce, the Bakufu's position has not been good; it has carried temporizing to extremes, and the arrogance of the barbarians has been rampant . . . Bakufu officials are afraid of them. . . . Even though only one barbarian was permitted to enter in the beginning, now several have pushed their way in. . . . Although trade is not yet three years old, the rising prices of commodities, the exhaustion of domainal resources, and the impoverishment of the lower classes must be viewed as disasters.[44]

Ōhashi was also convinced that the bakufu had systematically undermined the "brave and loyal samurai" of "courageous domains." The only solution, he reasoned, was a call to arms under the "banner of an imperial decree."

Like Yoshida, Ōhashi believed that the decision to take Japan out of the hands of the barbarians belonged to the imperial court. Hence, he declared, all people, out of love of the emperor, lay waiting for the "august movement of the court. . . . As with the booming clap of a thunderous voice, once an imperial decree is promulgated all men must act, since all will be inspired. It will be like the collapse of a dam holding back a lake." Ōhashi believed that the bakufu had violated the strictures of *meibun* and had acted out of contempt of the court. He

44 Ibid., p. 270.

was convinced that nine of every ten men were alienated from the Tokugawa exercise of power. "The people of the realm," he urged, "must abandon the Tokugawa before it is too late, deepen their devotion to the imperial court, and move toward a revival of the emperor's power. The time must not be lost."

Ultimately Ōhashi's views on restoration melded into the organization of a small group of plotters – grass-roots heroes, recruited from Mito and Utsunomiya, willing to execute a plan to assassinate the shogunal counselor Andō Nobumasa. The plot was carried out in 1862 and is known as the Sakashitamon incident. Ōhashi saw the assassination as the occasion for both a rising of patriots and the promulgation of an imperial decree condemning the bakufu. Although he played no direct role in the attempted murder (Andō was wounded), he was willing to accept responsibility for his part in its planning.

The failure of Ōhashi's theory of restoration prompted a shift to the second method, that of raising an army of loyalists prepared to embark on an imperial campaign. This method was developed chiefly by the Kurume priest Maki Izumi (1813–64), an enthusiastic follower of the Mito discourse. The locus of activity also shifted from Edo to Kyoto, the site of the imperial court and the emperor. Whereas Ōhashi stressed the more formal Neo-Confucian elements in the Mito discourse, Maki, owing to his Shinto education, emphasized the native mythohistorical dimensions of the discourse. Maki was also critical of the meditative and quietistic tendencies of Neo-Confucianism, which he felt contained little sense of practicality. Neo-Confucianism, like Zen, was too abstract to use in understanding the contemporary situation. It was his intent to replace passivity, meditation, and self-cultivation with direct action.

Maki also plunged into national politics in the early 1860s after spending years in house imprisonment for activities in the Kurume domain. Almost immediately, he began to develop a theory of an imperial restoration to arrest the "unceremonial" behavior of the barbarians and to punish the "effeminacy" of the wavering bakufu. He was convinced that it was the court's duty to seize the initiative and to act. This was the moment, he wrote in 1861, to encourage the emperor to promulgate an expulsionist policy that would announce the restoration of imperial authority. In a letter to a Kyoto courtier, Maki outlined the way to accomplish a restoration: (1) Select talented men for positions of political responsibility; (2) reward men who act for the court with status; and (3) preserve the "great polity of the realm" by "returning to the prosperity of antiquity." Here, Maki brought together two themes – *kokutai* and the heavenly ordinance, both familiar conceptions within the Mito discourse, and pressed them into the task of formulating a new theory of emperor. To see the emperor armed with the moral authority of heaven and the divinity of the national ancestors and personalized by history (a tactic that the Mito writers failed to promote) became the condition for Maki's call for restoration. His theory sought to actualize the Mito conception of representation by calling up the historical characteristics of ancient emperors (although Mito merely summoned the principle, not the principal, of imperial authority) and rescuing the sovereign from his seat "beyond the clouds," as he put it, in order to liberate him from court concealment and return him to the world of politics. He believed that this conception of the emperor, now conforming to hard, concrete elements derived from actual history, corresponded to the requirements of contemporary political reality more closely than to the bland and abstract image envisaged by the Neo-Confucians.[45]

Maki saw the present as the moment in which to implement what he called, in his *Kei-i gusetsu*, a "great enterprise." He later translated the "great enterprise" into an "imperial campaign" against the bakufu. The idea of such an "imperial campaign," pledged to bring about a restoration, was authorized by historical examples. Emperors in the past had satisfied heaven's requirements to act. "Jimmu tenno had erected the great feudal system, established the teachings of Shinto, and unified the public spirit. . . . Temmu tenno expanded the skills in a hundred ways. He planned for the central administration, swept away abuses in the court, established a prefectural system . . ." Ancient imperial precedents showed contemporaries that current conditions necessitated a comparable response, what Maki called the "labor of the august Imperial Body." But completing this act in the present demanded commitment and heroism. In 1860 and 1861 Maki conceived of a plan to organize an imperial campaign aimed at overthrowing the bakufu. In an essay called the *Record of a Great Dream* he argued that the time had arrived for the emperor to exercise direct authority by issuing an edict branding the shogun a traitor and usurper. The edict would also call for an imperial campaign led personally by the emperor from a new base of operations established in the Hakone mountains. There, the emperor would take up residence and assemble shogunal officials for punishment. Next, he would summon the young shogun Iemochi and demand from him the return of former

45 Matsumoto Sannosuke, *Tennōsei kokka to seiji shisō* (Tokyo: Miraisha, 1969), pp. 72–82.

imperial possessions. Finally, the emperor would enter Edo and seize the shogun's castle, which would become the new imperial capital, and issue a "proclamation announcing a great, new beginning." Because for Maki the whole purpose of the imperial campaign was to destroy the bakufu, he recommended a return to an antiquity before the shogun and military estates had appeared as a model for the present, even though he favored retaining the feudal order in form. As for the composition of the imperial campaign, the *Gikyō sansaku* (1861) advised that the first principle had to be the recruitment of loyal lords. Beyond appealing to feudal lords, Maki also looked to enlisting small guerrilla groups composed of samurai and upper-ranking peasants capable of carrying out lightninglike action. In the end, Maki, together with men from Chōshū, tried to bring about an imperial restoration in 1864 at the Imperial Palace in Kyoto. It was a desperate plan, and it failed. But Maki's concept for restoration was to become a rehearsal for a real and successful performance in 1868. In Maki, the Mito discourse, which had begun with Confucian statecraft for domain reform, had gone on to provide the validation of Shinto mythology for the organization of efforts for nationwide reforms and emperor-central revolution.

THE RESTORATION OF WORSHIP AND WORK

Just as the Mito discourse interpreted contemporary reality in order to establish the "real" and the "appropriate" as justification for the autonomous domain, so the nativists (*kokugakusha*) advanced a theory of the self-sufficient village as the substituted part for the unenvisaged whole. The nativists operated under similar constraints but sought, in contrast with Mito, to represent a different social constituency selected from the rural rich, such as the upper and middle peasantry and village leaders. They also proceeded from the assumption that the vast changes in the content of culture necessitated finding a political form adequate to the transformation. Like the Mito discourse, nativism originated at an earlier time in the late seventeenth century and initially concentrated on resuscitating the landmarks of the Japanese literary and aesthetic tradition. National studies represented an effort to structure what we might call native knowledge and matured under the guidance of scholars like Kamo Mabuchi (1697–1769) and Motoori Norinaga (1730–1801) in the eighteenth century. Toward the end of his life Motoori began to show sensitivity to contemporary conditions and recommended ways of averting social failure. Although he was the most gifted and original practitioner of *kokugaku,* a man whose range of interest was truly prodigious, it was one of his self-styled students, Hirata Atsutane (1776–1843) who virtually transformed the nativist discourse in the late eighteenth and early nineteenth century into a discipline of knowledge addressed to specific interests.

This transformation resulted in a radical shift from poetic studies (which were carried on by Motoori's adopted son and successor Motoori Ōhira) to practical religiosity and a preoccupation with daily affairs. Under Hirata's reformulation, nativism left the cities, where people like Motoori had lectured to wealthy townsmen and samurai, for the countryside, where the message was appropriated and even altered by the rural rich as a response and a solution to the apparent incompetency of the control system to provide security against disorder and assistance to the general peasantry. The immediate target of the peasants' discontent was invariably the village leadership and the rural rich. Thus nativism, as it became a discourse representing the leading elements in the countryside, constituted a break with its original purpose and character. This is not to say that Hirata and his followers abandoned their original tenets. Hirata had started his career as a conventional student of *kokugaku,* and his earliest writings in this idiom concentrated on poetry and aesthetics. Early in the nineteenth century he broke with the main line of *kokugaku* and began to emphasize a different position, but he was still very much dependent on earlier formulators like Kamo Mabuchi and Motoori Norinaga. Hirata tended to give weight and emphasis to ideas and elements in nativist thought that had, in earlier studies, remained recessive. The result was a new mapping of nativism and a plotting of its structure of thought to make it appear different. Hirata's mapping was virtually transformed into a new discipline, the study of the Japanese spirit (*yamatogokoro no gakumon*), whose subject would now be the "ancient Way" (*kodōron*) rather than language and poetry. Later followers like Ōkuni Takamasa (1792–1871) reshaped these new formulations into a systematic field of knowledge that Ōkuni called "basic studies" (*hongaku*) or into a unified doctrine that Yano Gendō (1823–87) referred to as "the study of basic doctrine" (*honkyōgaku*).

Adopted into a family of doctors, Hirata Atsutane appeared on the scene in the late eighteenth century and opened a school in Edo. He claimed to have studied with Motoori, but there is no record that he did. Almost immediately he became known as an outspoken critic of contemporary custom and urban mores. Intemperate to a fault, excitable but self-possessed, Hirata's special targets were scholars of all stripes, but especially Confucians (*bunjin*), whom he identified with writers of verbal fiction, and vulgar Shintoists. In his discussions on the practice of worship (*Tamadasuki*, 1828) he struck hard against contemporary preoccupations with poetic parody, wordplay, and *gesaku* fiction. Thus although he excoriated writers of verbal fiction for confusing people, his own concerns aimed at providing the ordinary folk with more useful instruction. Ordinary people served as both the subject of his lectures and the audience or object. He talked to them about themselves and their daily lives. Texts like the *Ibuki oroshi* and the *Tamadasuki* employed the language of daily speech, often the same idiom found in *gesaku*, and projected a vernacular voice studded with references to both the "ordinary person" (*bonjin*) and to things constituting their world. Yet it was precisely this juxtaposition between the "ordinary" and "extraordinary" (emphasized by Motoori in his discussions of aesthetic sensibility) that Hirata hoped to dramatize in his denunciations of contemporary scholars, poets, and writers. To underline this stance, he rejected the status of scholar for himself, as if by doing so he was cementing his ties to an audience of ordinary street people.

> This humble person hates scholars. . . . The scholars of Edo do not devote themselves to bringing people together. Still, the ordinary people are not nauseating. Because it is good to assemble people together, I am fond of this kind of association. If you ask a commoner, he will speak, but ordinarily he does not like (to listen to) a scholarly tale.

Hirata boasted that there were many like himself among the ordinary folk, who simply did not consider themselves as scholars.[46] Specifically, "scholars are noisy fellows who explain the Way. Such people as Confucians, Buddhists, Taoists, Shintoists, and intuitionists broaden a bad list indefinitely. . . . " Scholars feared obeying the "sincerity of august national concern" and avoid "emphasizing the court" in their studies. In the end, Hirata added, they poisoned the people's intention and neglected the emperor. "Even though there is an abundance of men in society who study, what fools they all are!" The reason for this "habit" was that there were simply too many men "who despise the eye and respect the ear." It was far better to study the "words and sayings of men who are nearby, men of our country, rather than the sayings of foreigners or only the deeds expressed by ancient men." Hirata's criticism sought to show that arcane knowledge monopolized by scholars had no relevance to large numbers of people; the immediate was more

46 Haga Noboru, "Edo no bunka," in Hayashiya, ed., *Kasei bunka*, pp. 183 ff.

useful than the mediate, and knowledge of what was "nearby" was prior to what was distant, remote, and foreign.

If Hirata left no doubt of his dislike for contemporary scholars who knew nothing about the present, he saw himself as a man devoted to studying the "true Way" and as one who possessed "extensive knowledge of the truth."[47] He believed that despite the army of erudite scholars inhabiting Edo, most were addicted to the good life, the arcane, and the strange. They all were essentially ignorant of the real goals by which ordinary people lived. His own lectures were first directed to reaching townsmen, but by the 1830s, the rural population. "Men of high rank have leisure time to read a great many books and thus the means to guide people; men of medium rank do not have the time to look at books and do not possess the means to guide people. . . ." Yet the ruled must be offered assistance and the opportunity to hear about the Way, as it was as relevant to those who might not be able to read well as to those who did have leisure time. "I would exchange one man who reads books for one who listens," he announced to his audience, "for those who hear the Way have realized a greater achievement than those who have reached it through reading."[48] Clearly Hirata was claiming the necessity of offering representation of a different kind of knowledge to the merely ordinary – those to whom Motoori had referred as ideal but rarely had specified or tried to reach. Hirata's tactic for creating a discourse designed for the ordinary person resulted in a shift to discussing the "ancient way" and showing that its content was no different from that of daily life. "Great Japan," he said, "is the original country of all countries; it is the ancestral country. From this standpoint the august lineage of our emperor has been transmitted successively and rests with the great sovereign of all nations. The regulations of all the countries are commanded and controlled by this sovereign." The bakufu and the managerial class were obliged to satisfy the "spirit of Japan," which came to mean fulfilling the "august obligation to the spirit of Tokugawa Ieyasu" by "serving" and "studying antiquity."

The immediate purpose of Hirata's thought was to allay popular fears concerning death and to provide consolation to the people. He believed that the popular mind had become confused by fashionable explanations that made people susceptible to the temptations of licentious and private behavior. It was for this reason, after the 1790s, that

47 Ibid., p. 184.

48 Muromatsu Iwao, ed., *Hirata Atsutane zenshū*, vol. 1: *Ibuki oroshi* (Tokyo: Hakubunkan, 1912), p. 2. Hereafter cited as *Hirata zenshū, 1912*.

he apparently turned his attention to the lives of the ordinary folk. Yet it would be incomplete to say that his only goal was to pacify the present. By centering on ordinary folk in discourse, Hirata provided a powerful warrant for independent action.[49]

Hirata's aim to offer consolation to ordinary folk involved a comprehensive strategy demonstrating the connection between all things and establishing a genealogy for that kinship. Connectedness showed family resemblances, and family resemblances revealed the relationship of all things, past and present, owing to the common and creative powers of the creation deities (*musubi no kami*). By promising unhappy contemporaries the prospect of consolation, Hirata and his followers resorted to a systematic classification capable of representing the relationship of all things. His own favored mode of relating was expressed in cosmological speculation (already pursued by a number of late-eighteenth-century thinkers) which presumed to explain why it was impossible for the spirits of people to migrate after death to the dreaded and foul world of permanent pollution (*yomi*). The purpose of this form of speculation was to provide comfort to the large numbers of ordinary folk who, Hirata believed, feared death and consequently expressed their anxieties and unhappiness in activities such as peasant rebellions, escape to the cities, and self-indulgence in the privatized pleasures of the culture of play. Hirata's explanation (articulated in *Tama no mihashira*, 1818) was rooted in a fundamental division between "visible things" (*arawanigoto*) and "matters concealed and mysterious" (*kamigoto*). Although this classification between the seen and the unseen had been initially authorized by the *Nihon shoki*, it now demanded apprehending phenomena as being related in the modality of the part–whole relationship, which permitted reducing one thing to function as a substitute for another. Nativists were able to make this move because they believed that both realms were ultimately produced by the creation deities. Yet they valued the world of "hidden things" more than the visible world of the living and made the latter dependent on the actions of the former. Because the invisible realm had been originally identified with the *kami*'s (deities') affairs, it was natural to see it as the source of the phenomenal world of living things. But by linking the visible to the invisible in this way and bonding conduct in the former to judgment in the latter, Hirata and his rural followers were able to offer representation and even meaning to the life

49 Despite Hirata's apparent valorization of the ordinary folk, many contemporaries would have agreed with the writer Bakin's assessment that he (Hirata) was less concerned with commoners than he was with self-aggrandizement.

of groups who had remained outside or on the margins of official discourse. Judgment of performance based on an asessment of morally informed behavior usually meant work and productive labor. Each individual was obliged to perform according to the endowment (*sei*) bestowed on him at birth by the heavenly deities. Whatever one did in life was important and necessary.

Hirata's elaborate cosmology did more than simply enjoin the ruled, the ordinary folk whom he now called by the antique name *aohitokusa,* to fall into line and work hard.[50] The significant result of his reformulation of the relationship between divine intention and human purpose was to transform what hitherto had been regarded as an object into a knowing and performing subject. Accordingly, the ordinary folk now occupied a position of autonomy through the valorization of their quotidian life and the productivity of their daily labor. By arguing that the living inhabited the invisible world where the spirits and deities resided, Hirata was able to demonstrate the existence of a ceaseless transaction between creation and custom. Even though each realm was considered separate from the other, they were nonetheless similar in all decisive aspects, as the living were descendants of the spirits and deities. If creation was initially the work of the gods, it was maintained by humans who continuously created to fulfill their divine obligation of repaying the blessings of the gods. The two primal creation deities established the connection of the two realms at the beginning of heaven and earth.[51] For thinkers like Hirata, the conception of *musubi,* creativity and productivity, established the divisions, the classes of events and things, inner and outer affairs, human and sacred, visible and invisible, yet such categories attested to the integrated wholeness of life and its continuation from one generation to the next. The archetypal example of the creation deities making the cosmos continued to manifest its "necessity" down to the present in manifold ways: the procreation of the species, the production of goods, and the constant reproduction of the conditions of human community. *Musubi* also denoted linkages, the act of binding things together, and union, an observation made by Ōkuni Takamasa that served as the leading principle in the formulation of the theory of harmony (*wagō*).

50 This is the argument of Matsumoto Sannosuke, *Kokugaku seiji shisō no kenkyū* (Osaka: Yūhikaku, 1957). Following Maruyama's interpretation of nativism as an irrational prop capable of eliciting voluntary submission of the ruled to the emperor, Matsumoto shows how *kokugaku* was made to serve the ideology of the managerial class.

51 Tahara Tsuguo, et al., eds., *Nihon shisō taikei*, vol. 50: *Hirata Atsutane, Ban Nobutomo, Ōkuni Takamasa* (Tokyo: Iwanami shoten, 1973), p. 18. Hereafter cited as *Hirata Atsutane, Ban Nobutomo, Ōkuni Takamasa*.

Above all else, the most explicit sign for the continuing activity of the creation deities was agricultural work. Work constituted the guarantee that the creation would be reproduced in every generation and appeared as the bond holding the community together. Here, nativists offered it as an alternative to securing social solidarity, fully as effective as mere political obedience because it was associated with the sacred. In this way Hirata and his followers succeeded in shifting the emphasis from performing specific behavior-satisfying norms to the essence of life activity itself, work, now authenticated by the archetypal event of creation, as the measure of all real conduct in the visible realm. By altering an argument based on abstract principles governing power relationships to valorize concrete and practical mundane activities, the nativists had found a way to highlight the means of social reproduction and its realization as the content of discursive knowledge.

In rural Japan this nativist intervention had great consequences. The hidden world, once the domain of the gods, now became synonymous with the departed ancestors of the living. This identification between the hidden and the space occupied by the spirits of the living increasingly served to encourage folk religious practices emphasizing guardian deities, tutelary beliefs, and clan gods. Yet it also induced the community to concentrate on its own centrality in the great narrative of creation and the reproduction in custom. In texts like the *Tamadasuki* and the starchy enjoinment to daily worship, Hirata outlined in some detail the way that the most mundane forms of daily life interacted with worship and how the lives and activities of ordinary people represented a religious moment. Summoning daily life to such a discourse and linking it to worship and religious observances made archaism (*kodōron*) meaningful to wider audiences in rural Japan. To be sure, Hirata imagined these mundane activities as living examples of the archaic precedent and authoritative proof that no real disjunction separated the present from the preclass, folkic past. In his exposition the ancient Way, once identified with sincerity and ethics in poetry and theater, forfeited its privileged status to the ordinary folk living in the present. When peasant leaders who had passed through Hirata's school juxtaposed this concentration on the unity of work and worship, life and labor with their perception of rural unease, it appeared to offer a solution to unrelieved fragmentation, divisiveness, and the threat of decreasing productivity, as well as conferring a form of representation on their leadership. By rescuing the ordinary folk from the margins of official discourse, *kokugaku* could enforce a community of interests among the upper and lower peasantry and overcome the apparent ambiguity stalking the relationship between the village leaders and their followers.

That link was provided by the status of the ancestors and the centrality accorded to the village deities in binding the various parts of the village into a whole. Together, they constituted a world of relationships more real and fundamental than those found in the visible realm of public power. For the flow of ties, transactions, and traffic between the hidden world of the ancestors and tutelary deities and the visible realm of work and social relations disclosed a commonality of interest and purpose that transcended ascribed status and mundane ethical duties. The logic for this connection between work and worship in the rural setting was plainly prescribed by Hirata's systematization of ancestor respect within the larger framework of folkic religious practices. In these lectures, he was able to link people with their ancestors and the creation deities, explain the central importance of the clan deities (*ujigami*) and tutelary gods (*ubusuna no kami*), and show why the creation deities were so vital to the agricultural project. These explanations also became elements in the formation of a theory of village rehabilitation and self-strengthening. By identifying increased productivity and agricultural labor with religious devotion, by making work itself into a form of worship repaying the blessings of the gods, and by projecting a theory of consolation that promised immortality to the spirits and certain return to the invisible realms after death, Hirata and his followers were able to strike deeply responsive chords in the villages of the late Tokugawa period and present the prospect of resolving the problems of the countryside and reconstituting life anew along different lines.

The most obvious contact with village life was provided by the creation deities and the necessity to continue agricultural work. A variety of writers like Satō Nobuhiro (1769–1850) and Mutobe Yoshika (1798–1863) pursued this connection further by showing how wealth originated in agricultural production and how rural life corresponded to cosmic categories. Hirata had already, in the *Tamadasuki*, established the necessary linkages among the creation deities, the ancestors, and the households (*ie*) as indispensable to reproducing the social means of existence. He argued that the spirits of the dead inhabited the same place as the living and that they fixed the essential similarity between the invisible and visible realms. In an afterword to his inventory of daily prayers, Hirata noted that it was as important to make observances to one's ancestors as it was to other deities. Men who carried out household duties properly were also obliged to pray to the deities of the *ie* and to the shelf reserved for the ancestors. One should also worship the various clan deities and the deities of occupations.[52]

If the household represented the most basic and essential unit in Hirata's conception of the invisible world, then the village defined its outermost limits. Village, household, spirits (ancestors), and distant deities reaching back to the creation gods constituted a series of concentric rings, one within the other, linked by kinship. As Hirata's prayers to the ancestors called for protection and good fortune of the household, so his invocation to the tutelary gods and guardian deities served to secure protection and prosperity for the village community. "Grant all protection to this village (*sato*)," the prayer intoned, "Before the great tutelary deities we offer prudent respect. Protect the village day and night, and grant it prosperity."[53] Hirata related these village shrines to the hidden realm. "Regional spirits (*kunitamashii*) and the tutelary deities have been directed to share the administration of the realm among themselves and to assist Ōkuninushi no kami, whose basis of rule is concealed governance." Authority was manifest in the tutelary shrines of the various locales. While the deities conferred protection and prosperity, a thankful community should offer prayer, supplication, and hard work. Prayer and work meant the difference between continued wholeness (order) and fragmentation and decreased productivity (disorder). Indeed, in Hirata's thinking it was natural to move from formal religious observance to more enduring forms of gratitude, work. This identification of worship and work was refined by others, but it is clear that Hirata figured work as another way of talking about worship. His conception of work was rooted in a concern for repaying the blessings of the *kami*. This meant returning trust to the deities who had bestowed benefits. This trust, as he pointed out, meant both the land that produced food and the material from which clothing and shelter were made.

This sense of a powerful, hidden realm directing the fortunes of the living represented a structural similarity with the world of the household and rural community. It was a world symbolized by the authority of the tutelary shrines (which themselves represented a manifestation of the invisible world) and hence the place of the village, hidden, powerless in the realm of public authority, but nevertheless vibrant with "real" activity. Here the nativists, who, like the Mito writers, turned away from Edo, pitted a horizontal realm, close to nature and origins, against the vertical world of the Tokugawa *daikan*, daimyo,

52 Hirata Atsutane zenshū kankōkai, eds., *Hirata Atsutane zenshū* (Tokyo: Meicho shuppan, 1977), vol. 6, pp. 4–19. Hereafter cited as *Hirata zenshū, 1977*. 53 Ibid., p. 217.

shogun, and even emperor. The hidden world of the village, deities, ancestors, and descendants was more "real" than was the visible world of power and consumption. Without the sanction of the hidden world, the idea of an autonomous village would not have been possible. At its most fundamental level, the world envisaged by the nativists was one of linkages and kin relationships. It was a realm where microcosm, the household and the village, served as a substitute for the macrocosm, the so-called national soil (*kunitsuchi*), where the emperor as a living deity met the tutelary deities and the ancestors administered by Ōkuninushi and where the vertical claim of public authority collided with the horizontal claims of village life.

In its rural appropriation, *kokugaku* sanctioned the elevation of the village as a substitute for the whole, as Mito had projected the domain. The argument for an autonomous and self-sufficient village, removed from the centers of power, relied on people's recognizing their duty to return the "blessings" to the creation deities from whom all things literally flowed. This meant replicating the archetypal act of creation through agricultural work and reproduction. Judgment and final authority lay in the hidden realm administered by Ōkuninushi no kami, not the "living deity" who was the emperor. Duty was described as a form of stewardship that, as stated earlier, referred to the actual event in which the creation gods gave something to the other deities, the imperial descendants, and the land itself as a trust. Trust required repaying the divine gift with work. Late Tokugawa *kokugakusha* like Miyauchi Yoshinaga (1789–1843), Miyao (or Miyahiro) Sadao (1797–1858), and Hirayama Chūeimon (?–?) (all priests or village leaders) saw the idea of entrustment as the means to emphasize the central importance of agricultural life. It was in this context that Miyao, a Shimōsa village leader, argued that the realm was founded on agriculture and that the village was the appropriate instrument for organizing people to work together in the countryside. Others saw the village and the household as one and the same. Miyauchi responded to what he believed were signs of fragmentation in rural life as an example of neglecting the imperial doctrine imparted by the two creation deities. Evidence appeared everywhere in "rebellion," "disorder," and "wastage," which Miyauchi attributed to improper leadership. Theoreticians like Ōkuni coupled this notion of proper village leadership with the idea of an administration pledged to taking care of the people (*buiku*). All agreed that *kokugaku* was a method for solving problems in the countryside. Even a high-ranking samurai nativist scholar like Ikuta Yorozu (1801–37) (who followed the route of rebellion) believed that peasant disturbances would cease if good doctrine and leadership were administered to the villages. Such a method was dramatized in the formulation of a conception of relief and assistance (used also by the new religious groups) that would program stewardship. In the end, stewardship or entrustment became the grounds for village self-sufficiency and the justification for secession from the center.[54]

According to the rural nativists, all of this would be possible if proper knowledge were available. Miyauchi, for example, saw knowledge as the proper definition of the boundaries of order, whereby all persons knew what they were required to do and what was sufficient for their livelihood. When people violated established boundaries, they invited disaster. "If one does not extend (through work) the boundaries imposed by the heavenly deities, one will surely neglect his productive duties and be impatient toward them. . . . In the end it destroys the household and is the source of disaster."[55] Miyauchi's *To-oyamabiko* (1834) is sensitive to the frequency of rebellions and disorder, and the text's apparent purpose was to understand their causes in order to arrest their occurrence. The question Miyauchi asked was how not to forget what one was supposed to do. Selfishness undoubtedly turned people away from the established divisions and tempted them to excess. Excess transcended boundaries and could lead only to unhappiness and ruin. Those who had "exceeded their own boundaries," neglecting "household duties," had gone beyond "endeavoring" and had ceased to work. Working for the household brought order; work out of that context meant disorder. Such duty represented "entrustment" from one's parents and beyond them from ancestors and deities. Following the lead of Hirata, Miyauchi enjoined people not only to work but also to worship the ancestral deities and pray at the tutelary shrines. Like other rural nativists, he tried to remind contemporaries that because people had become so habituated to the uses of money, they had forgotten the source of wealth. Treasure (*takara*) was the word that many nativists used to designate the peasants (*hyakushō*), and by that they meant people working in the fields. Such people reflected a blessing of the gods, whereas offenders of divine injunctions, men who committed polluting acts (*tsumibito*), resembled "annoying pests" who gathered together to destroy the house-

54 The idea of a self-sufficient village "movement" was developed by Haga Noboru in several essays and books but notably in "Bakumatsu henkakuki ni okeru no undō to ronri," in Haga Noboru and Matsumoto Sannosuke, eds., *Nihon shisō taikei*, vol. 51: *Kokugaku undō no shisō* (Tokyo: Iwanami shoten, 1971), pp. 675–84. Hereafter cited as *Kokugaku undō no shisō*.

55 Ibid., p. 333.

hold. Such concerns led Miyauchi to examine the function of tutelary shrines as a focus for life, work, and worship, with a constant reminder of the necessity to "repay the blessings" of continued good fortune.

So powerful was this impulse to restructure village solidarity around the tutelary shrine that it became the basis of a nationwide movement in the 1840s. Another Shinto priest, Mutobe Yoshika, devoted his major texts to elucidating the connection between such shrines and the two creation deities. In his cosmological *Ken-yūjun kōron,* he proposed that the creation deities responsible for the procreation of humans were indistinguishable from the gods associated with the tutelary shrines. "These . . . deities reside in their *gun, ken, mura,* native place (*furusato*), and it is decreed that their ordinances are to be regulated by the tutelary gods."[56] Elsewhere he argued that the division according to fixed boundaries and deities representing various regions in the country meant that each place had its own tutelary god. The purpose of these deities, he declared, was that they informed people regularly of the "secret governance" of procreation and its administration. "In these places people daily grasp in their lives both the spirit of activity and calm from . . . the shrines."[57] Although the invisible government was not seen by mortals, it was manifest symbolically in the precincts of the shrines. They represented a bonding between the invisible realm and the visible and a guarantee of the continuing presence of the former in the world of the living. "The shrines of tutelary deities are very important," Mutobe wrote in the *Ubusunashako.* "Because that is the case, we must first offer daily prayer to these deities; next we should make regular visits to these shrines."[58] When such devotion and respect was carried out faithfully, it would guarantee prosperity and abundance. Guided by this conviction, Mutobe was prompted in the 1840s to call for the establishment of a countrywide movement pledged to worship the tutelary deities.

Whereas writers like Miyauchi and Mutobe were shrine priests who emphasized the importance of worship, Miyao Sadao, who described himself as a "potato-digging village official," stressed the primary role of the village official. Yet his concerns for leadership and work reflected another way of talking about worship and respect and stressing the importance of making the village a self-sufficient economic and political unit. By advising peasants to understand and preserve the "commands of the *namushi,* which are no different from the public ordinances (of the

56 Mutobe Yoshika, "Ken-yūjun kōron," *Shintō sōsho* 3 (October 1897): 2–3.
57 Ibid., p. 3. 58 *Kokugaku undō no shisō,* p. 229.

lord)," Miyao was envisaging the role of village leadership (in the manner of Mito writers writing about domainal leadership) as a substitute for the entrustment represented by the emperor, shogun, and daimyo, not as a challenge to officially constituted authority. His intention was merely to recognize that within the jurisdiction of the village, officials "must make the administration of the peasantry their chief duty." Most rural nativists acknowledged that the village, especially in bad years, would have to take responsibility for the extension of relief and assistance. This idea had been promoted earlier by agricultural writers of such differing persuasions as Ninomiya Sontoku and Ōhara Yūgaku. But assistance and relief, real necessities for village survival in the hardship years of the 1830s and 1840s, also underscored the primacy of collective purpose over private interest. It was seen as a method whereby the village, following the model of the household, would rely on its resources and its own efforts to reproduce the necessities of social life and thereby achieve a sense of the whole. This preoccupation with relief and mutual assistance, leading to the achievement of village autonomy and self-sufficiency, logically drew attention to the quality of local leadership. Promoting policies of strict economy meant urging the peasants to increase productivity for the sake of the village community as a whole under the informed guidance of agricultural sages, usually village officials, elders, and local notables (*meibōka*), instead of simply tightening their belts. Yet such leaders – Ninomiya, Ōhara, and rural nativists like Miyao believed – had to possess the right kind of knowledge of rural affairs in order to validate their authority.

For the rural nativists, knowledge meant "knowing about the *kami*." But to "know" about the *kami* meant also knowing about the ordinary folk. In other words, knowledge of the customary life of ordinary people was equivalent to knowledge of the deities, and vice versa. Village leaders were obliged to know both the divine intent of the gods and the conditions of daily existence that might satisfy the purpose of creation. Miyao described his own appointment as a divine trust that bound him – and all officials – to the duty of promoting self-sufficiency and economic self-reliance. This formulation concerning the identity of divine and human knowledge represented a transformation of an idea introduced earlier by Hirata. Whereas Ōkuni Takamasa catalyzed the formula into a discipline of learning in the 1850s, the rural nativists had already made its "content" a criterion for proper and authoritative leadership. Miyao in his *Kokueki honron* advised that the wealth of the region properly instruct the people into the way of the *kami*. He shared with thinkers like Ninomiya and Ōhara the conviction that people had to be inculcated with the spirit of the work by showing them how their daily life related to a world larger than mere day-to-day subsistence and the paying of taxes. This meant teaching them about the necessity of producing children to increase the labor force and to ease the financial burden on the rural population.[59] By the same token, village leaders must attend to famines, natural disasters, and the general well-being of the community. "Uneconomical policies," he asserted, "result in shame for the village, and the shame of the village becomes the shame of the lord."[60] Improper leadership always revealed a lack of knowledge and lack of piety before the deities. What Miyao feared most was the ever-present threat of conflict and division within the village. Its officials should promote harmony and "guide ignorant peasants." Their trust to administer well was even greater in hard times because they had "replaced the *daikan*." "During times of bad harvests," Miyao stated, "one cannot rely on the assistance of the regional lords and officials. One helps oneself with one's own savings and effort. One must understand that one should not bother or depend on the leaders in bad times."[61] To say this was to recognize that local autonomy and authority prevailed in the countryside.

Suzuki Shigetane (1812–63), an independent student at the Hirata school and a casualty in the loyalist explosions of the 1860s, gave even sharper expression to this identification of trust and knowledge and the stewardship of local leadership. In *Engishiki norito kōgi* (1848) he presented the idea that officials do not differ from the emperor inasmuch as they are obliged to offer "mutual help and assistance in the great august policy . . . to preserve the household enterprises given by the gods and make substance for food, clothing, and shelter."[62] Suzuki was referring to the rural elite assigned to administer the communities under their jurisdiction. Although he accepted a division within society, he was convinced that each sector exercised a sacred trust to fulfill the divine obligations "to make things for other people in hard times." His student Katsura Takashige (1816–71), a village leader in Niigata, constructed an argument whereby Suzuki's conception of "making the *kunitsuchi* habitable for the people" was enlisted to promote the primacy of village administration. In fact, writers like Suzuki and Katsura simply spoke of the village as if it were the larger realm

59 Ibid., p. 293.
60 Miyao Sadao, "Minke yōjutsu," in *Kinsei jikata keizai shiryō* (Tokyo: Kyōbunkan, 1954), vol. 5, p. 317. 61 Ibid., p. 304.
62 Suzuki Shigetane, *Engishiki norito kōgi* (Tokyo: Kokusho kankōkai, 1978), pp. 13–14.

(*kunitsuchi*). In *Yotsugigusa tsumiwake* (1848), Katsura envisaged the village as the equivalent or adequate political form for the realm as a whole and local leaders as exemplars for peasants. This should require no reliance on coercive measures, laws, or ordinances, as trust bound ruler to ruled. Such trust was conveyed to the people through "preaching" and "exhortations" from elders and superiors. He explained how this was to be done:

> First, depend on the Great August intention (heart) which deepens and widens the *kami* learning of the people. . . . This learning is transmitted from court officials (priests) who have made their own intention identical with the Great August Heart, down to regional lords, county officials, village chiefs, and headmen, to the peasantry. The peasants also receive and transmit this intention to each household in the learning of the deities.[63]

The systemization of *kokugaku* into a discipline of knowledge was completed by Ōkuni Takamasa, who sought to show how "learning about the *kami*" amounted to "learning about the ordinary folk." The term, he believed, referred to the realm itself. In the age of the gods, he wrote in *Hongaku kyoyō*, there had been three instances of entrustment, and two in the age of men. The first of these was from the heavenly deities to Izanami and Izanagi; the second from Izanami and Izanagi to Amaterasu (the formation of the moon and sun); the third was Amaterasu's entrustment to the imperial ancestor Ninigi no mikoto.[64] For the human world, the two great grants were to Sukunobikana and Ōkuninushi to solidify the realm and to make it habitable. Here was the basis for a theory meant for local leaders searching for the authority to establish an arrangement of mutual assistance and relief in the interest of a productive and harmonious life, as well as the larger sanction for a restoration of antiquity. At the mythic level, this link was forged in the example of the grant to Ōkuninushi to render and restore the national soil to human cultivation and habitation, and at the historical level it appeared in demands for the local leadership and peasantry to live up to this trust.

Ōkuni structured these trusts and obligations within the framework of a discipline. He associated knowledge of the gods with knowledge of the ordinary folk, without whom the creation would be meaningless and "talk about ruling the realm useless." One must always view the times from the perspective of the ordinary people. No real distinction could be made between the customs of the gods and those of ordinary

63 Katsura Takashige, *Yotsugigusa tsumiwake* (Niigata, 1884), unnumbered pagination.
64 *Hirata Atsutane, Ban Nobutomo, Ōkuni Takamasa*, pp. 408–9.

people. In *Yamatogokoro* (1848) Ōkuni wrote that the human species was divided into two categories. The Chinese called these two categories "great" and "small" men, but in Japan it had been the learning of the gods and the customs of the ordinary people. "When one learns about the deities, then even the small person will become a lord and great man, and when the lord and great man learn about the *aoi-hitogusa*, they will become as ordinary people."[65] A knowledge of origins (*moto*) thereby taught that the official was the base, and one's body, the ends. Together, they formed a reciprocal relationship. Yet in recent times, he continued, the ordinary people had reversed the order of things and had begun to consider their "bodies as the base." To do so resulted in pursuing pleasure and neglecting household duties. Moreover, this habit had affected the lords as well. Ōkuni warned the lower classes against imitating upper-class habits and advised them to "learn well the customs of the deities." He worried most about conflict and disharmony, division and fragmentation. Even though men had different faces and appearances, they were fundamentally the same because they were human.[66] Owing to divine intention, all humans were linked to one another by "mutual concern." When people conformed to this intention, times were good, but when they went against it, disaster ensued.

"The deeds of the gods join base to ends." Actualizing divine intention in practice resulted in the organization of a human community. But the ends of human activity represented the making of products from the natural material of the land granted by the gods. If the "customs of the ordinary people" (work, mutual assistance, relief) were successfully reunited with the customs of the gods, as specified in the ancient texts, then the true meaning of a harmonious union would be recovered and made manifest in the present. Indeed, the customs of the gods were equivalent to the "desires of the deities." The human impulse to help others expressed the desire and deeds of the gods. If the identification of godly deeds and human nature comprised the core of Ōkuni's thinking about politics, the installation of a harmonious community, wherein all were united by mutual assistance, became the form he envisaged for it as a displacement for contemporary institutions and administration. Because this form of human community existed before the establishment of all historical political structures and ordinances but had been forgotten in time, the present generation was appointed to restore it from memory to resolve the contemporary "crisis."

65 Nomura Denshirō, ed., *Ōkuni Takamasa zenshū* (Tokyo: Yuko shakō, 1937–9), vol. 3, pp. 18, 43. 66 Ibid., vol. 5, pp. 32 ff.

The *kokugaku* conception of work and mutual assistance was brought to completion by another rural writer from the Shimōsa region, Suzuki Masayuki (1837–71). Suzuki's central text, written just before the Restoration, was the *Tsukisakaki*, which tried to demonstrate that work was fundamental to life and that activity and performance represented the fulfillment of the cosmic plan. He attributed the "generation of all living things" first to the primal creation gods and then to the ancestral spirits. The spirits, he believed, were actually *kami* who had formerly been humans. The meaning of creation was, therefore, related to the "generation of life." Since the beginning of time, all "have endeavored similarly for the enterprise of generating life." Such an enterprise prevented conflict and disharmony. Excesses everywhere, Suzuki noted, could be avoided if people pursued the completion of virtue by working to generate life. Yet the generating of life bespoke mutual assistance, much in the manner that it had been conceptualized by Ōkuni Takamasa. "To work by and for oneself," Suzuki wrote, "will, in general, fail to bring about an accomplishment" of the great enterprise.[67] Like many nativists, Suzuki appealed to the body as a model, not to specify never-ending pleasures, but to represent the unity symbolized by household and village. The eyes see, he declared, the ears hear, the mouth speaks, the hands hold, and the feet move; each part relies on "mutuality" in order for the whole – the body – to operate. Suzuki then projected this metaphor to describe people working together as the key to realizing the great enterprise. If any part fails to assist the other, the body will collapse into dysfunction, just as neglect of reciprocity in work will terminate the "generation of life" and plunge the realm into disorder.

Suzuki was convinced that destruction of the work ethic would drive the realm into riot and rebellion, forcing people to turn against one another and transforming Japan into the image of China. Ultimate responsibility for the interruption of life-generating activity, however, belonged to the lords, and not to village officials. Lords obstructed and often prevented people from performing work. Suzuki went further than most nativists to portray the disruption and discontinuity between ruler and ruled and showed how *kokugaku*, in creating a discourse centering on the producer – the ruled – would hold the leadership responsible for interfering in activities necessary to the continuation of life. The lord, like the parent, provided the conditions for life-giving activity; the land constituted the basis of this activity. But

67 Sagara Tōru, ed., "Tsukisakaki," vol. 24 of *Nihon no meicho* (Tokyo: Chūō kōronsha, 1972), p. 387.

although this arrangement reflected a positive good, it could also turn into evil. Work and productivity could be misused by the lord for private and selfish purposes. Private desire drove the realm into a "deep valley." Higher loyalties to the land and to the deities should be repaid with life-generating work. Suzuki's explanation of private desire rested on the conviction that confusion was caused by "evil doctrines." It was necessary to "jettison the evil and mistaken doctrines of foreign countries (China) and return to the original intention . . . to cast off contemporary abusive customs in order to study the ancient minds." In his last, post-Restoration text on local government, Suzuki pointed to the village as the crucible for carrying on life-generating activity and an autonomous administration as the surest defense of proper doctrine.

RELIGIONS OF RELIEF

Commenting on the contemporary religious situation, the author of *Seji kemmonroku* roared:

> In today's society, the representatives of Shinto and Buddhism resemble national traitors. All the *kami* have ascended to heaven; the Buddhas have left for the Western Paradise; and all present and other worlds have fallen into disuse. Providence and retribution have been exhausted. All the Buddhist priests have fallen into hell and have ended (their mission) by becoming sinners.

Buyō Inshi's astringent condemnation of religious life in the Bunka–Bunsei area, like his sweeping renunciation of social life, may have been hyperbolic, but it signified a general playing out of older, more established religious forms at a time when people were beginning to search for new kinds of meaning and faith. Hirata Atsutane was already in the streets of Edo denouncing the vulgar Shintoists, the deceiving Buddhists, and the "stinking Confucianists." Provincial life was beginning to show renewed interest in more basic, nativist forms of religious practice. In the spring of 1830 large numbers of people from several areas of Japan streamed toward the Grand Shrine at Ise. This mass movement, numbering in the hundreds of thousands, was the most recent of periodic pilgrimages to the shrine of Amaterasu. The pilgrimage disintegrated into disorder and violence. It had no disciplined structure (although many groups were organized as *kō* for this explicit purpose), and it is not clear who its leaders were. But people were prompted to leave their households and villages – men, women, even children – to make the long and often perilous trek to Ise. The greater portion of pilgrims were from the lower classes, and even though they were proscribed from making the visitation, they nonetheless felt compelled to leave their work, families, children, parents, wives, and husbands to make the journey to Ise. Some writers proposed that the pilgrimages represented an enlargement of the late Tokugawa impulse for travel. If it is true that the pilgrim experienced momentary release, freedom, or even a sense of unconnectedness while traveling on the road, the pilgrimage was nonetheless religious or political in its intensity. Travel, propelled by religious zeal, offered temporary release from the harsh uncertainties of everyday life, the very same life that *kokugaku* scholars had made the centerpiece of their new discipline of learning. It also heightened awareness of the power that large groups could command. "We have stimulated an earthquake and unleashed the august virtue of the Grand Shrine; the heart moves Japan. We have unleashed the august good omen in the pilgrimage, and it is called an earthquake; the heart moves the country of Japan," so announced a contemporary riddle.[68] The pilgrimage of 1830 also dramatized questions of social surplus, fragmentation, poverty, and the prospect of even greater disorder. People went on such pilgrimages for many reasons. Some even had a good time, but many were driven by hopes of divine relief, assistance, and the desire for good fortune. The experience signified both a new religious zeal and a concomitant search for new forms of community. It also disclosed what had become disturbing and disquieting about the tenor of life for large numbers of ordinary people.

It was in this context of a massive search for divine assistance and relief, and the quest for new forms of communitarian and voluntary association, that a number of new religious groups appeared in the late Tokugawa decades. Along with the establishment of new, syncretic religious organizations, some older sects, like the *nembutsu* sects and Fujikō, also underwent renewal and revitalization. But it is important to note that the new religions, like Mitogaku and *kokugaku*, represented a departure from past and more established religious forms that, many believed, had been played out. Like other discourses in the late Tokugawa period, the new religious message reflected the operation of a strategy that sanctioned bringing together older ideas, elements, and practices into new combinations. Organizationally the new groups like Tenri, Konkō, Kurozumi, and Maruyama sought to real-

68 Quotation from Fujitani Toshio, *Okagemairi to ee ja nai ka* (Tokyo: Iwanami shoten, 1968), pp. 168–9.

ize the promise of voluntary association (as against the involuntary association demanded by "nature") and horizontal relations by reconstituting themselves as autonomous communities. These new religions recruited their followers from the broad stratum of society but appealed largely to the lower classes. Their recruitment signified both the attempt of the people to represent themselves in a discourse, by centering themselves and their lives as its subject, and a criticism of Tokugawa social conditions. In this connection Professor Yasumaru Yoshio has written:

> In order to criticize society as a whole from the standpoint of popular thought, which tended to make humility, submission, and authoritarianism as its substantive element, a great leap was necessary. The mediation that made this leap possible took on a . . . character that was, in many cases, religious. The new popular religions offered an ideal . . . that transcended the authority of the contemporary feudal system.[69]

Like *kokugaku,* many of the new religions were disposed to blend elements of myth with contemporary history as a means to create new forms of expression and interpretation. Moreover, they were often driven by the same impulse to ascertain the "real." Their solution, which led to even more radical secessions, disclosed an obsession with autonomy and the desire to remove their followers from the contagions of contemporary history and the corruption of the center. The most extreme example of this obsession was the *yonaoshi* (world renewal) movements and *ee ja nai ka* (ain't it grand) outbursts of the last years of the Tokugawa period, whose constituencies were usually the same people against whom both Mito and *kokugaku* sought to find protection by granting relief and assistance. Recalling the intentionality informing both Mito discourse and nativism, the new religions consistently projected an unpolitical stance in the promotion of new programs and new relationships based on different conceptions of knowledge, even though their activities resulted in political consequences. Adherents to these sects often saw themselves as providing pockets of productivity and relief in a context of scarcity and unrelieved hardship, rather than as challenging the established world of politics and public authority. But when they sought to eliminate the divisiveness of politics by dissolving the collectivity into autonomous religious communities, they instead contributed to the very political fragmentation that they were seeking to displace. In the move to establish the principle of autonomy and wholeness, in which they apparently saw neither, the new religions withdrew

69 Yasumaru Yoshio, *Nihon kindaika to minshū shisō* (Tokyo: Aoki shoten, 1974), p. 90.

from the center and offered their own interpretation of contemporary history by rejecting it. At the periphery, they believed that they would find a place sufficiently removed from the corrosions of temporality to establish new political forms growing out of the content of culture. An apprehension of the world in this manner was equivalent to changing it in order to secure the necessary communal arrangements that conformed to the new forms of knowledge and conceptions of human nature. Nowhere was this commitment to act and change the world expressed in greater extremity than in those groups yearning for "world renewal" (*yonaoshi*).

If the new religions strove to recapture an original experience of wholeness, they also believed that the horizontal relationships that their belief authenticated came before the vertical ties demanded by the "discrimination of names" and the Tokugawa status system. This was their most distinctive and dangerous contribution to the general discussion in late Tokugawa society. All looked to the establishment of a genuine human order organized along horizontal relationships devoted to realizing equality. By the same token the new religions showed sensitivity to the way that distinctions caused social inequality. Consequently they announced their determination to find forms of organization calculated to diminish the reliance on hierarchy. The form favored by most recalled the traditional *kō*, groups of believers in which every member served as an equal partner, which characterized the groups participating in the *okagemairi* (i.e., Isekō) and merchant investment societies.[70] Under the sanction of an egalitarian organization, the new religions projected an image of relief, mutual assistance to all followers, and even reform of existing structures by calling for the equitable distribution of land and resources. At the heart of their programs was the valorization of daily life and its importance for maintaining the solidarity of community. Although their organizational principle emphasized human connectedness (the brethren) and the necessity of working and living together in mutual reciprocity as a solution to the fragmentation of more established social units that had taken place with the commercialization of the countryside, it also made equality the condition for sustaining community.[71] The new religions sought to console the spiritually and materially poor who occupied the lowest rungs of the social scale of Tokugawa Japan. In their understanding of the times, people who were "poor" were also

70 Murakami Shigeyoshi, *Kinsei minshū shūkyō no kenkyū* (Tokyo: Hōzōkan, 1977), pp. 21ff.
71 Yasumaru, *Nihon kindaika*, pp. 18ff.

"unhappy," and only association and mutual cooperation could alleviate that state.

What enabled the new religions to interpret contemporary reality in this way and to claim interest in the poor and unhappy was a special conception of knowledge and of learning. They all substituted faith and belief in the powers of deity for conventional sources of solace. Faith and belief appeared to be comparatively rational, as the new religions made an effort to discourage believers from relying on superstition and traditional magical practices.[72] In parting from the more structured sects of Buddhism in which Tokugawa regulations had required villagers to register, they also represented a direct search for new forms of knowledge and belief, often promising health and happiness, that met the needs of daily life. In this they could be related also to the focus on utility that characterized Mito and *kokugaku* thought. Thus Konkōkyō proposed that "learning (*gakumon*), without belief, never assists people," whereas the founder of Tenri, Nakayama Miki, advised her believers that only faith could enable people to know the exalted state and secure relief from contemporary suffering and hardships. Kurozumi Munetada, founder of the Kurozumi sect, constantly admonished his followers to stop "worrying about the Way" in order to "know and transmit the virtue of Amaterasu to people of the times."

It is important to note that many of the new religions originated in localities where newer commercial arrangements were in the process of disturbing older modes of production and social relationships and where economic distress seemed to be the most severe. In large part this observation describes the frequency and distribution of peasant rebellions as well and suggests why the new sects often ended up recruiting the same kind of people who were willing to join rural jacqueries. Owing to the regional nature of economic hardship, many of the new religions enlisted local nativistic practices and traditions to familiarize their messages when recruiting a followership. Yet, it is undeniably true that many struck deep roots in regional and village religious practices associated with Shinto and shamanism and that they derived their authority from a broadened base of shrine Shinto and religious conventions related to agricultural life.[73] But the appropriation of older, local practices frequently betrayed the limited appeal of such groups and revealed the initimate relation-

72 Kano Masanao, *Shihonshugi keiseiki no chitsujo ishiki* (Tokyo: Chikuma shobō, 1969), p. 138.

73 Miyata Noboru, "Nōson no fukkō undō to minshū shūkyō no tenkai," *Iwanami kōza Nihon rekishi*, vol. 13 (*kinsei* 5) (Tokyo: Iwanami shoten, 1977), pp. 209–45.

ship between regional hardship and the construction of consoling ideologies, even though many of these religions projected a universal message.

In general, these sects promoted doctrines calling for the regime of relief everywhere, according to the blessings of a single and all-powerful *kami* who represented a first principle (or principal), whether it was Amaterasu Ōmikami of Nyorai and Kurozumi, Tenri Ōmikami of Tenri, Tenchikane of Konkōkyō, Mt. Fuji of Fuji *kō*, or Moto no oyagami of Maruyama *kō*. Such deities supplied authority for claims promising to offer relief and assistance and contrasted dramatically with the rather discredited obligations of the feudal order to provide benevolence and aid in times of need. It is also true that nativists assigned a comparable role to the creation deities and to the tutelary shrines, even though they emphasized the human capacity for self-help. In many instances, these all-powerful gods were seen as creators of the cosmos and progenitors of the human species. And the reliance on a reliever who bore striking resemblance to the Buddhist Miroku (Maitreya) or simply one who possessed *kami* character explained to the poor and the beleaguered the necessity for help and assistance among humans and why it was absent in their time. The effectiveness of this explanation often depended on the powers of the founder of a sect to demonstrate the efficacy of his or her knowledge and charismatic powers. Unlike nativism, which often diminished the powers of the person for the spirit of the word (*kotodama*), the new religions relied principally on performance to validate the message. Part of this reliance on the performative act stemmed from a distrust for conventional forms of knowledge based on the primacy of words and abstractions, yet part of it was undoubtedly inspired by the emphasis on the body and on the importance of its movements, whether in play or in physical work, in late Tokugawa thought. What appears important is the emphasis on the performative powers of the body and its kinship with manual rather than mental activity. This projection, of course, reflected the primacy of daily life. It is, in any case, this factor that accounts for the difficulty in dissociating the religious career of the founders from the discourse that they helped construct and in separating actual demonstration and action from verbal utterance. Frequently, the performance model of the founder became a text for the followers to read, as a source for correct knowledge, just as the body served as a text in verbal fiction.

The founder's performance depended on a successful appropriation of elements from shamanistic practice related to *kami* possession and healing spiritual powers. Many of the new religions resorted to the convention of identifying the founder of the sect as a "living *kami*" (*ikigami*), a designation that the nativists reserved for the emperor. The act of describing the founder as a living god, mediating between the primal voice and the followers and supplying his or her body as a vessel to convey the deity's wishes to the faithful, added authenticity to the autonomous doctrine that each was trying to articulate. The process whereby in most cases this new persona was realized began with the founder's illness (later interpreted as time spent with the primal deity), followed by divine intervention and speedy recovery, which led to a change in personality, which in turn bore fruit in miraculous cures among the local inhabitants and was accompanied by periodic trances to reinforce the new charisma. The ritualization of the founder's life into a drama of living *kami* undoubtedly served the same purpose as the Mito celebration of the timeless presence represented by the Daijōsai and the nativist enshrinement of tutelary worship as a technique for securing continuous contact with the creation deities and the work of Ōkuninushi no kami.

To explain a world based on knowledge that only initiates could know (closely resembling *kokugaku*'s valorization of the activities of daily life) risked provoking conflict with the authority system, which had its own claims to a privileged knowledge entitling certain people to rule and its stated responsibility to provide benevolence. Even so, some of the new religions, like Tenri and Maruyama, developed doctrines announcing "world renewal" in the present and the beginning of a new heaven on earth. So powerful was the appeal of this ideal that by the end of the epoch, world-renewing rebellions and *ee ja nai ka* disturbances in cities like Kyoto and Osaka were proclaiming their cause in slogans of relief and assistance to the people. Despite the world renewal project, such revolutionary utopianism usually drew attention to this-worldly temporal orientations. All of the sects, including the revitalized *nembutsu* organizations like the *myōkōninden*, spoke of "extreme happiness in this world" and underscored the necessity to find contemporary answers to prayers requesting the *kami* to eliminate struggle and "correct illness and disease." Tenri insisted on making a "fresh start beyond death" and enjoined its followers to concentrate on their daily lives without fear or anxiety concerning their fate after death. Underlying this attitude was the conviction that humans, not nature, were the standard of action or behavior, just as the present, rather than some remote and transcendent sanctuary in the future or elsewhere, was the place for carrying out the duties of the daily life. Here again is a close resemblance to the claims of late Tokugawa verbal fiction and woodblock illustrations with its own elevation of human subjectivity as the maker of society and custom. In the case of the new religions, primacy of the human, regardless of status, was intimately related to the process of becoming a *kami*. Doctrines like Konkō and Tenri, for example, joined humans to the deities by employing such familistic metaphors as "children of the *kami*" or "family of the deities." Yet such reference to the divine merely reinforced the essential kinship that it was believed all humans shared, regardless of status, class, sex, or even race. To be human meant promoting programs of relief and assistance to all folk, whose destitute and often impoverished lives constituted the touchstone for recruitment into the new religions. Konkōkyō constantly dramatized the importance of "men who assist other men" as the major criterion of being human, whereas Nakayama Miki exhorted her followers to "never forget other men" – not just people of abundance, the rural rich, merchants, and managers, but the diligent and nameless people about whom official discourse had been silent, who now inhabited the "bottom of the valley" (*tanizoku*). Social division itself, it was held, set people against one another and created the circumstances of conflict and struggle between the rich and the needy. The purpose of programs pledged to relieving the poor was a radical presumption of the equality of all individuals and between the sexes and the promise to redistribute wealth and land. Behind this call was the sustaining power of human love for others and a dangerously optimistic belief in the essential goodness of human nature.

Among the late Tokugawa religions the most representative sects, which also captured the largest following, were Kurozumi, Tenri, and Konkōkyō. Kurozumi was the earliest and was founded by Kurozumi Munetada (1780–1850) in Okayama prefecture. He was born in a village in Bizen, the son of a Shinto priest of the Imamura Shrine, a guardian deity of Okayama Castle. His mother was the daughter of a priest. When Munetada was in his thirties, he contracted tuberculosis, after losing his parents who apparently also died of infectious disease, and was confined for a year and a half. His illness and confinement solidified his resolve to devote his efforts to securing assistance from the sun goddess for the ill, diseased, and downtrodden. It has been reported that he aspired to become a "living deity" and felt cheated because of the imminent threat of death, deciding that after death he would become a deity devoted to healing the ill. But Munetada survived and recovered after experiencing unity with Amaterasu while venerating the rising sun at the winter solstice. Upon recovering, he began a new ministry of cures, teaching his first followers the lesson he had learned about the sun and the benefaction and compassion of Amaterasu. Success led to disciples and the establishment of a formal organization.

Kurozumi's doctrine was based on conversion to the sun goddess. He advised people to know how to concentrate their devotion on the august virtue of Amaterasu; the light of the sun goddess had not changed for an eternity and wanted the "august intention of Amaterasu" and the people's intention to become united.[74] Like other founders, Kurozumi was convinced of the possibility of becoming identified with the deity. This devotion undoubtedly derived from his own religious background, but his focus on the singularity and superiority of the sun goddess also offered a way to overcome the claims associated with other deities prevalent among traditional agricultural believers. Hereafter relief and assistance were to be related to the saving powers of a single deity. In time such relief came to range from simple cures to the prolongation of life, abundance, having children, easy delivery, increased success in trades and business, bumper crops, and larger fishing catches, all things that would make life easier.[75] If Amaterasu were idealized as the sun and the source of life, then life itself would find meaning only within the confines of her powers. Hence Kurozumi advanced a conception of enclosure (found in other doctrines as well) bounded by belief and occupied by the faithful. In a letter he confessed that there "was no special way to relate this basic unity (between believer and sun goddess) outside this circle (○)."[76] This imagery of the circle was scattered throughout his writings and referred to an enchanted enclosure free from desire and misfortune. In the early 1840s he wrote:

> The Way is easy to serve, even though we can see that some do not serve it easily. To serve this Way is to live in it. This Way, as I have repeatedly stated, is Amaterasu Ōmikami. That is, it is the circular deity. As I have said before, things should be entrusted to this circle. It is easy to leave things to this Way, and it is very strange that people in China and Japan have not been aware of this. They are perplexed by the name of the Way. Men who have been separated from the true Way are all under heaven. Not to be separated from the true Way is the Way I have been talking about.[77]

If all things were done gratefully, the "august intention of Amaterasu Ōmikami" would be satisfied.[78]

74 Kano, *Shihonshugi*, p. 138. See also Helen Hardacre, *Kurozumikyō and the New Religions of Japan* (Princeton, N.J.: Princeton University Press, 1986). 75 Kano, *Shihonshugi*, p. 139.

76 Ibid., p. 140; also, Murakami Shigeyoshi and Yasumaru Yoshio, eds., *Nihon shisō taikei*, vol. 67: *Minshū shūkyō to shisō* (Tokyo: Iwanami shoten, 1971), p. 130. Hereafter cited as *Minshū shūkyō to shisō*. 77 *Minshū shūkyō to shisō*, p. 115. 78 Kano, *Shihonshugi*, p. 114.

To explain the grace provided by the circular enclosure made it appropriate to develop an idea of order faithful to its requirements. The central principle lay in the deity's capacity to fulfill all requests. When individuals entrusted themselves to the the sun goddess's ordinances, they were immediately relieved of evil. To enter the enclosure meant leaving the world of suffering and misfortune; and as the epoch came to a close, followers increasingly read that to mean the Tokugawa social system. Kurozumi's message presupposed the power of the deity to deliver people's requests. By locating all blessings in the sun goddess, he was able to place his principal emphasis on the believers' faith in the deity and their willingness to make the effort to improve conditions. Kurozumi held that the unification of the believers' intention with that of Amaterasu meant that people themselves had to show by faith and goodness that they were deserving. Failure to secure grace or blessing revealed only one's unworthiness and lack of real faith. Next came the idea that all people were brothers and sisters. This, too, resulted from the conception of a united intention. "When assisting," he wrote in a poem, "there is life."[79] Life was accessible to all. Kurozumi believed that all people were ultimately children of the sun goddess. "There are none who do not give thanks sincerely; one truth is that all in the four seas are brothers."[80] With the universalistic thrust of this idea, its immediate purpose was to stem contemporary conflict and distrust. The idea promoted a powerful sense of equality and sharing. Things are important, Kurozumi wrote, but they do not constitute criteria by which to separate people between the esteemed and despised. Neither life nor death, high nor low can separate people from one another. In this connection Kurozumi sought to juxtapose the spirit of sun (light and happiness) to the principle of darkness. According to Kano Masanao, the dark, or *in* (*yin*), principle was the symbol for the peasants' circumstances; it was precisely the association manifest in the status order that made the peasant low man in the hierarchy. "The august belief in the sun goddess (projecting the symbol of light – *yō* (*yang*) – increasingly dispells the spirit of darkness." If too much attention were devoted to darkness, to the exclusion of the principle of light, it would ultimately lessen and destroy the spirit of light. Kurozumi believed that a balance between the two would fulfill the expectation of a perfect and complete society, perhaps the circle he had drawn to dramatize the sacred space designated for believers. His

79 Ibid., p. 102. 80 Ibid., p. 116.

conception of the social order was revealed in his meditations on the circle. For the circle, the sun, light, Amaterasu represented fullness, plenitude, presence, perfection – surely an attractive alternative when juxtaposed to the received arrangement of authority. Kurozumi saw the installation of this new age of the *kami* as a veritable utopia glowing in the midst of progressive social darkness. "The age of the gods and of the present are one; they offer compassion to all at the end of the world."

More than Kurozumikyō, Tenri was implicated in the trials of the oppressed and conveyed the sense that the present constituted a time of crisis. It was founded by a peasant woman near Nara, Nakayama Miki (1798–1887), who was oppressed by her family and her husband and knew hardship, pain, and personal suffering. Miki's biographers have attributed her zeal for helping people to her personal experience. But Nakayama Miki also had a keen grasp of political realities; she was a sensitive recorder of the Tempō famine and an understanding witness of the *okagemairi* pilgrims who passed through her village on their way to Ise. The pilgrimage and the famine signified suffering for her and showed the necessity of finding ways to provide relief and assistance. As with Kurozumi Munetada, Miki's life unfolded as a series of cases of caring for the needy and the poor. Self-sacrifice, ascetic zeal, and a sense of injustice propelled her on her ministry. According to Carmen Blacker, Miki's ministry was marked by a number of important "tribulations" in which she was able to demonstrate her powers to heal the afflicted.[81] In time she was credited with the powers of a local shaman (*yamabushi*). In one session, when Miki was beginning to chant the incantatory spells, her face began to contort, and she fell into a trance. While still possessed by a deity she replied to a question that she was Ten no shōgun, "the true and original god who has descended from Heaven to save mankind."[82] In the presence of her husband and others, the *kami* who had come to inhabit her body asked Miki to abandon her family to serve as the vehicle and messenger for the divine work of assistance. Should her husband refuse to comply, the deity threatened to cast the family under the pall of a curse. This trance lasted three days, and only after Miki's husband consented to the divine demand did Miki return to normal. She experienced subsequent signs of divine origin as part of her passage into a new state. The sudden fits of possession and her erratic behavior as a condition for her

81 Carmen Blacker, "Millenarian Aspects of New Religions," in Donald Shively, ed., *Tradition and Modernization in Japanese Culture* (Princeton, N.J.: Princeton University Press, 1971), pp. 574–6. 82 Ibid., p. 575.

ministry led to ostracism and poverty, but her success in healing, especially with respect to painless childbirth, brought her followers and the beginnings of an organization.

Miki's transformation into a divine vehicle for relief began when, commanded to give up her possessions, she decided to distribute her family land. The act dramatized personal attachment to land and the belief that ownership itself was the source of all inequality. Because equal distribution under conditions of ownership is impossible to realize, true equality can be realized only through abject landlessness. Miki's behavior underscored her teaching that "one must fall into poverty." Poverty and relief from pain became the axis of her vision. This vision was further reinforced within the structure of a cosmological myth, derived from native myth, legend, and history. According to this, the world originated in a muddy ocean (the salty brine of *kokugaku*) inhabited by a variety of fish and serpents. Because the parent deities wished to create humans, they gave birth to myriads of people on the site of the Nakayama household in Japan. These grew to great size and died. After this, the deities had created birds and beasts and a variety of insects; these also died. All that was left were monkeys. From the monkeys, men and women were born; then heaven, earth, mountains, and plains were differentiated. Humans lived first in water for eons and eventually moved onto the land. It is interesting to compare this crudely evolutionary conception with Hirata's earlier assertion that all humans originated from the insect world. Although such notions were indispensable to the peasant experience, steeped as it was in a firsthand involvement in the cycle of growth, they also showed how earlier concerns for natural history had become part of a prevailing consciousness.[83] Moreover, such an evolutionary process demonstrated the common origins of equality among all people and validated Miki's articulation of a utopian vision in her hymn *Mikagurauta* (1869).

This long text, written in Nara dialect, focused on increased agricultural productivity. "The intention of everybody in the world requires fields and lands,"[84] "if there are good fields, everybody in a row will be cleansed of desire,"[85] and it would be possible to increase the abundance of Yamato through the unlimited powers of the deities.[86] Miki also sang her expectations of social reformation: "Drum beat, the New Year's dance begins/ How wonderful; if we erect a structure for teaching/ What prosperity! revering the body and securing health/ *yonaori*."[87] Related to the idea of "world renewal" was, of course, the

83 See Kano, *Shihonshugi*, pp. 147–8, for an account of the Tenri mythology.

84 *Minshū shukyō to shisō*, p. 184. 85 Ibid., p. 185. 86 Ibid., p. 181. 87 Ibid.

ideal of mutual assistance which was the central theme of both the *Mikagurauta* and her instructions (*Ofudesaki*). The hymn opens with a celebration that all people will be one when they assist one another. Assistance will also confer the blessings of the spirit of light: ". . . If one speaks the faith in the wider world, one and then two will be cleansed by helping each other." Assisting people will bring freedom and an eternal abode in the heart of the *kami*. Disturbances can be dispelled by recognizing the fundamental equality of all humans. "When one compares humans from the standpoint of the body," Miki wrote, "they all are the same, whether high or low." Once more, it should be noted, we encounter the metaphor of the body and its centering as subject, known by acting; it is the body, not status, that confirms humanity; not the trappings of civilization, but the blessings of the gods.

To neglect the ordinances of the *kami* and to fail to work for universal relief and assistance was to incur divine wrath. In order to ward off anger and forestall misfortune, repentance was necessary. In this context Miki pointed to the quality of late Tokugawa leadership and its failure to deliver relief and help. She characterized the leadership as high mountains, remote and distant from the ordinary folk who dwelt in the valleys and in the real world. But the power of the *kami* was vastly stronger than the power of "those who are high and make the world's conditions as they are; will they know about the misfortunes of the deities?"[88] Indeed, she had no hesitation in calling attention to the "contrast in intention between the *kami* and those in high places." The false division between high and low constituted a sign of the way that things were and the conditions of life that had to be overcome. People would change, she was convinced, because humans were "the children of the gods" and possessed a good nature. Their problem was pride (*hokori*). Pride, for Miki, was the basic human evil and produced the "eight dusts" – desire, regret, sweetness, avarice, arrogance, hatred, rancor, and anger – qualities she associated with the powerful. The powerless were advised to trust themselves to the deity of world renewal, who held out for them the promise of a renovated moral life. How the gods were to bring about this idealized world was already prefigured in Miki's conception of assistance and relief. It was, as Yasumaru Yoshio explained it, the world vision of small cultivators and encompassed diligent and frugal peasants bound together in a community of cooperation.[89]

88 Yasumaru, *Nihon kindaika*, p. 83. 89 Ibid.

Konkōkyō was established by a peasant named Kawate Bunjirō (Konkō Daijin) (1814–83) in Bitchū, also part of present-day Okayama Prefecture. Adopted into a rural family, Kawate, unlike Kurozumi and Nakayama, was deeply versed in agricultural affairs. The area was marked by commercialization and a subsequent decline of small-holding farmers. The founder experienced a long life punctuated by hardship and poverty, and this undoubtedly prompted his deep concerns for the unrelieved hardship among cultivators of the vicinity. The boundaries of his own thought were marked by his desire to secure relief from contemporary circumstances and a zeal for bringing about order and prosperity. His religiosity was early revealed in a decision to make the trek to Ise with fellow villagers during the Ise *okagemairi* of 1830. Several years later (1846) Kawate made still another pilgrimage to the Grand Shrine. His personal ministry was interrupted by bouts of illness, and it ultimately brought on a trance that disclosed to him his true identity as the brother of Konjin, one of the calendar gods of the yin–yang tradition observed in rural areas. In folk belief this deity was capable of inflicting great harm or abundant prosperity, depending on how he was worshiped. Kawate received the ordinances of this god into his body which, as with Nakayama Miki, became the instrument for the "august intelligence" (*oshirase*). Kawate also received permission from the deity to be called the "family Kane no kami's lower leaves" and to take the divine appellation of "Bunji Daimyōjin."

Once Kawate, or as he now came to be called, Konkō Daijin, served as the vessel of Konjin's *oshirase*, the popular understanding of that *kami* was transformed. A figure that had been associated with curse and calamity became a *kami* of love who brought good fortune and abundance to those who followed his commandments. As the instructions of the *kami* proliferated and encouraged agricultural activity among believers, the cult spread.[90] In 1859 Konkō Daijin, on instructions from the *kami*, went into concealment. Empowered as a *daimyōjin*, Konkō Daijin now functioned as a living *kami*. Like Miki, he gave up all his possessions to demonstrate his faith in Tenchi Kane no kami. His new organization coincided with the critical events of the pre-Restoration decade. In an environment charged with political struggle and shogunal failure, a saying went, "How many distressed *ujiko* (members) there are in society! But if the *kami* help, the people will be able to live."[91] Nine years before the Restoration, when he returned from his concealment, Kawate established a formal religious organization.

90 Murakami, *Kinsei minshū shūkyō no kenkyū*, p. 177. 91 Ibid., p. 179.

More than other founders, Konkō Daijin stressed the importance of knowledge in the form of the *oshirase*. This is not to say that other groups were not interested in the question of knowledge. But Kawate was more systematic about the kind of knowledge that his followers should possess. While he served as the agency to transmit divine knowledge, the revelations he made in response to specific problems were not sudden. He received instructions in a conscious state, not in the circumstances of a trance, but he alone was able to recall the content of the divine instructions and interpret them to others.[92] Sharing with the founders of the other sects a profound distrust of conventional knowledge, Kawate's central text for the faithful condemned learning (*gakumon*) as something that "consumes the body" and as the product of mere "cleverness" and contrivance.[93] He freely granted that he did not have much formal learning and was not very literate:

> Today's society is one of wisdom and knowledge. By permitting humans to become clever, we risk losing the virtue of the body. In this age the principal pollutant is desire. Let us be released from the use of the abacus. It is said that we are clever but have no skills. We show off our cleverness and rely on artifice. Let us separate ourselves from cleverness, contrivance, and wisdom. Let us depart from the assistance and customs of society. By leaving society, we will be able to entrust our body to the *kami*.[94]

Accordingly, acts of "listening" and "understanding" were supremely important. In the operation of listening and understanding, the body became the reservoir for intentionality and knowing similar to the way Konkō used his own body as agency for divinity. It was the action of the body, not the contrivances and ruses of mere knowledge extracted from books and conventional instruction, that promised to secure people relief from society's afflictions. The *Konkō Daijin rikai* reported that the founder disapproved of religious austerities and advised that "eating and drinking are important to the body."[95] The body required strength if it was to express its faith and belief by working and acting.

The knowledge valued by Konkō Daijin related to how people were to assist others. Like the other new religions, Konkōkyō stressed relief and assistance for others as the condition for faith. No other kind of knowledge was required. Here again, this idea pertained to contemporary society and custom which had failed to provide relief to the distressed. Konkō Daijin constantly called on people to leave society,

92 Seto Mikio, "Minshū no shūkyō ishiki to henkaku no enerugi," in Maruyama Teruo, ed., *Henkakuki no shūkyō* (Tokyo: Gendai jaanarizumu shuppankai, 1972), p. 67.

93 *Minshū shūkyō to shisō*, p. 364. 94 Ibid., p. 376. 95 Ibid., pp. 400, 404.

with all its contrivances and fragmenting propensities, and to entrust themselves to the *kami*, whose grace would manifest itself in people helping people. "Men, assisting men, are human."[96] Mutual help distinguished humans from other species and represented a special form of thanks to the *kami*. Just as the deities, at times of illness and disaster, offered assistance to humans, so humans should assist the needy in times of distress.

Such assistance was also based on the idea of human equality. Here Konkō proposed two interrelated notions: All people are members of the "family of the deity" (*kamisama no ujiko*), and they are capable of becoming deities themselves. Together they represented a new concept of community. "All under heaven," he advised, "are the *ujiko* of the deities of heaven and earth. There are no other kinds of men."[97] Because all were potentially *ujiko*, "one cannot look down on humans or befoul them." Closely associated with this sense of equality was the new status assigned to women. All the new religions elevated women to a status equivalent to men, and some, like Konkō, even tended to exalt them. "Women are the rice fields of the world," Konkō Daijin announced, and in the "teachings of the deities, if the rice fields are not fertilized and enriched, they will be of no value."[98] Life itself would not be possible. Hence Konkō proposed, employing familiar metaphors of samurai politics and power, that women were the *karō* (principal retainers) of the household; if there were no *karō*, there could be no castle. Thus women and peasants, precisely because they lacked access to the established disciplines of learning, became exemplars of what was truly human. Belief came from women; they were close to the deities. No doubt valuing women in this way stemmed from an idealized agricultural respect for productivity. Both Kurozumi and Tenri also showed real concern for women physiologically, especially with reference to problems and pain incurred at the time of childbirth.

Yet ultimately all people were capable of becoming godlike. "Deity and man," Kawate announced, "are the same." Whatever deity one worships, if he fails to correspond to the heart of man, he will not correspond to the heart of the *kami;* and if he fails to correspond to the heart of the deity, he will not conform to the heart of man."[99] Konkō Daijin wrote that as he had received the "august principle of *yin* (*okage*) to become a living deity, so you (*anatagata*) will receive the principle as well." A living *kami* was nothing more than someone

96 Ibid., p. 420. 97 Ibid., p. 401. 98 Ibid., p. 416. 99 Ibid.

doing the work of the deity in a human moment and was a status available to all. Hence he constantly played down his own exalted status as an intermediary and acknowledged personal "ignorance," as he was simply a man who "tills the soil and does not know anything." Irony notwithstanding, Konkō Daijin possessed the kind of knowledge necessary to make him and all followers living *kami*. The community of believers thus constituted a divine assembly, as "all receive their bodies from the *kami* of heaven and earth."[100]

In its elaboration of a new community of believers serving one another and withdrawn from official society, Konkō stressed, not least of all, the primacy of household work and agricultural cultivation. As he himself was a committed farmer, he paid close attention, as did the rural *kokugakusha,* to growing conditions and agricultural techniques. He was particularly interested in weather ("wind and rain" as he put it) but linked such conditions to the presence or absence of belief. He rejected the idea that a mere visit to the shrine would bring wind and rain at the right time. Proper conditions could be secured only if faith allowed the *kami* to enter one's body. Evidence of such faith was shown by attending to one's household duties. The believer's sense of joy, he noted, would make him feel obliged to tend to his household duties.[101]

DEFENSE AND WEALTH

In the late Tokugawa period, Dutch studies, as it was first called, combined with eighteenth-century discussions on political economy (*keisei saimin*) to create the possibility of a new discourse. Dutch studies expressed an interest in the new sciences of medicine, anatomy and physiology, natural science, astronomy, physics, and geography. Political economy aimed at uncovering the sources of wealth. As it was formulated in the early nineteenth century, the new discourse first emphasized maritime defense and related science and technology and then moved on to discuss national wealth. The impulses underlying such a discourse was the increasing presence of foreigners who were searching for adventure, trade, and empire, and the domestic economic failures, which the Tempō reforms were seeking to arrest. At the heart of this new discourse was a dissatisfaction, bordering on outright criticism, with the shogunal political arrangement and its evident incapacity to act decisively and effectively to find adequate sources of wealth for relieving the people (*saimin*).

100 Ibid. 101 Ibid., p. 366.

Writers at the turn of the century had already alerted contemporaries to the foreign menace and the need for adequate coastal defense and a firm national policy. Discussions on defense turned on the question of adequate military technology, but any consideration of science and technology invariably raised the issue of political decision making. An early proponent, Kudō Heisuke (1734–1800), saw the installation of new maritime fortifications as the fundamental condition for a new policy. "The first aim in governing the realm," he wrote, "is to deepen the power of our country. To deepen the strength of the country, we have first to allow the wealth of foreign countries to enter Japan." Trade was an absolute necessity, as it generated the wealth that many came to recognize as the key to a proper defense. Kudō went on to advocate the opening of new lands like Hokkaido and the systematic search for gold, silver, and copper. Another contemporary, Hayashi Shihei (1738–93), author of a famous geographic miscellany, *Sankoku tsūran zusetsu*, shared a similar view and was even more insistent about the merger of defense and the search for wealth.

It was Honda Toshiaki (1744–1821) who first grasped in global terms the problem of wealth and formulated a coherent statement yoking wealth to defense:

> Because Japan is a maritime nation, crossing the ocean, transport, and trade are the primary vocations of the realm. In governing with the power of only one domain, the national strength weakens increasingly. This weakness affects the peasantry, and it is a natural condition for them to yearly decrease their productivity.[102]

He was convinced that policy must reach beyond a single domain to represent and employ the resources of the whole. Trade and markets were also necessary. Once Japan was thrown into the global market network, it would have to compete with other countries in a struggle for scarce resources. Appearing as a good mercantilist, Honda was persuaded that the search for trade and markets was prompted by the domestic scarcity of goods, products, and natural resources. Yet it was in Japan's national interest to promote foreign trade if the realm was to survive and overcome chronic domestic difficulties. Honda noted that Japan differed from other Western nations only in its scientific and technological inferiority, but he was convinced that the gap could be closed.[103]

102 Quoted in Maeda Ichirō, ed., *Kōza Nihon bunkashi* (Tokyo: Misuzu shobō, 1963), vol. 6, p. 58.

103 Tetsuo Najita, "Structure and Content in Tokugawa Thinking," unpublished manuscript, p. 54.

More than any other political economist, Honda recognized the relationship between trade as a source of national wealth and Japan's technological backwardness. To rectify both, he proposed in an unpublished essay, *Keisei hissaku* (1798), four urgent priorities: (1) the systematic manufacturing of explosives for military and civil purposes; (2) the development of mining, as metals were the backbone of the nation's wealth; (3) the establishment of a national merchant marine that would enhance the national treasury by selling products abroad and help avoid domestic famines; and (4) the abrogation of seclusion for a policy of colonial enterprises in nearby territories.[104] Collectively, these proposals were meant to show that Japan had pursued an unnatural course that had led to an economic dead end. Isolation was anachronistic, territorial decentralization destructive to the national interest, and agricultural primacy was a fiction in view of Japan's maritime position. Japan should promote a policy directed toward the opening of trade in order to meet, rather than to be subdued by, the European thrust in Asia.[105]

Any consideration of defense and wealth entailed employing a new knowledge capable of developing military technology and finding new sources of wealth. When thoughtful men turned to this question, they embraced a form of inquiry that validated the investigation of first principles, but they were also mindful to balance the inherent formalism of first principles with a conception of historicism that accounted for changing circumstances. As did other contemporary discourses, Western learning used a strategy that required reducing things to origins in order to demonstrate how the principle of the past authorized changes in the present. Whereas Mito, *kokugaku,* and the new religions resorted to primal deities and archetypal events to specify first principles, Western studies referred to paradigmatic heroes in the remote past whose accomplishments reflected the conviction that each age demanded policies adequate to its requirements. The discourse on defense and wealth, owing to its commitment to defend the realm as a whole rather than as a domain or a region, inched toward abandoning feudalism for a conception of a larger political unity. Ultimately, the cultural content of the discourse came to suggest the political form of the early modern state to satisfy the imperatives of national wealth and defense. If other discourses searched for ways to deliver relief and assistance to the needy, the discussions on defense and wealth saw a

104 Ibid., pp. 54–5; and Donald Keene, *The Japanese Discovery of Europe* (Stanford, Calif.: Stanford University Press, 1969), for a partial translation of *keisei hissaku*.

105 Najita, "Structure and Content," p. 60.

mercantilist state as the form most able to realize this goal. Honda early perceived in the state the agency to supply such services when he observed that the "several European nations are kingdoms that provide assistance to people; it is a heavenly duty of the kingdom to relieve hunger and cold with trade, overseas transport, and passage."[106] The state that such writers came to conceptualize was more mercantilist than despotic or absolutist and was based on social labor and productivity, manufacturing, and trade. In this regard, it was also more ethical than merely political, which many writers identified with the privatism of the Tokugawa bakufu. Although the practitioners of this discourse, as good mercantilists, shied away from thinking about an equitable redistribution of national resources, as did the Mito writers, they displaced the egalitarian impulse by turning to merit, talent, and ability as criteria for recruitment and advancement. The demonstration of talent (*jinzai*) depended on the mastery of expert knowledge useful to the necessities of the day. The discourse on wealth and defense envisaged human subjectivity as the maker of custom and history and agreed that the human species, even though people held different stations in life, originated from a single source. Although Western studies rejected the existence of qualitative distinctions among people, it did believe that status derived from the acquisition and demonstration of useful knowledge which constituted the only acceptable criterion of social and political preferment. But it also agreed with Mito that such knowledge was not available to all, even though it resisted making this conceit into a principle of preemptive closure. It is, furthermore, important to note that its followers frequently came from small and medium-sized domains, often *fudai* houses, and sometimes large merchant houses, men who were no doubt convinced that transforming the bakufu into a national organization devoted to promoting wealth and defense would save them as well.

The maturation of the discourse on wealth and defense occurred in 1830, with the establishment of the Shōshikai, two years after the famous Siebold incident. Two of the members of this group had previously been Siebold's students. By resorting to examination of the foreign scientist as a "spy" and condemnation for his chief contact, Takahashi Kageyasu, the authorities had raised the stakes for anybody desiring to pursue the new knowledge independently. One of the

106 Maeda, *Kōza Nihon bunkashi,* vol. 6, p. 59.

casualties of the incident and a former student of Siebold, Takano Chōei (1804–50) remarked in the wake of the persecution that because of the bakufu's policies, the "school of Western scholars was momentarily frightened, and Western studies began to decline."[107] As a result, organizing an independent study group in Edo years later constituted an act of calculated risk.

The Shōshikai's agenda was to explore new kinds of knowledge that promised to yield practical solutions to contemporary domestic and foreign problems; its heyday coincided with the Tempō famine, mounting peasant disturbances, violent urban uprisings, and Ōshio's Osaka rebellion. Writing years later in *Bansha sōyaku shoki,* Takano Chōei explained that the society aimed to supplement traditional samurai learning which, emphasizing elegance and ornamentation in expression rather than substance, prepared people for purely literary careers. He commented that this tradition "has not been useful for the relief of society" and recalled that when the group was founded, many believed it was necessary to "understand how to mend social abuses."

> Since 1833, famines have occurred among the lower classes in the cities and the countryside. One can only conjecture at what is happening in the countryside. In response, there have been expressions of regret, and many have produced books concerning relief and ruin. Because many of these [books] investigated specific conditions relating to political economy, several domains implemented policies [to rectify the conditions] and tended to question the nature of political affairs itself. But because the problems have become exceedingly complex and so difficult to resolve, we decided to establish the Shōshikai.[108]

In addition, news concerning the intention and appearance of foreign ships, though frequently incorrect, seemed to appear more frequently during the 1830s and was used increasingly by shogunal critics to justify their demands for new policies.[109] One such rumor circulating throughout Edo prompted Takano and Watanabe to question the bakufu's expulsion policy. Takano's *Yume monogatari* (Tale of a dream) and Watanabe Kazan's report on foreign policy resulted in shogunal action leading to the dissolution of the society, imprisonment of its principal members, and Watanabe's eventual suicide. The inci-

107 Kitajima Masamoto, *Bakuhansei no kumon,* vol. 18 of *Nihon no rekishi* (Tokyo: Chūō kōronsha, 1966), p. 367.

108 Satō Shōsuke, Uete Michiari, and Yamaguchi Muneyuki, eds., *Nihon shisō taikei,* vol. 55: *Watanabe Kazan, Takano Chōei, Sakuma Shōzan, Yokoi Shōnan, Hashimoto Sanai* (Tokyo: Iwanami shoten, 1971), p. 190. Hereafter cited as *Watanabe Kazan, Takano Chōei, Sakuma Shōzan, Yokoi Shōnan, Hashimoto Sanai.*

109 Ibid., pp. 192, 193.

dent became known as *bansha no goku*, or the purge of barbarian scholars.[110]

It is important to note that the society, many of whose members had begun in Dutch studies with some proficiency in medicine, anatomy, and natural history, shifted its focus to investigating knowledge that might be put into the service of the country. Guiding this decision was the belief that appropriate policy could not be formulated unless it were informed by knowledge adequate to its objectives. This apparent coupling of knowledge and power was fully acknowledged by the society when it demonstrated how policies concerning famine relief drew attention to political conduct or when it made public the official insensitivity to questions relating to maritime navigation and defense. Yet it is important to add that the society's leading figures envisaged political criticism as an effect of a new conception of culture. Takano Chōei, for example, explained in his *Wasuregatami* (*Torii no nakune*) that it was possible to imagine changes in the content of culture and necessary to pursue a critical course if such changes were to be enacted. As evidence, he offered the example of his associate Watanabe Kazan who had been transformed from the status of a high-ranking samurai noted for his literary and artistic interests into a serious and committed student of Western learning. Despite his considerable achievements in traditional disciplines, art, composition, and his exquisite sensibilities, Watanabe had changed, Takano reported, after observing places marked by disaster and famine in recent years.

What provoked Watanabe to make this cultural "sea change" was his search for reasons explaining contemporary hardship and disorder. The rich, he observed, seemed to get richer, while the poor slipped farther down the scale of poverty. Everywhere the poor were resorting to rebellion. "Because tumult has spread throughout the society for one reason or another," Takano wrote, "he [Watanabe], impelled by a grieving heart, began excerpting selections from Dutch books on the *kokutai* of all countries and political affairs and circumstances revealing social conditions and the way people felt." Next, he had turned to examining the pros and cons of contemporary affairs, writing essays on the issues of the day and discussing these matters with other thoughtful men. "Even though he had studied the way of old, he had

110 The novelist Ishikawa Jun wrote a moving account of this complex and concerned intellectual: *Watanabe Kazan* (Tokyo: Chikuma shobō, 1964). Marius B. Jansen, "Rangaku and Westernization," *Modern Asian Studies* 18 (1984), also described this early Westernizing impulse, based on a survey of the recent secondary literature.

become a person whose doubts could no longer be concealed."[111] In place of the traditional learning that served him so well before but that now fell short of providing an understanding of contemporary conditions, he sought to substitute science and technology. Watanabe himself confessed as much in a letter in 1840 to Maki Sadachika in which he asserted that no division existed between the Way and the reality of custom.[112]

Watanabe's views on Western culture confirmed the efficacy of this new content. Western learning represented a new orientation, he believed, and thus required new methods to achieve it. In *Gekizetsu wakumon*, he complained that the traditional discrimination between "civilized" and "barbarian" was bound to cause serious trouble for Japan in the future as it affected Western nations. Times changed, and the present could never be the same as the past. Men who apprehended the present from the standpoint of the past tried to anchor the *koto* (Japanese harp) to a support and were obliged to pull both harp and support when they moved. The learning of T'ang China was inapplicable to Japan's current needs and resembled a "dream within a dream." Watanabe relied on the explanatory powers of historicism to explain that great changes have occurred since antiquity. Among these changes, one of the most important had been the Western use of "things" (in physics). Although he plainly recognized a differentiation between practicality and doctrine (morality) in the *Shinkiron*, he also acknowledged that each could assist the other and form a complementary relationship. When juxtaposing the "Way of the West" to the "Way of Japan," it might be supposed that they were different, but because both were informed by reason (*dōri*), they were ultimately one and the same. Study showed that what distinguished Western societies from Japan was their discovery and development and science and technology, not their favorable climates (as Honda Toshiaki had thought), rich lands, or even vast populations. Western superiority disclosed the difference between diligence and indolence. For Watanabe, diligence meant wisdom, knowledge, and effort. Western schools prospered in subjects like political studies, medicine, physics, and religion, whereas Chinese learning was moribund. "Because the Western barbarians have concentrated chiefly on physics, they have acquired detailed knowledge of the world and the four directions." Fearing the West, the Japanese "hear the thunder and block their ears. The greater evil is to shut one's eyes because one detests listening. It is

111 *Watanabe Kazan, Takano Chōei, Sakuma Shōzan, Yokoi Shōnan, Hashimoto Sanai*, pp. 179–80. 112 Ibid., p. 123.

our duty to investigate not only the principles of creation but also the principles of all things and opinions."[113] Technology, the application of scientific principles, as Watanabe understood them, was particularly important to this new endeavor, because it showed how to transform the physical landscape through methods of construction and excavation, to put up schools, hospitals, and poor houses; technology pointed to the way that culture might be changed.

Watanabe's faith in the practical use of science and technology inspired specific proposals. The foreign question had become particularly irksome, and Japan was the only country that did not have a relationship with the West. As a result, Japan has come to resemble a "piece of meat left along the roadside. How can the attention of wolves and tigers be avoided?" Without proper knowledge, Japan's security had acquired all of the "contentment of a frog in a pond."[114] Politics originated on the basis of what was considered reliable, whereas misfortune ushered in the smug assumption that nothing was wrong. Today, Japan existed only because of the happy accident of geography that offered protection by distance and the seas. But it was no longer possible to depend on what others had relied on in the past and to be consoled by solutions that had worked before. China, once a vast and powerful land, was already heaving under the impact of seaborne Western intrusions. Hence, the first task for Japanese was to abrogate the seclusion policy and then to embark on a program of maritime trade and defense.

Watanabe saw that the globe had become a competitive arena for struggle among nations, but Japanese leadership had failed to see that Japan would involuntarily be drawn into this contest. T'ang learning had come to Japan in remote antiquity. Since that time empty studies had prospered continuously to divert men's minds from the real tasks at hand. The new learning demanded a commitment to preparing for the defense of Edo Bay. The bakufu's failure to recognize the necessity for such preparations revealed an even more basic incapacity to grasp the power offered by Western knowledge. Not even the bakufu's most reliable allies had yet been deployed to the region of the bay. Caustically, Watanabe described the situation as a sign of "domestic catastrophe" (*naikan*), rather than "external disaster" (*gaikan*): a failure of nerve rather than an outside threat.[115]

The threat of an invasion imperiling a defenseless Japan haunted Takano Chōei as well. Unlike Watanabe, Takano was a professional

113 Ibid., p. 78. 114 Ibid., pp. 69, 72.

115 Satō Shōsuke, *Yōgakushi no kenkyū* (Tokyo: Chūō kōronsha, 1964), p. 168.

student and translator of Western learning and a leading proponent of the utility of the new learning. This interest in medicine fostered in the discourse on Western studies continued even after many of its adherents shifted their focus to questions concerning defense and military technology, and it represented an impulse comparable to the effort of relieving the ill and diseased found among the new religions. As a principal participant in the Shōshikai, Takano had begun in the 1830s to direct his own interest toward resolving the perceived disjunction between the domestic policy of feudal fragmentation and the question of national defense. Upon learning of a proposed visit of an English ship in the late 1830s, he drafted an essay to express his alarm at the probable rejection of such a probe. Takano charged in *Yume monogatari* (Tale of a dream, 1838) that expelling the *Morrison* would be considered by the British as the act of a belligerent country that understood neither right nor wrong. The loss of virtue resulting from this action would result in untold disasters.[116] Years later, Yokoi Shōnan transformed this reading of national moral conduct in international affairs into a classic defense of trade and peaceful foreign relations against the noisy claims of xenophobic expulsionists.

While others joined the discussion on maritime defense in the early 1840s, the issue came to command serious attention by shogunal officials, who understood that a decision on defense meant a prior commitment to a different conception of knowledge. Even as Watanabe and Takano were trying to establish the outer boundaries of the discourse on defense, bakufu officials like Egawa Tarōzaemon and Torii Yōzō turned to formulating appropriate proposals for policy after making their inspections of Edo Bay. Egawa's views corresponded closely to those held by Watanabe, but Torii rejected any suggestion of entering into relations with countries like England. Torii (who has sometimes been portrayed as the archetype of malevolence) was not a simple witchhunter; his memorandum late in 1840 disclosed a keen awareness of weapons manufacture. But he also recognized that a new conception of the world was at the heart of the problem of defense. Unlike many contemporaries, he was not convinced of British technological superiority at this time and thought the English victory over China to be inconclusive. What distressed him about proposals calling for new measures of defense and the implementation of Western technology was that they were linked to a larger view of the world whose acceptance he rejected as vigorously as he denounced colonialism. Although the cannons used by

116 *Watanabe Kazan, Takano Chōei, Sakuma Shōzan, Yokoi Shōnan, Hashimoto Sanai*, pp. 168–9.

the West performed efficiently, he wrote, and might be especially useful for coastal defense, in Japanese warfare there had been little utilization of weapons useful chiefly for a precision strike applied in places where large numbers of men were concentrated in close quarters.[117] This difference dramatized the profound distinction between Japanese and Western customs. The West planned only for the pursuit of profit, in contrast with a society intent on rites and rituals; it waged war to compete, rather than to defend morality. Owing to the disparity between these two social orders, it was inappropriate for the Japanese to have any faith in Western science and technology. What Torii implied was that any acceptance of Western technique necessarily meant adopting the culture that had produced it. Writers like Watanabe and Takano had already demonstrated that their interest in the West was not restricted merely to cannons but included the whole matrix of education and customs on which its culture was based. The dangers of a policy aimed at incorporating Western culture, Torii warned, were great. "The first principle of defense entails encouraging the strengthening of traditional military and civilian skills. At the same time, it is important to eliminate frivolous military discipline and esteem competence."[118]

In response to Torii's critique of the new Western learning, Egawa argued that Torii had deliberately misrepresented the nature of British activity in China and had misunderstood the knowledge they employed. Although wise planning always involved the study and mastery of military skills, it also included an evaluation of methods that were strange and effective. In accord with the ancient advice to "know the other in order to know oneself," it was imperative for the Japanese to learn as much as possible about the English before formulating a policy. When the Chinese were confronted by the British, they had no knowledge of the adversary they faced. How could they have devised a wise plan? China's failure and its subsequent defeat by the British reflected a reliance on empty theories and useless knowledge. Egawa was confident that importing cannons and other hardware would not constitute a faddish whim. It was common knowledge that Confucianism and Buddhism had been imported from abroad, and it was well known that there were many foreign products esteemed for their convenience and value. If such goods had a useful purpose, they were not fads. To favor trifling and useless toys might be a waste, but it was not whimsy to adopt useful items.

In the ensuing debate, the real problem clearly lay in the relation-

117 Sugiura Mimpei, *Nihon no shisō*, vol. 16: *Kirishitan, rangakushū* (Tokyo: Chikuma shobō, 1970), p. 353. 118 Ibid., p. 354.

ship between employing foreign military technology for defense and adopting the whole system of knowledge that produced it. Torii rightly considered this enabling knowledge as a threat to the legitimacy of the Tokugawa order, and he derived little solace from Egawa's thinly disguised effort to justify importing discrete items rather than the whole cultural matrix. Provoked less by charges of official incompetence (which he could easily acknowledge) than by the threat to Tokugawa claims to legitimacy, Torii recognized that the importation of military technology would inevitably lead to incorporating the enabling culture and jeopardizing the foundations of the traditional world order. His fears were systematized in classic manner by Ōhashi Totsuan years later in a last-ditch defense of the Neo-Confucian conception of a natural order.

In the last decades of the Tokugawa era, the discourse on defense was transmuted into a coherent theory of cultural purpose capable of combining the claims of a traditional world view with the principles of scientific discovery. This task was accomplished by Sakuma Shōzan (1811–64) and Yokoi Shōnan. Although they were initially prompted by the project to find a fit between Neo-Confucianism, however they understood it by this time, and Western learning, they contributed to reinforcing the primacy of the new knowledge as the fundamental condition for understanding the world and acting in it. Their effort to secure entry into the new knowledge through the agency of received philosophical idiom attests to the importance they assigned to finding a way of using both. Yet their ultimate solution was to lay the foundations for the subsequent dismissal of nature in favor of a history that was crucial to later Meiji efforts to establish a system of useful and instrumental knowledge.

The key to this vast transformation lay in Sakuma Shōzan's decision to recognize in Western knowledge a source of power as great as morality. Both Watanabe and Takano had taken steps in this direction, but neither of them went as far as to propose systematically the equivalence between two different forms of knowledge. The nature of international events in the late 1840s and 1850s had changed considerably, and the frequent appearance of Western ships in Japanese waters undoubtedly persuaded Sakuma to conclude that the world had come to represent a stage on which nations acted out their claims. If Japan failed to compete in this struggle for power, it would be eliminated. Accepting Western learning under these circumstances, "controlling the barbarians with their own methods," resolved the problem of acquiring the necessary strength and power to compete effectively in the coming contest. But power really referred to knowledge and its enabling cultural matrix. It was necessary to grasp the very principles that produced the techniques that now promised to protect the realm against Western colonialism. Without it, Sakuma warned, Japan was doomed.

It is important to note that Sakuma's commitment to study Western weaponry failed to follow the usual course of appraising Neo-Confucian metaphysics first. During the 1830s he made two extended trips to Edo. On the first he studied with the prominent Confucian teacher Satō Issai (1772–1859), the mentor of many late Tokugawa figures. His second trip coincided with the controversy over the alleged *Morrison* visit, shogunal punishment of Watanabe and Takano, news of the first Anglo-Chinese war, and the continuing debate over the defense of Edo Bay, a debate fueled by Takashima Shūhan's memorial calling for a new program of cannon casting. During his residence in Edo, Sakuma also witnessed at firsthand Mizuno Tadakuni's shogunal reforms, which included the appointment of Shōzan's lord Sanada Yukitsura to the post of naval defense. Sanada selected Sakuma as his adviser and commanded him to begin studying military technology. In response, Sakuma enrolled in Egawa Tarōzaemon's school. This sequence of events suggests that Sakuma did not enter into Western studies through Neo-Confucianism, as if it constituted a logical extension of his philosophical position, but found himself involved in the immediate and practical problem of coastal defense and cannon casting, thanks to the initiative of his lord. The identification of power as a new element in global policies, and the urgency to define practical programs enabling Japan to compete, prompted him to think about the relationship between the claims of the new knowledge and Neo-Confucianism, his own intellectual endowment. Sakuma's appraisal of Neo-Confucianism proceeded from his encounter with the new knowledge.

Through his contact with Egawa, Sakuma learned of the imprisonment of members of the Shōshikai and secured knowledge of Watanabe Kazan's writings. His own thoughts concerning European kingship appear to be a replay of Watanabe's elaborate explanation of kings and their importance in the expansion of the state. Disappointed in Egawa, Sakuma soon left the school after deciding that it had nothing to offer comparable to the views articulated by Watanabe.

Following a lead forged first by Egawa, Sakuma argued that the promise of an investigative method (*kyūri*) had been smothered by excessive concern for textual studies and that the true meaning of "the investigation of things" had been lost. Since antiquity, the Japanese and Chinese had therefore been robbed of the fruits of investigation and had forfeited the means to build national power. He advised that it was essential to national survival to make the effort to know the enemy, even though such knowledge had been forestalled by cultural conceit and complacency. "The urgency for preparing to meet a foreign invasion does not begin just by knowing them (the foreigners). The method by which you know them lies not just in exhausting their skills but in combining their learning with ours."[119] If they had large ships, Japan should construct large ships; if they had large guns, so should Japan. Sakuma warned against using outmoded and ancient methods that could not ensure victory. To use new technologies from the West was the condition for containing the foreigner. The expansion of the West and the war in China had shown that mere ethical propriety was no longer an adequate defense against colonization. By recognizing the centrality of power over morality alone, Sakuma distanced his discussion from the Mito discourse and made the crucial distinction between the opportunity of power and moral opportunity.[120] His recognition of power drove him to abandon a view that foreigners were mere barbarians who knew nothing of the niceties of morality and civilization.

And yet Sakuma's concern with power compelled him to minimize the substantive difference between Japanese and Western societies. He condemned the Chinese for having lost to the British because of their unwillingness to see foreigners as something more than barbarians who were no different from birds and beasts. To slight the great powers as barbarous, he wrote to his lord in 1849, "is a principle of great injury and small benefit to the state." Ultimately, he saw no incompatibility between "customs of the West and Japan's conventions." "When . . . foreign studies are carried on prosperously, the beautiful customs of our country will gradually change," but "if there is distrust and doubt, then they (foreign studies) will be impeded."[121] Received learning, like any learning, had to demonstrate its universality before its validity could be established. Attachment to rites and propriety should not be restricted to China and Japan alone. Knowledge knew no boundaries; nothing was foreign if it proved useful in preserving the independence of the realm.

Thus Sakuma viewed the new knowledge as a form of power.

119 Shinano kyōikukai, eds., *Shōzan zenshū* (Nagano: Shinano Mainichi shimbunsha, 1922), vol. 1, p. 128.
120 Uete Michiari, *Nihon kindai shisō no keisei* (Tokyo: Iwanami shoten, 1974), pp. 39–40.
121 *Shōzan zenshū*, vol. 2, p. 710.

Knowledge of military technology guaranteed power, and its mastery was mandated by the "welfare of the state." Although this view originally restricted the adoption of Western learning to military matters, (trade, he still believed in 1843, would result in the importation of useless products), Sakuma was to change his mind. The positive inducement of Western scientific technique would result in the expansion of contact with other nations. If "strength" was the criterion, then any policy, including opening the country, would be justified if it led to the realization and completion of national power. This opinion marked Sakuma's thought after the Perry mission (1854) and the subsequent signing of commercial treaties. In the wake of these events, he began to advocate maritime travel and foreign trade. He considered the opening of trade between Japan and the outside world as a corollary to his conception of power. Military prowess needed a sustaining source of wealth, and trade was the only policy by which a small Japan could accumulate national power to strengthen its military capacity. In one of his last petitions (February 1862) Shōzan eloquently made the case for greater contact with the West. "The skills and techniques of foreign countries," he wrote, "especially the inventions of Newton and Copernicus and the discoveries of Columbus, have progressed long distances and extended to things like physics, geography, shipbuilding, cannon casting, and the construction of fortifications." From their prosperous study of the steam engine, the Europeans had navigated steam-driven ships at sea and steam-driven trains on land. Such accomplishments depended on exploring for resources at home: iron for railways, and coals for foundries. "How can we enrich and strengthen the national power? We must deduce from the facts." In Japan, he continued, neither the bakufu nor the domains had made much of a start. "If, however, Japan exerts itself for the profit of trade, strengthens its national power, attends to preparing ships, casting cannons, and building warships, it will be able to resist any country. . . . Should we not unite with the great countries and formulate a plan . . . ?" Knowledge and superior technology, he believed, would lead to "mutual refinement" and "mutual growth."[122]

This argument rested on the conviction that countries such as Japan and China were inferior to the West in more than military ways. If Japan was to withstand the peril of the Western presence and preserve its independence, it would have to proceed from the basis of powerful knowledge and powerful learning. In the past the trouble had stemmed

122 *Watanabe Kazan, Takano Chōei, Sakuma Shōzan, Yokoi Shōnan, Hashimoto Sanai*, pp. 322–3.

from the failure to identify the essence of useful learning. This perception was linked to Sakuma's understanding of the "investigation of principles." He now tried to restructure Neo-Confucianism by rescuing an earlier tradition of philosophic monism and by superimposing the idea of *kyūri* on Western natural science. Rather than investigating to satisfy the needs of ethics, he emphasized grasping the "principle of things" in the natural, material world. What he proposed was a "correspondence" between Chu Hsi Confucianism, which he never rejected, and Western natural science.

> The meaning of Chu Hsi's thought is to penetrate principle in conformity [with the needs of] the realm so as to increase knowledge. When the meaning of the Ch'eng-Chu school corresponds to such things as the investigation of Western conditions, the explanations of those two teachers will correspond to the world. If we follow the meaning of the Ch'eng-Chu school, even Western skills will become part of learning and knowledge and will not appear outside our framework.[123]

Sakuma saw no real conflict between Neo-Confucian claims to knowledge and Western skills. If conflict appeared, it would have meant postulating two distinct cultures, a "we" and a "they," which were foreclosed by his conception of power and global struggle. In a letter to a friend, he stated that "there are not two principles of the universe residing in different places. The learning skills developed in the West are conducive to the learning of the sages. . . ."[124] And to the shogunal official Kawaji Toshiakira, he wrote that because the Western science of investigating principles conformed to the intention of Ch'eng-Chu, their explanations should apply correspondingly elsewhere. In this reformulation of the traditional epistemology, Sakuma expanded the meaning of investigation to include measurement, proof, and evidence and concluded that they constituted the real bases of all learning, which was mathematics. All learning was cumulative, "refinement," as he put it. Because Sakuma saw no conflict or duality of principles but, rather, a correspondence, he was able to couple Eastern morality with Western science. His famous phrase in *Seiken roku*, bonding Eastern morality and Western science, was not an acknowledgment of a division but, rather, a recognition of particularistic manifestations of a universal science.

Sakuma's view of knowledge as power and his construction of a scientific culture implied a conception of politics. At one level his constant admonition "to explore the five continents" for knowledge put

123 *Shōzan zenshū*, vol. 2, pp. 549–51.
124 Miyamoto Chū, *Sakuma Shōzan* (Tokyo: Iwanami shoten, 1932), p. 53.

Japan in a wider world. Greater knowledge of that world prompted him to accept what it could offer to bolster Japan's strength. Although he never went as far as Yokoi Shōnan did to recommend complete political and social reorganization, he was willing to alter his view of political possibility to adhere to the requirements of a scientifically based culture. Even though he willingly acknowledged that Japan was weaker than the Western nations, he added that such weakness was physical and material and demanded systematic correction. However good the "American political system was," he wrote, "it could not be carried out in Japan" because history inhibited such a transfer.[125] The acceptance of Western knowledge did not mean abandoning the moral way. Just as science was universal, so, too, was the morality of the five relationships. Western nations did not yet possess these truths. By retaining the idea of a natural order with its specific sense of politics, Sakuma was prevented from envisaging a larger social entity. Ethics always ruled the inner realm, whereas the outer, the world of politics and history, was changeable and could be served only after making a proper investigation of contemporary conditions. Although the idea of a prior natural order militated against actually substituting society for nature, Sakuma's commitment to science resulted in consequences for the Tokugawa social imagination that he could not have foreseen.

Contemporary events required new attitudes. Japan was facing an emergency. "However important the rules of the past have been," Sakuma announced, "they have to be replaced because of the hardships they have brought." He was referring here to seclusion; it was natural to "reform the august laws that have been erected for the realm," as "it is a moral principle of Japan and China to follow ordinary law and procedures in ordinary times, and emergency measures in time of emergency."[126] His advice to abandon "old standards" (remarkably similar to Watanabe's earlier plaint) foresaw the possibility of a new political form. He imagined something higher than the "dignity of the Tokugawa house" and the court itself and pointed to what he called the "welfare of the realm" as a principle of legitimation. From this point he constructed an image of a nation-state, no doubt derived from his observations of Western countries, devoted to defending the wider realm and not just protecting the Tokugawa family. Sakuma, like many contemporaries, saw in Western knowledge the promise of immediate relief and assistance. The solution was a national community (*tenka kokka*) that could compete with comparable

125 Uete, *Nihon kindai shisō keisei*, p. 61. 126 *Shōzan zenshū*, vol. 1, pp. 98–9.

nations "throughout the five continents." Ultimately, he proposed the establishment of some sort of comity of nations, whereby each country would retain a uniqueness insofar as it would not disturb the continuation of harmonious relations. The "divine land" would become the Japanese state, and Japan would earn for itself a place among the nations of the world through the exercise of the "correct principles of civilization." This conviction led him to propose internal reforms. These fell short of total reorganization, but the core of his program was rooted in the recognition that proper and able leadership preceded all other considerations. Although he retained the imperial office, he identified its occupants with national kings like Peter the Great and Napoleon. Here, Sakuma came close to earlier views that had linked national strength to the power of kings who could lead their countries to power and wealth.

The intervention of Yokoi Shōnan (1809–68) in the discourse on wealth and defense resulted in refashioning this conception of king and country into a theory of political formation that favored the mercantilist state. If Yokoi shared a discursive world with Sakuma and Hashimoto Sanai, his predecessor in Fukui *han,* he differed significantly from these two thinker-activists in crucial areas of experience and study. Sakuma and Hashimoto had immersed themselves in the study of foreign languages and rudimentary science, but Yokoi had had only the slightest exposure to these disciplines. Yokoi was more deeply committed to a traditional Confucian metaphysic, and his examination of its claims derived from an internal struggle with its philosophical propositions rather than an awareness of a national crisis. Like Hashimoto, Yokoi served as an adviser to the lord of Fukui, Matsudaira Yoshinaga (Shungaku), who was himself a prominent figure operating at the center of national politics during the late 1850s and early 1860s.

Yokoi's philosophic differences with Sakuma are instructive and help explain the decision to denature the social as a condition for establishing a modern state in Japan. Whereas Sakuma envisaged the act of investigating principle as a form of natural science and even tried to reinterpret the scientific discipline as inquiry based on a rational and empirical method, Yokoi, closer to a received metaphysic, grasped the investigation of principle and the concomitant "examination of things" (*kakubutsu*) as the vital connection between "true intention" and a "correct heart."[127] As a result, Sakuma moved toward an "investigation of the

127 See Uete, *Nihon kindai shisō keisei,* p. 83.

natural world," whereas Yokoi rejected any tendency that sought to "make morality a small consideration and imprudent and to transform knowledge into extensive reading and memorization." This attitude toward knowledge would lead only to "vulgar Confucianism" and "mere uselessness." In actuality, the investigation of principle and the examination of things referred to grasping the "physics of daily use." Despite Sakuma's decision to couple *kyūri* with empirical investigative methods, he was never able to overcome the dilemma of studying a primary natural order with the techniques of a natural science. Undoubtedly Sakuma recognized that the two categories of nature differed substantively, even as he tried to bring them together in an impossible synthesis. But Yokoi, who declared his fidelity to the true tradition by summoning the exemplar of the three dynasties and the ancient sages, found a transcendent way valid for all times and places. At the heart of his discovery was a reconstituted conception of the social now free from the responsibility of mirroring nature, which he believed conformed to the experience of the archetypal sages of antiquity, Yao and Shun. Their great achievement, Yokoi proposed, was to construct a viable social and political order adequate to the needs of their time alone and thereby to bequeath to future generations the universality of this particular experience, not a timeless arrangement of authority. In this manner, the universalism of the ancient precedent liberated Yokoi from the Sung conceit of defending the idea of a static natural order as if it constituted a norm for all times to come. Even though Sakuma came close to making this move by positing his conception of universalistic principles, he failed to follow through on its consequences. By contrast, Yokoi explored the possibilities inherent in the universalizing of the ancient precedent and went on to conceptualize a new social image for Tokugawa Japan based on the production of wealth and the deployment of power.

Yokoi shared Sakuma's conviction concerning the relationships between knowledge and power. Early in his career, he drew attention to what he called the "vulgar learning of the useless" which he discerned in the contemporary practice to separate forms of knowing from political affairs. The essence of learning required disciplining the self for governance. If men failed to understand the site on which the ancients inaugurated their own project, they would inevitably become "slaves of antiquity." In Yokoi's thinking, the logic that identified knowledge with politics was provided by a commitment to understanding the practical details and necessities of daily life. That life itself exemplified the great lesson of antiquity and validated the very historicism authorizing men in each generation to change and to prepare for new requirements. Scholars of later generations, especially since Sung times, had missed grasping the importance of daily use because they had been consumed by efforts to understand books:

> When thinking about how one should study Chu Hsi today, you must think about how Chu Hsi himself studied. Without doing so, you will become a complete slave of Chu Hsi when you take to reading books. When one thinks about composing a poem and how it should become, you have to consider the kind of things that Tu Fu studied, which means going back to the Han, Wei, and Six dynasties.

Underlying this approach was the deeper conviction that texts are constituted and subsequently implicated in the very time they have been produced. But their identity is not fixed for all times to come. Active thinking, not blind acceptance of established precedents and morally irrelevant pieties, must become the essential condition for all learning seeking the mastery of principle. Yet Yokoi recognized that the decision to abandon old precedents and cast off ancient abuses would not necessarily lead to an understanding of the "physics of the daily" unless it were accompanied by the proper intention, sincerity, and honesty, a kind of good faith motivating thoughtful men to investigate themselves first. Writing to a colleague, Yokoi asserted that despite living in a universe that is the proper place for "our thinking, our minds have not yet investigated the various things we encounter and penetrated their principle." When one practiced sincerity and relied on "daily experiences, then one will have movement or the exercise of minds."[128] Self-examination prompted by sincerity invariably demands an investigation of the outer world and, accordingly, distinguishes between the act of merely knowing and genuinely understanding.

By constantly exercising the mind, men would reach a "true understanding of the governing principles that are brought out from thought." The Sung theorists, Yokoi complained, remained mired in the pursuit of mere knowing and wrote learnedly about the act of investigation but never understood it as a technique for "improving the welfare of the people."[129] In their hands, the examination of things and the investigation of principle, *kakubutsu kyūri*, served as an instrument for speculation and never as a tool for grasping the external world in its constant flux and inducing men to make the appropriate responses. Under the sanction of this conception of knowledge and

128 Ibid. 129 Yamazaki Masashige, ed., *Yokoi Shōnan ikō* (Tokyo: Meiji shoin, 1942), p. 922.

understanding, there could be little room for the idea of a timeless and fixed natural order.

"The conditions of past and present are different," Yokoi announced in his discussions with Inoue Kowashi at Nuyama, when he was under house arrest, "and although today and yesterday correspond to principle, they are not the same." Here, following the historicist impulse of eighteenth-century political economism, he differentiated principle (*ri*) from conditions (*sei*).[130]

Principle consistently guided men during times of change and enabled them to grasp the reality of circumstances in order to devise appropriate courses of action. Compelling men to overcome the temptations of an inactive subjectivism, the idea of sincerity would motivate them to know their times and to "assist nature's work," which now meant political administration or what the classic of the Great Learning called "outward pacification." In this discussion, Yokoi revealed his own conception of political form. If a culture were ethical, as he surely believed, informed by sincere intent, "good faith," prompting men to meet changing conditions head-on, then its form should also be ethical. Practical action undertaken to confront the challenge of changing conditions must always aim to actualize benevolence, which in the context of late Tokugawa times had become widely synonymous with the "public interest." What Yokoi was to imagine as the nation-state was principally an ethical space in which rulers pursued the public interest by serving the people's welfare. In this way, he realigned the conduct of political affairs with the larger conception of an ethical imperative. Behind this reformulation of place and purpose were the classic formulae that the "realm belongs to the public" and the "people are the base of the realm." "If there are no people," Yokoi asked rhetorically, "how would it be possible to erect a realm? But if there is a realm, it must serve the people who make it up." In an 1860 text, *Kokuze sanron,* Yokoi specified this conviction by calling attention to the Tokugawa failure. The Tokugawa household had acted as despots, he explained, demanding financial support from the several regions even when resources were scarce, thereby embarking on a "private management" that served only the "convenience of one family." Political doctrine alone never managed to tranquilize the realm by making people into children. "Perry was correct when he called this a nonpolitics." Real politics always assisted the people.

130 *Watanabe Kazan, Takano Chōei, Sakuma Shōzan, Yokoi Shōnan, Hashimoto Sanai,* p. 506.

> [For to] govern the realm means governing the people. The samurai are the instruments used to govern the realm. Even though it is fundamental to the way to teach filial piety, honesty, and loyalty to the samurai and the people, doctrine must also aim at bestowing wealth. . . . Wealth must be the most important task.[131]

Good leadership must always make sure that its conduct and policies conform to the public interest. Profit should exist only on behalf of the people. "The usefulness of benevolence . . . reaches men in the form of profit. . . . To abandon the self is to profit the people. The ideograph for profit is the name for unprincipled (action) when it is used privately. When one profits the people, its use is benevolent."[132] In these circumstances, the realm should encourage trade and maritime commercial relations in order to realize the requirements of the public interest.

According the *Kokuze sanron,* agriculture remained the source of livelihood, even if it were only one aspect of it. Without the innumerable products that people needed for their daily use, life would be impossible. These products were obtained through exchange. Trade and the circulation of currency affected the whole country. Because such a system had not been put into practice, contemporary Japan was a comparatively poor country. As a result, every effort should be made to prepare for the development of a variety of products in several areas. But before this could be accomplished, there had to be a system of markets for the distribution of goods. A market system and the flow of currency would prevent stagnation by regulating the exchange and distribution of products. It would keep in check the activities in the economic realm. In fact, Yokoi's writings show a gradual shift of emphasis to the market over the national defense among Western enthusiasts once the opening of the country had made international relations possible. Yokoi chose the *han* (especially Fukui) as the unit in which the new economic arrangements should be implemented, but he also believed that the form of *fukoku kyōhei* could be extended to other domains because the "proper administration of one realm can be expanded to the whole country." On the national level, Yokoi, like Sakuma, supported the project of large domains striving to bring about a reconciliation between the court and the bakufu in the establishment of a new conciliar arrangement. The importance of his mercantilist program was that it could be applied to the broader national

131 Ibid., p. 444. *Kokuze sanron* is translated by D. Y. Miyauchi in *Monumenta Nipponica* 23 (1968): 156–86.

132 *Watanabe Kazan, Takano Chōei, Sakuma Shōzan, Yokoi Shōnan, Hashimoto Sanai,* p. 504.

scene. At this time, Takasugi Shinsaku was already seeking to establish a comparable program in Chōshū, and Ōkubo Toshimichi was trying to transform Satsuma into a wealthy and powerful domain. Eventually, as Yokoi became committed to finding ways to account for the existence of plural interests, he drew his political model from the example of the United States.

Yokoi developed a coherent argument justifying claims for broader participation in issues relating to the welfare and security of society as a whole. The idea of "public discussion" (*kōgi yoron*) signified an effort to formalize this claim to speak about society's business. This arrangement meant that the bakufu should summon all talented men of the realm to Edo (because the "great urgency of the day is to confide in sincerity") "to bring together the able of the realm and its political affairs." This policy would "seek out the words of the people in the realm and transmit people's intention on benefit and injury, gains and losses."[133] Yokoi particularly envisaged the form of a unified structure that still allowed for the expression of domain interests, resembling most the American Federal Republic which he came to admire. He hoped to install a hedge against the divisiveness of the *bakuhan* system, which inevitably invited "private management," by resorting to the idea of public discussions that would equate ability with efficacy or utility, informed by expert and specialized knowledge, and mediated by an awareness of changing times and a concern for the people's will and feelings. He believed that he had found the appropriate means to express the Confucian imperative that made the private morality of the lord ("disciplining and cultivating oneself") equivalent to governing the realm in the public interest. Knowledge came to replace morality as the necessary criterion for leadership. This was revealed in his recommendation to Matsudaira Yoshinaga (Shungaku) of Echizen in 1862 which urged "the abandonment of the selfishness that the Tokugawa bakufu has shown since it acquired countrywide authority." It was the season to "reform the nonpolitics of the Tokugawa house" and to "govern the realm" in the interest of a larger public.

CULTURAL PRACTICE AND THE TRIUMPH OF POLITICAL CENTRALIZATION

Among late Tokugawa writers and activists, none came closer than Yokoi Shōnan to grasping in the "current situation" the play of differ-

133 Uete, *Nihon kindai shisō keisei*, p. 83.

ences represented by new discourses, the destruction of received political identities, and the need to find a way to accommodate the plural claims that were being made in the explosive environment of the 1860s. Yokoi's "reading" of contemporary circumstances proposed a resolution of the problems of security and assistance that involved installing a hegemonic arrangement capable of stabilizing the political order while retaining the differing articulations. In fact, the conjuncture of discursive claims ultimately became the terrain for a new hegemonic political practice.

Since the turn of the century, the steady increase of discourses augmenting distinctly articulated practices presented the spectacle of a ceaseless play of what might be called cultural overdetermination,[134] a process whereby multiple causes and contradictions reappeared regularly in condensed form to shape an image of rupture and fragmented meaning. The new practices all announced the importance of "difference" which, since the late eighteenth century, had been associated with blurred social identities that demanded accommodation. The culture of play reflected an experience of fragmentation and division as the starting point of literary, artistic, and intellectual production. The collapse of a view that divided political space between ruler and ruled, the gradual dismissal of a meaningful cosmic order within which people occupied precise and determined places, and the replacement of this view by a self-defining conception of the subject combined to launch Japanese society on a constant search to reconstitute its lost unity. Each discourse, including Mito, acknowledged in its way the end of a simple division between ruler and ruled, which had authorized a hierarchic order accountable only to itself and directed by a metaphysic based on the paradigm of nature. Under the sanction of Neo-Confucianism, the social body had been conceived as a fixed whole. As long as such a holistic mode of social imagination prevailed, politics would remain a mere repetition of the hierarchical social relations. What the several discursive "interpretations" disclosed was the recognition of the incessant need to find instruments for restructuring that society by identifying and articulating social relations. Each dis-

134 The term *overdetermination* has a venerable genealogy that, for our purposes, goes back to Sigmund Freud's *Interpretation of Dreams*, in which he applied the concept to describe the process when a dream's elements appear to have been represented in dream thoughts many times over. I am using *overdetermination* to refer to the presence of plural discursive representations during the late Tokugawa period, whereby the same elements appear time and again in different form. In brief, those elements (fear of disorder, concern for productivity, anxiety over questions of security, the idea of community free from fragmentation, new concepts of authority and legitimacy, and the like) that seem to have the most numerous and strongest supports acquire the right of entry into the content of discourses.

course revealed an overdetermination implied in annulling the contradiction among a growing number of differences, a plethora of meanings of the "social," and the difficulties encountered in any attempt to fix those differences as moments of a stable structure.

All of the discourses proceeded from the presumption that the issues they sought to understand and speak to constituted society's business, not other people's business. Henceforth, questions relating to order, security, productivity, relief and assistance, the centrality of daily life, and the practical knowledge needed to reproduce social conditions of existence required a concept of the social capable of being mobilized for the realization of its goals. The creation of public opinion in late Tokugawa discourse as a condition for considering issues vital to the collectivity made it possible to conceptualize a new political space. All of the discourses shifted the terms of legitimation from cosmic and natural principles to the agency of human performance and productivity. In this they contributed their greatest challenge to the established Tokugawa order, whose claims rested first on metaphysical principles and only second on the instruments of production. Driven by a common impulse to overcome the division between ruler and ruled, the several discourses all sought to place daily life in the forefront of attention by emphasizing the tangible and sensuous against the abstract. As a result, all of the discourses aimed at showing how knowledge derived from the daily life of a certain social constituency entitled its knowers to the power to make decisions affecting their lives. An effect of these new systems of knowledge was the disciplining of the body, whereby the proper mental attitude was made to correspond to certain mutual intentions, in order to offset the baneful influence of received arrangements that insisted on separating mental from manual and more recent customs in which the body played and performed, often to excess.

To make other people's business one's own required finding a different form of authority that would validate the act of centering on the activity of people who had hitherto been disenfranchised. Any discussion of politics or administration, as officially defined, among groups long considered ineligible because they lacked the proper knowledge risked danger; it also challenged the officials' claim to designate objects for political discourse. This move entailed displacing the center from politics to culture and rethinking the identity of social relations in areas of religion, science and technology, and economics in order to locate an arena capable of offering representation to such groups. By the same token the move to imagine a new arena of this sort permitted conceptualizing different political forms. Each one of the new discourses produced a vision of political form consistent with the social identity of the group that it wished to represent and that, it was believed, had emerged from the new content of culture. Mito emphasized the autonomous domain; the nativists projected the self-sufficient village; the new religions installed the sacred enclosure or community of believers; and the proponents of defense and wealth promoted the nation-state. Yet for the most part the institution of envisaging a stable system of "differences" had become overdetermined, was directed at solving the problem of the whole by substituting a part for it.

As a distinct process of articulation, the several discourses tried to move away from the center to a periphery, or envisaged a plurality of centers by creating a larger public space as a forum for discussing issues that affected society as a whole. This signaled both the dissolution of a politics in which the division of identities between ruler and ruled had been fixed for all time and a transition toward a new situation characterized by unstable political spaces, in which the very identity of the contesting forces was submitted to constant shifts and calls for redefinition. In the late Tokugawa period the discursive field was dominated by a plurality of practices that presupposed the incomplete and open character of the social. This signified challenging closure and finding a form of mediation between the general need to stabilize order and promote productivity and a local demand to guarantee the preservation of the various social identities produced by the will to discourse. Only the presence of a vast area of semiautonomous, heterogenous and unevenly developed discourses and the possibility of conflict made possible the terrain for a hegemonic practice competent to satisfy both order and difference. For many who belonged to the new discourses, the Restoration vaguely promised the possibility of accomplishing a hegemonic formation committed to stabilizing the social and preserving interests and fixed identities. Yet the existence of these various claims to interest and projections of social identity would soon become the problem, not the solution.

In a sense, the initial stage of the Meiji Restoration, or as it was called, *ōsei fukko*, appeared at the moment when many believed it was necessary to find a form that would contain and even represent the various interests that undermined Tokugawa control. It should be noted that each of the movements discussed, in its efforts to discredit the center and replace it with centers, supplied its own conception of political restoration: Mito had already announced the goals of *chūkō* (restoration); nativism lodged its appeal in an "adherence to foundations" (*moto ni tsuku*); the new religions epiphanized their image of a new order in calls for "world renewal"; and proponents of wealth and defense sought in some sort of conciliar arrangement (*dai kakkyo*) a way of rearranging the constellation of political forces that existed in the 1860s. Nor least important, all could easily support a restoration symbolized by the emperor and court that promised nothing more binding than a return to the age of Jimmu tenno, a "washing away of all old abuses" and a search for new knowledge throughout the world. Here, for a brief moment, was the necessary fit between the forces that combined to bring down the Tokugawa and a hegemonic political structure that promised to reinstate order and security and to distribute relief while preserving regional autonomy. Uncertain as to its future goals, *ōsei fukko* could project the image of a hegemony willing to take into account the interests of all groups by presupposing a certain equilibrium among the various forces. So powerful was the appeal of an *ōsei fukko* in 1867 that writers like Suzuki Masayuki were encouraged to declare (significantly in a *chōka*, an archaic long poem): "Even the despised people, will not be lacking/ The emperor (*oogimi*), hidden in the shade like a night flower, will flourish increasingly/ Everyone will rejoice in the prosperity of the august age."[135] This sentiment seemed to be shared widely throughout society, and people everywhere saw in the Restoration, albeit momentarily, a representation of their own hopes and aspirations.

Yet before long, other voices were beginning to condemn the Restoration as a deception and a deathblow to their most cherished ideals. In Yano Gendō's short, elegiac lament for the vanished glories of Kashiwara and the promise of returning to its golden age, all that was left by 1880 was a "dream that will never be."[136] Almost immediately after *ōsei fukko,* the prospect for a hegemonic formation of the Restoration polity disappeared in the construction of a modern bureaucratic state – the Go-Ishin – pledged to eliminating precisely the fragmentation, difference, and overdetermination that had defeated the Tokugawa system of control. The reorganization of an ensemble of bureaucratic administrative functions arranged by criteria of efficiency and rationality after 1870 aimed at removing the very antagonisms that had surfaced in the discursive articulations of late Tokugawa and that were necessary for the installation of a hegemonic order. The very conditions that produced new political subjects demanding order, relief,

135 Itō Shirō, *Suzuki Masayuki no kenkyū* (Tokyo: Aoki shoten, 1972), pp. 287–8.
136 This quotation from Yano's poem is from Hirose Tamotsu, ed., *Origuchi Shinobu shū* (Tokyo: Chikuma shobō, 1975), p. 386.

assistance, security, and the subsequent withdrawals from the center now constituted a problem that many believed had to be resolved. The contest down to the 1890s consisted of an opposition between proponents of discursive practices insisting on preserving a measure of autonomy, usually expressed in movements calling for local control, and a new leadership committed to the rational centralization of power and the elimination of all articulations requesting the reinstatement of a hegemonic arrangement in a genuinely constitutional policy.[137] This is not to say that the Meiji Restoration successfully terminated the several discourses. Mito had already taken itself out of the political field as a result of a destructive civil war in the early 1860s, even though the later Meiji government appropriated parts of its program. Through the support of courtiers like Iwakura Tomomi, nativism briefly sought to control the course of events in 1867 and 1868 by proposing the implementation of a new restorationist polity based on ancient models, but it was too late for the construction of an order more religious and mythic than political and more self-consciously archaic and agricultural than modern and industrial. As a discourse, it was dissembled into a state-controlled sect promoting the worship of Ōkuni no nushi, the god housed in the Izumo Shrine. Later it was transformed into a Japanese science of ethnology that once again was formulated to forestall the power of the new bureaucratic state. The new religions continued a checkered course of withdrawals, staging confrontations with the state, recruiting larger numbers of followers, and generating newer and more radical communities like Maruyamakyō and Ōmotokyō. Finally, the older discourse on defense and wealth continued its own efforts to curb the centralization of the Meiji state by trying to give substance to ideas of broader political participation and local autonomy, ending with a systematic attempt to "civilize" and "enlighten" Japanese society in the 1870s and 1880s as the condition for a permanent moral and rational order.

Yet the Meiji state, as it was completed in the 1890s, was also a solution to the *bakumatsu* problems that have been addressed. It was precisely the loss of control in late Tokugawa decades that catalyzed a contest over how the center, and hence the whole, was to be reconstituted. Fear of the continuing failure to arrest the disorder – first in the

137 The terms of this contest between *center* and *periphery* are documented in Michio Umegaki, "After the Restoration: The Beginnings of Japan's Modern State," forthcoming. New York University Press, while the proponents of the localist inflection have been romanticized in Irokawa Daikichi, *The Culture of the Meiji Period*, translation edited by Marius B. Jansen (Princeton, N.J.: Princeton University Press, 1985).

countryside and the cities – and of the inability to meet the foreign threat, plus the clear need to put an end to centrifugal forces set in motion by secessions and withdrawals served to impel a search for more effective ways to restructure society. In this restructuring, the struggle was seen increasingly as one between authority and community, between the effort of various groups to attend to society's business and the belief that that business was too important to leave to the public. The modern state managed to exclude surplus social meaning, by fixing the identity of the public interest in its quest for order and security while relegating communitarian claims to the margins of otherness. It should be recalled that all the late Tokugawa discourses projected an image of assistance and relief, even when, as in Mito, that image was an ambiguous mix of loving and caring for the people while treating them as dependent children. But the Meiji leaders recognized that politics must determine the content of culture, rather than the reverse, and felt that social identities must be made to comply with the necessity of the state because an opposite course would have encouraged a continuous generation of new subjectivities and divisive antagonisms. Once the state had arrogated to itself the modes of cultural production, it was possible to remove culture from play and employ it as an ideological instrument to depoliticize the masses. That act required reducing the polyphonic discourses of the late Tokugawa, with their many voices speaking about the same things, to the single voice of an authoritative discourse.

CHAPTER 3

THE MEIJI RESTORATION

The Meiji Restoration stands as one of the turning points of Japanese history. Although the actual events of 1868 constituted little more than a shift of power within the old ruling class, the larger process referred to as the Meiji Restoration brought an end to the ascendancy of the warrior class and replaced the decentralized structure of early modern feudalism with a central state under the aegis of the traditional sovereign, now transformed into a modern monarch. The Restoration leaders undertook a series of vigorous steps to build national strength under capitalist institutions and rapidly propelled their country on the road to regional and world power. Thus the Restoration constituted a major event for Japanese, East Asian, and world history. The process whereby this came about has inevitably become a central issue in Japanese historiography, for verdicts on its content and nature condition all appraisals of the modern state to which it led. The work of historians has been undergirded by a vast apparatus of sources preserved by a history-minded government concerned with its own origins, and the scholarship that has been produced illuminates the intellectual history of Japan's most recent century.

TROUBLES WITHIN, DISASTER FROM WITHOUT

Japan's political crisis of the 1860s was preceded by serious internal difficulties and foreign danger that brought to mind formulations of Chinese historians who habitually coupled internal decline with border incursions made possible by that decline: "troubles within, disaster from without" (*naiyū gaikan*). A great deal of historical inquiry has been directed to the questions of how severe the first would have been in the absence of the second. Once the ports had been opened, there was no mistaking the complementary vibration between internal and external problems, but in the absence of foreign aggravation, the possibility of an internal upheaval sufficient to bring about the collapse of the feudal order remains uncertain. What is clear, however, is that the almost total isolation of Japan before its "opening" by the West served to magnify the consequence of the foreign impact in the public imagination.

The regime's internal difficulties came into striking focus during the years of the Tempō period (1830–44), which receive detailed treatment in Chapter 2. During those years Japan was devastated by crop failures that caused ruinous famines in central and northern areas. These combined with governmental inefficiency and unresponsiveness to encourage or provoke popular resistance. The most spectacular revolt of this period was one led by a model Confucian samurai official in Osaka, Ōshio Heihachirō, whose emotional call to insurrection made him a hero for later historians who sometimes dated the loyalist revolts from his manifesto. Ōshio's uprising resulted in little more than the burning of large areas of Osaka, but the striking incompetence shown by bakufu officials in its suppression contrasted with his own courageous (though equally maladroit) performance to symbolize what was wrong with the regime. Ōshio's revolt, led by samurai and centered in the second most important city of the land, provided a national shock,[1] but it was only one of many risings in that period. Peasant insurrections and urban "smashings" had tended to grow in size with the interrelationships of Japan's increasingly close-knit economy, and popular risings often moved rapidly along lines of communication. An added phenomenon of the period was the increase of chiliastic and millenarian movements. The world renewal (*yonaoshi*) uprisings were frequently led by a self-sacrificing individual who willingly martyred himself for the eventual good of his fellows. Ōshio, too, came to take on such an appearance in popular thought.[2]

Nevertheless, the insurrections of the period proposed few alternatives to the social and economic system that gave them birth. Manifestoes and petitions usually focused on recent or threatened violations of what had come to seem as acceptable, though admittedly burdensome, government demands. Communication routes were natural conductors for such protest, as the villages along the right of way were ex-

1 Tetsuo Najita, "Ōshio Heihachirō (1793–1837)," in Albert M. Craig and Donald Shively, eds., *Personality in Japanese History* (Berkeley and Los Angeles: University of California Press, 1970), pp. 155–79; and Ivan Morris, *The Nobility of Failure: Tragic Heroes in the History of Japan* (New York: Holt, Rinehart and Winston, 1975), pp. 180–216, provide the best coverage in English of the man and his revolt.

2 Two essays that suggest the dimensions of the problems in such uprisings are Irwin Scheiner, "Benevolent Lords and Honorable Peasants: Rebellion and Peasant Consciousness in Tokugawa Japan," in Tetsuo Najita and Irwin Scheiner, eds., *Japanese Thought in the Tokugawa Period: Methods and Metaphors* (Chicago: University of Chicago Press, 1978), pp. 39–62; and Sasaki Junnosuke, "Bakumatsu no shakai jōsei to yonaoshi," in *Iwanami kōza Nihon rekishi*, vol. 13 (*kinsei* 5) (Tokyo: Iwanami shoten, 1977), pp. 247–308.

pected to provide the *sukegō* porter service that moved travelers and transport on human and animal backs. Needs for such services increased in late Tokugawa times.

Rural order was also reinforced by an interesting group of nonofficial rural reformers whose teachings of sobriety, thrift, mutual cooperation, and agricultural improvement were designed to give farmers a better livelihood. The agricultural technologist Ōkura Nagatsune (1768–1856), the rural reformers Ninomiya Sontoku (1787–1856), with his plans for mutual cooperatives, and Ōhara Yūgaku (1798–1858) all worked to restore the health of the rural areas. Significantly, all three focused on the reclamation of land left fallow, whether by bad government or famine or migration. Their teachings were usually moralistic and pietistic, stressing the maintenance and care of land as an essential part of filial piety and ancestral obligation. Such efforts, though surely helpful to the government, were also evidence of the government's inability to fulfill the paternal role it had long ago set for itself. Equally important, the appearance of genuine rural leaders of this sort testified to a rising level of scholarship and leadership among the commoner elite throughout the Japanese countryside.[3]

The bakufu's response to these troubled times took the form of the Tempō reforms launched by the *rōjū* Mizuno Tadakuni in 1841. As Harold Bolitho points out in Chapter 2, the reforms, which included edicts against migration from country to city, provided relief for bakufu retainers' debts, abolished merchant guilds, and attempted to rationalize and concentrate bakufu landholdings within a set radius of Edo and Osaka, struck at vested interests of townsmen and vassals, and ended in failure. Simultaneous reforms in some of the larger domains, notably Satsuma and Chōshū, were somewhat more successful, but none fully met its goals. The bakufu's failure was particularly important, for its inability to raise its revenues augured ill for the greater crises that lay ahead. Nevertheless the ambitious, though abortive, plans for more intensive bureaucratic control of society have provided the basis for some historians' interpretations of the Tempō years as inaugurating late-feudal nineteenth-century "absolutism." Although judgments of these issues differ sharply, undoubtedly the future Meiji leaders, "men of Tempō" who experienced that turmoil in their early years, built on those lessons to their loss or gain.

The bakufu that had to deal with these problems was in many ways

3 Thomas C. Smith, "Ōkura Nagatsune and the Technologists," in Craig and Shively, eds., *Personality in Japanese History*, pp. 127–54; and Miyata Noboru, "Nōson no fukkō undō to minshū shūkyō no tenkai," in *Iwanami kōza Nihon rekishi*, vol. 13 (*kinsei* 5), pp. 209–45.

a less flexible and less adequate instrument of government than it had been. Although the eighteenth-century administrators had felt able to experiment rather widely within the pattern of the past, the language of the nineteenth-century leaders increasingly stressed the "obligations of the past" (*sono sujisuji no gohōkō*) in a rigid adherence to tradition. Central authority, as Harold Bolitho's study of the *fudai* daimyo points out, had not grown;[4] if anything, the shift from strong to weak shoguns had resulted in bureaucratic immobility. Mizuno's effort during the Tempō reforms to reclaim some vassals' holdings roused a storm of complaint, and yet his abortive efforts anticipated the measures that would be found necessary by future reformers when the crisis deepened in the 1860s. The once pragmatic bakufu had become a rather fine-tuned instrument that found it difficult to proceed without the cooperation of a number of distinct interest groups. Institutionally it remained premodern. The senior counselors (*rōjū*) served on cycles of monthly rotation, and the adoption of regular responsibilities and the abolition of the rotation system came only on the eve of the Tokugawa fall in 1867. Internal disaffection and bureaucratic rigidity may not have reached the levels that characterized contemporary China, but both regimes operated in a setting in which custom and precedent placed limitations on central power. More important, both regimes were limited by an inadequate governmental share of the nation's product. The precedents set by the ancestors and the barriers set by established and deeply routinized patterns of administration made it difficult to initiate radical change. The bakufu, though charged with the responsibility for the national defense, had access to only the income of its own lands. A shogunal procession to Kyoto in the 1860s required most of its regular cash income for that year, and the cost of restoring traditional preparedness and purchasing modern arms was soon to become prohibitive.[5]

The crisis in foreign affairs that followed the Tempō years is treated by William Beasley in Chapter 4. As he points out, it was a crisis that had been developing for decades. A growing consciousness of the foreign danger had been one of the unsettling elements in the nineteenth-century climate of opinion among informed intellectuals. The defeat of China in the Opium War of 1838–42 brought this conscious-

4 Harold Bolitho, *Treasures Among Men: The Fudai Daimyo in Tokugawa Japan* (New Haven, Conn.: Yale University Press, 1974).

5 Conrad Totman, *The Collapse of the Tokugawa Bakufu, 1862–1868* (Honolulu: University of Hawaii Press, 1980), provides excellent brief discussions of bakufu finances in the 1860s, pp. 190ff.

ness home to a far larger public. The Japanese had ready knowledge of that disaster through the messages brought by Dutch and Chinese merchants to Nagasaki, and Chinese accounts of the problem, notably Wei Yüan's *Hai-kuo t'u-chih,* went through many editions in Japan, where they were immediately accessible to all who had received formal education. In a secluded island country whose great metropolises were collection points for the literate elite of all sectors, speculation inevitably led to uneasy fears that imperialist flotillas would next come to Japan.[6]

Such consciousness had also been advanced by changes in the world of thought, which are treated by Harry Harootunian in Chapter 3. The nativist thought of national scholarship (*kokugaku*) moved in increasingly extreme directions in the nineteenth century. In the teachings of Hirata Atsutane and his disciples, it combined an increasingly assimilative and syncretic utilization of non-Japanese thought with a religious fervor focusing on the sun goddess Amaterasu as a national deity. A new and compulsive ethnicity was in formulation. Still premodern and perhaps only protonationalistic, this thought lay at hand as a potent incitation to alarm and indignation when once the sacred soil and sparkling waters of Japan might be sullied by foreign boots and hulls.

Knowledge about the West, and consequently informed awareness of its capability, was also available through the rise of Western learning (*rangaku*). A practice of translating Western books, launched in 1771 with the discovery by several doctors that the human anatomy conformed more closely to Dutch than to Chinese anatomical charts, grew so rapidly that at the time of his death in 1817 Sugita Gempaku, one of the doctors involved, compared it with the translation movement from Chinese a millennium earlier. The bakufu did its best to channel such learning and also to appropriate that part of it that seemed useful, but restless minds and figures soon carried it beyond the bound of the permissible. In the *Morrison* incident of 1837 a group of "Dutch scholars" concluded that the rude rejection of an English emissary would subject Japan to great danger. The ship in question had in fact already been repulsed successfully, but political criticism of this sort provided the impetus for political repression of the scholars in the purge of 1839.

A third, and ultimately the most important, development in the thought world of the nineteenth century was a growing concern with the imperial institution, which was the product of the *kokugaku* tradi-

6 Ōba Osamu, *Edo jidai ni okeru Chūgoku bunka juyō no kenkyū* (Tokyo: Dōhōsha, 1984), pp. 388 ff., for bakufu orders of Wei Yüan's work.

tion. This cut across all groups, but it found its most forceful and powerful formulation in a blend of ethnic and Confucian teaching that associated loyalism with morality and justified – and even required – participation in the political process under its imperative. In the slogan "revere the emperor, drive out the barbarian!" (*sonnō-jōi*), loyalism wedded to antiforeignism became the most powerful emotion of mid-century Japan.

Historical scholarship has often limited its consideration of emperor-centered thought to treat it as a political tactic without considering its substance, in good measure as a result of and in reaction to the use made of the institution by the modern state.[7] In fact, however, it can be demonstrated that the development of loyalist thought had a long continuity in Tokugawa intellectual history and was not without its roots in Chinese thought as well. The dominant stream of Tokugawa Confucianism drew on the Neo-Confucian thought of Sung China, which developed at a time when the foreign danger in the form of northern barbarians was at the forefront of scholars' consciousness. The antiforeign thrust of Chu Hsi Neo-Confucianism became blunted in a China ruled by Manchus, but in Japan the nonfunctioning throne became idealized, and it ended as the focus of ethnic nationalism. In samurai minds the identification of "country" with "virtue" tended to make absolutes of duty and action. "Loyalty" (*chūgi*) became a "great duty" (*taigi*) and the supreme test of the moral individual. This primacy of political values became the more powerful because, as Maruyama Masao has pointed out, it carried with it the implication that it was the vassal's responsibility to "correct" or "admonish" as well as to "obey" his superior.[8] In the nineteenth century, Tokugawa Confucian scholarship stressed a hierarchical scheme of obligations in which sovereign came to stand above shogun. Chinese civilization gradually came to seem distinct from the country of its birth, particularly after the fall of the Ming to the Manchus in the seventeenth century. Indeed, many nineteenth-century writers referred to Japan as the central country.

There were also trends in Tokugawa policy that gave impetus to this trend of imperial loyalism. In the eighteenth century, the bakufu, increasingly responsive to Confucian morality, demonstrated its respect for the court by protecting and maintaining the imperial tombs

7 Nagahara Keiji, "Zenkindai no tennō," *Rekishigaku kenkyū* 467 (April 1979): 37–47; and Bitō Masahide, "Sonnō-jōi shisō," *Iwanami kōza Nihon rekishi*, vol. 13 (*kinsei* 5), pp. 41–86. See also Hershel Webb, *The Japanese Imperial Institution in the Tokugawa Period* (New York: Columbia University Press, 1968).

8 Maruyama Masao, "Chūsei to hangyaku," in *Kindai Nihon shisōshi kōza* (Tokyo: Chikuma shobō, 1960), vol. 6.

and by increasing the miserly stipends that the early shoguns had provided for the court and courtiers. Whereas Ieyasu and his immediate successors had taken care to sever the ties the court had had with the military class up to that time,[9] awards of imperial rank and title to the Tokugawa cadet houses now became expected. Gradually extended to other leading daimyo, such titles became a matter of prestige and pride and helped lead to daimyo–court connections against which the early shoguns had guarded. Gradually and almost imperceptibly, the bakufu's "virtue" came to be identified with its ability to protect and insulate the court and country from outside contact. *Sakoku,* begun as a measure to ward off domestic dissidence in the mid-seventeenth century, ended by becoming a criterion of shogunal loyalty and performance.

Intellectually this package of patterns and ideals found its most persuasive setting in the writings of a group of scholars in Tokugawa Nariaki's domain of Mito. Aizawa Seishisai's *Shinron* (1825) provided in particularly compelling form a warning of the power of the West, insistence on the sacred nature of Japan and its imperial polity, and reminders that that superiority was based on the benefits of the imperial family. Mito thought, and especially Aizawa's book, became widely read in the 1840s and 1850s, at a time when the Mito daimyo began to take a vigorous part in urging measures of moral and material rearmament and in extending his political contacts to the Kyoto court.

THE HARRIS TREATY AND ITS AFTERMATH

The opening of Japan to international contact, described by Professor Beasley in Chapter 4, produced problems that were made more difficult by these strains. Economic difficulties and military unpreparedness made it important for Japan to avoid military conflict until preparations had been advanced. This required information (gathered by the Bansho shirabesho, the new Institute for Western Learning established in 1855), money (collected through new taxes, forced loans, and government economies), and political consensus to provide a time of quiet during which plans could be prepared. The search for that consensus brought efforts to consult, and thereby to educate, the daimyo and the Kyoto court. That consultation had the effect of activating first them and then their vassals and subordinates. A broadening circle of concern among people who were often poorly informed about for-

9 See Asao Naohiro with Marius B. Jansen, "Shogun and Tennō," in John W. Hall et al., eds., *Japan Before Tokugawa* (Princeton, N.J.: Princeton University Press, 1980), pp. 248–70.

eign affairs but who were anxious to use those issues for internal affairs came close to paralyzing government processes.

The bakufu's first response to the news of the Opium War was to relax its standing orders for the prompt repulse of foreign vessels and to order that supplies be provided for them when they requested them. This order, issued in 1842, brought a reminder from Emperor Kōmei four years later to be careful about coastal defense. However mild its wording, it was an early indication that the court would consider itself involved in matters of foreign policy and defense. A letter of warning from the king of Holland in 1844 and the Biddle mission of 1846 were successfully turned aside, but no one doubted that more such would follow. Bakufu orders to daimyo to be vigilant about coastal defenses were issued in 1849, but because of the general financial stringency of the times, no real advances had been made when the Perry mission arrived in 1853.

Abe Masahiro, an able conciliator who had been *rōjū* since 1845, sent the Perry letter to the court for information and to the Tokugawa vassals with requests for advice. Abe was aware of the need for change; he had promoted a number of low-ranking officers to key posts. He also had a keen awareness of Japan's military weakness and had established an office of coastal defense over which he himself presided and which he manned with his own followers. Abe tried to outmaneuver the leading exponent of exclusion, Tokugawa Nariaki of Mito, by appointing him to a key defense post. The opinions that the bakufu received from daimyo and lesser vassals revealed a wide range of views on the American request, but for the most part they agreed that conflict should be avoided. The bakufu made its decision without a great deal of reference to the views that came in; it was a full year before it sent the text of the Shimoda treaty that its negotiators had worked out with Perry to the daimyo and the court. At the same time its orders to the daimyo had sharp reminders of the importance of coastal defense, and police officials (*metsuke*) were given sharp warnings about the importance of quick and ruthless action to prevent contacts between foreigners and ordinary Japanese. Abe seemed to have resolved the first step, but even his political agility could not conceal the change that was to come. In 1854 the court issued an order to melt down temple bells for guns, the first time in the entire Edo period that Kyoto had taken it upon itself to issue a national directive. Matsudaira Shungaku (Yoshinaga, Keiei), the collateral house (*shimpan*) daimyo of Fukui, Abe's father-in-law, and a leading figure in national politics from then on, wrote to remind Abe that daimyo respect for the bakufu was contingent on the bakufu's respect for Kyoto. In the future, the bakufu's desire for daimyo support in difficult decisions would find it consulting them more frequently, and the court itself developed the tactic of suggesting that daimyo, or at least leading Tokugawa vassals like the *gosanke,* should be consulted again.[10]

The Commercial Treaty of 1858 negotiated by Townsend Harris marked the real opening of Japan to trade and residence. Harris drew his most effective arguments from the disasters that China met in the second round of warfare (the *Arrow* war) that ended with the Tientsin treaties in 1858. Oddly enough, the bakufu's fear of following the course of China into foreign subjection led it to accept treaties almost identical to those inflicted on China.[11]

The debates about the Harris treaty next became inextricably interwoven with the problem of shogunal succession. Tokugawa Iesada, who died in the summer of 1858, had no successor, and so adoption procedures had to be set in motion. The leading candidates were Hitotsubashi Yoshinobu (Keiki), an able young man who was in fact one of the many sons of Tokugawa Nariaki of Mito, and a still-immature descendant of the Tokugawa house of Kii (Wakayama), the future Tokugawa Iemochi. Iemochi's selection would be the more conventional, and in the maneuvering that took place, reference to an "able" heir was code language for choosing Hitotsubashi (later Tokugawa) Yoshinobu.

Hotta Masayoshi, who had succeeded Abe Masahiro as chief bakufu official, informed Townsend Harris that the regime would need the formality of court approval of the new treaty before signing it, and he arrived in Kyoto to secure that approval in the spring of 1858. To his astonishment, the court instructions he received a half-month later instructed the bakufu that because this was of utmost importance to the country, it should take up the matter once more with the three cadet houses (*gosanke*) and the daimyo. This marked the first time in the Tokugawa years that the court had presumed to disagree publicly with bakufu policy. What had happened was that a number of leading daimyo, among them Tokugawa Nariaki, had recognized in the com-

10 Abe's tactics and ability have received poor marks from most historians, but more appreciative verdicts are rendered by Conrad Totman, "Political Reconciliation in the Tokugawa Bakufu: Abe Masahiro and Tokugawa Nariaki, 1844–1852," in Craig and Shively, eds., *Personality in Japanese History,* pp. 180–208; and Bitō Masahide, "*Bushi* and the Meiji Restoration," *Acta Asiatica,* 49 (Tokyo, Tōhō Gakkai, 1985): 78–96.

11 The point is Ono Masao's in "Kaikoku," *Iwanami kōza Nihon rekishi,* vol. 13 (*kinsei* 5), pp. 1–39. Nakamura Tetsu, "Kaikokugo no bōeki to sekai shijō," however, points out that the Ansei treaties were superior to the Tientsin treaties because they did not legalize opium or permit missionaries and provided better tariff arrangements, pp. 108–9.

mercial treaty an issue on which they could use the court's xenophobic instincts to influence bakufu policy in the matter of shogunal succession. Henceforth they would propose that the court couple reluctant approval of the treaty with the condition of selecting an "able" and mature heir to the shogun.

When Hotta addressed his second request for approval to the court, he was close to having his way when eighty-eight Kyoto nobles joined to protest. As a result, instructions to consult the vassals were handed down a second time. With this the lines were drawn for a showdown. House succession went to the heart of Tokugawa policy and was an internal Tokugawa matter. As the *fudai* daimyo of Hikone, Ii Naosuke, put it in a letter, selection according to ability might be the "Chinese way," but it was not the way things were done in Japan. Last-minute bakufu lobbying blocked a court plan to call for an able shogun.[12]

The court's second rebuff came in a context of growing exasperation with Kyoto xenophobia and obstruction, and it brought hard-liners to the fore in Edo. Shortly after Hotta's return from Kyoto, Ii Naosuke of Hikone became regent (*tairō*) and took over the leadership role in the Edo councils. He now began a period of personal leadership that had no real precedent in the history of shogunal ministers. It seemed to him that the reassertion of bakufu control over dissidents was a matter of the highest priority and that other issues were secondary.

On June 25, Harris was promised that the treaty would be signed by September 4. Once again letters were sent off to the daimyo in apparent conformity with imperial instructions. But when Townsend Harris brought word of the Treaty of Tientsin and speculated that the British and French warships would probably proceed to Japan next, the treaty was hastily signed on July 29 before the results of the new survey were in hand and without court approval. Ten days later the bakufu announced that shogunal succession had gone to the young Iemochi of Kii. Thus Ii Naosuke had decided the two burning questions of the period within ten days, and quite on his own authority.

Ii now moved against the opposition. Bakufu moderates and foreign affairs specialists who had come to office under Abe and who had favored a cooperative and conciliatory policy toward the daimyo were dismissed, demoted, or moved to less important posts. The great

12 George Wilson, "The Bakumatsu Intellectual in Action: Hashimoto Sanai and the Political Crisis of 1858," in Craig and Shively, eds., *Personality in Japanese History*, pp. 234–63, quotes Ii's retainer Nagano: "To nominate a lord because of his intelligence is to have inferiors choose their superior and is entirely the Chinese style . . . the custom of our empire must be to respect the direct line of descent," p. 260. But Nagano was too dogmatic in this; the adoption system permitted great flexibility in succession to secure ability.

daimyo who had lobbied through their agents in Kyoto for the succession of Yoshinobu as heir were driven into retirement and, usually, house arrest. Matsudaira Shungaku of Fukui, Tokugawa Nariaki of Mito, Tokugawa Yoshikuni of Owari, and Yamauchi Yōdō of Tosa were only the most eminent of those punished.

Emperor Kōmei was furious at this flouting of his sentiment and even considered abdication to demonstrate his frustration. He ordered that the head of one of the three cadet houses (*gosanke*), or the *tairō* himself, come to Kyoto, only to receive the response that the house heads were being punished and that the *tairō* was too busy with national affairs to absent himself from Edo. A lesser *rōjū*, Manabe Akikatsu, was designated as emissary, and even that worthy delayed almost two months before setting out for Kyoto. The court struck back; its directive to the bakufu, in a totally unprecedented breach of channels and security, was transmitted to the Kyoto representative of Mito and sent on to Edo by him to the consternation of the bakufu, which forbade Mito to divulge its contents to other quarters. At Kyoto, low-ranking agents of the daimyo who had favored the Hitotsubashi cause urged on inexperienced courtiers in misguided efforts to have the court insist on a reversal of bakufu policy, the dismissal of Ii, and a reversal of the Harris treaty. Ii Naosuke had his own agent in Kyoto, one Nagano Shuzen, who reported all this activity to Edo and helped provoke the counterstrokes that followed.

By October, bakufu arrests of those agents began. Umeda Umpin, Mito agents, and others were arrested in Kyoto. Hashimoto Sanai, Matsudaira Shangaku's chief emissary, was arrested in Edo. The men arrested in Kyoto were transported to Edo in cages and under heavy guard, and once there they were severely interrogated by a judicial board of five that sat for only the most serious offenses. The sentences handed down were unexpectedly severe and made this one of the largest crackdowns in the history of the bakufu. Over one hundred men were sentenced. Eight were condemned to death, and six of them were beheaded like ordinary criminals.

While all this was in progress, *rōjū* Manabe was working to wring approval from a sullen and reluctant court for the treaty that had already been signed. His hand was strengthened as bakufu punishments approached the court itself, with a round of changes and retirements in courtier positions there. In the end the reluctant sovereign agreed that because the treaties had been signed, it was too late to stop them.

Ii Naosuke has had harsh treatment at the hands of historians, especially those who wrote before 1945. His personal rigidity and harshness were untypical of bakufu procedure and, indeed, of most of Japanese administrative history with its preferences for collegial decision making. Moreover, his victims included some of the ideal types revered by the future Meiji state. The Fukui counselor Hashimoto Sanai, trusted assistant of Matsudaira Shungaku, was clearly carrying out instructions from his lord. In character and attainments he had won universal respect and admiration. Despite this, his sentence read: He "should have remonstrated with his lord that this was a serious matter . . . and he acted without respect for Bakufu will."[13]

Even more serious and tragic in popular imagination was the fate of the Chōshū scholar-teacher Yoshida Shōin. Yoshida began as a low-ranking but brilliant student of military science. After traveling to Nagasaki and elsewhere he concluded that these places would not suffice to protect Japan. He came under the influence of the modernizer Sakuma Shōzan and tried to persuade Perry to take him back to America with him for a period of study in 1854. After Perry maintained his commitments to the shogunate and refused this request as illegal, Yoshida was discovered, arrested, and sent back to Chōshū. There he was given partial freedom to teach in a village academy that came to number among its students many of the future Meiji leaders. Furious at what he considered bakufu disrespect to Kyoto and the servility to foreigners shown in signing the Harris treaty, Yoshida schemed with Umeda Umpin to engineer the assassination of Manabe on his way to Kyoto. Arrested and extradited to Edo, Yoshida was executed after his fellow inmate Hashimoto Sanai. He became posthumously exalted as a martyr for emperor and country.

Postwar historians, however, have been kinder to Ii Naosuke. Freed from the compulsion of earlier historiography to side with those who fell in the "Ansei purge" and able to see courage and intelligence on both sides of the struggle that was to rend the political fabric of mid-century Japan, later writers have softened their denunciations. Yet in any case, Ii Naosuke did not long survive his triumph. On a snowy day in March 1860, as his entourage approached the Sakurada gate of the great Edo Chiyoda Castle, a group of swordsmen, seventeen from Mito and one from Satsuma, cut through his guards, whose swords were covered to protect them from the late winter snow, and took the *tairō*'s head. The assassins' manifesto attacked the regent personally rather than the government he had headed, but it made it very clear

13 Wilson, "Bakumatsu Intellectual: Hashimoto Sanai." The Japanese text charges Hashimoto with disrespect for the *kōgi*.

that Ii's crime had been that of indifference to the imperial will, and it urged all Tokugawa retainers to turn with shame to the sun goddess of Ise in penitence. The loyalist years had begun.

THE LOYALISTS

The purge that Ii Naosuke carried out had resulted in his murder; the persecuted loyalists had retaliated by assassinating the chief bakufu minister. These events ushered in a period of violence and terror that transformed the setting of late Tokugawa politics. The loyalists, known to their contemporaries and to history as *shishi* – men of high purpose – became an explosive element in local and national affairs and ended by serving as ideal ethical types for the ideology of the modern imperial state and also as models for young radicals in future periods of instability.

Shishi tended to be of modest rank, status, and income. Lack of status meant that they were little encumbered by official duty and office, which were reserved for higher samurai rank. They lived in a world that was less structured by ritual than was that of their superiors, and communication with men from other domains was also easier for them than it was for their superiors. Because the *shishi* were at the outer circumference of the ruling class, frustrations of limited opportunity and ritual humility often made them suspicious and critical of their cautious superiors. Poorly informed about the context of national diplomatic and political issues, they were inclined to the simplistic solutions of direct action. Calls for preparedness that accompanied the opening of Japan produced a lively expectation of war and led to a setting that was alive with rumor and that put new emphasis on the importance of the martial arts. Swordsmanship academies were crowded as never before with students, and together with tournaments they became settings for political bravado and self-assertion. The *shishi* were men of the sword.

The lower samurai's frustrations often meshed with the discontent of the rural samurai and village leaders. In the countryside, pseudo-samurai pretensions were symbolized by swords, surnames, and rudimentary scholarship. These could combine with the experience of administrative responsibility to encourage critical attitudes toward urban-based but underemployed samurai, sometimes with the conclusion that it was the leadership of the farm villages that really mattered. In Tosa, for example, a Shōya League of the 1840s produced complaints that summed up many of the frustrations and that harked back to a past order in which village leaders had carried out the court's commands without interference from castle town samurai. Tosa *shishi* included sons of rural leaders as well as lower samurai.[14]

Shishi learning varied widely, but it tended to include assertion of the primacy of sincerity demonstrated through action. The Satsuma hero Saigō Takamori was steeped in the views of Wang Yang-ming Confucianism which stressed the identity of knowledge and action. Others drew on popularized teachings of Chu Hsi and Mencius to emphasize the meaning of sincerity and a well-ordered polity and to draw quick conclusions from bakufu concessions to the imperialist powers and its apparent disregard of the wishes of the court. Although they were drilled in the virtue of loyalty and subordination (*meibun*) as the highest duty (*taigi*) of all, the *shishi* also accepted the retainer's obligation to correct his superiors when convinced of their errors. The bakufu itself accepted this in its death verdict against Hashimoto Sanai. He "should have remonstrated with his lord" instead of blindly carrying out his instructions in Kyoto. By the same logic, the *shishi* were ready to condemn bakufu officials for carrying out shogunal instructions in defiance of the sovereign's wishes. A popular history of Japan that was written from the standpoint of Confucian loyalism, Rai San'yō's *Nihon gaishi* (Unofficial history of Japan) circulated in increasing volume, first in its Chinese original and then in Japanese translation, to spread the praise of loyal servants of the court in former days. Rai Mikisaburō, a younger son of the historian, was executed in 1859, one of the victims of Ii Naosuke's purge.

The *shishi* began as loyal retainers, convinced of the identity of their lord's wishes and the desires of the court. Ii Naosuke's punishment of the daimyo who had advocated the Hitotsubashi cause and did their best to block the Harris treaty turned them against the bakufu minister in the name of loyalty to their lord. In the southwestern domain of Tosa, for instance, an oath signed in blood committed a group of young swordsmen to a loyalist party in the fall of 1861 with a statement that combined indignation at the humiliation of Japan by the barbarians and the punishment of "our former lord . . . who, instead of securing action, was accused and punished." "We swear by the gods," the statement concluded, "that if the Imperial Flag is once raised we will go through fire and water to ease the Emperor's mind,

14 Marius B. Jansen, "Tosa During the Last Century of Tokugawa Rule," in John W. Hall and Marius B. Jansen, eds., *Studies in the Institutional History of Early Modern Japan* (Princeton, N.J.: Princeton University Press, 1968), pp. 340–1.

carry out the will of our former lord, and purge this evil from our people."[15]

At the outset, ethnic nationalism, retainer loyalty, and imperial reverence could be combined in a devotion that was relatively free of moral dilemma. But once feudal loyalty seemed at variance with imperial reverence – when the daimyo chose the path of caution and pulled back from the loyalist cause – the *shishi* faced a difficult personal choice. Large numbers resisted renewed subordination to their superiors through flight from the domain jurisdiction, seeking protection and employment under the aegis of a domain perceived as more committed to the imperial cause (Chōshū long served as a protector of men from all over the country) or entering the employment of court nobles in Kyoto who had need for bodyguards, agents, and messengers as the political cauldron heated up. Participation in politics in this way was dangerous and often tragic for men who gave up the security of family, home, and safety, but it also proved stimulating and ennobling for many who contrasted the excitement of their new life with the tedium of the ritualized subordination that they had known at home. The Tosa activist Sakamoto Ryōma wrote his sister to contrast the importance of his activities with this old life at home, "where you have to waste your time like an idiot"; at another time he asserted that "the idea that in times like these it is a violation of your proper duty to put your relatives second, your domain second, to leave your mother, wife, and children – this is certainly a notion that comes from our stupid officials. . . . [But] you must know that one should hold the Imperial Court more dear than country, and more dear than parents."[16]

The loyalists did not have a structured view or program toward which they were working. They had slogans (of which the most important was *sonnō-jōi* – revere the emperor! drive out the barbarians!) but not programs. They were opposed to their authorities but not to authority; they were full of ethnic nationalism but only dimly aware of the possibilities of a true nation-state in which the two-sworded class would not stride forth as a special repository of virtue and privilege.

This point requires further comment. E. H. Norman's pioneering study of the Restoration[17] perceived a coalition of "lower samurai" and "merchants" at the center of the political movement, with implications

15 Marius B. Jansen, *Sakamoto Ryōma and the Meiji Restoration* (Princeton, N.J.: Princeton University Press, 1961), pp. 108–9. 16 Jansen, *Sakamoto*, pp. 174–5.

17 E. Herbert Norman, *Japan's Emergence As a Modern State: Political and Economic Problems of the Meiji Period* (New York: Institute of Pacific Relations, 1940 and later printings).

for future social change, but more recent writers have differed sharply over the utility of this as an analytical distinction. The "merchant" participation has proved even more difficult to examine, much less establish. W. G. Beasley's masterly summary of Restoration politics examined the evidence in a number of the most important domains to conclude:

There is, therefore, a valid connection between low-rank – rank below that of hirazamurai, which qualified a man for domain offices of some responsibility – and rebellion, terrorism, or the threat of violence. The rōnin who were the placard-posters, the demonstrators, the conspirators, the assassins were characteristically men of lower standing than the "politicians."

The same argument extends, Beasley wrote, to others whose "claim to samurai status was tenuous or even nonexistent: the village headmen, rich farmers, and merchants who had perhaps bought the right to use a family name and wear a sword."[18] Tokugawa status divisions had no provision for the political participation of such individuals, and to participate at all was to set aside authority and to ally oneself with kindred spirits who had at least some claim to status. Thus the Tosa loyalists included a goodly number of rural samurai (*gōshi*) (including Sakamoto) and village heads or their sons whose normal horizons of political awareness would have been expected to be limited to the valley within which their acreage lay.

Albert Craig, who restricted his focus to Chōshū, found the "lower samurai" phrase imprecise and without analytical value. "Almost any large movement of samurai would by necessity be a lower samurai movement," he wrote, and the conventional definition of "upper" would fit only seventy or eighty (out of five thousand, or counting rear vassals, ten thousand) Chōshū samurai families. Moreover, in Chōshū there were high-ranking loyalists and low-ranking conservatives. "The samurai class," Craig concluded, given its disparity, "could not act as a class, a gentry class, with common class interests."[19] Thomas Huber, who also studied Chōshū but limited his attention to the students of Yoshida Shōin's academy, defined "lower" as an income of two hundred *koku* or less to conclude that the Chōshū movement, which included commoner village administrators, represented the interests –

18 W. G. Beasley, *The Meiji Restoration* (Stanford, Calif.: Stanford University Press, 1972), p. 171.

19 Albert B. Craig, *Chōshū in the Meiji Restoration* (Cambridge, Mass.: Harvard University Press, 1961), pp. 112–13; and "The Restoration Movement in Chōshū," in Hall and Jansen, eds., *Studies in the Institutional History of Early Modern Japan*, pp. 363–73.

or at least the discontents – of the "service intelligentsia," thus refining and improving Norman's argument and position.[20]

Even when one grants the frustration and occasional fury of low-ranking members of the Tokugawa military elite and grants the importance of their enthusiasm and violence in energizing a political situation theretofore torpid and somnolent, one is reminded that the story that unfolded after the loyalist years was one of action and decisions taken by domains. Loyalists *as such* were brought under control after 1864 and required the cooperation of men who held power. *Han* policy was set by men of rank with access to the narrow elite that monopolized the highest offices. That elite seldom moved until it was convinced that the perils of inaction outweighed the risks of participation. At the last, the danger of failing to join a common front was that of exclusion from a new political order and structure. Regional and family self-interest had to be calculated with the greatest precision by men who inherited status, authority, and wealth. The *shishi* helped create an atmosphere in which movement was possible. Many, perhaps most, of them, perished in that work. Those who inherited the fruits of their labors were for the most part middle- and upper-ranking samurai who moved their *han* into positions in the years that followed.

Han policy and the logic of events seemed to enroll most samurai in some domains, notably Chōshū, under the loyalist banner before the Tokugawa fall. But in 1867 Chōshū had the most to lose and the most to gain. In other areas the scales were balanced differently. But just as many – indeed, far more – similarly placed samurai in other domains responded differently in other contexts, remaining aloof or following other banners. The bakufu responded to disorder and terror in Kyoto and Edo by recruiting and organizing *shishi* or *rōnin* who, seeing the Chōshū–Satsuma force as regional and "selfish," proved potent instruments of counterviolence. Lower samurai of the Tokugawa domain of Aizu, who served to keep the peace in Kyoto through the final Tokugawa years, were subject to the same class interests and frustrations as were their Chōshū counterparts and probably included as many advocates of exclusion and imperial loyalism among their number. But they responded to different regional and historical affiliations, and their domain provided the single most effective counter to Satsuma and Chōshū military strength until the Aizu Castle was put to the torch in

20 Thomas M. Huber, *The Revolutionary Origins of Modern Japan* (Stanford, Calif.: Stanford University Press, 1981).

the desperate siege of Wakamatsu in 1868 that ended the Aizu presence on the national scene.

COURT AND CAMP, DAIMYO STYLE

The domains of Satsuma, Chōshū, Tosa, and Saga furnished the early Restoration leadership. With the notable exception of Mito, which destroyed its strength in a civil war, remarkably few other *han* achieved a clear-cut presence or identity in the Restoration movement. Among these, Saga was a latecomer and was co-opted only after 1867. It may have joined the charmed circle chiefly because its proximity to the port of Nagasaki, which it was required to defend, helped bring some able and experienced leaders to the fore. Consideration of the sources of Restoration leadership therefore leads immediately to inquiry into the special characteristics of a very small number of domains. If samurai constraints and frustration were roughly comparable in all parts of Japan, what additional factors distinguished those southwestern domains and the few others that counted in the late Tokugawa years?

Factors of size and location come to mind immediately. Satsuma was second, Chōshū ninth, Saga tenth, Mito eleventh, and Tosa nineteenth in assessed productivity among the feudal domains. Distance and tradition helped create pride and autonomy. Large-scale resources were necessary for mounting a significant military force through the purchase of Western ships and guns in the 1860s. Satsuma, Chōshū, and Tosa also had disproportionately large numbers of samurai. Satsuma and Chōshu had been on the losing side in the struggles that brought the Tokugawa to power in the early seventeenth century; they suffered a loss of territory and had compressed a large military force into a reduced area. Also, the three domains were integrated territorial units with defensible borders along land communication routes that permitted vigilance over contacts with contiguous areas. Satsuma, at the extremity of southern Japan, was particularly famous for its own exclusion system. Each was a *tozama* domain, although Tosa's status was special because the Tokugawa founder had installed a man of his own selection after expelling his predecessor. Consequently, the Tosa lord sought some way of combining gratitude with warning and worked out the suggestion for shogunal resignation. Elsewhere, compunctions of loyalty were weaker. The entire samurai class of Satsuma and Chōshū and the lower ranks in Tosa, many of them rear vassals who had served the previous daimyo, harbored a centuries-old resentment of Tokugawa rule.

Remoteness and secure borders made for a greater degree of autonomy and of self-consciousness. "Han nationalism," to use Albert Craig's term, guaranteed that strong competitive urges operated to drive men on and to exacerbate fears of being left behind or out of whatever new political order might eventuate. Remoteness also made for a smaller role and presence in Edo, for higher costs and greater inconvenience attached to the central bakufu control mechanism of *sankin-kōtai*, and for reliance upon the Osaka market over that of the shogunal capital. Distance and size made possible relatively autonomous responses to bakufu and imperialist demands, as when Satsuma refused to make amends for the murder by its retainers of an English trader who happened along its line of march on horseback (the Richardson, or Namamugi incident), and when Chōshū tried to expel the foreigners by shelling ships along its shores without bakufu authorization. These incidents brought both domains face to face with the superiority of Western military technology, demonstrated by the British fleet against Kagoshima in 1863 and a foreign flotilla against the Chōshū Shimonoseki batteries the following year.

Remoteness had other consequences. At a time when money economy, economic change, and social dissolution were making the domains along the main-traveled parts of the Osaka and Edo plains, most of them held by Tokugawa houses, less feudal, social and economic relationships in southwestern Japan were still backward and traditional. The higher ratio of samurai to commoners in southwestern Japan could also be used to inhibit commoner complaint or participation; this was particularly so in Satsuma. Traditional authority structures provided an effective base for efforts to bolster the domain economy, tap more of its surplus for the regime, and speed military reforms. The Tempō reforms failed in bakufu territory, but Tempō fiscal and economic reforms in Satsuma and Chōshū left those domains in much stronger position for the competition that lay ahead. In Saga, too, the mid-century decades witnessed a successful campaign to redistribute land equally once again on the lines of the old Heian *kunden* system, a "land reform" program that spoke volumes for the ability of the feudal administration to control its most important resource.[21]

At mid-century the great fiefs of the southwest also enjoyed strong and able leadership. Throughout Japan able daimyo were few and far between in the late Tokugawa years, and in Edo itself shogunal power

21 See, for Chōshū, A. M. Craig, *Chōshū in the Meiji Restoration;* for Tosa, M. B. Jansen, *Sakamoto Ryōma;* and for Satsuma and other *han*, Ikeda Yoshimasa, "Bakufu shohan no dōyō to kaikaku," in *Iwanami kōza Nihon rekishi*, vol. 13 (*kinsei* 5), 174–207.

was entirely in the hands of surrogate bureaucrats during the reigns of Iesada and Iemochi. In Satsuma and Tosa, however, a fortunate accession to power of able men, products of the adoption system, introduced strong direction at the center. Saga too had an able daimyo, though the Chōshū lord was a cypher. What counted was the presence of a generous number of unusually able and adroit subordinates in each fief, men who did not hesitate to speak their minds.

This combination of historical, geographical, and economic circumstances helps to account for the few domains that took leading roles. But it does not explain why so few other domains, some more or less comparably endowed, took vigorous part in national politics. In Mito, where the loyalist teachings of the Confucianists and the personal prestige of Tokugawa Nariaki made for a leading role in the 1850s, an internal power struggle that destroyed domain unity combined with a Tokugawa affiliation to remove the *han* once Tokugawa Yoshinobu became a bakufu leader. In Fukui, also a related Tokugawa house (*shimpan*), Matsudaira Shungaku's early leadership gave way to watchful waiting and hoping for the moment when political conciliation would again be possible. But most daimyo – and indeed most upper samurai – witnessing the dangers that could accompany wrong judgments, preferred to conserve their resources and keep their counsel until the situation was clarified. There was no "anti-imperial" party, but there was a good deal of suspicion, much of it well founded, that those who professed loyalty to Kyoto were chiefly interested in their own advantage. For Tokugawa adherents, on the other hand, the twists and turns of bakufu policy made it both difficult and dangerous to follow a consistent and active line.[22]

The assassination of Ii Naosuke was followed by a series of efforts to bring court and bakufu together in a new and more cooperative structure. It did not succeed. For Edo, as Beasley points out, it meant "a bolstering of bakufu authority by the use of the imperial prestige," while to the great lords involved "it implied a renewed possibility of intervening in politics in the Emperor's name so as to achieve, among other things, an increase in baronial privilege."[23] Yet these efforts were important, for they led to the Bunkyū reforms of 1862, reforms which so changed the political balance of power that a recent study begins its consideration of the Tokugawa fall at that point. Meanwhile for others the hopes they engendered returned at the last to inspire the

22 Totman, "Fudai Daimyo and the Collapse of the Tokugawa Bakufu," *Journal of Asian Studies* 34 (May 1975): 581–91.
23 Beasley. *Meiji Restoration*, p. 177.

Tosa proposal under which the last shogun agreed to surrender his powers in 1867.

The proposals are usually grouped under the slogan *kōbu-gattai*, for reconciliation of court (*kō*) and camp (*bu*). The first of these to be proposed was put forward by Chōshū, where the official Nagai Uta persuaded his daimyo to urge that a new agreement make it clear that the shogunate ruled "in accordance with the orders of the court," which would thus set policy while the bakufu carried it out. Having secured agreement with this in Kyoto, Nagai proceeded to Edo for negotiation. But there he was soon overtaken by a Satsuma proposal and mission that seemed to promise Kyoto a good deal more. This proposed pardon for all those who had been punished by Ii Naosuke in 1858 and dismissal of the principal bakufu leaders who had held office since then. More important, the court would designate certain daimyo to represent its interests in Edo; the two principal figures of the succession quarrel, Matsudaira Shungaku, daimyo of Echizen (whose vassal Hashimoto Sanai had been executed for advancing the candidacy of Tokugawa Yoshinobu), and Tokugawa Yoshinobu (Keiki) himself were to be appointed to newly created offices. Yoshinobu, who had been denied the shogunate, would serve as guardian (*kōken*) for young Iemochi, while Shungaku would be Supreme Councillor (*seiji sōsai*). This set of proposals was brought to Edo by the court noble Ōhara Shigetomi, and the escort was provided by a large Satsuma military force headed by the regent Shimazu Hisamitsu.

These plans had antecedents in thinking that began in the years following the arrival of Townsend Harris under the urgency of military reform. The great lord who had lobbied for the succession of Tokugawa Yoshinobu wanted cooperation to replace the costly control measures of the Tokugawa system. Yamauchi Yōdō, the Tosa daimyo, had proposed a seven-year moratorium on *sankin-kōtai* duty for daimyo at that time, and many large domains had developed steps for financial reform to make military spending possible. Saga had pushed the implementation of its land division program, and Tosa and Satsuma had developed programs for central merchandising of regional specialties to increase domain income – Satsuma with sugar from its southern islands and Tosa with its camphor and indigo. Modification of the ritualized alternate attendance at Edo would be the best possible economy measure.

Unfortunately the strains generated by Ii Naosuke's purge and the enforced absence through punishment of several of the daimyo who were most important to the Ansei reforms had changed this pattern of planned cooperation into one of competitive assertion and rivalry. The

Ōhara-Satsuma mission itself was soon followed by a third, this time accompanied by troops from Tosa.

While Yamauchi Yōdō was still in forced retirement, his chief minister had been assassinated by loyalists, who promptly moved to the center of the decision structure that surrounded the young successor daimyo. Takechi Zuizan, the leader and founder of the Tosa Loyalist Party, now proposed in his young lord's name that the court nobles Sanjō Sanetomi and Anenokoji Kintomo proceed to Edo with orders from the court that the bakufu prepare to expel the foreigners immediately. These plans went on to propose establishing the Osaka-Kyoto (Kinai) plain as the private realm of the court, granting the court clear political primacy, ending *sankin-kōtai* so that the daimyo could spend their money for defense, establishing seven or eight of the daimyo of southwestern Japan in Kyoto as support for the court, and establishing a private defense force of courageous *rōnin* from all parts of the country to defend the court. Costs of all this would be met by ordering wealthy merchants in the Osaka area to put up the money. This proposal was one of the most sweeping the loyalists put forward, and it serves to illustrate the way thinking became radicalized. But it did not get much farther, for much to Takechi's surprise his former daimyo, Yamauchi Yōdō, moved skillfully to oust the Tosa loyalists after he was released from house arrest. After lengthy interrogation Takechi was ordered to commit suicide in 1865 for insubordination.[24]

The Chōshū and Satsuma initiatives, however, produced results before the Sanjō-Tosa procession had reached Edo, and the changes that came are known as the reforms of the Baunkyū era. These changed the political setting so basically that a recent study of the Tokugawa fall begins with the assertion that "the Tokugawa bakufu's time of troubles began early in 1862 . . . [when] a series of political changes . . . reduced the bakufu to a secondary role in national politics."[25] In terms of politics, the most important changes were the implementation of the Ōhara mission proposals: Matsudaira Shungaku of Fukui was appointed *seiji sōsai* (Supreme Councillor) and Hitotsubashi (Tokugawa) Yoshinobu *kōken* (guardian), the latter appointment specifically announced as made at "imperial request." Japan's problems with the imperialist powers, the extent of court disaffection, the insecurity of top-level bakufu officials, several of whom had been assassin's targets, and the appearance of the strong Satsuma military force in Edo to accompany Ōhara had combined to suggest to

24 Jansen, *Sakamoto Ryōma*, pp. 131–7, and Ikeda, "Bakufu shohan," pp. 184–6.
25 Totman, *Collapse of the Tokugawa Bakufu*, p. 3.

bakufu officials the wisdom of retreating from Ii's insistence on traditional bureaucratic direction of bakufu and national affairs. Shungaku and Hitotsubashi were in any event from Tokugawa houses, and the appointments did not at first seem an undue participation by outsiders in bakufu and national affairs.

Unfortunately for those who thought in these terms, Shungaku saw his appointment as a first step in a sharing of power by the great lords who had been his allies in the succession dispute a few years earlier. He began by insisting on a general pardon for those who had been punished by Ii; having carried his point he went on to demand punishment for the bakufu officials who had helped direct the purge. There followed a stream of demotions. The house of Ii lost its mandate as protector of Kyoto, and Ii's retainer and adviser Nagano Shuzen was ordered to commit suicide. Soon additional pressures represented by the Sanjō-Tosa mission persuaded bakufu officials of the need to show good faith with the court by extending the punishments to almost all officials who had worked with the successor governments that followed the murder of Ii and to the men who had negotiated the treaties with the foreigners. In considering the remarkable equanimity with which most Tokugawa fudai saw the bakufu collapse a few years later, it is well to keep in mind the demoralizing effect that turnabouts of this sort must have had on vassals' loyalty and resolution.

The 1862 reforms went on to a series of steps that were cumulatively disastrous to bakufu primacy. The first of these was the moderation and virtual abolition of the system of *sankin kōtai,* undertaken in order to permit economies to facilitate domain military preparedness. The period of daimyo residence at Edo was reduced to one hundred days in three years. Many of the lords, freed from duty at Edo, now transferred their attention to Kyoto, which thereafter competed with Edo as center of a national politics. Within a year bakufu officials were trying to undo the effects of this; two years later the bakufu asked all daimyo to send their families to Edo as before. Some lesser lords complied, but the more important domains showed no interest in returning to the restrictions of earlier times. By 1865–6 the great lords hardly granted the bakufu the courtesy of a reply to its summons, and a bakufu survey of Edo mansions turned up the fact that some of the lesser lords had gone so far as to rent their residences to commoners.[26]

Another step that was undertaken to repair relations with Kyoto involved a visit to the imperial court by the young shogun Iemochi.

26 Ibid., p. 141.

No shogun had visited Kyoto since the third shogun Tokugawa Iemitsu had traveled south with a mighty retinue in 1634 to demonstrate his power. Iemochi's trip to Kyoto was a dramatic contrast to that of his ancestor. Iemitsu had gone to Kyoto to show his might; he had acted to sever daimyo connections with the court, and redirected daimyo residence and attendance from Kyoto to Edo.[27] Iemochi, however, went to Kyoto as part of an attempt to gain strength from reconciliation at a time when daimyo attention was shifting from Edo back to Kyoto. In one point the visits were comparable. Iemitsu had taken an imperial princess as consort, and the same course was now suggested for Iemochi. In an effort to further cement relations with the court an imperial princess (Kazu no Miya) was proposed as consort for the young shogun. The arrangements were made in apparent disregard of her own reluctance and that of the Emperor Kōmei, and the matter served to inflame loyalist indignation further as a demonstrate of shogunal disrespect.

Iemochi's trip was planned to be a short one for reasons of economy and politics; bakufu optimists hoped that his presence would serve to reestablish the awareness of bakufu primacy in Kyoto. It worked out quite differently; before the young shogun could be extricated from the intrigues at the imperial capital four months had gone by. He was obliged to show ritual humility in processions to imperial shrines, and his ceremonial deference to the emperor left little doubt of his subordinate position. In 1634, in contrast, it was the emperor who had called at the shogun's Nijō castle. The shogun's position had always depended in the last analysis on force; it was therefore significant that bakufu ministers now thought it desirable to secure a specific court authorization of shogunal authority. Unfortunately, that commission included orders to drive out the barbarians. Further instructions reminded Iemochi to consult with daimyo on major questions and to respect "lord and vassals" relations. "Not since the Muromachi period," Totman observes, "had a shogun been given such a patently empty title of authority."[28]

The shogun's visit was an important step in the growing transfer of political centrality of Kyoto. Within months of his return to Edo proposals for a second visit were underway; he was to die at Osaka, still a youth, on his third visit in 1866. More and more daimyo now established headquarters in the ancient capital. Kyoto became a prime

27 Asao Naohiro, "Shogun seiji no kenryoku kōzō," in *Iwanami kōza Nihon rekishi*, vol. 10 (*kinsei* 2), pp. 13ff.
28 Totman, *Collapse*, p. 58.

object of political and military planning for the southwestern domains. It was preeminently the preserve, at least until 1864, of the radical loyalists and *shishi* who made its streets unsafe for suspected enemies. In one celebrated instance of symbolic rebellion, they lopped the heads off statues of the Ashikaga shoguns. In order to retain control of the capital the bakufu appointed Matsudaira Katamori, young lord of Aizu, protector (*shugo*) of the city in 1862, and as a result he became an important actor in the politics of the next decade. So important did Kyoto become to Edo policy that the fifteenth and last shogun, Tokugawa Yoshinobu, spent his entire period in office in the Kyoto area and never once felt free to take time for a return to Edo. All this added urgency to the bakufu's economic problems. The Kyoto visits of Iemochi were ruinous for bakufu finances, and the necessity of maintaining an ever larger force and presence three hundred miles from the Tokugawa heartland worsened an already difficult situation.

A fourth product of the Bunkyō reforms was cooperation with the great daimyo. This has had indeed been at the very heart of the program of proposals grouped as *kōbu-gattai* from the first, and it constituted the platform on which the last shogun based his resignation in 1867. The great lords that mattered included, in addition to Matsudaira Shungaku and Tokugawa Yoshinobu, a number of leading lords: Yamauchi Yōdō of Tosa, Shimazu Hisamitsu of Satsuma, Date Munenari of Uwajima, Mōri Yoshichika of Chōshū, and Matsudaira Katamori of Aizu. They were intermittently drawn into conference to discuss court-bakufu relations and displomatic problems. In theory this was supposed to prevent unilateral, "selfish" bakufu direction. But the meetings, which began in 1862 and continued sporadically thereafter, produced no real results. There was no agreed-upon program of procedure, and the lords themselves were at least as "selfish" as the bakufu, usually retiring to their domains when things did not go well. The Tokugawa members, meanwhile, inherited the suspicion of bureaucratic "regulars" in Edo. The first attempt ended particularly badly when Matsudaira Shungaku, Supreme Councillor who had brought the whole program into being, resigned and returned to Fukui, followed by a bakufu order that he place himself under house arrest. He was pardoned by the summer of 1863 and remained a major figure, but then and later his program of conciliar cooperation had no real basis in regional interest and bureaucratic politics. As far as bakufu leaders in Edo were concerned, Shungaku and the others were outsiders whose interest in and loyalty to the Tokugawa cause was quite different from their own. In addition, haughty daimyo had great difficulty in controlling irritation and overcoming disagreement. Confrontation was not a congenial mode of resolution for them. A system without provisions for retreat and conciliation found them bargaining by absence and boycotting meetings. Most important of all, however, was the fact that the Western pressure left no slack for the resolution of differences. The insistence of court xenophobes on undoing the treaties clashed directly with the deadlines that had been agreed upon with the Western powers.

The Bunkyū program foundered most importantly on the issue of foreign policy. Throughout most of the negotiation about restructuring power between Edo and Kyoto, Japan was facing diplomatic problems and military threats that required more effective central-government decision making at the very time that power was becoming more diffuse. Important figures at the Kyoto court never wavered in their distaste for the treaties that had been signed with the Western powers, and an inevitable effect of the increased attention to court wishes in the rhetoric of 1862 and 1863 was subscription to promises, however ambiguously worded, to get rid of the foreign plague.

The Ansei treaties opened to foreign trade Yokohama (Kanagawa), Nagasaki, and Hakodate; within four years (by January 1863) Osaka, Hyōgo (Kobe), Niigata, and Edo were to be opened. Hakodate proved of little importance, and foreigners soon lost interest in Niigata, but Osaka was a national center and located, together with Hyōgo, close to the imperial court at Kyoto. In the spring of 1861 the bakufu sent a mission to Europe to ask for delay in the opening of additional ports, and an attack on the life of Andō Nobumasa, just after the mission had sailed, underscored its assertions about domestic difficulties as grounds for the request. Trade had not yet assumed major proportions, and even Rutherford Alcock, British consul general and later minister, thought the request reasonable. A protocol delaying further openings until 1868 was worked out as a result.[29]

The agreement unfortunately unraveled quickly. Within Japan competitive jockeying for favor at court produced more extreme demands for exclusion of foreigners, while on the spot "exclusion" in the form of samurai and *rōnin* terrorist attacks on foreigners (and, in 1863, on the British legation itself) produced a negative response on the part of the imperialist powers. At Kyoto demands for exclusion were set in motion to embarrass the bakufu, which then confounded its critics by

29 Beasley, *Select Documents on Japanese Foreign Policy 1853–1868* (London: Oxford University Press, 1955), pp. 1–93, provides the most incisive account.

agreeing to exclusion even after many great lords had backed away from the prospect of unsuccessful war.

The Satsuma regent, Shimazu Hisamitsu, emerged as a force for moderation. On his way into Kyoto in 1862 his men crushed a *rōnin* conspiracy in which his retainers had taken a leading role, and upon his return from Edo (whither he had conducted the court noble Ōhara) he warned of the impossibility of exclusion. Unfortunately his samurai had also taken a major step in strengthening English policy by their murder of Richardson on the way back to Kyoto. Thereafter Hisamitsu was preoccupied with the impending threat of British reprisal (which took the form of shelling and burning of his castle town of Kagoshima), and he helped destroy the hopes for a successful council of great lords by leaving Kyoto for Satsuma.

In Chōshū during this same period the pendulum swung from conservatism to radicalism. The initial Chōshū initiative represented by the proposals of Nagai Uta had failed before the more sweeping counter initiative of Satsuma; Nagai was disgraced, retired, and ultimately ordered to commit suicide. By summer of 1862 Chōshū stood as the principal protector and instigator of radical *shishi* and *rōnin* activities at Kyoto. In the latter part of 1862 Chōshū strength was joined by that of Tosa after the loyalists had taken control of that domain.

Thus it happened that, as has been described, the Tosa-Sanjō mission to Edo carried with it the clearest call yet for immediate and unconditional exclusion of foreigners from Japan. The chief bakufu representatives in Kyoto, Matsudaira Katamori (guardian of Kyoto) and Tokugawa Yoshinobu (shogunal guardian), were inclined to the view that the bakufu would have to announce agreement with this demand to show sincerity, and meanwhile look for some way of delaying its implementation, but the regular bakufu officials at Edo were aghast at the dangers involved in even a verbal pledge of exclusion. Edo leaders were operating under the guns of foreign warships in Edo bay and in fear of an English bombardment of their city when they hurriedly agreed to pay over to Great Britain an indemnity for the murder (by Satsuma men, it will be remembered) of Richardson in the spring of 1863, just as Tokugawa Yoshinobu was returning from Kyoto where he had agreed to a court demand for a promise of expulsion. It seems probable that Yoshinobu and other officials hoped they could avoid a clear deadline for action, and that even when they accepted, reluctantly, the court-imposed date (June 25, 1863) they thought of it as a date on which negotiations would commence (and inevitably fail). In any event they passed it along to the daimyo but with instructions to avoid hostilities.

In Chōshū, however, the extremist-dominated administration seized the opportunity for full compliance and opened fire on an American merchant ship at anchor in the Shimonoseki straits and later on French and Dutch vessels as well. Thus the *kōbu-gattai* program ended in a shambles: the Satsuma lord in Kagoshima vainly trying to prepare for a British attack on his city; Matsudaira Shungaku, author of the program, in retreat in his domain in Fukui; the bakufu verbally committed to exclusion at the same time that it was paying damages to Great Britain for actions it had not committed; and a defiant Chōshū determined to carry out exclusion on its own.

THE TREATY PORTS AND FOREIGN INFLUENCE

The Western powers had created the bakufu's political problems, and they remained to complicate them by their presence in the ports that had been opened. From the time that Yokohama, Nagasaki, and Hakodate were opened to trade in 1859, the bakufu found itself faced with insoluble dilemmas in having to yield to foreign pressures at the same time that it was being pressured to end the foreign threat. The foreign presence, however, also contained elements of hope for the bakufu: Tariffs provided a new source of central income, and the purchase of foreign weapons and foreign assistance in training soldiers and sailors was more easily available to the bakufu than to other governments in Japan. But arrangements for capitalizing on these opportunities were slow in being planned and worked out, and long before they might have helped restore Tokugawa political and military primacy, the negative aspects of the foreign presence had dealt mortal blows to some of the institutional aspects of Tokugawa power.

In some ways, however, the Tokugawa political institutions proved surprisingly resilient in their capacity to accommodate the problems that the mid-nineteenth century brought, for the tradition of seclusion contained few of the expectations of international hierarchy and national centrality that bedeviled contemporary Chinese efforts to accommodate institutions to international society.[30]

From the first, Abe Masahiro entrusted negotiation with the Americans to men he had selected for their ability. By the summer of 1858 a new magistracy was set up to specialize in foreign affairs, the *gaikoku*

30 See, for China, Immanuel C. Y. Hsu, *China's Entrance into the Family of Nations: The Diplomatic Phase, 1858–1880* (Cambridge, Mass.: Harvard University Press, 1968); and Masataka Banno, *China and the West: 1858–1861, The Origins of the Tsungli Yamen* (Cambridge, Mass.: Harvard University Press, 1964).

bugyō, with the appointment of five men to serve in a collegial capacity. From then until 1867, when a more streamlined and responsible structure was worked out, a total of seventy-four officials served in it. This also demonstrates a difficulty: Institutional flexibility was there, but political instability and uncertainty made the post hazardous to occupy. Policy shifts required new teams, and the magistracy changed its occupants like a revolving door. The individual and career patterns of virtually all late-Tokugawa high officials show the political hazards. The board of *rōjū* showed a 100 percent turnover with the substitution of Ii for Hotta. Ambassadors sent to the United States in 1860 to ratify the Harris treaty disappeared into a (probably well deserved) obscurity upon their return to Japan. Lower-level interpreters and "technicians" like Fukuzawa Yukichi and Fukuchi Gen'ichirō, on the other hand, survived to travel again and become the commentators and pundits of the future.[31]

The bakufu sent a series of missions to the West in the 1860s. They became more frequent, more professional, and more serious. The first, in 1860, included seventy-seven men. The discovery that life was possible in the West without mountains of straw sandals and the full panoply of ritual that accompanied Tokugawa society made it possible to be more selective with future missions. In 1882, thirty-eight men went, the interpreters for a second time; this group stayed longer, worked harder, and learned more. Mission followed mission, and a sixth was abroad at the time of the shogun's fall in 1867. By then a number of leading domains, including Satsuma and Chōshū, had smuggled students abroad to study. It will be remembered that Yoshida Shōin, the Chōshū martyr, had himself wanted to sail with Perry to learn about the West. The shogunate too sent students to Leiden to study. Upon his return, one, Nishi Amane, was charged with drawing up a modern charter for the shogunal regime. Japan had an exhibit at the Paris Exposition of 1867, as did Satsuma, which sent its own exhibit and tried to work out independent status as ruler of the Ryūkyū Islands. The bakufu rescinded its ban on the construction of oceangoing ships as early as 1853: It permitted Japanese exhibitors to go to Paris and buried the last of the seclusion provisions in June 1866 with a tariff convention that removed all restrictions on Japanese trading at the open ports, on Japanese purchase of foreign ships and employment of foreigners, and on Japanese travel abroad. In legal

31 For figures of officials, *Dokushi sōran* (Tokyo: Jimbutsu ōraisha, 1966), pp. 648–51. Eiichi Kiyooka, trans., *The Autobiography of Fukuzawa Yukichi* (Tokyo: Hokuseidō Press, 1948), and many other studies. For Fukuchi, James L. Huffman, *Fukuchi Gen'ichirō* (Honolulu: University of Hawaii Press, 1979).

and institutional terms, in other words, the bakufu was able to move speedily to dismantle the barriers it had established between Japan and the outer world.

Politically it was another matter. The readiness of the bakufu officials to build bridges with Kyoto at the cost of the careers of the officials who had negotiated and approved the early stages of the opening meant that foreign affairs specialists' careers showed a dizzying, roller-coaster sequence. Obscurantism and xenophobia among the two-sworded men who cursed the foreign presence meant that it was dangerous to be known as an expert in the new specializations associated with the West. Fukuzawa Yukichi found himself in fear of his life when he returned from Europe and America with the material that he made into his best-selling book, *Seiyō jijō* (Conditions in the West). Prominent consultants like Sakuma Shōzan and Yokoi Shōnan who had the ear of decision makers were murdered on suspicion of being pro-Western and even, in Yokoi's case, pro-Christian. The most trusted retainer could find himself ordered into suicide when the wind changed for his lord.

Yet for those who had access to foreign travel or, in time, the products of such travel in books like Fukuzawa's, the power of Japan's overseas adversaries provided convincing proof of the need to open Japan in order to strengthen its institutions and arms. Nor was the evidence all baleful. Fukuzawa found much in the West to praise: George Washington was almost a culture hero in late Tokugawa Japan; so, too, was Peter the Great. The West offered attraction as well as repulsion. Repulsion was close to hand on the Shanghai coast. Japanese who traveled to Shanghai on missions to buy ships and arms for their domains saw in the conditions at Shanghai a glaring example of humiliation and insult they were determined to avoid for their own country. Others recognized power: Inoue Kaoru, a Chōshū loyalist and future Meiji leader, recognized in the "forest of masts" in the Shanghai harbor sure evidence that exclusion could never succeed, and Takasugi Shinsaku, his superior in that movement, was shocked by the incidence of Western arrogance and superiority he encountered in Shanghai.

Nevertheless few Japanese made that trip, and none were more consistent in xenophobic instincts than the court nobles and their loyalist allies. Iwakura Tomomi, who had worked for the success of a reconciliation with the bakufu and helped arrange the shogun's marriage with Kazu no Miya, found himself out of office and forced into hiding to protect himself from angry *shishi.*

The representatives of the Western powers were quick to credit the erratic course of Japanese politics to dishonesty and deception. Rutherford Alcock, who initially favored accommodating the bakufu's requests to delay the openings of additional ports, changed from an advocate of accommodation to one of retribution. Japan's inability to protect foreigners was seen as bakufu unwillingness to do so, and security was sought in the presence of foreign detachments – Britain's came to number fifteen hundred men, and French units added several hundred more. These inevitably brought new problems and resentments with them. In 1864 the arrival of Harry Parkes as British minister brought to Japan one of the most vigorous and choleric of the China-coast specialists in gunboat diplomacy. Parkes soon developed contempt for the bakufu's inability to control the daimyo and domestic violence, and before long he added doubts about the bakufu's *de jure* authority to the clear evidence of its deficiencies in de facto authority. Leon Roches, the French minister who preceded Parkes by a few months, on the other hand, never showed the slightest doubt about bakufu legitimacy and detected an opportunity for French leadership in providing military assistance, economic advice, and institutional suggestions to the Tokugawa leaders. Yet even Roches was quick to join his colleagues in joint demands for bakufu concessions, and he warned Tokugawa officials that it would be folly for them to try to stand against the foreigners' wishes. The foreign presence thus provoked antiforeign incidents, which in turn brought demands for additional concessions, with the result that the imperialist presence became a one-way ratchet opening Japan. It was a process that wounded the bakufu more than it did the daimyo, for it was the bakufu that claimed, but could not exercise, full authority. Meanwhile, the evidence of foreign influence and the fears of more to come stimulated and fed a sense of danger and crisis among the Japanese elite. This was only natural. In addition to the background information about the fate of China, there were stories closer at hand. There was a Russian "occupation" of Tsushima for several months in 1861, and the possibility of future danger in a contest between Great Britain and France for leadership, the one favoring the great lords and the other helping the bakufu.

The economic impact of the opening of the ports on the social unease and political turbulence of mid-century Japan requires particular attention. Japan entered the world trade system at its point of greatest growth and at a time when the English Industrial Revolution was the chief locomotive of the trade expansion. The nineteenth century saw an exponential growth in the rate of world trade: Beginning with the 1820s, the growth rates for the successive decades were roughly 33 percent, 50 percent, 50 percent, 80 percent (for the 1850s), and 44 percent for the 1860s, when the Civil War in the United States slowed trade. Exports constituted an ever-larger part of England's product, surpassing 60 percent in the 1850s. The unequal treaties with non-Western countries were important instruments of that advance. Persia (in 1836 and 1857), Turkey (in 1838 and 1861), Siam (in 1855), China (in 1842 and 1858), and Japan (in 1858), entered that system in quick succession. Commercial arrangements that had been worked out for other areas were easily and speedily applied to Japan. The Peninsula and Oriental Steamship Company (founded in 1840) steamers added Yokohama to their calls. At Yokohama and, secondarily, at Nagasaki, the trading houses, agencies, and banks that had been set up along the China coast extended their networks and assigned their men to the newly opened ports of Japan.

From the first the Japan trade exceeded the modest expectations that had been held of it. In 1860, imports stood at 1.66 million and exports at 4.7 million Mexican dollars, respectively; five years later, exports had quadrupled, and imports were up ninefold. At a time when world trade was complicated by the American Civil War and the China trade was disturbed by the Taiping Rebellion, the unexpected growth of Japan drew pleased surprise from British consular and trading representatives and doomed any hopes that bakufu optimists might have had of Western willingness to accept reduction or forgo the planned opening of additional ports.[32]

Japan's trade grew rapidly because of the integration and efficiency of the national market. Goods flowed naturally and easily to the new markets at the new ports. The same flow complicated and ultimately defeated bakufu efforts to control the course of trade and channel its profits into politically desirable hands. Indeed, foreign trade in open ports served to accelerate a shift from metropolitan commerce, channeled through authorized guilds, to regional centers of production. This shift was long in process, and it had long been a subject of contention and dispute.[33] Unfortunately for the bakufu, the metropolitan guilds were important to its control of the economy and to the profits of the merchant houses whose forced loans (*goyōkin*) it called on to meet the rising need for cash. An effort was made to channel trade through Edo in 1860, when "five products" (thread, cloth, wax, hair and lamp oil, and grains) were to be shipped through Edo. But as the

32 Nakamura Tetsu, "Kaikokugo no bōeki to sekai shijō," in *Iwanami kōza Nihon rekishi*, vol. 13 (*kinsei* 5), pp. 95–6, 111.

33 For a dispute of 1823 in which 1,007 villages resisted the jurisdiction of Osaka guilds, see William B. Hauser, *Economic Institutional Change in Tokugawa Japan: Osaka and the Kinai Cotton Trade* (New York: Cambridge University Press, 1974), pp. 97ff.

trade grew, its largest items were raw silk and tea. In 1863, at a time when the bakufu was ostensibly committed to closing Yokohama, the silk thread guild sought relief from taxes levied on its products that did not move through Edo, and for a time it virtually managed to close Yokohama by boycotting shipments. A year later the bakufu tried to reassert its authority by banning the planting of additional mulberry trees on lands under its control. Such efforts drew quick protests from the representatives of the foreign powers, so much so that some historians suggest that the naval demonstration against Chōshū in 1864 had as a secondary aim the intimidation of the bakufu's efforts to channel trade. The foreigners' demand coincided with that expedition and brought abandonment of the ruling that products move through Edo channels. The following year the powers succeeded in getting tax and tariff agreements against the imposition of internal transit taxes on goods bound for the ports. Foreign trade thus had the effect of weakening the bakufu's ability to control domestic commerce and opened Japan to the ports as well as opening the ports to the foreigners.[34]

The market for Japanese silk was made larger by the European silkworm blight that resulted in large exports of cards of silkworm eggs in 1865 and 1866. The consequence was a dramatic rise in the price of eggs and thread for the Nishijin weavers of Kyoto, whose raw material prices doubled almost overnight. The unemployment that resulted became an element in several urban riots. Urban handicraft laborers and fixed-income groups were the chief victims of price instability in products that had long seemed stable.

Foreign trade was, however, only one element in a wild inflation that sent the prices of all essentials spiraling upward in the early 1860s. The major element in this instability was the bakufu's need to recoin. A closed country had been able to maintain a 1:5 gold-to-silver ratio as long as neither could be exported. But the open ports brought in a flood of Mexican silver dollars from nearby Shanghai, where the international rate of 1 to 15 prevailed. The disruption that followed, in what one author called the "great gold rush," was countered by the bakufu in a basic recoinage program that was punctuated by charge and countercharge between foreigners and Japanese officials. Gold, silver, and copper coinage all were devalued. At the same time the hard-pressed bakufu grew more liberal with its permission to the daimyo to mint their own coin and to print paper currency. Currencies of this sort were not supposed to circulate beyond domain borders, but the integration of Japan's commercial economy guaranteed their

34 Ishii Takashi, *Bakumatsu bōeki shi no kenkyū* (Tokyo: Nihon hyōronsha, 1943).

spread. Satsuma, for instance, minted millions of copper coins and profited hugely from them. Counterfeit coinage added to the problem. At the time of the Restoration there were sixteen hundred issues of paper money in addition to the multiple varieties of coinage in circulation.[35] An economy that had always known a multiplicity of issues – the bakufu had first debased its coinage in the late seventeenth century and did so fairly periodically thereafter – in the short space of a decade now enormously increased the number, variety, and quality of its issues. Regular requirements of large payments to the foreign powers – for equipment, military needs, and indemnities – worsened the problem by skimming off a significant fraction of the gold and silver bullion available; such payments were assayed with the greatest care and exactness.

The consequence of all this was a galloping inflation that drove up the price of essentials, particularly rice, For the daimyo and upper samurai who measured their income in *koku,* this posed no discomfort, but the vast majority of the warrior class had long since had their incomes commuted to money. Emergency levies in the form of stipend reductions added to the injury. City dwellers were equally distressed. As early as 1862 the Edo city magistrate reported that inflation had raised commoners' living costs by 50 percent. Placards denouncing merchants and foreigners contributed to the tension and growing level of violence. During one month in 1863, "some twenty people were murdered in the city (Edo), and uncounted others were attacked and threatened. . . . One worrisome aspect of the situation was the extent to which the keepers of the peace were becoming the breakers of the peace."[36] In addition to undisciplined members of *rōnin* units, the bakufu had coopted to cope with policing problems, "members of the new Bakufu infantry units were suffering from demoralization, and some of them also became engaged in brawls and abuse of city folk." Open ports also brought disease. A major cholera epidemic coincided with the opening of the ports. Nationwide, births in 1861 were 12 percent fewer than the year before, and in some central provinces they were as much as 80 percent lower.[37] If one adds the earthquakes in Edo in 1854 and 1855 and the severe crop failures in 1866 and 1869, it becomes clear that the last years of Tokugawa rule were difficult for most Japanese.

35 This astounding count of currencies reflects the fact that none was ever fully withdrawn or retired, so that the money chargers had a constantly changing ratio to work out. See John McMaster, "The Japanese Gold Rush of 1859," *Journal of Asian Studies* 19 (May 1960): 273–87; and Peter Frost, *The Bakumatsu Currency Crisis*, Harvard East Asian Monographs, no. 36 (Cambridge, Mass.: Harvard University Press, 1970). 36 Totman, *Collapse*, p. 94.

37 Akira Hayami, "Population Movements," in M. B. Jansen and G. Rozman, eds., *Japan in Transition: From Tokugawa to Meiji* (Princeton, N.J.: Princeton University Press, 1986).

Finally, mention must be made of the monetary payments that the bakufu had to make to the foreign powers. The Richardson indemnity, paid for Satsuma's violence, came to £100,000. The Shimonoseki indemnity was set at an astounding 3 million Mexican dollars. "During the early days of the seventh month of 1865," Conrad Totman noted, "officials at Edo secretly transported to Yokohama some 30,000 to 40,000 *ryō* per day for delivery to the foreigners as another $500,000 payment on the indemnity."[38] Even this was only part of the very large sums that were shipped to the ports to pay for costs involved in new shipyards, guns, batteries and missions abroad in the next few years. National politics, the visits of the shogun to Edo, support to needy daimyo, rebuilding the Kyoto palace (destroyed by fire in 1854) and Edo Castle (destroyed by fire in 1863), and the movement of troops to the Kyoto area – all, or most such expenses, could be described as direct or indirect consequences of the opening of the ports. As the inflation worsened, all impoverished the city dwellers and also those on fixed incomes, and all weakened the political posture of the bakufu. Confidence can hardly have been raised by the series of impressive drives for special loans from merchants that were launched between 1862 and 1867; some specified numbers and amounts expected, and others established classes of contributions, for a total of 2.5 million *ryō* of gold, or three times the bakufu's regular annual income in specie.

BAKUFU RALLY

In 1863, loyalists at Kyoto and in the domains overplayed their hand. Satsuma recalcitrance against the English brought on the bombardment of Kagoshima, and Chōshū insistence on implementing exclusion without waiting for bakufu instructions resulted in the four-power naval demonstration at Shimonoseki and doomed the bakufu's efforts to stave off the opening of additional ports and to take up the closing of Yokohama. The Tosa loyalists' efforts to seize the initiative in the name of their former lord resulted in their punishment and elimination on grounds of insubordination after Yōdō was free to turn his attention again to the direction of domain affairs.

This series of miscalculations enabled the bakufu leaders in Kyoto to claim to be more effective implementers of the imperial orders for exclusion programs and to oust the loyalists from Kyoto. Their colleagues at Edo took heart from these developments and tried to

38 Totman, *Collapse*, p. 193.

reassert Tokugawa control more broadly. The latter part of 1863 and most of 1864 saw the bakufu leaders advocating reconciliation with the court, but this time to their own, and not to the great lords', advantage.

The loyalist military and political setbacks came in quick succession. In September 1863, Aizu troops staged a successful coup with the assistance of Satsuma to drive Chōshū units out of Kyoto and thereby make it impossible for Chōshū loyalist leaders to communicate with and claim the authorization of the court. In the Kyoto area two loyalist risings, one led by a Tosa figure and the other by a Fukuoka *shishi,* were crushed by bakufu units when they tried to rally rural leaders to the loyalist cause and set up a regional political base. Nearer to Edo, in the summer of 1864, a loyalist movement led by elements of the Mito samurai class that began as the product of confusion over bakufu purposes was exacerbated by obtuse leaders and erupted into full-scale civil war. When it was finally crushed five months later, the domain of Mito was for all practical purposes eliminated as an effective political force. Over one thousand men died in the fighting, and hundreds of the holdouts who had been taken prisoner were executed the next year. Also during the summer of 1864, Chōshū loyalist units tried to avenge their setback by staging a military invasion of Kyoto that was driven back, though at immense loss of property in the fighting and fires that swept through the ancient capital. Leading loyalist court nobles fled to Chōshū with the defeated loyalists, thus ridding the court of some of its most troublesome elements.[39] Though discomfited by the way that suppression efforts had revealed its military ineptness, the bakufu stood to gain from this new evidence of loyalist rashness and insubordination, and it now tried to demonstrate its own loyalty to the court's instructions. During the shogun's first visit to Kyoto, the bakufu had accepted the imperial order for exclusion, and Tokugawa Yoshinobu had been named supreme commander of Imperial Defense. Yoshinobu now assumed a steadily larger role in Kyoto, though not without incurring the suspicions of Edo bureaucrats that his apparent acceptance of expulsion was wrongheaded and impractical.

For a few months after the shogun's return to Edo in the summer of 1863, the bakufu basked in the discomfiture of its Chōshū critics. Unfortunately, however, Kyoto's approval still hinged on the imple-

39 The fullest account of the Mito rebellion in English can be found in Totman, *Collapse*, pp. 108–21. Chōshū loyalist reverses can be followed in Craig, *Chōshū in the Meiji Restoration*, pp. 208–46; Tosa in Jansen, *Sakamoto*, pp. 145–52; and loyalist reverses more generally in Beasley, *Meiji Restoration*, pp. 197–240.

mentation of promises of expulsion that were clearly impossible to keep. Within months the shogun was in receipt of an imperial order directing him to return to Kyoto to report on the progress he was making in closing Yokohama. Edo bureaucrats put off compliance as long as they could, citing the pressure of diplomatic efforts and national politics. Their arguments had a good deal of substance, for the early stages of the unrest that would result in the Mito rising were evident, and a disastrous fire had reduced much of the shogunal castle complex to ashes. But by early 1864 the shogun was back in Kyoto, now in much higher favor, privileged with a number of audiences with Emperor Kōmei and able, through his appointment of Matsudaira Katamori of Aizu as guardian of the capital and the exclusion of Chōshū, to exert exclusive authority over access to the court.

Unfortunately these "gains" were still premised on promises of expulsion. When the bakufu informed the daimyo that it had been decided to work toward the closing of Yokohama, it encouraged some to press for stronger measures at the same time that it convinced the foreign emissaries of its mendacity. And when bakufu bureaucrats tried to extend their reassertion of control over Kyoto with steps to move toward a return of daimyo residence at Edo, they received lame excuses that should have told them that their old political primacy could not be restored.

The high point of the new bakufu enthusiasm for *kōbu-gattai* – on its own terms – came in 1864 after the impetuous attack of the Chōshū loyalists had resulted in a devastated Kyoto and an indignant court purged of its most extremist nobles. Ironically, the bakufu's decision to punish Chōshū, which was demanded by the court in late summer, was made more attractive because of the prior demands of the foreign powers, who wanted retribution for the shelling of their vessels. At first the bakufu tried to tie that punishment to the closing of Yokohama, only to have the imperialist powers respond that they would then undertake it themselves at bakufu expense. They did so in late summer, before the bakufu expedition got under way, and submitted as their bill the demand for the indemnity of three million Mexican dollars, which they offered to waive in return for immediate opening of an additional port. Bakufu administrators, committed by their promises to the court to have fewer and not more ports, saw no alternative but to agree to pay the indemnity, although doing that also strained their understanding with the court.

The court now insisted that the bakufu go ahead with its own punishment of Chōshū, thereby adding further expenses to the heavily burdened regime. A ponderous allied force commanded by the Tokugawa daimyo of Owari, with Saigō Takamori of Satsuma as his chief of staff, got under way and seemed for a brief moment to represent the return of the kind of Tokugawa-led coalitions that had been formed in earlier centuries. Yet the conditions were very different; it was not in the interest of allied daimyo to deplete their own forces for bakufu purposes or to provide precedents for the future by crushing the Chōshū dissidents. Consequently, a compromise, one that disappointed both court hard-liners and Edo traditionalists, was worked out. The expedition was declared a success, and the armies were disbanded before Edo had given its full approval. Under the terms, Chōshū was to offer a formal apology, suppress the irregular militia companies that had attacked Kyoto, turn over the loyalist court nobles who had fled to Chōshū to Fukuoka for custody, and order the suicide of the three domain elders (*karō*) who had been responsible for the mistaken loyalist attacks. The nobles were duly transferred and the apology delivered, together with the heads of the three *karō*.

This settlement was acceptable to the bakufu leaders in Kyoto, but men in Edo anxious to reassert full Tokugawa primacy did not find it punishment enough. They wanted the terms strengthened to include the bringing of the Chōshū daimyo and his heir to Edo, as a symbol of submission and as a prelude to the return of other major daimyo to residence there. In short, the squelching of loyalist dissidence in the Kyoto and Edo areas and the encouraging evidence of ascendancy over Chōshū had brought personnel shifts that saw the hard-liners again take over bakufu policy positions. Some were seasoned specialists in foreign affairs, wanted an end to the charade of exclusion, and thought the time had come for closer coordination of policy planning and implementation. *Fudai* traditionalists in Edo were fully supportive of this and desirous that the influence of the "outsiders" who represented the Tokugawa cause in Kyoto be lessened. This medley of purposes produced a consensus that led to the preparation of a second Chōshū expedition, the death of young Iemochi in Osaka where he had gone to "lead" his armies, and the disasters of the second Chōshū campaign of 1866. By then daimyo awareness of Tokugawa purposes had also produced a very different political climate, one that made all such plans depend on a convincing military victory.

REGIONAL REFORM

With central power diminishing, the future of Japan was to be decided by a contest among regional powers, and the chief contestants were the great domains of southwest Japan and the bakufu itself. Preparation for the struggle was primarily military and secondarily administrative. What counted was the ability to marshal resources and to use them effectively within a social context of obsolescent status distinctions.

Military reforms had been anticipated in some of the frantic preparations for possible war that followed the coming of Commodore Perry. In the domain of Tosa in the 1850s, for instance, desperate efforts were mounted to procure and produce better weapons. Officials were sent to Satsuma to study efforts that had been made to build a reverbatory furnace for arms production. The most important Tosa innovation was probably the decision to form a people's corps (*mimpeitai*) made up of commoner formations commanded by rural samurai (*gōshi*). But these efforts were abandoned after a few years' experience; war with the West had not eventuated; and Yoshida Tōyō, the administrator who had sponsored these efforts, was assassinated by the loyalists. The loyalists who succeeded him in control of domain fortunes were men of the sword and not of the gun.

In Chōshū, however, loyalist extremism accommodated Western arms and methods. In that domain, military reforms began in the 1860s, and as extremism drove the *han* into solitary opposition to the bakufu and its allies, the sense of crisis served to speed up military reform. The innovation for which Chōshū was to become best known was the recruitment of militia companies (*shotai*) with complements drawn from both samurai and nonsamurai; of these the Kiheitai are the most famous. Some of these companies were set up by government action, and others collected around extremist samurai who lived away from the castle town. All the companies were made up of samurai and commoners. The commoners showed a wide range of origin (hunters, mountain priests, townsmen, and fishermen), but the largest category seems to have been sons of village headmen. Thus the leaders of these companies were the sort of men who exercised effective, as opposed to formal, authority in the countryside. The companies also included *rōnin* from other areas. In the fighting that followed in 1866 and 1868, these units fought with tenacity and even ferocity. They must have known that if they failed, neither the bakufu victors nor the highly placed Chōshū conservatives would have shown much compassion. More than any other domain, Chōshū was becoming a small-scale "nation in arms" of the sort that the Meiji modernizers wanted.

The capitulation of the Chōshū government to the first expedition mounted by the bakufu displeased loyalists of many sorts in Chōshū, but none more so than the military units that were to be disbanded by the terms of the settlement. One of these, led by Takasugi Shinsaku, revolted and seized a government office in Shimonoseki before the ink was even dry on the agreements, thereby producing an offer from the bakufu negotiators to provide a body of troops to help the domain regulars suppress them. The Chōshū administration, confident in its own ability to subdue the militia, declined, but its confidence proved misplaced. Within a short time, additional *shotai* victories had produced an advance on the castle town itself and a strong sentiment of criticism against the domain administration that had let the civil war come about. This situation was resolved by the emergence of a new domain administration in the early spring of 1865 that represented a coalition of extremist and moderate samurai. This group led the domain on its collision course with the bakufu and into the early Restoration government.

The Chōshū violence had elements of class or at least of status conflict, and yet it was not a contest between upper and lower in any simple sense. The new administration produced a commitment to the loyalist cause, yet it was also staunchly Chōshū centered in values and objectives. It was nominally antiforeign and exclusionist in its goals, and yet places of influence were beginning to be found for individuals who knew the West. Itō Hirobumi, one of the future leaders of the Meiji state, symbolized the course of a leadership generation in the shifts of his career: a student of Yoshida Shōin, then a student in England, an interpreter and translator in the concluding stages of the foreign bombardment of Shimonoseki, next a commander of a militia company, and finally a protégé and trusted lieutenant of Kido Takayoshi, probably the single most important figure in the new Chōshū administration. Itō was of modest rank and origin. Responsibility and opportunity sobered judgment, and information about the outer world gradually moderated the extremism of the young warriors. Yet what seemed to their elders reckless "extremism" had brought them to power within Chōshū, and their pursuit of the bakufu was not likely to be more conciliatory.

Satsuma, unlike Chōshū, experienced no internal violence or political upset. Its samurai numbers were large and needed no supplement of commoners; distinctions of rank and income within its samurai ranks were so large that rifle-bearing companies could be mounted with little of the status compunctions that hampered the bakufu levies. Most importantly, however, the Satsuma regent Shimazu Hisamitsu was able to maintain political control and enlisted the talents of Saigō Takamori and Ōkubo Toshimichi, men who had been tempered by danger and punishment in 1858. They helped suppress Satsuma extremists at the beginning of the *kōbu-gattai* movement in 1862, and by 1865–6 they recognized and acted on the need for the domain to know more about the West. Fourteen students were selected and sent to London under the guidance of domain officials. Once in Europe the students were set to studying a variety of technological and military specialties. Before long they were joined by a second group. Satsuma officials in Europe tried to secure for their domain status as an independent country for the Paris Exposition of 1867, citing as reason the domain's control of Okinawa. They negotiated a number of agreements for industrial and mining operations, and although little came of most of these, the purchase of five thousand rifles added important strength to the Satsuma military. Thus, whereas Chōshū, under great military pressure from without, underwent a political upset that placed power in the hands of "extremists" who had use for the advice of the Western-experienced Itō and Inoue Kaoru, Satsuma, without the goad that military crisis provided for administrative change in Chōshū, was, thanks to the English bombardment of Kagoshima, no less alert to the need for Western equipment. Expulsion, one may conclude, was now a dead letter (though it remained a useful slogan) after the shellings of Kagoshima and Chōshū. The overthrow of the bakufu, which was not a practical proposition before the reforms of 1862, had become a goal of many men by 1865.

The changes of the early 1860s had made the bakufu itself a regional power. No set of reforms was more impressive and more extensive than the changes that the Tokugawa leaders initiated in their Kinai and Kantō territories. The Osaka and Edo plains were under full foreign and Japanese observation and hence subject to all the interference that national and international politics could provide. These territories were also divided between those under direct bakufu administration and the lands of minor daimyo and *hatamoto* who administered their holdings independently. Cumulatively the largest holdings of any daimyo in the Tokugawa structure, the Tokugawa *tenryō* was also the most affected by urban and national commerce and communications, the most "modern" in economic developments, and the most lightly invested by resident samurai. In Tokugawa lands, samurai as a percentage of domain population were relatively few and highly urbanized. The bakufu thus faced particular problems in its military modernization.

The bakufu's Bunkyū reforms of 1862 included administrative and military changes as well as the relaxation of daimyo controls that have already been discussed. On the whole, the administrative changes were more successful than the political changes. New procedures were developed for the rapid promotion of able men. Unessential jobs were eliminated; so many, in fact, that the unemployment that resulted required special programs of aid and relief for the newly unfortunate.

Military reforms found the bakufu (and its rivals) struggling to acquire the most lethal weapons at a time when firearms were undergoing rapid change in the Western world. A second problem was to transform the corps of house retainers (*hatamoto* and *gokenin*) into rifle companies. This last was easier to do in theory than in practice, for the urbanized samurai, who were essentially an army of occupation that had spent many generations in peace and quiet, often resisted drill.[40]

Extensive plans were worked out for a modern army and navy within the confines of the troop strength that retainers were expected to be able to provide. Efforts were made to correlate income to the rank structure of the modern forces, and planners set the goal of drawing one-half of those forces from the bakufu's house retainers. Thus it was assumed from the outset that it would be necessary to augment samurai with commoner strength.

Naval training got its start when a small Dutch training contingent came to Nagasaki in the 1850s; in the early 1860s Katsu Kaishū was assigned the responsibility of organizing a naval training school at Hyōgo. Katsu's tendency to recruit his men from many areas alarmed bakufu conservatives, who saw the institution becoming a nest of loyalists, and so Katsu was replaced in 1864. The point is significant: Bakufu reformers tended to draw on men of many areas, but the great southwestern *han* could be exclusive and probably had more esprit de corps. Sustained efforts were devoted to the land arm of the new military structure. By 1864 some ten thousand weapons had been imported through Yokohama, and from then to the end of the bakufu, gunrunning to Yokohama and to Nagasaki (for the southwestern domains) proved one of the most lucrative aspects of trade at the ports. As the second expedition against Chōshū drew near in 1865, bakufu leaders were beginning to realize that their reliance on their retainers (and especially the landholding *hatamoto*) would have to change. First they tried to get them to provide conscripts as part of their feudal military service requirement, but before long it became clear that a better system of recruiting commoners was needed. As the forces took shape, the composition of the principal rifle-bearing units gradually

40 For Satsuma, Beasley, *Meiji Restoration*, p. 246; for bakufu military reforms, Totman, *Collapse*, pp. 25–7: (for Bunkyū), p. 182 (for 1864), and p. 199 (for 1865). Totman's discussion of technological changes involved in muzzle loaders, Minie rifles, breech-loading rifles, and multishot pistols, p. 25, is particularly useful.

became commoner based. By degrees, *hatamoto* military service requirements were becoming commuted to a money tax that was used to cover the costs of conscripting and training peasants. All of this affected only part of the Tokugawa vassal armies, but it was that part that indicated future trends.[41]

The Tokugawa military reforms required extensive foreign cooperation, but as the nominal government of the entire country, the bakufu had the best access to foreign assistance. Its first moves were by way of the traditional link with Holland, and in the fall of 1864 three navy officers were sent to the Netherlands to study shipyards and other Western military developments. Negotiations for a shipyard were begun with the Dutch and also for a warship; talks also began for the building of a warship (the future *Stonewall*) in the United States.

But the most important channel of foreign assistance was that with France. Minister Leon Roches, who arrived in Japan in April 1864, worked unceasingly to consolidate for his country the role of principal source for military – and, he hoped, political – reform in Japan. Those plans developed gradually; they represented Roches' enthusiasm and not that of his government. Foreign aid never assumed the dimensions that the bakufu's domestic rivals feared it would, because neither Tokugawa nor French leaders were prepared to take risks. Yet the plans were extensive and stand as reminders of the possible impact that imperialist competition could have had on a developing Japan.[42]

Roches began with specific goals: The French silk industry was in dire need of help from Japan because of a silkworm blight, and that made him the bakufu's most importunate customer. But he was free with additional suggestions. Before long he had secured the appointment of Kurimoto Joun as special liaison officer between himself and the *rōjū*, and by the end of 1864, bakufu officials had requested his help in planning for the construction of a naval yard and arsenal at Yokosuka. Gradually confidence in Roches' intentions developed. In 1865 a mission was sent to Europe to seek military assistance as well as machinery and equipment for Yokosuka. Arrangements for a mint and a military training mission took shape, and bakufu officials began to develop hopes of a special source of access to the technology and training they knew they needed.

41 Totman, *Collapse*, p. 182. For purposes of brevity, this discussion telescopes changes that came at different speeds in different periods and areas.

42 Mark David Ericson, "The Tokugawa *Bakufu* and Leon Roches," Ph.D. diss., University of Hawaii, 1978, p. 243, improves on the earlier work of Meron Medzini, *French Policy in Japan During the Closing Years of the Tokugawa Regime* (Cambridge, Mass.: Harvard University Press, 1971).

These experiments gathered momentum with proposals for an officially sponsored trading company that would generate funds for bakufu purchases abroad. The banker Fleury-Herard was invested as the bakufu representative in Paris and put in charge of purchasing equipment for a foundry and mint. French advice (though not, it should be noted, French money), began to pour into Tokugawa circles about ways to restructure Japan's economy and administration in order to speed modernization and build up power. Long before much could come of this, however, the Tokugawa forces were gathering in Osaka to carry out the second punitive expedition against Chōshū. When hostilities broke out in the summer of 1866, it was still a largely traditional congeries of bakufu vassal forces that tried to contest the issue with the more highly motivated Chōshū units.

The second war with Chōshū proved a disaster. Although elements of the bakufu's new units were employed, they were fielded together with old-style units from other *han*. The bakufu army was a coalition of vassals' armies, as had always been the case, enabling the Chōshū warriors to select their target and attack the Tokugawa forces where they were weakest. Bakufu efforts to attack Chōshū at each of its borders were poorly coordinated, and the forces were poorly led. While all this was in progress, the young shogun Iemochi died at Osaka.

When the full scale of the military disasters became clear, Tokugawa Yoshinobu, now the ranking figure on the bakufu side, reluctantly decided that the battle would have to be broken off and seized upon the shogun's death as a face-saving reason for a cease-fire. Yet the cease-fire left Chōshū troops occupying areas of bakufu and *fudai* land, and it dealt the shogunate a blow in prestige from which it never fully recovered.

The defeat of the bakufu armies by Chōshū gave the Tokugawa modernization movement new urgency. The last year of the Tokugawa shogunate saw sweeping changes that portended centralization, rationalization, and bureaucratization. Once Yoshinobu was fully invested as shogun, with full honors and titles, the reconstruction of the bakufu began in earnest. Foreign relations were regularized. Permanent missions were set up in capitals. Yoshinobu's younger brother Akitake was sent to France as the bakufu representative at the Paris Exposition of 1867, and plans called for him to spend years of study there to prepare him for future leadership. Appointive changes brought to office some of the most effective of the modernizing officials of the recent half-decade. The entire foreign diplomatic corps was invited to Osaka for an audience with the new shogun, who entertained them at a dinner prepared by a newly employed French chef. Western dress replaced Japanese at the shogunal court for that occasion.

Numerous requests for advice were addressed to Roches, and he answered during long sessions with senior officials and a private audience with the shogun Yoshinobu himself. The list of questions covered administrative changes, taxes, military development, mineral resource development, economic growth, queries about Switzerland and Prussia, and questions about the abolition of feudalism by European countries.[43] Administrative reforms followed; these set up a sort of cabinet system with specialized responsibilities replacing the monthly rotation of all-purpose generalists that had been the pattern. New personnel practices were designed to facilitate the selection of competent officials, with a regularized salary system for government departments. A great deal of time went into the preparation of diagrams laying out specific administrative responsibilities and procedures, and initial steps working toward the commutation of vassal lands and stipends developed. Shogunal power in the Edo area was strengthened by measures to call in small nearby fiefs in order to rationalize and centralize administrative procedures. Military reforms were pushed particularly rapidly. A French military mission arrived in January 1867. Western uniforms were adopted; obsolete forces were disbanded; and steps were taken toward the substitution of a monetized tax on house vassals as the basis for a peasant conscription system. Nishi Amane, newly returned from study in Holland, was ordered to draw up a more modern scheme of government and produced a parliamentary draft that envisioned a division of power among the court, an executive branch, and a bicameral legislature with an upper house of daimyo empowered to dissolve the lower house.

As a result, it can be asserted that the bakufu leaders were launching a modernization program – perhaps a "Tokugawa restoration" – that would in time have emulated at many points the programs adopted by their successors in the Meiji government. Seen in this light, it can be said that the civil war of 1868 was fought over the issue not of whether Tokugawa feudalism would survive but whether its demise would be presided over by Tokugawa or anti-Tokugawa leaders. It was no longer a matter of saving the bakufu system but of replacing it, now that it was collapsing. As Totman said of the period immediately before the summer war, "there was no longer in Japan an authority

43 Ericson, "The Tokugawa *Bakufu* and Leon Roches," pp. 238ff.

symbol capable of moving the feudal lords. There was no national polity; the *bakuhan* system no longer existed."[44] Ironically, however, these needs were probably seen more clearly by the bakufu leaders than by the southwestern lords who opposed them.

RESTORATION

The changes launched in Edo are difficult to evaluate, for they did not mature in time to help the bakufu; it is always easier to sketch reforms than to carry them out. Nevertheless, the fear that they would result in a greatly strengthened shogunate was an important factor in impelling leaders in Satsuma and Chōshū to try to anticipate such success with efforts of their own to overthrow it. What they particularly feared was that the administration of Yoshinobu would use French military and administrative assistance to build a central government capable of destroying the daimyo, with the shogun serving as its chief executive officer.

In 1867, the death of Emperor Kōmei of smallpox brought changes at the court as well. Though consistently antiforeign, Kōmei had usually been well disposed toward the bakufu as represented by Tokugawa Yoshinobu, with whom he had established relations of considerable trust. With the succession of the boy Mutsuhito, the future Meiji emperor, court nobles had a new field for political maneuver. The most able and important of those courtiers was now Iwakura Tomomi, a shrewd judge of events and possibilities. By the fall of 1866 Iwakura was writing that the court had the choice of siding with the bakufu against Chōshū and, possibly, Satsuma, or maneuvering to make itself the center of a new united polity. Because bakufu prestige and power were in decline, he suggested that "the Emperor should issue orders to the Bakufu that from now on it must set aside its selfish ways, acting in accordance with public principle; that imperial rule must be restored; and that thereafter the Tokugawa house must work in concert with the great domains in the Emperor's service." To restore national prestige and handle the foreigners, the country would have to be united, and "for policy and administration to have a single source, the Court must be made the center of national government." In additional documents Iwakura sounded more and more like the Satsuma leaders with whom he communicated, as when he wrote: "In the heavens there are not two suns. On earth there are not two monarchs. Surely

44 Totman, *Collapse*, p. 291.

no country can survive unless government edicts stem from a single source. . . . Hence it is my desire that we should act vigorously to abolish the Bakufu" and relegate the Tokugawa house to the ranks of the great domains.[45] Some of this language was echoed in future proposals, as in a Satsuma–Tosa document worked out in the summer of 1867:

> There cannot be two rulers in a land, or two heads in a house, and it is most reasonable to return administration and justice to one ruler. . . . It is evident that we must reform our regulations, return political power to the court, form a council of feudal lords and conduct affairs in line with the desires of the people . . . only then can we face all nations without shame and establish our national polity.[46]

These notes of national danger, international prestige, and the need for an effective, single center of government recur in many pronouncements of late Tokugawa days. In fact Japan now had not only two governments but even two bakufus, given the presence of Yoshinobu in Osaka/Kyoto and the more Tokugawa-centered world of the bureaucrats at Edo.

Although such divisions of power seemed impossible to men like Iwakura and many others, they also made it troublesome for foreign representatives who wanted firm guarantees of their privileges and a clear understanding as to the channels of power. Roches accepted the bakufu as a legitimate national government and devoted his efforts to help it become a more effective one. His British counterpart Harry Parkes was not sure and suspected that Japan would not have a real government until basic changes in Edo–Kyoto relations took place. Though junior to Roches in time of residence, Parkes proved a ruthless competitor, on one occasion forcing his way into a private meeting between Roches and Yoshinobu to insist on equal treatment as Her Majesty's representative. When the bakufu requested postponement of the second installment of the enormous indemnity exacted for Shimonoseki because of the costs that had been incurred in the preparation of the second campaign against Chōshū, Parkes demanded an accounting of those costs. When the bakufu argued court opposition as grounds for delay on Hyōgo, Parkes demanded – and secured – explicit court approval of the treaties by staging a demarche at Osaka in November 1865. When he saw the bakufu's difficulties with its recalcitrant daimyo, Parkes concluded that England, in a spirit of neutrality, should cultivate those daimyo as possible future power

45 Beasley, *Meiji Restoration*, pp. 261, 266–7. 46 Jansen, *Sakamoto Ryōma*, p. 300.

holders, and he alarmed bakufu officials by visiting several castle towns in the southwestern domains, including Kagoshima. Parkes's interpreter Ernest Satow, probably the best informed foreigner in late Tokugawa Japan, maintained close friendships with the leaders of the southwestern *han* and wrote a pamphlet (which was immediately translated into Japanese) arguing that English policy should work toward the creation of a council of great lords, of whom the Tokugawa head would be one, under the emperor, in order to secure binding guarantees of foreign privileges and rights. This private opinion was widely taken to represent English policy and seemed to be in the process of implementation by the actions of Harry Parkes. Thus foreign as well as court and daimyo opinion was working to exacerbate unstable national politics.

As the great domains shook off their subordination to bakufu leadership, they began to negotiate private agreements among themselves. These were no longer the personal discussions of daimyo, as in the early years, but policy decisions reached by the bureaucratic leaders who staffed *han* administrations. The most important of these was an agreement between Satsuma and Chōshū that was worked out early in 1866 to lessen the possible dangers for Chōshū in the approaching second bakufu punitive campaign. The agreement was made possible by the efforts of Sakamoto Ryōma and Nakaoka Shintarō of Tosa who provided their good offices. In February 1866, Kido Takayoshi, for Chōshū, and Saigō Takamori, for Satsuma, agreed that Satsuma would provide its help in mediating for Chōshū at court; it would do its best to prevent the bakufu from crushing Chōshū; it would secure Kyoto if necessary; and it would join with Chōshū, once that domain had been pardoned, in working for "the glory of the Imperial country."

After the defeat of the bakufu armies at the hands of Chōshū, the Satsuma–Tosa agreement that has been mentioned added another agreement. The two domains agreed on a program for politics: The court should have full authority, and a council with two houses would be established in Kyoto, one chamber staffed with daimyo and the other made up of "retainers and even commoners." The shogunate as such would be abolished. New treaties would be drawn up with the foreign powers "on the basis of reason and justice"; institutions would be revised and brought up-to-date; and self-interest was everywhere to take second place to the consciousness of the larger national good.

This optimistic view of an unselfish future, clearly a legacy of the *kōbu-gattai* persuasion, represented a Tosa plan to secure a peaceful solution to Japan's political crises. Chōshū, flushed with its victories in the summer war, was still technically under the ban of both court and bakufu and determined to exploit its military advantage in further violence. Simultaneously, the treaty powers were demanding action on the opening of Hyōgo, which was scheduled for the summer of 1867. Once again the great lords assembled to discuss the crisis. Matsudaira Shungaku, Shimazu Hisamitsu, Yamauchi Yōdō, and Date Munenari proposed to Yoshinobu that the bakufu combine a solution to the two and proposed to the court a pardon of Chōshū together with court approval for the opening of Hyōgo. Yoshinobu, however, was inclined to hold out for the impossible condition of an apology from Chōshū, but because Hyōgo could not wait, he preceeded to wrest approval from the court for that opening on grounds of pressing national danger.

This stance confirmed Satsuma's discouragement with even a reformed bakufu and helped produce a new Satsuma–Chōshū agreement for a military coup against the shogunate in the summer of 1867. The Tosa leaders, holding a median position, still tried to head this off with a peaceful solution. Tosa's size made it fearful of losing out in a military showdown. Its relationship to the bakufu, which had treated the Yamauchi house favorably, was also one of obligation and loyalty. All this reinforced hopes of a negotiated settlement by which the shogun would agree to step down and become one of the great lords in a new conciliar structure under the aegis of the throne. Similar hopes had been at the heart of the *kōbu-gattai* movement since 1862. Matsudaira Shungaku reappeared on the scene once again. Sakamoto Ryōma, once a Tosa loyalist and then an associate of the bakufu official Katsu Kaishū, subsequently sheltered by Satsuma and central to the Satsuma–Chōshū agreement of 1866, now worked out an eight-point program that contained Tosa hopes for a negotiated settlement. The Satsuma leaders who willingly subscribed to this program in endorsing the Satsuma–Tosa compact in the summer of 1867 were quite willing to help propose the bakufu's voluntary dissolution and were prepared to use force if a peaceful settlement should fail.

These currents converged in November 1867. While Edo modernizers were pushing reforms to produce a more effective bakufu and Chōshū and Satsuma leaders were readying their troops for a military showdown, Tosa representatives in Kyoto presented Yoshinobu with Yamauchi Yōdō's proposal that he resign his office and titles. The proposal contained eight parts: The court would rule, but a two-house council, made up of daimyo and court nobles, would be established; new treaties would be worked out; an imperial army and navy would be established;[47] "errors of the past" in procedure and institutions would be abolished; "wrong customs" in the court would be reformed; and once again, self-interest would be put aside.

Yoshinobu accepted the proposal. He did so without consulting the Edo government leaders and after almost no consultation in Kyoto. Clearly he saw it as a way of escaping his predicament of responsibility without power and retaining the power base that his reforms were building at Edo. Once the court accepted his resignation as shogun, the Tokugawa polity of 267 years formally came to an end.

But there was still nothing to replace it. The council of daimyo did not materialize, for uncertainty was so widespread that only sixteen daimyo arrived in Kyoto in response to a court request for attendance. *Kōbu-gattai* proved no more viable in 1867 than it had been in 1862. Soon large contingents of samurai were being sent to Kyoto; parts of the Chōshū domain army, still unpardoned, were nearing the city. The Satsuma–Chōshū plans for a military coup were still intact, and tension grew steadily. On January 2 and 3, 1868, an assembly at the court was convened, dominated by Iwakura and Satsuma men. Yoshinobu and his closest supporters, suspicious of what was planned, declined to attend. The meeting resolved to transfer the palace guard from bakufu to non-Tokugawa hands, to abolish old offices, and to demand the surrender of Tokugawa domains to the "court." Yoshinobu, in doubt as to his next step, withdrew to Osaka.

For over three weeks, things were at a standstill. Court representatives ordered Yoshinobu to appear in formal contrition and surrender, only to have him propose that all daimyo dedicate a comparable fraction of their income and land to the court. Roches offered Yoshinobu such French aid as he could muster, an offer that was not accepted, but neither was the advice of bakufu leaders who wanted to fight. A powerful document from Yoshinobu to the court calling attention to Satsuma's duplicity and his own exemplary behavior was kept from the young emperor. The former shogun's indecision began to cost him the support of even Tokugawa houses. Finally, in late January 1868, Yoshinobu decided to return to Kyoto with a body of troops to remonstrate. His commanders did not expect to have to fight their way back; their formations and composition represented an unlikely mixture of modern and premodern companies. To their misfortune they were opposed and ambushed by modern Satsuma and Chōshū units that

47 The proposal read: "We must have a force which will have no equal in the world."

stopped them and drove them back. The civil war had begun; force would decide the issue.

Fighting at Fushimi-Toba went on for four days and produced a casualty count of five hundred dead and one thousand to fifteen hundred wounded. On both sides, units fought well, but the leadership and determination of forces committed to the Kyoto cause was superior to that on the bakufu side. The bakufu commanders seem to have let a fear of popular disorder keep them from using all their Western-trained and armed troops at the front, whereas their adversaries had their best units at the right places. The bakufu units, trying to advance along two narrow roads, one on either side of the Yodo River, had the harder task to carry out. In some units, morale was a problem, but others, notably those of Aizu, fought with dash and courage.

When the dimensions of this new disaster were apparent, Tokugawa Yoshinobu and his bakufu army headed north for Edo. Within two weeks the former shogun had decided against further resistance to his enemies, despite Roches' encouragement and advice that he try again. The bakufu army was dismantled as the daimyo took their units to their own domains, some to join and others to apologize and submit to the "imperial" armies that advanced from the south. In the spring of 1868 Edo itself was surrendered by the bakufu official Katsu Kaishū to an imperial army commanded by Saigō Takamori.

But the war was not over, for the fighting known as the Boshin conflict went on until May 1869, when the Tokugawa naval units that had sailed to Hokkaido and held out there under the command of Enomoto Takeaki surrendered. The war in the northeast had been carried on by a daimyo alliance headed by the Sendai domain. Its cause was really not that of the Tokugawa, which was clearly doomed, but, rather, that of its region against the distrusted southerners from Satsuma and Chōshū. This "Northeastern League," in fact, claimed that its members were more loyal to the emperor than were the "selfish and self-serving" southerners. The most fierce battle of the campaign came at Aizu Castle in Wakamatsu, where the men of Matsudaira Katamori, former *shugo* of Kyoto and long a thorn in the side of Satsuma and Chōshū, fought desperately. The castle was put to the torch, and Aizu lost almost three thousand samurai in the war, more than the combined total of the opposition. After its defeat, the domain was broken up, and its ruling family was moved to a niggardly and inhospitable plot of ground unable to support the remnants of its former retainer force. Katamori himself was made a Shinto priest, guardian of the Tokugawa burial shrines. No other domain was treated as harshly, though a number of recalcitrant daimyo were forced into retirement and others into house arrest. Tokugawa Yoshinobu himself was ordered to retire as house head and withdrew to Numazu in Shizuoka where he did his best to maintain his retainers. By the 1890s he had been received by the emperor and restored to honor. His successor, Iesato, was first head of the House of Peers.

The regime that replaced the bakufu, as Chapter 10 makes clear, underwent many changes before becoming the Meiji government.[48] Its first institutional probings came in the January meetings that maneuvered Yoshinobu into opposition. The same meeting that declared bakufu offices abolished established a new three-tier structure of *sōsai, gijō* (councilors), and *san'yo* (junior councilors) and named Prince Arisugawa *sōsai* in order to make the greatest possible use of imperial legitimacy. Gradually, however, status and office filtered downward to the samurai leaders of the southwestern *han* whose lords dominated the original table of organization, and as that process matured, the Meiji government took form.

In a basic sense, the program of the new government was enunciated as early as the spring of 1868, at a time when the regime was still seeking to reassure the doubtful and to enlist the wavering. In April, one day after Katsu and Saigō negotiated the surrender of Edo, the young emperor was presented with what became known as the "Charter Oath," five articles that bridged the transition from the Tosa proposals of 1867 to the constitutional order of the modern Japanese state. These articles promised the creation of "deliberative councils" and the determination of policies on the basis of "general opinion," the cooperation of all classes in carrying out the administration of affairs of state, full opportunity for commoners as well as for officials, and the abolition of "evil customs of the past." They also proposed basing everything on the "just laws of nature." Finally, a search for knowledge "throughout the world" would follow in order to "strengthen the foundation of imperial rule." This was a document couched in terms sufficiently general to conform to the social structure of its day, but it also held out the possibility of changes so basic that it could still be cited as authorization for the democratic institutional changes that followed World War II.

48 See Albert Craig, "The Central Government," Marius B. Jansen, "The Ruling Class," and Michio Umegaki, "From Domain to Prefecture," chaps. 2, 3, and 4 in Jansen and Rozman, eds., *Japan in Transition*.

THE RESTORATION IN HISTORY AND HISTORIOGRAPHY

If the definition of the Meiji Restoration is limited to the events of 1867 and 1868, it constituted little more than a coup that shifted rule from one sector of the ruling class to another. But when it is considered as a larger process, one that began before mid-century and that culminated in the modern state at the century's end, it can be seen to have brought revolutionary changes in Japanese society. Studies of these events during the century that followed them have inevitably been intertwined with the climate of opinion within which they were carried on. The nature of the nineteenth-century historical process, and the motive forces involved, have provided basic problems of classification and analysis.

The orthodox view of Japanese history before 1945, and one that is by no means dead, was based on interpretations that emphasized the maturization of currents of imperial loyalism through the Tokugawa period. With the coming of Perry and the foreign danger, the textbooks explained, selfless patriots – the *shishi* – fought to reverse their *han* policies and to defeat the bakufu by wakening long-slumbering imperial and national consciousness. Saigō, Ōkubo, Iwakura, Kido, and all the heirs of Yoshida Shōin were portrayed as though foretold by anguished loyalists of earlier times. Laudatory biographies told their stories as they themselves would have wished to be remembered. Official historiographical institutes provided proportional representation for the southwestern *han* to make certain that the praise would be allocated equitably. These views were spread by a modern education system that was centered on patriotism and loyalty, reinforced by the popular press, and fortified by scholarly compilations. So brief a summary risks distortion. There was enough of substance in the commitment of Restoration figures, enough romance and color in what they did, and enough national pride in what they produced to retain for the loyalist leaders a secure place in any historiography. But the identification of their success with morality and patriotism also introduced a strong bias in much that was written in a highly nationalistic setting.

Yet the nationalist emphasis of prewar history had developed in a context of much more critical writing. By the 1880s, historians had begun to fit Japan's experience into international models of liberal and capitalist societies, and some were becoming troubled by the disparities they sensed between the "deliberative councils" that had been promised and the reality of the Imperial Diet they saw approaching.

Japan seemed to be eclipsing the timetable of other countries in modernization, but the reforms granted "from above" were somehow different from the reforms won from below. By late Meiji times the conservative and pragmatic government leaders in power also seemed quite unlike the hotheaded, two-sworded idealists of romantic memory. To some, they were becoming Japan's new problem, and judgments of the bakufu softened as a result. By the early twentieth century a new generation of writers had begun to separate the leaders from what they had brought about, to minimize the conflicts, and to explain the Restoration and modernization programs by showing the material advances that had taken place in Japanese society under Tokugawa rule. Tokutomi Sohō argued that it was not the Meiji leaders but inexorable trends that had created the new Japan. He and others stressed the fragility of feudal society, and the growing independence of stouthearted rural leaders, as the critical factors in the overthrow of Tokugawa feudalism. In turn, such interpretations were usually related to political advocacy and the desire to find legitimacy for liberalism and to advance social reform in Japan.[49] By the 1890s, however, the flush of victory over China, soon to be followed by the conquest of Russia, the maturation of the ideology of the imperial state, and the completion of the network of national schools all combined to reinforce the official orthodoxy with its sanctification of the modern state. Tokugawa Yoshinobu himself, in his memoirs (1915) and in an authorized biography (1918), became a loyalist.

After World War I, Marxist analysis provided a new and powerful teleological expectation of what the Restoration should or could have produced. Economic instability culminating in the world depression, increased political and intellectual surveillance consequent to the formation of the Japan Communist Party in the form of the Peace Preservation Act of 1925, and the aggressive course of Japanese foreign policy all combined to encourage new evaluations of Japan's recent past. Marxist historians divided into the Labor-Farmer (Rōnō) group, which was prepared to describe the Restoration as a basically bourgeois movement that had ended feudalism in Japan, and the gloomier Lectures (Kōza) group which held that feudal relationships had lived on in the countryside through noneconomic and non-contractual

49 See Jiro Numata, "Shigeno Yasutsugu and the Modern Tokyo Tradition of Historical Writing," in W. G. Beasley and E. G. Pulleybank, eds., *Historians of China and Japan* (London: Oxford University Press, 1961), pp. 264–87, for the evolution of Meiji historiography within inherited, Chinese tradition; and Peter Duus, "Whig History, Japanese Style: The Min'yūsha Historians and the Meiji Restoration," *Journal of Asian Studies* 33 (May 1974): 415–36.

restraints on tenants as the basis of a new "absolutism" built around the "emperor system," a term that was utilized in the Japan Communist Party theses of 1932. Like their Meiji predecessors, these historians were directing and relating their views to problems of political advocacy.[50]

Japan's surrender in 1945 freed the air of "emperor system" orthodoxy (although it replaced it with equally compulsive derogation for a time) and produced immensely important work that retained some of the Marxist categories without repeating the simplistic formulas of much of the earlier writing. Nevertheless, the presentist orientation of historical evaluation continued, and many writers' concerns were to identify and eliminate feudal remnants and advance democracy.[51]

When the focus of research is brought closer to the decade in which the bakufu was toppled, problems still outnumber answers. The principal actors among the leaders have been clearly delineated, but the source of their backing remains a matter of dispute. Shibahara Takuji, after summarizing movements of popular discontent and disorder in Restoration times, did not hesitate to term agrarianists the "moving force" of the Restoration and saw popular antifeudal sentiments as the key historical ingredient in the events of the decade. On the other hand, Conrad Totman's analysis of the bakufu's fall, though recognizing commoners' antifeudal attitudes, concludes:

> This anti-feudal mentality did not become an anti-Bakufu mentality, however, and the reason seems to be that the political contest of the 1860s was pitting some parts of the ruling or feudal elite against others. . . . In conse-

50 The immediate prewar years saw publication of authoritative summaries of the positions mentioned here: Tokutomi Iichirō, *Kinsei Nihon kokuminshi* for Duus's "Whig History"; the monument of government historiography, *Ishin shi*, 6 vols., (Tokyo: Meiji shoin, 1941); and the definitive statement of the *kōza* position that gave the school its name, *Nihon shihonshugi hattatsu shi kōza*, 7 vols. (Tokyo: Iwanami shoten, 1932–3). For a recent and cogent analysis of the Marxist struggle, see Yasukichi Yasuba, "Anatomy of the Debate on Japanese Capitalism," *Journal of Japanese Studies* 2 (Autumn 1975): 63–82. See also Germain A. Hoston, *Marxism and the Crisis of Development in Prewar Japan* (Princeton, N.J.: Princeton University Press, 1986), for its analysis of prewar Marxist writing.

51 See, for a brief comment on the contributions of Maruyama Masao, Ōtsuka Hisao, and Kawashima Takeyoshi in the postwar climate, Nagahara Keiji, *Rekishigaku josetsu* (Tokyo: Tokyo daigaku shuppankai, 1978), pp. 51ff. The most influential postwar summary of Restoration scholarship was Tōyama Shigeki, *Meiji ishin* (Tokyo: Iwanami shoten, 1951), which argued the "absolutist" thesis. Most recent and influential is a "people's history" that emphasizes the indigenous and internal development of Japanese history, focusing (as did Tokutomi to some extent) on rural elites at mid-century. Carol Gluck, "The People in History: Recent Trends in Japanese Historiography," *Journal of Asian Studies* 38 (November 1978): 25–50. An important statement of this school, Irokawa Daikichi's *Meiji no bunka* (Tokyo: Iwanami shoten, 1970), has appeared in translation as *The Culture of the Meiji Period*, ed. Marius B. Jansen (Princeton, N.J.: Princeton University Press, 1985).

quence one finds commoners in all camps and on all sides of major disputes. . . .[52]

One statistical examination of the incidence of popular revolts between 1865 and 1871 (a total of 545) found that they were least prevalent in future "Restoration-led" areas and most common in Tokugawa-ruled or related areas and related this to the relative prosperity and productivity of the Tokugawa areas and the relatively depressed and suppressed state of the antibakufu domains. Effective anti-Tokugawa *political* action cannot be related to such popular discontent, but Tokugawa efforts to maintain control and counter nonsamurai resistance were, presumably, hampered by the relatively less stable social base of the Tokugawa territories.[53]

No one can doubt the evidences of commoner restlessness and movement. Recent studies of a bizarre movement that swept the principal communications routes of central Japan during the final months of Tokugawa rule provide fascinating evidence of a widespread and rather joyous spirit of revelry and mischief that was so troublesome for Tokugawa forces of order that some were prepared to blame the outbreaks on loyalist suggestion and stimulation. Yet the mood of the crowds was overwhelmingly optimistic, more appropriate to festival than to fury, and more social than political. The wealthy, who were expected to provide food and entertainment because the gods had favored them with talismans of good fortune, paid the bills.[54] Nonetheless, it is clear that the bakufu leaders interpreted such movements as threatening their control of society. Spontaneous, large-scale febrile movements like this also related to the rising trend of popular pilgrimage to Ise in the nineteenth century. Occasionally they became associated, at least briefly, with sentimental homage to loyalist *shishi* killed in the Restoration violence.[55] There was much political satire in occasional wall writings and shrine placards, but these phenomena do not seem to have been sufficiently focused to grant them a very significant role. The search for an independent merchant interest and role has also been unprofitable. Some merchants did assist the *shishi:* Shiraishi Shōichirō, a Shimonoseki shipping guild merchant, was a man

52 Totman, *Collapse*, p. 458; Shibahara Takuji, "Hanbaku" shoseiryoku no seikaku," in *Iwanami kōza Nihon rekishi,* vol. 14 (*kindai* 1) (Tokyo: Iwanami shoten, 1962), pp. 169–212.

53 Yoshio Sugimoto, "Structural Sources of Popular Revolts and the Tōbaku Movement at the Time of the Meiji Restoration," *Journal of Asian Studies* 34 (August 1975): 875–89.

54 Takagi Shunsuke, *Eejanaika* (Tokyo: Kyōikusha rekishi shinsho, 1979), pp. 209–34.

55 Onodera Toshiya, "Zannen san kō: Bakumatsu Kinai no ichi minshū undō o megutte," *Chiikishi kenkyū* 2 (June 1972): 46–67, discusses pilgrimages to the tombs of Yoshimura Toratarō and Yamamoto Bunnosuke around the time of the Restoration.

of culture and means whose diary includes the names of four hundred *shishi*, to whom he was generous with food, drink, and lodging. But even more merchants, whether or not by choice, assisted the bakufu, which based a good deal of its emergency financing on massive loans. It seems logical to conclude that in a setting of widespread disaffection with the state of political and social order, many commoners favored those who promised change. But it is also true that regional loyalty – and distrust – affected commoners as well as samurai.

Another series of debates centers on the foreign threat. The increasing intimacy of Leon Roches with the bakufu leaders in the closing years of their regime and the bluster with which Harry Parkes obstructed that contact have led many to emphasize the danger of imperialist competition for influence in Japan. There was at one point negotiation for a French loan that would be predicated on Hokkaido's resources, and Roches apparently offered Yoshinobu the services of the small French military mission after the Fushimi–Toba disaster in January 1868. But the danger of foreign intervention has probably been exaggerated. Satow's influential pamphlet on English policy was written, as his memoirs make clear, without the knowledge of his short-tempered chief, and Roches seems consistently to have extended his personal diplomacy, as he called it, beyond the authorization of his government, which had all the imperialist problems it could handle in Mexico and in Southeast Asia during those years. Even if the bakufu leaders had decided to commit themselves to French assistance, they would have found that there was very little to be had: Far from being able to negotiate loans, they had to pay for everything in advance and in cash. Yet it has also to be granted that none of this lessens the perceptions of foreign danger that the Japanese held in the 1860s. That impression itself was a fact impelling men to action, and the fear of entangling loans and foreign leverage lasted throughout the decades of nation building in the Meiji period.

The importance of the imperial institution and the role of the court present further problems for historical analysis. The policy of the Meiji government to keep that court area sacrosanct and to accept it as a basic element in national character and history produced an understandable reaction in post–World War II days when authors minimized its substance and stressed its use as a tactic and artifice of the Meiji planners. Yet clearly there was more than tactic involved. Although the Restoration leaders frequently lamented popular indifference to the existence of the court, they themselves clearly kept it uppermost as the quintessential center of national identity, and that emphasis was later diffused among the people through centralization, mobilization, and education. The emotion generated among the *shishi* by charges that the bakufu had somehow allowed the emperor to be disturbed – heightened at court, where nobles knew that the emperor was in fact indignant – was a powerful solvent of ordinary discipline and restraint. Yet the court itself, after the loyalist frenzy of the early 1860s, was much less a factor than it had been at the beginning of the process. As Totman put it: "It was *shishi* who gave effective voice and real content to this *sonnō-jōi* rhetoric, and so the prominence of the imperial role is primarily attributable to *shishi* success in making their views heard."[56]

The historian turns finally to the Restoration leaders, men of modest rank but immodest self-assurance, who gloried in the opportunity to establish for themselves, their friends, and their domain a visibility that had been denied them under the constraints of feudal discipline and status, and who saw their cause as pure and selfless because it held out the hope of winning for their emperor and country the place they felt they deserved among the nations. Those hopes were great and almost the reverse of the circumstances of their time. For a country humiliated by Western powers, they wanted a leading role in the world; for a sovereign restricted to secluded impotence, they demanded full authority over a country his ancestors had once ruled; for their domain, they wanted a full share in national politics instead of second-class vassalage and, for themselves, honored status as imperial servitors instead of vassals' rear vassals.[57]

Yet in the final analysis, most of this concerned the locus of leadership and not its goals. Most Tokugawa partisans wanted much the same thing. One is struck by the convergence of planning between bakufu and Restoration leaders in the last decade of Tokugawa history. Indeed, the bakufu leaders, charged with responsibility, approached the steps that their adversaries worked out later. Discussion of shogunal resignation and substitution of a council of great lords began in Edo quarters, found its way into Tosa councils by that route, and came to fruition in the Charter Oath's promise of "deliberative councils"; later it was integrated into Meiji political institutions. Military reforms found the bakufu, like its southwestern vassals, discover-

56 Totman, *Collapse*, p. 462.

57 Hopes and expectations of course changed dramatically with the intensification of political conflict and the revelation of bakufu incapacity during the 1860s. See Yoshio Sakata and John W. Hall, "The Motivation of Political Leadership in the Meiji Restoration," *Journal of Asian Studies* 16 (November 1956): 31–50; and Sakata Yoshio, *Meiji ishinshi* (Tokyo: Miraisha, 1960).

ing that samurai hauteur went poorly with the discipline and drill required for infantry companies and substituting, by steps, a personnel and then a money tax as basis for a conscription system that would displace the samurai altogether. The bakufu planners who worked this out were, like their adversaries from the southwestern *han*, of middle rank within their status hierarchy, *hatamoto* or petty daimyo who set about disestablishing their fellows. Needs of administrative retrenchment and rationalization produced programs for integrating the vassal domains nearest to the metropolitan centers, leading to rumors that a system of postfeudal, effective centralization was being prepared. The Meiji government, which used the Tokugawa lands as its own without parceling them out to daimyo after the civil war of 1868–9, kept them as the core for the centralization that was consummated by the return of feudal registers in 1869 and the establishment of prefectures in 1871. In brief, the pressures posed by opening and reconstruction revealed to friend and foe alike the impossibility of long continuing with the institutional structure of the *bakuhan* system and the need to replace it with the structure of a central state.

CHAPTER 4

OPPOSITION MOVEMENTS IN EARLY MEIJI, 1868–1885

Like all the great revolutions of the modern era, the Meiji Restoration generated intense opposition from groups and classes displaced and disadvantaged by revolutionary change. What sets the Meiji Restoration apart, however, is the apparent ease with which opposition to the revolutionary regime was defeated or co-opted. Peasant riots over the new conscription law, village protests against the land tax revision, revolts by disaffected samurai, early campaigns for representative government, and uprisings by dispossessed farmers all were contained or suppressed. The original leadership group stayed in charge and did not change its basic policies. Viewed positively, Japan enjoyed extraordinary continuity and stability in government; viewed negatively, conservative and bureaucratic politics prevailed.

Japanese and Western historians disagree sharply when explaining the failure of opposition movements to oust the ruling oligarchy or force changes in its agenda. Scholars in America and Great Britain influenced by modernization theory have generally viewed Japan as a model of peaceful transition from feudalism to modernity, a transformation in which core values of consensus and loyalty to emperor kept dissent within manageable bounds.[1] On the other hand, most Japanese and some Western historians credit the failure of the opposition movements to the authoritarian character of the Meiji state, emphasizing the incorporation of oppressive semifeudal structures into the Meiji polity and the oligarchy's control of the new state's efficient state security apparatus.[2]

Although there is some truth to both interpretations, neither of which is as simple as this summary might suggest, neither adequately explains the complex interaction between modernizing reforms and

1 John W. Hall, "Changing Conceptions of the Modernization of Japan," in Marius B. Jansen, ed., *Changing Japanese Attitudes Toward Modernization* (Princeton, N.J.: Princeton University Press, 1965), pp. 7–41.

2 E. Herbert Norman, *Japan's Emergence As a Modern State* (New York: Institute of Pacific Affairs, 1940); and Roger W. Bowen, *Rebellion and Democracy in Meiji Japan* (Berkeley and Los Angeles: University of California Press, 1980).

class interests, and neither takes into account the diverse nature of the social forces represented within the various opposition movements. The following analysis focuses on the social factors involved in political mobilization and the structures and conditions that restricted mass collective action.

EARLY RURAL PROTESTS

If the number of village protests and disturbances is a meaningful indicator of the degree of social unrest, rural Japan was anything but peaceful in the aftermath of the Meiji Restoration. According to Aoki Kōji's data, there were 343 incidents between 1868 and 1872.[3] Peasant protests, which had increased steadily at the end of Tokugawa, reached a historical peak of 110 in 1869. Beginning in 1870, however, the number of incidents declined rapidly, and in 1872 only 30 incidents were recorded.

What does this large number of rural disturbances signify? To put the data into perspective, nearly half of the incidents were local conflicts engendered by the malfeasance of village headmen, landlord–tenant relations, hoarding of rice, foreclosure of loans, and other issues that affected the popular welfare but did not directly involve the central government. Of the remainder, the most frequent cause was the land tax. It can be argued that in these protests, the peasants expressed their frustration that the overthrow of the Tokugawa bakufu had not brought relief from feudal levels of taxation. Shortly after the imperial coup d'état of January 1868, the new government, at the urging of Saigō Takamori, issued an edict promising tax reductions of up to 50 percent in territories belonging to the shogun. Subsequent edicts promised that the emperor would "alleviate the suffering of the people," and commoners were invited to petition the proper authorities in order to rectify the "evil practices" of the Tokugawa bakufu.[4] These early expressions of benevolent concern for the farmers' welfare were commendably Confucian and reflected a degree of genuine concern for the plight of poor peasants. The promise of tax reduction, however, was a deliberate strategy to foment rebellion in the shogun's home provinces and thereby weaken the bakufu's capacity to wage war. After the Tokugawa family and most vassal daimyo surrendered in the spring of 1868 without fighting a single battle, no more was said on the subject, for with victory assured, the new government's most

3 Aoki Kōji, *Meiji nōmin sōjō nenjiteki kenkyū* (Tokyo: Shinseisha, 1967), p. 36.
4 Ibid., pp. 15–16.

urgent need was to pay its bills. Meiji officials temporarily lowered taxes in districts where extraordinary conditions made relief unavoidable. In Aizu, for example, the war had disrupted farming and devastated crops, and farmers were granted reductions of 50 percent in that year's taxes.[5] Moreover, in areas that had experienced climate-related crop loss, officials accepted petitions for tax relief. Thus, the policy initially adopted by the Meiji government with respect to the land tax was to leave the feudal fiscal structure in place and permit traditional appeals for temporary aid.

If early Meiji tax officials were in fact behaving very much like their feudal predecessors, did protests over the land tax signify the farmers' discontent that things had not changed for the better? In some petitions, the villagers respectfully but forthrightly reproached the government for unfulfilled promises. A January 1869 petition from villages in the Chichibu district began by citing two years of destructive floods in requesting tax reductions and also commented on the government's failure to carry out a general tax reduction: "A benevolent order was issued at the time of the Restoration that the [tax] rate be made lower than last year's, but it was not carried out; in the end nothing more was heard of it."[6] However, the language, content, form, and sentiments of these petitions were identical to those of the peasant appeals of the Tokugawa era that asked for tax reductions when forces beyond their control drastically reduced harvests. Because of generally high rates of taxation under the *kokudaka* system, peasants farming small, subsistence-size holdings depended on daimyo benevolence to mitigate the effects of natural disasters, for without tax reductions and loans, many small farmers would be forced to mortgage their land or leave farming altogether. Realizing the daimyo's interest in retaining population and thereby protecting his tax base, the peasants frequently organized illegal "direct appeals" (*osso*) and staged large and raucous demonstrations (*gōso*) before the castle in the expectation that public embarrassment and fear of greater disorder would move the authorities to grant concessions.[7] Economic conditions in fact explain the large number of land tax–related protests in early Meiji. Beginning in 1867, Japan experienced three consecutive years of crop failure; by 1869, the peak year for disturbances, many rural districts were eco-

5 Shōji Kichinosuke, *Yonaoshi ikki no kenkyū* (Tokyo: Azekura shobō, 1970), pp. 319–22.

6 Aoki, *Meiji nōmin sōjō*, p. 17.

7 Especially in the early Tokugawa period when new land was being brought into cultivation, it was in the interest of the daimyo to provide sufficient aid and tax relief to keep peasants on the land. Stephen Vlastos, *Peasant Protests and Uprisings in Tokugawa Japan* (Berkeley and Los Angeles: University of California Press, 1986).

nomically exhausted, although famine was rare. We find the greatest concentration of protests in the districts of western Japan that had suffered the most severe crop losses, and in general the incidence of rural protests in early Meiji correlates with the timing and extent of crop failures.[8] Indistinguishable from the Tokugawa peasant movements in most respects, these protests did not indicate opposition to the Meiji Restoration.

Beginning in 1870, agriculture revived, and the number of protests and disturbances declined dramatically. However, during the first years of Meiji, farmers gained little from the change in government. Indeed, in some districts administered directly by the new regime, taxes had actually increased. When the government abolished feudal domains in 1871 and appointed governors to replace the daimyo, farmers sometimes protested. For example, in August 1871 villagers in Hiroshima tried to prevent the daimyo's entourage from leaving the domain. In September there were demonstrations in Takamatsu and Fukuyama, and in November over three thousand people gathered in Okayama to demand both the reinstatement of the former daimyo and lower taxes. However, in these and other demonstrations, the villagers linked their appeals for the return of their daimyo to the issue of taxation, much like the Tokugawa peasants who protested when the appointment of a new daimyo presaged higher taxes.[9] But their actions did not signify a preference for feudal administration as such.

The Conscription Act of January 10, 1873, gave rise to the most violent rural disturbances of this period. The law decreed compulsory military service of three years in the regular army and four in the reserves for commoners, thereby ending the long tradition of a hereditary (and privileged) warrior class. Many samurai were naturally displeased by the loss of an ancient birthright. But why did the farmers protest?

Most of the sixteen antidraft protests occurred in the spring and summer of 1873, soon after the law was made public.[10] Although the circumstances of each disturbance differed, the uprising in Misaka district illustrates their salient features. First, the villagers misunderstood the meaning of a passage in the edict and charge that "Western people call this a blood tax. This is because one protects his country verily with blood." The intended meaning of the wording of the edict, of course, was that the citizen soldier should be prepared to die in

8 Aoki, *Meiji nōmin sōjō*, pp. 39–40.
9 See Shōji Kichinosuke, *Tōhoku shohan hyakushō ikki no kenkyū: shiryō shūsei* (Tokyo: Ochanomizu shobō, 1969), pp. 186–8.
10 Aoki, *Meiji nōmin sōjō*, p. 38.

battle to defend his country. As one of the leaders of the Misaka riots testified, however, many believed that the army drained the blood of conscripts for sale to foreign countries. Even before publication of the conscription law, villagers in Misaka had become greatly agitated by recent edicts that either imposed additional financial burdens or offended local custom. They objected to the cost of compulsory education, the slaughtering of cows, the liberation of the outcaste communities, and new hair styles. When they first learned of the Conscription Act, the villagers discussed the possibility of voicing their concerns through traditional grievance procedures but concluded that petitions to officials in Tokyo would surely go unanswered. Suddenly rumors abounded that men dressed in white were coming to round up conscripts. Anxious farmers met and resolved to organize a demonstration. A few days later, amid new rumors of the imminent arrival of the "blood tax man," they convened a mass meeting at a local shrine at which the villagers also complained vociferously of the outrageously presumptuous behavior of former outcastes and demanded a return to old customs. According to a prearranged plan, someone reported having seen a man walking in the nearby mountains dressed in white and carrying a large glass bottle. Great commotion ensued, and those assembled were easily persuaded to march to the district magistrate's office. On the way, they attacked the homes and shops of wealthy farmers, moneylenders, and merchants; entering the town of Tsuyama, they surrounded the prefectural office. When officers appeared and attempted to quiet the crowd, farmers armed with hunting rifles and bamboo spears attacked, killing one official and injuring a second. As soon as the police fired back, the crowd scattered, but subsequently disturbances spread to every district in the prefecture, as crowds attacked schools, slaughterhouses, village headmen, outcaste communities, and government buildings.[11]

Ignorance and prejudice contributed to the Misaka "blood tax" riots and violent "antimodernization" protests triggered by laws that offended local customs and beliefs. If we look only at the immediate causes, we can dismiss such incidents as irrational reactions to modernization. Examined more closely, however, the demonstrations reveal a complexity of motivations and objectives. In Ikuno and Harima villages near the present-day city of Kobe, farmers first protested laws relating to outcastes but went on to demand tax reductions; next they drew up an eight-point list of grievances and vented their anger at the

11 Tanaka Akira, *Meiji ishin*, vol. 24 of *Nihon no rekishi* (Tokyo: Shogakkan, 1976), pp. 275–9.

government by destroying machinery at nearby state mines. Finally, they destroyed the property of wealthy commoners, especially moneylenders, merchants, and village officials. Thus one finds in these incidents a mingling of political and social grievances, for to some degree ordinary farmers harbored suspicions, which were not entirely groundless, that the new laws benefited the rich. Although the draft law contained a provision for hardship cases, poor farmers realized that the burden of conscription would fall most heavily on their shoulders. A wealthy farmer could buy exemption from military service for his sons by paying ¥270, a luxury that no ordinary farmer could possibly afford. But if a poor farm family lost a son's labor for three years, its very survival would be threatened.

These protests reveal understandable suspicions regarding laws that, it must be remembered, were promulgated by the central government without public discussion or consultation. To understand why poor farmers in Misaka called for a return to the old ways, we should recall that the Meiji Restoration did not bring popular participation in the political process. If anything, the centralization of authority made it more difficult for the villagers to influence the very policies that most affected them. With respect to the land tax, the most frequent cause of conflict, the Meiji state was infinitely better prepared to resist protest than was the bakufu or daimyo. Not infrequently, the peasants' protests in the Tokugawa period had succeeded in wringing concessions from lords, even though the leaders of illegal protests might be severely punished. However, the creation of an efficient national bureaucracy and modern police and army drastically undercut the efficacy of traditional forms of protest. In the case of the Misaka riots, the villagers considered petitioning the Tokyo government but decided that their appeals would be fruitless and so took matters into their own hands instead. Hence, the apparently irrational "blood tax" riots and related disturbances stemmed from the peasants' justified fears that political centralization had actually increased their powerlessness and vulnerability to the new government's arbitrary decisions.

THE MEIJI LAND TAX AND VILLAGE PROTESTS

After abolishing the feudal domains in 1871, the Meiji leadership grappled with the problem of how to reform the feudal land tax system to meet the demands of national development. The enormous financial costs of pensioning off the daimyo and samurai made their task all the more difficult. How the government persuaded daimyo to surrender peacefully their ancient rights and powers will be discussed in the next section. What concerns us here is the economic constraints on fiscal policy incurred by pensioning off the ruling class, for stipends and domain debts alone consumed most of the government's revenue in the early 1870s.[12]

There were few sources of additional revenue that the government was willing or able to tap. It rejected borrowing abroad because of the obvious perils to national security in case of subsequent default, and it was determined to tax commerce and industry as lightly as possible in order to speed capital formation. Meanwhile, the commercial treaties forced on Japan by the West had fixed tariffs at uniform low rates that limited the revenue from foreign trade.[13]

Although the leaders saw no alternative to maintaining the high taxes on agriculture, they could not afford to alienate the farmers' allegiance to the state. There was little reason to fear rural revolution. But even passive resistance in the form of withholding taxes would strain the treasury, and small, nonviolent protests always had the potential to escalate. Memories of *yonaoshi* (world rectification) and *uchikowashi* (urban smashing) uprisings that had erupted in the mid-1860s were still fresh. If the farmers violently protested the new tax, prefectural officials would be forced to mobilize ex-samurai bands to restore order. Unemployed retainers were only too willing to unsheathe their swords, but the central government judged the risks of unleashing them to be unacceptably high. Whatever the changes made in tax and property rights, the government needed the farmers' acquiescence.

The dilemma facing the Meiji government was how to ensure the farmers' cooperation with the new tax system without substantially reducing land tax revenues. Part of the solution involved eliminating feudal restrictions on landholding and legalizing capitalist relations of production, changes welcomed by most farmers and particularly beneficial to large landholders. In 1871 the government abolished the customary restrictions on land use. Early in 1872 it legalized the sale of private holdings and prohibited the daimyo and retainers from expropriating farmland in their former domains. Next, new land surveys were ordered, and certificates were issued. Finally, in July 1873 the government promulgated a law that fundamentally restructured the

12 Niwa Kunio, "Chiso kaisei to chitsuroku shobun," in *Iwanami kōza: Nihon rekishi*, vol. 15 (*kindai* 2) (Tokyo: Iwanami shoten, 1962), pp. 145–6.

13 The United States and the other major Western imperialist powers had forced the bakufu to sign commercial treaties that limited import and export duties to a flat rate of 5 percent.

land tax system while maintaining the old levels of taxation. It deserves closer scrutiny.

The Meiji land tax established uniform procedures for assessing taxes based on the market value of land as a fixed investment. The Tokugawa land tax had been based on estimates of productivity measured in output of rice, and both nominal and real rates of taxation varied considerably from fief to fief. However, the new tax was set at a uniform 3 percent of the monetary value of each parcel of land as determined by a complex formula that included estimates of land fertility, commodity prices, fixed production costs, and reasonable rate of return. The tax was paid in cash directly to the state by each owner; it was a fixed tax that initially made no provision for reduction in the event of natural calamities. In return, taxpayers were given title deeds that conferred full rights of ownership. No attempt was made to regulate landlord–tenant relations: Landlords were responsible for paying the yearly tax, after which they were free to charge whatever rents the market would bear.

Inasmuch as the 1873 revision of the land tax altered every feature of the old tax system, we should expect conflicts to have arisen. According to Arimoto Masao's data, there were ninety-nine rural protests between 1874 and 1881, the period during which the reform was carried out. Why did farmers protest, and how did they mobilize?

Initially, the most frequent complaint was not the tax rate itself but the way that the local tax commissions had determined land values and interim taxes. Often villages disputed the prices used to calculate the cash value of crops and to commute taxes previously collected in kind; for the lower the price, the lower the assessment. And because rice prices fluctuated from year to year and from one district to the next, some villages were likely to feel unfairly treated, especially if local soil, climate, and market conditions lowered the price of their crop.

One of the larger protests occurred in the Naka district of Wakayama Prefecture in 1876.[14] In February, Kodama Shōemon, the eldest son of the mayor of Nakayama village, petitioned the governor to complain that in commuting taxes formerly collected in kind, the tax commission had overcharged villages by assuming an unrealistically high rice price. Spurred by Shōemon's appeal, the mayors of twelve neighboring villages petitioned jointly and voiced the same complaint. When the governor responded by rejecting the petitions, Shōemon made yet another appeal in which he insisted that although the official

14 Arimoto Masao, *Chiso kaisei to nōmin tōsō* (Tokyo: Shinseisha, 1968), pp. 600–10; and Gotō Yasushi, "Chiso kaisei hantai ikki," *Ritsumeikan keizaigaku* 9 (April 1960): 109–52.

price accurately reflected conditions in other districts of Wakayama, the prices in his district were in fact considerably lower. Anticipating the objection that the procedures must be uniform, he lectured the governor on the proper function of laws: "Laws are made for the people, not people for laws."

At first, the villages disputed only the assessment of interim taxes, but they soon broadened their demands to include land values. As before, they insisted that the official rice price was too high and cited examples of more favorable treatment afforded by other tax commissions. In their petitions they also played on the fears of popular disturbances. Reminding the governor that the mayors stood "between the officials and the people," they warned of the hardship caused by the tax revisions, hardships so severe that "even the blind can stir up the people."[15]

Only after twenty-nine mayors and assistant officials had tendered their resignations did the governor attempt a compromise. He refused to accept the resignations and authorized a 5 percent reduction in the official price, about half of what the mayors had requested. However, instead of ending the protest, his actions stirred the hope of even greater concessions and swelled the ranks of the protesters. In April, 177 village officials jointly petitioned the governor to demand that prices be determined on a case-by-case basis according to the conditions in each district.

By contesting the use of uniform procedures, the protest threatened to cause interminable delay. As compromise had not produced a settlement, the governor now took a hard line. The mayors were summoned to a meeting and admonished; when they still objected, he fired them and arrested five ringleaders. Although the arrest of popular village officials provoked a large demonstration, within a few days the local authorities had restored order without resort to force. A company of infantry had been dispatched to Wakayama, but it was not necessary to deploy it in the countryside. Later large-scale arrests were made to set an example: Over 1,000 people were arrested, and 688 were convicted of encouraging public disturbances.

The protest of Wakayama was unusual in that most disputes that arose in conjunction with the tax law revision were resolved without fines or mass arrests. How, then, did the tax officials gain the consent of recalcitrant villagers, for the law required owners to agree to new assessments? The fate of the protests in Tottori suggests some of the answers.[16]

15 Arimoto, *Chiso kaisei*, p. 605. 16 Ibid., pp. 618–29.

In Tottori, more than twenty villages in the Yatsuhashi and Kume districts rejected the new tax assessments, and an equal number postponed making a decision. Hoping to quell the resistance before the revolt spread, the tax commission ordered representatives of the villages to the prefectural capital where they were subjected to intense pressure to give their consent. Most of the bullying was verbal, but one man reported being held ten hours a day in the back of the jail for eight consecutive days. Not surprisingly, some of the representatives gave in and agreed to the assessments; soon only seventeen holdouts remained. But then several villages that had previously consented reversed their decision and joined the protest. In December, thirty-six villages filed suit in the district court challenging the assessments, and the pendulum swung the other way. By February 1876, 112 villages were holding out. Again, the officials did their best and convinced eight powerful landlords to break ranks and sign individual consent orders. Because their holdings spanned many villages, the effect was to undermine resistance, especially by their tenants.[17] As a result, the number of holdouts had dropped in half by spring.

Opposition collapsed in July when the local tax commission invoked a recently adopted amendment to the land law that authorized binding on-site assessments as a last resort.[18] The commission appointed a committee of local notables to investigate conditions in the eight villages that had been at the forefront of the protest. To the surprise of no one, they reported that conditions in the villages did not warrant special consideration, a finding that gave ample warning of what to expect from on-site assessments. Soon after, most of the villages abandoned the protest. The reduction of assessments for seven of the remaining holdout villages ended all opposition. By December the tax commission reported to the main bureau in Tokyo that its work was done.

The largest number of protests occurred in the latter half of 1875 and 1876. Although revision of the land tax had begun in the spring of 1874, initially there were few protests, for in areas such as Hiroshima, Chikuma, and Yamaguchi local notables participated in the commissions, and the new assessments were generally lower than the old. However, in May 1875 a special agency was established in Tokyo to supervise the work of the local commissions and to speed implementa-

17 Almost half of all the land in the Yatsuhashi and Kume districts was tenant cultivated, and a few landlords controlled immense holdings. Their acceptance of the commission's assessments undermined resistance in all of the villages.

18 The law was amended in April 1876 to authorize assessments without consent when based on inspections carried out by the local commissions. Because the new assessments were generally lower than the old, in most cases it was necessary to invoke this provision.

tion. Thereafter, state interests tended to predominate.[19] Assessments were less generous to the farmers, for the commissions were given target quotas that, though not absolute, influenced their decisions. And to discourage villages from protesting, in May 1876 an amendment authorizing on-site inspections was adopted.

The tougher policy produced a sharp increase in protests. At the same time, however, samurai revolts erupted in southwestern Japan, and soon the government adopted a more conciliatory posture toward the farmers.[20] In January 1877, the land tax was lowered from 3 percent of market value to 2.5 percent, a reduction of 17 percent in the yearly tax. Later in the year, the law was further amended to permit reductions when crop loss due to natural disasters exceeded 50 percent. Finally, farmers in villages distant from marketing centers were allowed to pay part of their tax in produce.

The adoption of these measures was followed by a noticeable decline in protests, but it did not eliminate all resistance. The most stubbornly contested dispute over revised assessments occurred in the summer of 1878 in Ishikawa Prefecture.[21] Initially, 232 villages in seven districts refused to accept the newly published assessments, but as the prefectural commission applied pressure, resistance dwindled. In the 28 villages that continued to hold out, opposition was led by a group of very wealthy local notables who did not back down when the tax commission invoked the threat of on-site inspections, a tactic that had worked well against poor villages in Tottori. Rather, they borrowed the rhetoric of natural rights to justify their refusal to accept the new assessment, lecturing the authorities that "if liberty be our right, we will never accede to what is not just." To strengthen their hand, they sought outside support and made contact with the Risshisha, a liberal political society headed by Itagaki Taisuke that was campaigning for an elected national assembly and that sent Sugita Teiichi to help their movement. Experienced in legal matters, Sugita filed various suits on behalf of the villagers, and it is likely that the linking of the two movements caused the government considerable alarm.

Perhaps because the government feared the involvement of the Risshisha in land tax–related protests, the dispute was settled in Tokyo by Ōkuma Shigenobu, chief of the Finance Ministry, who ordered that the entire process be redone, starting with new surveys. When

19 Niwa Kunio, "Chiso kaisei," in Nihon rekishi gakkai, ed., *Nihonshi no mondai ten* (Tokyo: Yoshikawa kōbunkan, 1965), pp. 297–8.
20 Fukushima Masao, *Chiso kaisei* (Tokyo: Kyōbunkan, 1968), pp. 188–92.
21 Arimoto, *Chiso kaisei*, p. 631.

these were completed one year later, the result was not an unqualified victory for the landowners, for although the new assessments were substantially lower, the administrative costs charged to the villages amounted to more than twenty times the yearly savings in the land tax.[22]

What does this brief survey of resistance to land tax revision reveal? What can we conclude with respect to rural opposition to the Meiji land tax, an institution that fundamentally shaped the development of the Meiji state?

First, the revision of the land tax must be judged a political as well as an economic success. Given the magnitude of the changes and the interests involved, conflict was inevitable. It was naturally in the farmers' interest to seek lower assessments, although the government could not afford substantial reduction in revenue. In the light of these facts, the total number of protests was small: ninety-nine incidents between 1874 and 1881, of which thirty-seven were landlord–tenant conflicts and did not directly involve the state. Most of the disputes over assessments were eventually settled through negotiation and compromise without arrests or resort to armed force. In a handful of cases, the local officials were sufficiently alarmed to call in the national army and mobilize samurai bands. But compared to the "blood tax" uprisings, these were tame and orderly affairs.

The principal effect of the Meiji land tax was to equalize and rationalize tax assessments according to market value and thereby to eliminate the arbitrary factor in Tokugawa taxation. Under daimyo rule, the actual rates of tax extraction varied considerably depending on the rigor of fief administration; rice fields (*suiden*) were more heavily taxed than was unirrigated land (*hatake*), as was arable compared with residential and commercial land. By making the land tax fall more equally, Meiji tax assessments provided some relief to the majority of landholders.[23]

Not all classes of landholders benefited equally, however. The Meiji land tax caused special problems for the poor.[24] The tax had to be paid in cash, a provision that forced subsistence producers into greater dependence on the market and increased the risk of bankruptcy. Sub-

22 The land tax is discussed in economic terms in Kozo Yamamura, "The Meiji Land Tax Reform and Its Effects," in Marius B. Jansen and Gilbert Rozman, eds., *Japan in Transition: From Tokugawa to Meiji* (Princeton, N.J.: Princeton University Press, 1986), pp. 382–99; and is described in James Nakamura, *Agricultural Production and the Economic Development of Japan 1873–1922* (Princeton, N.J.: Princeton University Press, 1966), pp. 177–96.

23 Arimoto, *Chiso kaisei*, p. 637.

24 Norman, *Japan's Emergence As a Modern State*, pp. 138–44.

sistence producers also lost the protection previously afforded by daimyo benevolence – the granting of tax reductions to mitigate the effects of crop failure. Farmers on the margins of the market economy had the greatest need of short-term aid, as they did not have the resources to withstand severe shortfalls. The Meiji land tax, however, initially allowed no exemptions at all and, when amended, permitted reductions only if the crop loss exceeded half of the harvest.

At the same time, the revised land tax system worked to the advantage of large farmers and especially landlords. The corporate features of the Tokugawa land tax were eliminated, as was payment in kind, and both of these changes gave capitalist farmers greater access to the market. Second, the feature of the Meiji land tax that caused the greatest hardship to poor farmers – the fact that taxes were held constant – proved highly profitable to those farmers who, through investment and technological innovation, boosted output and income, for taxes were not tied to profits. Of course, innovation and production for the market were not limited to the wealthy. Nevertheless, landlords and farmers with large holdings naturally reaped the greatest benefits of the decline of the land tax as a fixed cost of production. Third, as noted earlier, taxpayers were given full rights of ownership, even to the mortgaged land and paddy fields that tenants (or their ancestors) had brought into cultivation, and conditions of tenure would no longer confer customary right to permanent tenancy. Finally, landlords were legally free to sell land and renegotiate rents. Although the landlord who cared about social esteem was unlikely to put out all his holdings to the highest bidder, the courts and police – both vastly more efficient than were their feudal counterparts – would back him up if he did.

It is not surprising, therefore, that in the latter phase of land tax revision, and particularly after the general reduction ordered in 1877, the number of disputes between tenants and landlords increased. Between 1877 and 1881, twenty-nine of the forty-nine incidents recorded were landlord–tenant conflicts. The major issues of contention were rents and the customary rights of cultivators. The issue of rents was connected to the revised assessments because tenants expected reduced rents when taxes were lowered, but tended to resist rent increases if the tax had been increased. Customary rights were a more volatile issue. The best-known, and certainly the bloodiest, dispute over proprietary rights involved tenant farmers in Shindo village, Kanagawa Prefecture, who had mortgaged land "in perpetuity" – a

Tokugawa practice whereby the mortgagor retained use rights.[25] When the tax commission awarded title to the mortgage holder, a powerful landlord and village mayor, the tenants contested the ruling through the courts, persisting with appeal after appeal over a two-year period. Finally, after a direct but fruitless appeal to the Ministry of Finance, they attacked the landlord's house in frustration, killing him and seven of his relatives and servants. Despite the murders, it was the dispossessed cultivators who won the sympathy of local opinion. When they were brought to trial, fifteen hundred villagers signed a petition pleading for leniency.

Taken as a whole, village protests against land tax revision reveal the pivotal role of the local notable (*gōnō*) class of farmers in representing to the state the interests of the rural communities. With the exception of disputes between landlords and tenants, opposition to land tax revision was spearheaded by mayors and local notables. That they assumed this role is not surprising, for throughout the Tokugawa period, headmen had represented the village in all dealings with fief authorities. Under the Tokugawa tax system, taxes were assessed on the village rather than on individual householders, and it was the responsibility of the headman to see that they were paid. Legally responsible for all financial relations between the corporate village and the state, headmen were also perceived by the community to be, and themselves felt, morally responsible for safeguarding their communities' well-being. If landholders suffered crop failure or the lord increased taxes, it was the headman's duty to petition the authorities; if permissible appeals failed to achieve redress of grievance, the village head had a moral obligation to continue the petitioning process, even if this entailed breaking the law. Hence, we find the tradition of *gimin*, the extreme case of leaders who risked (or lost) their lives protesting onerous taxes and officials' malfeasance.[26]

To understand the political dynamic of village protest against land tax revision, we should remember that the headmen and notables had traditionally assumed responsibility in all matters involving the village's fiscal obligations and other financial dealing with the state. Thus, majors and notables acted out a familiar role when they

25 Irokawa Daikichi, "Konmintō to Jiyūtō," *Rekishigaku kenkyū*, no. 247 (November 1960): pp. 5–6.

26 Irwin Scheiner, "Benevolent Lords and Honorable Peasants," in Tetsuo Najita and Irwin Scheiner, eds. *Japanese Thought in the Tokugawa Period* (Chicago: University of Chicago Press, 1979), pp. 39–62; and Anne Walthall, "Narratives of Peasant Uprisings in Japan," *Journal of Japanese Studies* 42 (May 1983): pp. 571–87. See also Yokoyama Toshio, *Hyakushō ikki to gimin denshō* (Tokyo: Kyōikusha rekishi shinsho, 1977).

participated in the implementation of land tax revision by overseeing the enormously elaborate and time-consuming work of surveying, grading, and registering the thousands of parcels of land in their communities. Although the Finance Ministry determined policy objectives, prefectural commissions necessarily relied on the cooperation of village heads and prominent citizens to supply the data used to calculate the new assessments. This gave heads and notables both power and responsibility to ensure a satisfactory outcome. Hence, most of the disputes between villages and local tax commissions involved issues that affected the interests of all farm households, regardless of the size of their holdings. The collective interests of villagers in lowering land evaluations and interim taxes permitted political mobilization within the tradition of Tokugawa village protests. As we saw in the conflicts in Wakayama, Tottori, and Ishikawa prefectures, when principled mayors and notables felt that the commissions had done them an injustice, these otherwise law-abiding citizens resisted stubbornly.

We can now analyze the political dynamic in village protests against land tax revision. First, responsibility for initiating protest rested with the village heads and local notables, and they acted only when the interests of all landholders were affected by the rulings of the tax commissions. The relatively small number of protests is therefore explained by the fact that the revised assessments, though higher than desired, were usually somewhat lower than the Tokugawa tax rates. Second, because high-status villagers assumed responsibility for representing the community's interests to the state and relied on petitions and legal process, the protests tended to be orderly and restrained. Generally, they did not mobilize the village poor – the most volatile and potentially most militant social class. With few exceptions, village protests against tax revision were settled through negotiation and compromise. Despite confrontation and the testing of wills, conflict occurred within the larger context of economic reforms that were welcomed by the majority of rural producers. One does not see villages protesting the principal provisions of the Meiji land tax, only specific rulings of the prefectural commissions. This limited the scope and intensity of the conflicts.

The real hardships caused by the Meiji land tax did not readily lead to collective action. The social classes affected most adversely – subsistence farmers forced into bankruptcy and cultivators dispossessed of customary rights – were relatively powerless. Because capitalist farmers profited from the system of unqualified ownership rights and fixed monetarized taxes, the village as a whole did not share a common interest in opposing these provisions of the Meiji tax. Moreover, the political obligations of the headmen and notables did not extend – or did so in only attenuated form – to hardship arising out of contractual and commercial relations; as landlords and moneylenders, they themselves might be party to such disputes. Thus the dispossessed were left to fend for themselves. Although *uchikowashi* and *yonaoshi* uprisings provided a model of collective action by the poor against both the rich villagers and the state, conditions favorable to the mass mobilization of small farmers did not materialize until the mid-1880s, well after the revision of the land tax had been completed.

SHIZOKU REVOLTS

In contrast with the generally peaceful and limited opposition movements of rural commoners during the first decade of Meiji, samurai opposition initially took the form of armed uprisings that sought to topple the government. The underlying cause of the rebellions was profound discontent and considerable economic distress within the former warrior class caused by early Meiji reforms that dismantled the feudal polity and all but abolished samurai elite status. To the extent that the rebellions expressed the frustration and resentment of former samurai, they represented the clearest and most forceful example of resistance to modernization in the early Meiji period. Viewed as the organized, political response of a dispossessed social class, the half-dozen *shizoku* rebellions between 1874 and 1877 can be explained as the predictably violent reaction of a traditional elite displaced by a modern revolution. There can be no doubt that materially and psychologically the samurai bore the major burden of rapid modernization; and because they were systematically disadvantaged by early Meiji reforms, they had an obvious interest in joining counterrevolutionary movements.

Nevertheless, important aspects of *shizoku* rebellion do not readily fit the mold of counterrevolution. The leaders of the rebellions were not defenders of the ancient regime, nor had they lost power and status as a result of the Meiji Restoration. Without exception, the rebellion leaders were young samurai from southwestern Japan who had early joined the anti-Tokugawa movement and continued to identify passionately with the imperial cause. Outstanding members of the revolutionary elite that seized power in 1868, they had been richly rewarded for their services. In fact, the leaders of the largest rebellions – Etō Shimpei, Maebara Issei and Saigō Takamori – all had served on the Council of State, the highest decision-making body, before breaking with the government. Before resigning in 1873 to protest the cancellation of the Korean invasion, Etō and Saigō supported, if somewhat grudgingly, sweeping reforms that all but ended feudalism and laid the foundations for subsequent modernization.

As we shall see, the *shizoku* rebellions were complex events that incorporated various political impulses. Insurrections led by disaffected leaders, they reflected personality conflicts and bureaucratic rivalry within the ruling elite; local protests against the increasing power and assertiveness of the government in Tokyo, they expressed sectional opposition to political centralization. Nevertheless, at least among the rank and file, the underlying impetus to armed resistance was the opposition to the loss of traditional warrior status and class privilege. Whatever the motivation of individual leaders, the social basis of antigovernment *shizoku* ferment in the mid-1870s was resistance to early Meiji reforms that, by dismantling the feudal polity and building a modern army and a centralized state bureaucracy, eliminated samurai class privilege.

The young samurai who came to power in 1868 had experienced the frustration of subordinate rank in feudal society, and they quickly ended the social distinctions based on hereditary status.[27] Having come to the realization that the traditional status system was an obstacle to national unity, they dismantled it one step at a time. Beginning in 1869, the government ordered the profusion of hereditary ranks within the samurai class reduced to two, *shizoku* (knight) and *sotsu* (foot soldier), and ended the archaic division of commoners into status groups – peasant, merchant, and artisan – based on occupation. Two years later, it freed outcaste communities from legal prescriptions that had enforced strict segregation. All commoners were required to adopt surnames and were informed that public acts of deference toward samurai, such as prostration, were no longer necessary or desirable. Samurai, on the other hand, were told that they need not wear swords in public, an oblique request that they abandon their swaggering ways of old. For the first time, warriors were authorized to take up farming, industry, and trade and were offered capital for starting new enterprises if they gave up their hereditary stipends. Samurai were also advised to cut off their topknots and adopt Western headdress, and

27 Some of the leaders of the *sonnō jōi* movement were discontented with the Tokugawa class system and ideologically committed to a meritocracy. See Thomas M. Huber, *The Revolutionary Origins of Modern Japan* (Stanford, Calif.: Stanford University Press, 1981).

soon Western-style clothing was encouraged – indeed required of certain government officials, as a final step toward eliminating the visible marks of traditional status.

The abolition of the feudal domains in 1871 accelerated the decline of the warrior class. Overnight, the samurai lost their traditional perquisites as retainers and sinecures as soldiers, functionaries, and administrators. The most dramatic and far-reaching of the early Meiji reforms, the transformation of the polity from feudalism to centralized nation-state did not so much spring from a social critique of feudalism as from a concern for national strength. The Meiji leaders realized that the Tokugawa political order, based on parcelized sovereignty, was fundamentally incompatible with the political and military mobilization required to preserve Japan's independence in the world of nineteenth-century imperialism. Kido Takayoshi, who among Restoration leaders was the most conscious of Japan's precarious international position and need to "hold its own in the world," early advocated greater centralization of state power and soon convinced Ōkubo Toshimichi of Satsuma and Itagaki Taisuke of Tosa. The central government was still too weak to compel the daimyo to give up power, but Kido, Ōkubo, and Itagaki persuaded the lords of their respective domains – who were moved as much by traditional rivalry as by patriotic duty – to surrender voluntarily their *han* registers, symbols of daimyo authority, to the emperor. As other daimyo followed their example, they were appointed "governors" and granted one-tenth of fief revenue as personal income, and the Tokyo government paid all the administrative costs. If anything, the daimyo were probably better off financially, and outwardly their power had not diminished drastically.[28]

Nevertheless, not all diamyo agreed to give up their hereditary rights and privileges, and the government waited two years before compelling compliance. In the meantime, Chōshū, Satsuma, and Tosa combined forces to create the embryo of a national army, the ten-thousand-strong Imperial Guard subject to the sole authority of the Tokyo government. With an army at their command, the Meiji leaders felt sufficiently secure to abolish the fiefs entirely. In August 1871, the emperor issued an edict that proclaimed the end of daimyo rule. Daimyo were offered various inducements: appointment as governors of their former domains, generous pensions, state assumption of fief debts, and, in time, titles of nobility in a new peerage. Later in 1871, the government eliminated the last vestiges of daimyo administration.

28 W. G. Beasley, *The Meiji Restoration* (Stanford, Calif.: Stanford University Press, 1972), pp. 335–49.

Daimyo were ordered to take up permanent residence in Tokyo; fief armies were disbanded; and many local officials were dismissed. Governors appointed by the Home Ministry, who were often outsiders and protégés of leading ministers, now administered the countryside.

Even a cursory account of the process by which the Tokugawa feudal polity was abolished suggests some of the reasons for the slow development of counterrevolution in the Meiji period. First, the daimyo class, which had little capacity for collective action, was divided vertically along traditional sectional lines as large southwestern fiefs, whose clansmen dominated the national government, were played off against one another, and then against the more numerous, but smaller, fiefs of eastern and northeastern Japan. Second, and more importantly, the preferential treatment of the elite ranks divided the warrior class horizontally, thereby vitiating the *kashindan* – hierarchically organized corps of retainers – as a vehicle of antigovernment mobilization. Daimyo and fief elders received lavish pensions, in addition to ranks and titles, and possessed a strong material incentive to accept the loss of traditional status without protest. On the other hand, the pensions of most samurai were less than subsistence livings, and even these were commuted to interest-bearing bonds in 1876. Thus, nonelite samurai had every reason to resist, but without the sanction of the domain leaders they could not use the existing (feudal) structures of collective action. Before the samurai could act in defense of their traditional rights as warriors, they would have to find a new basis for collective action.

If *shizoku* privilege was to be preserved, the new national army was the logical place. A minority within the leadership clung to the feudal ruling class conceit that as the inheritors of a thousand years of military service, the samurai were uniquely endowed with the requisite martial virtues – courage, loyalty, and honor. Maebara Issei wanted the army to be entirely *shizoku*. Kirino Toshiaki and Shinohara Kunimoto, Saigō's chief lieutenants and commanders of the Imperial Guard, violently opposed the induction of commoners and resisted all attempts to integrate conscripts into their force. Others saw the drafting of unemployed *shizoku* as a solution to a pressing social problem. Torio Koyata, a general from Chōshū, proposed that 20 percent of the revenue be set aside to create a standing army and national reserve large enough to enlist all *shizoku* between the ages of twenty and forty-five. Tani Kanjō of Tosa advocated first conscripting the sons of *shizoku* and, only later, after all able-bodied *shizoku* had been inducted, opening recruitment to commoners.[29] However, majority opin-

29 Masumi Junnosuke, *Nihon seitō shi ron* (Tokyo: Tokyo daigaku shuppankai, 1965), vol. 1, p. 113.

ion within the oligarchy supported universal conscription – in part because it was the system used in the West but mainly because of its intrinsic merits. Yamagata Aritomo, who succeeded Maebara Issei as head of the army, foresaw that samurai virtues were a mixed blessing in a modern army. *Shizoku* might well be fierce and brave fighters, but they were also likely to be fractious, undisciplined, and more loyal to their clansmen than to the central government. High regard for ascriptive status and particularistic loyalties were as much as part of *bushidō* as was unflinching courage. Yamagata correctly anticipated that the first task of the national army would be to suppress internal revolts and reasoned that among the *shizoku,* their strong emotional identification with fief and clansmen impaired unity.[30] Even as soldiers of the imperial army, the *shizoku* might act and think in terms of old loyalties.

Promulgated on January 10, 1873, the Conscription Act made all twenty-year-old males liable for seven years of military service – three in the regular army and four in the reserves – and required men between the ages of seventeen and forty-five to register for possible call-up. The immediate aim was to create a truly national army loyal to the central government and suited to the highly regimented military system recently adopted from the West, but the adoption of universal conscription widened the distance between conservatives who insisted that the *shizoku* remain the military and political elite and those who viewed ascriptive status as being incompatible with modern national development.

Saigō Takamori was the leading conservative in the Meiji government. In 1871 he submitted two memorials outlining a model of economic and political development very different from the "iron and coal" model favored by the majority of the oligarchs. The first memorial advocated not only the adoption of Shinto as the state religion but also the proscription of Buddhism and Christianity; a national tax on agriculture based on the feudal norm of half to the lord and half to the people; and a tax on manufacturing to pay in full all warrior stipends under 100 *koku*. The second memorial proposed specific measures to revitalize the rural economy: hiring foreign experts; appointing especially diligent farmers as headmen to instruct villagers in the virtues of filial piety, frugality, obedience, and sincerity; setting up agricultural research stations; selecting the best technologies of traditional farm practices and Western agronomy; invest-

30 Roger Hackett, *Yamagata Aritomo in the Rise of Modern Japan, 1838–1922* (Cambridge, Mass.: Harvard University Press, 1971), p. 61.

ing public funds in irrigation and flood control; and providing credit to individual farmers.[31]

Whatever the merits of specific proposals aimed at improving agriculture, Saigō's conception of political economy was thoroughly traditional. The 50 percent land tax he proposed would impoverish all but the richest farmers and inhibit investment and growth. Instead of promoting industrialization, the manufacturing sector would be heavily taxed to support the socially unproductive *shizoku*. In later proposals, Saigō came to support and even advocate reduction in the level of *shizoku* support, but there remained little common ground between his thought and the "iron and coal" school of modernization.

The issue that split the original leadership group ostensibly involved foreign relations rather than domestic policy. When Korea refused to open diplomatic and trade relations with Japan, Saigō proposed a venture in gunboat diplomacy that he secretly hoped would lead to war and the immediate mobilization of unemployed samurai.[32] He was supported by Itagaki Taisuke and Gotō Shōjirō of Tosa and Etō Shimpei and Soejima Taneomi of Hizen, who agreed that Japan should invade Korea and impose diplomatic and trade relations, as the West had done to Japan fifteen years earlier. However, Iwakura Tomomi, Ōkubo Toshimichi, and Kido Takayoshi, who had recently returned from an extended tour of the United States and Europe, argued forcefully against Saigō's plan. They did not object on grounds of principle: They agreed that it was Japan's destiny to rule the backward nations of Asia, if only to protect them from the predatory West. But they realized that despite the abolition of feudal political institutions, Japan remained weak and vulnerable compared with the countries that the Iwakura mission had visited between 1871 and 1873. The possibility of Chinese or Russian intervention if Japan invaded Korea raised the stakes considerably, for the costs of fighting a prolonged war would jeopardize the development of the very institutions on which Japan's future as a major power depended. Although initially outvoted, the "peace" party managed to reverse the vote in the Council of State in October after Iwakura was appointed chairman. With his group now in the majority, Iwakura reintroduced Saigō's plan, which, of course, was voted down; and despite vehement protests from the war party, he immediately presented the results to the emperor. Humiliated and outraged by tactics that violated the spirit, if

31 Gotō Yasushi, *Shizoku hanran no kenkyū* (Tokyo: Aoki shoten, 1967), p. 28.

32 Saigō volunteered to head an uninvited diplomatic mission to Korea, fully expecting to be attacked and very possibly killed, thereby precipitating war.

not also the letter, of collective rule, Saigō, Itagaki, Gotō, Etō, and Soejima resigned from the Council of State and left Tokyo. So did many of their followers in the bureaucracy and army.

Underlying the debate over policy toward Korea was the acute social crisis confronting the *shizoku* class. Even though the pensions paid to the *shizoku* provided less than a subsistence living, they drained the treasury of revenue needed to finance national development.[33] Clearly, the government could not live indefinitely with this arrangement; in 1873, before the debate over Korea, the Finance Ministry had introduced a plan for the voluntary conversion of pensions into lump-sum payments in interest-bearing bonds. Ideally, the *shizoku* would invest in farming, trade, or manufacture and thereby enhance economic development while freeing tax revenues for public investment. But relatively few *shizoku* accepted the offer, and of those who did, many soon lost all their money. As their economic situation deteriorated, they became increasingly alienated and restive. Saigō had earlier written to Ōkubo, who was in London with Iwakura, that he felt as though he was "sleeping on a powder keg," because of the dissatisfaction of the Satsuma men in the Imperial Guard. Perhaps he exaggerated; nevertheless, the prospect of immediate employment and the excitement and adventure of war seemed to offer a temporary solution. The army had only just begun to conscript commoners, and the *shizoku* constituted the only segment of the population with military training. In addition to providing immediate employment and salary, mobilization for war promised to resuscitate traditional martial values and to restore the *shizoku* to a position of honor and respect. War might also strengthen the hand of Saigō and Itagaki, the "old soldiers," against the professional bureaucrats.

Of the six councilors who resigned in the fall of 1873, all but Soejima ended up leading antigovernment movements. In January 1874, Itagaki and Gotō submitted a memorial to the emperor (Etō and Soejima also signed) asking the throne to establish an elected national assembly. Rebuffed, they returned to Tosa and began a national campaign for constitutional government. Saigō immediately sailed for Kagoshima. Renouncing all political involvement, he retired to the Satsuma countryside. Although three years later he would lead the greatest of all *shizoku* revolts, the 1877 Satsuma Rebellion, his first inclination was to withdraw entirely from politics.

After resigning from the Council of State, Etō Shimpei returned to

33 Masumi, *Nihon seitō*, p. 124.

Saga where he led the first major rebellion against the Meiji state. By birth a lower-ranking Hizen samurai, Etō had defied the orders of his daimyo while still a young man to leave Saga to join the ranks of activists leading the loyalist cause against the Tokugawa shogunate. He rose steadily within revolutionary circles, even though as a native of Hizen, he was something of an outsider. Appointed to the Council of State in 1873, Etō also held key posts in the ministries of Education and Justice. During his tenure as chief of the Ministry of Justice, he oversaw work on legal codes that laid the foundation of the Meiji legal system. He was personally responsible for several humanitarian reforms: outlawing the sale of women into prostitution and putting restrictions on contracts of indentured laborers.[34] However, he advocated an aggressive foreign policy in the belief that only forceful demonstration of Japan's military power would end extraterritoriality. Convinced that Japan's failure to chastise Korea would be interpreted as a sign of weakness, Etō sided with the war party.

The decisive factor in Etō's move from opposition to rebellion was his involvement with the Seikantō (Attack Korea Party), one of two *shizoku* groups in Hizen openly critical of the Tokyo government. The larger group, the Yūkokutō (Party of Patriots), was headed by Shima Yoshitake. Shima was also a veteran Restoration activist, revolutionary, and after the defeat of the bakufu he initially held several middle-ranking posts in the Meiji government. Unlike Etō, however, he lacked the skills and temperament to be a successful bureaucrat. He was also violently opposed to reforms that smacked of Westernization. The political program of the Yūkokutō was xenophobic and reactionary. In addition to restoring fiefs and warrior rule, the party advocated the proscription of Christianity to prevent contamination of the national gods, the revival of traditional martial arts as part of a program of moral self-strengthening, and a massive military buildup. The Seikantō, on the other hand, focused its criticism of the government entirely on foreign policy. It was made up mainly of young *shizoku* who hoped to escape poverty and tedium by enlisting for the war with Korea; they were sufficiently desperate to resolve to carry out an invasion on their own, even without government authorization. Meeting for the first time in December 1873, the society enrolled more than one thousand members. Soon after it sent a delegation to Tokyo to confer with Etō, who agreed to assume leadership.

It is by no means certain that Etō returned to Hizen with the intent

34 Sonoda Hiyoshi, *Etō Shimpei to Saga no ran* (Tokyo: Shin jimbutsu ōraisha, 1978), pp. 89–92.

of leading a rebellion. Rather, the government, alarmed by reports of an imminent uprising in Saga, forced his hand by sending an expeditionary force into the prefecture. Previously, the Yūkokutō disdained any association with the Seikantō, but its members too felt compelled to resist the entry of government troops. Ironically, Shima had gone back to Saga at the express request of Iwakura to forestall rash action by his compatriots when he learned en route that the government had already sent a force to occupy the prefectural capital. Meeting at Nagasaki on February 12, Shima and Etō agreed to organize armed resistance, even though they realized that they faced certain defeat. Etō had already received word of Saigō's refusal to join forces, and without Saigō, it was hopeless to expect the support of Itagaki and the Tosa faction. Although a rebellion limited to Saga could not possibly succeed, Etō decided the issue by exclaiming that because the government had already ordered troops into Saga, "we have reached that point where there is no room for discussion. Rather than die with hands at our sides, isn't it better to seize the initiative?"[35]

Two days later the Seikantō set up headquarters at a temple five miles north of Saga. There was little consultation with the Yūkokutō, which had commenced its own preparations. The rebellion started by chance at dawn on February 16 when a party of Yūkokutō warriors exchanged fire with sentries posted by the vanguard of the government force that had entered the city a few hours earlier. A successful attack on the army garrison followed, but this was the only rebel victory. Three days later the main body of the expeditionary force led by Ōkubo in person linked up with the garrison troops, which had managed an orderly retreat. The Imperial army counterattacked and quickly gained the upper hand. In addition to more than five thousand soldiers from the standing army, the government had enlisted an equal number of *shizoku* volunteers from neighboring prefectures who were more than willing to aid in the suppression of the rebellion. Regional and class loyalties helped the Saga rebels not at all. In fact, at least several hundred Saga *shizoku* led by Maeyama Ichirō turned against their clansmen and joined the government forces.[36]

The revolt lasted less than two weeks. Faced with certain defeat, the rebel soldiers surrendered or deserted after the first pitched battle. Etō and his lieutenants fled to Kagoshima where they made a final appeal to Saigō. They went on to Tosa where they were tracked down and returned to Saga, brought to trial, and summarily executed. Punish-

35 Ibid., p. 154. 36 Ibid., p. 157.

ment of the rank and file of the rebel force was relatively lenient. Of the several thousand who took up arms, about one hundred were given sentences ranging from three to ten years.

Two and a half years elapsed between the Saga rebellion and the next major *shizoku* insurrection, the Shimpūren uprising. That the Saga rebellion was not the last attempt by the *shizoku* to overthrow the Meiji government should not surprise us. During the intervening years the position of *shizoku* had become increasingly insecure financially and psychologically as the government pushed ahead with policies that eliminated the last vestiges of warrior privilege. Moreover, Western culture and customs were spreading beyond the treaty ports and largest cities to the provincial towns and even villages. The expansion of diplomatic relations with the West caused great displeasure to nativists for whom the pre-1868 revolutionary slogans, "revere the emperor" and "expel the barbarian" were not separable. At the same time the central bureaucracy, now dominated by Chōshū and Satsuma men, asserted itself in more conspicuous and decisive ways in local affairs. Thus, a variety of factors fed *shizoku* discontent in the mid-1870s.

The leaders of the Shimpūren were lower-ranking samurai in Kumamoto who had joined the movement to overthrow the bakufu but remained passionately committed to Shinto nativism. Their mentor, Hayashi Ōen, was a Shinto priest and scholar who had advocated resisting all demands from the West to enter into trade and diplomatic relations, whatever the short-term consequences. Like many loyalists in the *bakumatsu* period, he acknowledged Japan's military inferiority and foresaw initial defeat but held that defeat would prove salutary: Samurai of all ranks would unite in the traditions of old, and fierce resistance would make occupying Japan too difficult and costly for distant invaders to maintain for long. Having expelled the West, Japan could then freely decide the terms on which it would relate to the outside world.[37]

Hayashi died shortly after the Meiji Restoration, but his disciples founded a nativist political society in Kumamoto and remained true to his teachings. Many were Shinto priests who vehemently opposed Westernization and denounced diplomatic relations with the West as dangerous, offensive, and cowardly. They were especially aroused by the arrival in Kumamoto of a young American, Leroy L. Janes, the first teacher at the newly established foreign school. Janes was a dy-

37 Araki Seishi, *Shimpūren jikki* (Tokyo: Daiichi shuppan kyōkai, 1971), p. 123.

namic and popular teacher and impressed many of his students with the virtues of Christianity. Not only staunch conservatives were shocked when in January 1876, thirty-five of Janes's pupils publicly swore an oath to "enlighten the darkness of the empire by preaching the gospel," if necessary at the sacrifice of their lives.[38]

In mid-1876 the government eliminated the last privileges and vestiges of warrior elite status. First, the commutation of *shizoku* pensions with bonds was made compulsory; in March the wearing of swords in public was prohibited, and in June schoolchildren were required to cut off their topknots and wear their hair short in the Western fashion.

For the Shimpūren the provisions outlawing swords provided the final impetus for rebellion. The sword was the very soul of the samurai, they declared, and carrying two swords was a sacred national custom without which life was not worth living. Recent government policies threatened to destroy Japan's unique polity, but if they rose up in the spirit of righteousness, brave and loyal warriors would rally from all sides. Even if the revolt failed and all perished, this was their destiny. After consulting an oracle and receiving an affirmative response, they began active preparations that initially included efforts to coordinate their rising with insurrections in neighboring prefectures. Shimpūren leaders met with Miyazaki Kurunosuke of Akitsuki and with leaders of bands of disaffected *shizoku* in Saga, Fukuoka, Tsuruzaki, and Shimabara. In Chōshū they made contact with Maebara Issei, a former leader of the Chōshū *shishi* movement who had left the government in the early 1870s. These efforts met with some success as both Miyazaki and Maebara promised support.

However, the Shimpūren leadership placed more faith in the wisdom of gods than in the benefits of acting in concert. After again consulting the oracles, they advanced the date of their uprising to October 24, which did not give their confederates in Akitsuki and Chōshū sufficient time to complete their preparations. They also refused to use rifles in the assault on the army garrison because firearms were of foreign origin. Nor did they enlist the support of the Gakkōtō, a rival conservative *shizoku* party in Kumamoto equally committed to overthrowing the Tokyo government. As a result, the uprising proved to be little more than a suicidal insurrection. Striking without warning, they succeeded in killing the commanding officers of the Kumamoto garrison and mortally wounding the prefectural governor. But vastly outnumbered and outgunned, they were quickly defeated, with

38 F. G. Notehelfer, *American Samurai: Captain L. L. Janes and Japan* (Princeton, N.J.: Princeton University Press, 1985).

most members committing *seppuku* to avoid capture. The Akitsuki and Hagi uprisings were also quickly suppressed.

The last *shizoku* revolt, the 1877 Satsuma Rebellion, was by far the greatest. Unlike the minor insurrections that preceded it, the Satsuma Rebellion is rightly considered a civil war.[39] Commanded by Saigō Takamori, the Satsuma army fought unrelentingly for seven months. Although confined to the southern half of Kyushu, the scale and intensity of combat were far greater than in the Restoration wars. Defeat proved to be decisive, for the annihilation of the Satsuma army extinguished the threat of counterrevolution in the foreseeable future.

The leader of the "war party" in the debate over relations with Korea, Saigō had resigned from the Council of State and given up his commission as supreme commander of the armed forces immediately after his proposal for armed intervention was defeated. Enraged by the tactics employed by Iwakura and Ōkubo, Saigō realized that in the near future he would have little power to influence policy. If he remained in the government, his principal role would be the unrewarding and morally distasteful task of reconciling former comrades at arms in the army and bureaucracy to policies that further undercut the position of the *shizoku* class.[40] Saigō was disgusted by the pretentiousness, venality, and vanity of many of his colleagues. He had publicly insulted Inoue Kaoru, Kido Takayoshi's protégé, over his unsavory connections with the business world, and his relations with Yamagata, whom he respected, had recently become strained owing to the Yamashiroya incident.[41]

After resigning, Saigō insisted that he wanted nothing more to do with politics and refused to support either Etō's revolt or Itagaki's campaign for an elected national assembly. However, whatever his initial intentions may have been, the possibility of his living out his life as a gentleman farmer was greatly diminished by the actions of his followers. As soon as Saigō's break with the government became known, a large contingent of officers and soldiers from the Imperial Guard picked up their weapons and followed him back to Kagoshima. Soon they were joined by more than three hundred clansmen from the newly formed national police, who, like the guards, pointedly ignored appeals from the emperor not to desert. Together they formed the

39 Japanese historians use the term *seinan sensō* (southwestern war) rather than Satsuma Rebellion. 40 Masumi, *Nihon seitō*, p. 116.

41 Hackett, *Yamagata*, p. 71. Yamashiroya, a military supplier that Yamagata had trusted and favored, had embezzled funds.

nucleus of a potential rebel army; the only question was what Saigō would do.[42]

Saigō had not encouraged his followers to defect and may have been, as some argue, more dismayed than pleased by their actions. Nevertheless, six months after returning to Satsuma, he established a system of "private schools" (*shigakkō*) which closely resembled military academies. The success of the *shigakkō* was due in no small part to Saigō's patronage: He provided funds for the schools from the large salary he still collected from the government; his popularity among the Satsuma *shizoku* had only been enhanced by the circumstances surrounding his break with the government; and his status as a "founding father" of the Meiji Restoration contributed to the schools' prestige. Equally important was the support of the *shigakkō* system provided by local government officials. Governor Ōyama Tsunayoshi, a close friend of Saigō, used prefectural funds to pay the salaries of the schools' staff and to provide rations to students, and he even purchased guns and ammunition which were distributed throughout the *shigakkō* system. The directors of the schools served under Ōyama in the prefectural administration, and many graduates of the schools were appointed to positions in the lower ranks of the provincial bureaucracy. Before long the entire administrative apparatus of Satsuma was staffed by *shigakkō* people or by senior officials like Governor Ōyama who were in complete sympathy with the antigovernment movement.[43]

As the line separating public and private institutions became increasingly blurred, the authority of the central government in Kagoshima all but disappeared. Satsuma officials openly criticized, and even disobeyed, the policies and directives of the central government. Governor Ōyama ignored instructions from the Finance Ministry to pay the *shizoku* stipends in cash rather than rice, and he refused to impose a surtax on *shizoku* income. Opposed to universal primary education and the progressive features of the Meiji land tax, he refused to implement either law. But most egregious was the use of the *shigakkō* to recruit, equip, and train an army hostile to the central government. The first academies established in Kagoshima were known as the "infantry" and "artillery" schools; the teachers and most of the students were former officers and soldiers of the Imperial Guard. The curriculum included academic subjects such as the study of Chinese

42 Tamamuro Taijō, *Seinan sensō* (Tokyo: Shibundo, 1958), p. 11. See also Charles L. Yates, "Restoration and Rebellion in Satsuma: The Life of Saigō Takamori (1827–1877)," Ph.D. diss., Princeton University, 1987.

43 Tamamuro, pp. 29–39.

classics, but the daily regime stressed physical fitness, military tactics, drill, and troop maneuvers conducted on land donated by the prefecture. By 1876, branch schools had been set up in every district to enroll *gōshi*, rural samurai. For military-age males, attendance became practically compulsory.[44]

Nearly one-quarter of the population of Satsuma were *shizoku* who provided a very large pool of potential recruits to the antigovernment movement. The extraordinarily large proportion of the population in Satsuma that claimed samurai status was due to the fief's policy of including *gōshi*, "rustic warriors," within the warrior class.[45] In most fiefs the *gōshi* had lost their warrior status at the beginning of the Tokugawa period and were assimilated into the wealthy farmer (*gōnō*) class. However, the Satsuma *gōshi* were accorded elite status and continued to think and act as warriors. They served the fief as rural administrators – district magistrates, policemen, and, most commonly, village headmen. *Gōshi* headmen governed hamlets of up to twenty households and lorded over the peasants like the estate managers of the medieval period. Elsewhere in Japan during the Tokugawa period, villages enjoyed considerable autonomy, and peasants acquired de facto proprietary rights to the land they cultivated. However, in Satsuma, the *gōshi* headmen strictly supervised the village economy and treated the peasants like tenant farmers. They had the authority to assign land to individual cultivators and adjusted the tax rate from year to year to take from the peasants all but what was needed for subsistence.[46]

Meiji reforms struck at the very heart of *gōshi* privilege. Like castle town samurai, they were accustomed to thinking of themselves as an elite, superior in status, if not always in wealth, to commoners. And as the lowest-ranking status group within the warrior class, they perhaps felt even more keenly the loss of the symbols of elite status, such as the right to bear arms. More concretely, the 1873 land tax revision threatened their socioeconomic power in the village. By conferring ownership rights on peasant farmers and taxing individual proprietors, the Meiji land tax eliminated the feudal role of the Satsuma *gōshi* as petty overlords. Not surprisingly, they flocked to the *shigakkō* once branch schools were established outside the city and later joined the rebel army in large numbers.

44 Masumi, *Nihon seitō*, p. 156.
45 Elsewhere, samurai numbered 5 or, at most, 10 percent of the population.
46 Tamamuro, *Seinan*, pp. 18–20; and Robert K. Sakai, "Feudal Society and Modern Leadership in Satsuma-han," *Journal of Asian Studies* 16 (May 1957): 365–76.

The government did not attempt to counter the *shigakkō* movement until late 1876, in part because it remained ignorant of the actual state of affairs. Prefectural officials, who would normally inform Tokyo of antigovernment activity, were in complete sympathy with the movement; they remained silent and, if questioned, denied that there was any cause for alarm. Furthermore, Ōkubo and the other Satsuma men in the oligarchy did not want to believe that Saigō and their clansmen in Kagoshima were capable of sedition. As late as November 1876, Ōkubo argued that Saigō's refusal to support the Shimpūren, Akitsuki, and Hagi uprisings was sufficient proof of his loyalty and honor and held that as long as Saigō remained in command, Satsuma would never rebel. Events soon proved Ōkubo wrong, but he was not entirely mistaken in his estimation of Saigō's character, for Saigō authorized rebellion only after the actions of government agents forced his hand.

Late in 1876, the government sent police spies into Kagoshima to infiltrate the *shigakkō*. It appears that their mission was to gather intelligence, foment dissention, and in other ways undermine the movement. A few weeks after arriving in Satsuma, the spies were exposed and apprehended. Under torture, one agent confessed that he had been sent to assassinate Saigō. The only evidence was his confession, but the officers and many of the students of the *shigakkō* desperately wanted an excuse to go to war, and Saigō appears to have believed the facts as reported to him.

Because of the increasingly tense situation in Satsuma, the government next tried to remove munitions stored at the Kagoshima arsenal. Although a commercial steamship and civilian crew were employed to disguise the operation, *shigakkō* students soon discovered what was going on. Without Saigō's knowledge, they broke into the arsenal and began carting off guns and powder. The local police did not try to stop them; emboldened, the students went one step further and forcibly prevented the ship's crew from loading cargo. The captain immediately set sail and, upon reaching Kobe, telegraphed the news to Tokyo.

Although angered by the students' rash action, upon learning of the raid on the arsenal, Saigō met with his lieutenants and authorized preparations for war. His intention was to topple the ruling oligarchy headed by Ōkubo. Believing that opposition to the oligarchy was sufficiently great to realize this goal with a minimum of force, he tried with vague public announcements to maintain the appearance of legality. On February 9, Saigō, Shinohara, and Kirino formally notified Governor Ōyama that they would "shortly leave the prefecture," taking with them "a number of former troops." Ōyama obliged by announcing that Saigō was proceeding to Tokyo in order to investigate the plot against his life, that a large force of former government troops would accompany him, and that the emperor had been fully informed. Although clearly in rebellion, Saigō and his officers wore their old Imperial army uniforms, and Saigō issued orders as commander in chief. At first he even refused to enlist volunteers from neighboring prefectures in order to avoid charges of having entered into a confederacy.[47]

By using the *shigakkō* system, mobilization was carried out with great speed. By the end of the first week in February, even before Saigō had notified Ōyama of his intentions, armed men from the schools had begun to assemble in Kagoshima. Within a week, the vanguard and a four-thousand-strong First Division completed mobilization and departed the capital; soon after, the Second Infantry Division, rear guard, artillery, and finally Saigō's bodyguard started the march north. On February 20 the Satsuma army crossed into Higo Prefecture. Defeating an advance party of troops from the Kumamoto garrison, they marched into the city and laid siege to the former domain castle that now served as the army headquarters. Almost immediately, two local bands of *shizoku* – the Gakkōto and the Kyōdōtai – came over to Saigō's side. It was an auspicious beginning.

After a final attempt to dissuade Saigō, the government mobilized for war. Three thousand troops from the Tokyo garrison were immediately transported by ship to Kobe, and the Osaka and Hiroshima garrisons proceeded directly to Fukuoka in northern Kyushu. Prince Arisugawa assumed command of the hastily assembled army and immediately dispatched two divisions to block further advance by the rebel force. Thereafter, the Imperial army steadily gained the upper hand. Despite being outnumbered, the Kumamoto garrison did not capitulate, and contrary to Saigō's expectations, it repulsed repeated assaults. Meanwhile, the government not only mobilized the standing army and called up reserves, but it also enlisted thousands of *shizoku* volunteers as "police" auxiliaries. Fresh units arrived daily, and the well-equipped Imperial army counterattacked. After several days of fierce fighting, on March 20, the government forces captured the key pass at Taharazaka. Both sides suffered heavy losses. The Satsuma army executed an orderly retreat and set up a new line of defense. During the next two weeks, the Imperial army assaulted this line while additional units advanced on Kumamoto from the south. Threatened

47 August H. Mounsey, *The Satsuma Rebellion* (London: Murray, 1879), p. 119. Reprinted by University Publications of America, Washington, D.C., 1979.

with encirclement, Saigō abandoned the siege and retreated. Although not yet defeated, the rebellion had clearly failed. The government controlled all of northern and central Kyushu, which severely curtailed the recruitment of additional forces. Most ablebodied *shizoku* from Satsuma had already enlisted, and Saigō was forced to conscript peasants, who had little incentive to fight on behalf of the *shizoku*, and convicted criminals, who were not likely to be dedicated soldiers. Nevertheless, Saigō and what remained of his army continued fighting through the summer. By September, only Saigō and a few hundred troops were still in the field. On September 23, 1877, confronted by a vastly larger government force in the hills north of Kagoshima, Saigō refused a personal plea from Yamagata to surrender. The next day the army attacked; the rebel force was annihilated; and Saigō committed suicide on the battlefield rather than allow himself to be captured.[48]

Unlike previous *shizoku* uprisings, which were small and poorly organized, the Satsuma Rebellion severely tested the government's capacity to wage war. To defeat the large and well-trained rebel forces, the government had to mobilize the entire standing army and reserves and enlist an additional 7,000 *shizoku* as "police" auxiliaries. Of the 65,000 soldiers sent to the front, 6,000 were killed in action, and 10,000 were wounded. The financial cost of prosecuting the war was staggering. Direct expenditures totaled ¥42 million, a sum equal to 80 percent of the annual budget.

However costly the war had been to the government in men and coin, the oligarchy had reason to view the outcome with considerable satisfaction. The annihilation of the Satsuma army – eighteen thousand rebel troops were killed or wounded, and Saigō and his lieutenants died in battle or by suicide – eliminated the only *shizoku* force capable of threatening the central government. Moreover, the performance of the Imperial army vindicated the government's decision to adopt universal military conscription. Approximately two-thirds of the Kumamoto garrison were conscripts; although outnumbered and short of supplies, they withstood a fifty-day siege, thereby preventing Saigō's army from moving into northern Kyushu. To say that the victory proved commoner conscripts to be superior to samurai is nevertheless an oversimplification, for the majority of government soldiers were also *shizoku*. The Imperial Guards and "police" auxiliaries, which were exclusively *shizoku*, bore the brunt of the fiercest fighting. Nevertheless, the overall efficiency with which the govern-

48 The most detailed account of the military campaigns of the Satsuma Rebellion is contained in Mounsey, *The Satsuma Rebellion*, pp. 154–217.

ment prosecuted the war amply demonstrated the advantages of military modernization and particularly of centralized command and national recruitment.

The Satsuma Rebellion marked the final attempt by disaffected *shizoku* to overthrow the Meiji government. What does the failure of the greatest revolt reveal about the limits of *shizoku* rebellion?

After the first three weeks, Saigō's army was outnumbered and outgunned. The core of the Satsuma army consisted of six infantry regiments of 2,000 men each, in addition to artillery and the rearguard. After entering Kumamoto, they were immediately joined by two bands of local *shizoku*, the politically conservative Gakkōtō and the Kyōdōtai (an association of nominally progressive *shizoku* affiliated with the Popular Rights movement) and an additional 5,000 volunteers from nearby provinces.[49] Thus, at peak strength the rebel forces numbered no more than 22,000.

In contrast, the government initially fielded an army of 33,000 and sent an additional 30,000 before the end of the war. The rebel army was short of guns and munitions throughout most of the war. The looting of the Kagoshima arsenal secured an initial stock of guns and powder, but when the army marched out of Kagoshima in February, each soldier carried only one hundred bullets, enough for two to three days of combat. Attempts were made to purchase arms abroad, but even if the negotiations had succeeded, the Imperial navy's control of the sea would probably have prevented their delivery. The government occupied Kagoshima in April, cutting off the overland supply of munitions that were manufactured locally.

Tactical miscalculations, and especially the decision to lay siege to Kumamoto Castle, undoubtedly hastened defeat. Because of the strategic advantages enjoyed by the government forces, it was unrealistic to expect victory in a prolonged war. The best hope lay in a rapid advance to link up with sympathizers and create the impression of success before the government had time to mobilize. If Saigō had proceeded directly to Fukuoka and thereby carried the rebellion into northern Kyushu, additional groups might have declared for the rebellion. As the Shimpūren, Akitsuki, and Hagi uprisings of the previous autumn had demonstrated, *shizoku* disaffection was intense, and the decision of the "liberal" Kumamoto Kyōdōtai to join Saigō when it appeared that the rebellion might succeed suggests that the timing was indeed a critical factor. How long would Itagaki and the Risshisha

49 Tamamuro, *Seinan*, p. 139.

have held off if Saigō's army had crossed the Inland Sea? One does not have to be a cynic to recognize that opportunism was a powerful determinant of political alignments in the early Meiji period. But by failing to stay on the offensive, Saigō forfeited his one chance of victory – a general uprising against the Tokyo government.[50]

However, military defeat was inevitable given the very narrow political base of the rebellion. Although Satsuma had been made into a bastion of counterrevolution, the high level of mobilization achieved there between 1874 and 1877 depended on a combination of factors unique to the domain: size and composition of the warrior population, virtual autonomy from central authority, sanction and support of prefectural officials, and Saigō's prestige as a "founding father" of the Meiji Restoration. Because these conditions could not be duplicated, Satsuma stood alone. In fact, its strength was also its weakness, for the leadership's parochial political loyalties stood in the way of horizontal alliances. From Saigō's return to Kagoshima in the fall of 1873 until the attack on the Kumamoto garrison in February 1877, mobilization had been carried out entirely within the prefecture; no effort was made to encourage, aid, or link up with like-minded *shizoku* bands outside Satsuma. As we have seen, Saigō steadfastly held aloof, even in the autumn of 1876 when the disaffected *shizoku* in nearby Kumamoto, Akitsuki, and Hagi went on the offensive. When Saigō finally moved against the government and authorized sending emissaries in search of allies, the optimal moment for a general uprising had passed. Potential allies had already committed themselves to local uprisings, which produced little more than suicidal insurrections. Lacking advance notice of Saigō's rising, in some cases sympathizers were not able to act quickly enough.[51]

In short, Saigō failed to capitalize on his greatest asset. Arno Mayer observed that counterrevolutions are similar to revolutions in that both "feed on socio-economic dislocations, discontents and cleavages."[52] But despite widespread disaffection, frustration, and despair among the *shizoku* nationwide, the antigovernment movement in Satsuma remained stubbornly parochial. This doomed it to defeat. Because mobilization was restricted to Satsuma and did not tap *shizoku* discontent nationwide, Saigō's rising produced a formidable, but geographically limited, military threat. As Gotō Yasushi has observed, despite geographical proximity, similar grievances, and a common

50 Ibid., pp. 134–5. 51 Gotō, *Shizoku hanran*, pp. 174–84.
52 Arno J. Mayer, *Dynamics of Counterrevolution in Europe, 1870–1956* (New York: Harper & Row, 1971), p. 59.

enemy, the *shizoku* rebels were incapable of acting in concert; dispersed and isolated, each was defeated.[53]

The Satsuma leaders also failed to mobilize politically disaffected commoners. Class itself need not determine the scope of counterrevolutionary mobilization. Historically, recruitment to counterrevolution has depended on the degree to which "segments of different classes experienced or were apprehensive about declassment, defunctionalization, or alienation." It is not simply displaced elites and formerly dominant classes who make up the cadre of counterrevolution, but strata of all classes, "whose fears and anxieties [are] heightened by crisis conditions."[54] However, the Satsuma leaders showed no interest in propagandizing and agitating the rural poor, who, no less than the impoverished *shizoku,* constituted a "crisis stratum" whose grievances and fears might have been turned against the government. As we have seen, small landholders and tenants gained little benefit from Meiji land policies; indeed, in some areas they had violently opposed its social, educational, and religious policies. How great the potential was for inciting rural uprising and what effect extensive social disorder might have had on the outcome of the Satsuma Rebellion cannot be known. But when the Satsuma army first entered Higo and laid siege to Kumamoto, the poor farmers in the Aso district carried out widespread attacks against the homes and property of local landlords and moneylenders. Although not encouraged in any way by the rebel army, they apparently assumed that the Satsuma army represented the poor and disadvantaged and associated the Imperial army with the rich. Against a background of resentment of the new land tax and allegations of malfeasance by village headmen, rumors circulated that Saigō had abolished the land tax and canceled outstanding debts. But the Satsuma army showed no interest in the peasants, except as suppliers of food, labor, and draft animals. In fact, they treated the local population so roughly that before long opinion swung against them.[55]

Counterrevolution was defeated because none of the rebellions drew on more than a fraction of the potential recruits to the antigovernment cause. Because the leaders did not develop models of collective action suited to mass mobilization, they failed to tap the vast reservoir of discontent among the declassed samurai nationwide. Generally, the revolts replicated the patterns of mobilization that characterized the *tōbaku* (overthrow the bakufu) movement: voluntary associations of like-minded men, on the one hand, and the domain as the territorial

53 Gotō, *Shizoku hanran,* p. 64. 54 Mayer, *Dynamics,* p. 41.
55 Tamamuro, *Seinan,* p. 157.

and emotional unit of collective action, on the other. However, whereas limited mobilization of *shishi* (men of spirit) and militant action by Chōshū succeeded in toppling the Tokugawa bakufu in the crisis conditions of the mid-1860s, a decade later the fully centralized Meiji state managed to suppress any single group that rose up against it.

THE POPULAR RIGHTS MOVEMENT

Liberal opposition to the Meiji oligarchy can be traced back to the splintering of the original leadership group in October 1873. Unlike Saigō Takamori and Etō Shimpei, Itagaki Taisuke and Gotō Shōjirō, the leaders of the Tosa faction, rejected rebellion; instead, they organized a public campaign to establish an elected national assembly. Calling themselves the Aikokukōtō, "Public Party of Patriots," in January 1874, they enlisted a handful of prominent Restoration leaders – among them Etō Shimpei and Soejima Taneomi – and drafted a memorial urging the adoption of "a council chamber chosen by the people."[56] Although it was rejected by the government, the memorial raised for the first time a liberal challenge to the incumbent leadership and signaled the opening round in what became a decade-long campaign by a socially and politically diverse coalition known as the "People's Rights" (*jiyū minken*) movement. Espousing liberty, equality, and the right to elect government officials, the People's Rights movement brought together at various times former Restoration leaders and intellectuals, urbanites and villagers, *shizoku* and wealthy commoners, and, finally, radicals and impoverished farmers – all who shared an interest in opposing oligarchic rule.

As suggested by the circumstances leading up to the Aikokukōtō petition, Japan's first "liberals" were members of the original leadership who had lost out in the power struggle of 1873. Indeed, there is reason to question the depth of their commitment to liberalism as a political doctrine, for their interest in representative government coincided with their loss of power. Moreover, they were prone to jingoism and rarely passed up an opportunity to denounce the government's handling of Japan's international relations, insisting on early revision of the "unequal" treaties, an aggressive pursuit of national interests in Asia, and favorable resolution of territorial disputes with Russia. They also repeatedly protested high taxes, especially the land tax. What,

56 Text in Walter W. McLaren, "Japanese Government Documents, 1867–1889," *Transactions of the Asiatic Society of Japan* 42 (1914): pr. 1, p. 428. Hereafter cited as *JGD*.

then, was the connection between specific grievances and advocacy of an elected national assembly?

The most prominent feature in the Aikokukōtō memorial was its criticism of the oligarchic and cliquish character of the government. The petitioners charged that the incumbent leadership, much like the hateful Tokugawa bakufu, monopolized power, thereby excluding both the emperor and the people. "When we humbly reflect upon the quarter in which the governing power lies, we find it lies not with the Crown (Imperial House) on the one hand, nor with the people on the other, but with the officials alone."[57] Officials acting in the name of the emperor ruled in an "arbitrary" and "partial" manner, to the detriment of the imperial institution, which was losing prestige, and of citizens, who could not express legitimate grievances. The consequence, the memorial asserted, was internal conflict and discontent which imperiled the nation; the remedy lay in government by "public discussion." Representative government, it was urged, would fortify the nation, for national strength depended on "the people of the empire being of one mind."[58] If entrusted with political rights, the people of Japan would willingly assume the many duties of citizenship, manifest a new unity of purpose, and develop the spirit of enterprise that was known to exist among the populations of fully civilized countries.

One finds in the Aikokukōtō memorial many of the themes and contradictions that permeated liberal thought in the Meiji period. In support of representative government, the petitioners emphasized the likely benefits to national strength rather than the value of individual rights. Instead of directly challenging the principle of absolute monarchy, they denounced "despotic officials" who stood between the emperor and the people. By claiming the imperial and popular will to be harmonious, they argued that the expression of public opinion would eliminate dissension between ruler and ruled. To this extent they implicitly invoked Confucian concepts to justify liberal reforms. At the same time, however, they called on the authority of natural rights theory, boldly citing the "universally acknowledged" principle according to which payment of taxes conferred rights of representation on citizens.

Although rightly criticized by modern scholars as shortsighted and opportunistic, the tactic of evoking the emperor's authority to legitimate demands for representative institutions reflected the realities of the contemporary political landscape.[59] Although theoretically abso-

57 Ibid., pp. 427–8. 58 Ibid., p. 430.

59 Gotō Yasushi, *Jiyū minken: Meiji no kakumei to hankakumei* (Tokyo: Chūō kōronsha), p. 43.

lute in every realm of public life, imperial authority had not yet been marshaled against progressive forces by conservative politicians and ideologues; the process of associating the throne with specific authoritarian structures had only just begun. On the other hand, the Meiji emperor symbolized the recent triumph over feudalism and Tokugawa-style despotism. Liberals, therefore, could make a strong claim to being the legitimate heirs of the 1868 revolution. After all, the first article of the Meiji Charter Oath – the most authoritative, if deliberately vague, statement of Restoration aims – promised deliberative assemblies and public debate of affairs of state. Nor were out-of-power politicians the only proponents of liberal reform. Generally, officials not aligned with the dominant Satsuma and Chōshū cliques favored broader political participation. In fact, the Sa-in, the lower chamber of the state council, formally adopted the Aikokukōtō argument, declaring that "the subject of the establishment of a council chamber chosen by the people is an excellent one" and urged the Council of State and Home Ministry to take appropriate steps.[60]

However, the oligarchs were not yet prepared to share power with elected officials. They ignored the Sa-in's favorable recommendation and replied that the great majority of the people were "ignorant and unlearned." Although some segments of the former warrior class were advancing intellectually, "the peasant and merchant classes are still what they have always been . . . satisfied in their stupidity and ignorance, and it has not yet been possible to arouse in them the spirit of activity."[61] To avoid disaster, public opinion would have to be guided and educated before representatives of such people could be entrusted with the power to make laws. Although they admitted that government in principle existed for the people, not the people for government, the most they were prepared to offer was an experiment with prefectural assemblies chosen by *shizoku* and well-to-do commoners that would be allowed to discuss, but not legislate, local matters.

Nevertheless, the oligarchs were sufficiently astute to recognize that the issue of representative government was a likely rallying point for the opposition, and they tried to forestall the growth of a broadly based movement by co-opting key leaders. They were most concerned about the activities of Itagaki Taisuke, who, after Saigō, ranked second among the military heroes of the Restoration. Itagaki and his clansmen had returned to Kōchi in February 1874 to build up a local party. There they founded the Risshisha, an association that functioned both as a

60 McLaren, *JGD*, pp. 432–3. 61 Ibid., p. 436.

self-help society for former samurai and as a vehicle for promoting liberal political thought. The Risshisha charter proclaimed that all Japanese were equally endowed with rights to life, liberty, property, livelihood, and the pursuit of happiness – rights that "no man can take away." To educate members to this new political philosophy, the association sponsored public lectures and talks that introduced the thought of Locke, Mill, Rousseau, and Bentham. Although the society was generally unsuccessful in managing economic enterprises, which included forestry, tea plantations, and credit unions, it attracted a large and enthusiastic following among the Tosa *shizoku*.[62] Consequently, the government became worried when the Risshisha tried to link up with other groups of disaffected samurai, as it did in 1875 by organizing the Aikokusha, a national "association of patriots." To deflate the challenge and restore a semblance of unity within the leadership's ranks, Ōkubo Toshimichi, the dominant figure in the oligarchy, agreed on the eve of the conference to issue an imperial edict promising "gradual progress" toward an elected national assembly. In return, Itagaki, Gotō, and Kido Takayoshi of Chōshū reentered the government.[63]

The agreement between Ōkubo and Itagaki is noteworthy, less for its immediate consequences than for what it revealed of the oligarchy's attitude toward the liberal opposition. The majority of the top leaders were not opposed to a constitution, or even in principle to limited representation. They were, however, determined to dictate the substance and pace of liberalizing reforms and to keep executive and bureaucratic power in their hands; as pragmatists they had no difficulty making token concessions to recent colleagues.

The announcement of the agreement between Ōkubo and Itagaki and the promise of progress toward an elected assembly upstaged the first meeting of the Aikokusha. However, inasmuch as Ōkubo and his colleagues had a very restricted notion of what constituted "progress," renewed conflict was inevitable. In October, Itagaki, by now convinced that he would have no real influence in the government, resigned once more and returned to Tosa. The stage was set for a resurgence of liberal agitation.

During the first phase of the People's Rights movement, that is, from 1874 to 1878, the Tosa leaders did not actively seek the support

62 Nobutake Ike, *The Beginnings of Political Democracy in Japan* (Baltimore: Johns Hopkins University Press, 1950), pp. 61–5.

63 Kido, the senior member of the Chōshū faction, had resigned in 1874 after failing to dissuade Ōkubo from sending a punitive expedition to Taiwan. Bringing Kido back into the government was essential to preventing a further narrowing of the oligarchy.

of commoners, for they too believed that former samurai, those with education and experience as administrators, were the people worthy of political representation. However, as wealthy farmers and local notables took up the liberal cause toward the end of the decade, the political and social character of the movement changed dramatically. The turning point came in the summer of 1879 when Sakurai Shizuka, a commoner farmer of moderate means from Chiba, published an appeal in which he denounced the oligarchy's failure to institute representative government and invited prefectural assembly delegates and concerned citizens throughout the country to join forces in a new campaign. Sakurai published his appeal in the *Chōya shimbun*, a Tokyo daily newspaper, and mailed thousands of handbills. The response was immediate and overwhelming. In Okayama, the prefectural assembly unanimously endorsed Sakurai's plan and authorized a mass petition campaign. From Iwate Prefecture in the northeast to Hiroshima in the west, assemblymen raised their voices in support and began circulating similar petitions.[64]

The stunning success of the petition movement was largely due to the broad support it received from the traditional village elite – headmen, landlords, and small-scale entrepreneurs who lent their prestige and influence to the campaign, thereby ensuring its success.[65] In March 1880, when the Aikokusha convened its semiannual meeting, ninety-six representatives from twenty-four prefectures attended, bringing petitions bearing a total of 101,161 signatures. Reconstituting themselves as the Kokkai kisei dōmei, "League for Establishment of a National Assembly," they authorized Kataoka Kenkichi and Kōno Hironaka to present the petitions to the government. Supremely self-confident, the delegates pledged to carry the campaign to a successful conclusion. Recognizing the importance of grass-roots support, they vowed to organize up to fifty new societies of over one hundred members each.[66]

With the national petition campaign of 1879, the initiative within the People's Rights movement passed to hundreds of local political societies, many located in villages and small towns. Among the earliest of the societies was the Sekiyōsha, established in 1875 in Ishikawa, a small and out-of-the-way mountain town in southern Fukushima. Kōno Hironaka, the founder of the Sekiyōsha, had been born into a once-prosperous *gōshi* family of Miharu fief and began his political career as a

64 Ei Hideo, *Jiyū minken*, vol. 25 of *Nihon no rekishi* (Tokyo: Shogakkan, 1976), pp. 80–5.
65 Irokawa Daikichi, *Jiyū minken* (Tokyo: Iwanami shoten, 1981), p. 26.
66 Gotō, *Jiyū minken*, pp. 100–1.

district officer in Ishikawa. If we can believe Kōno's autobiography, he read a translation of John Stuart Mill's classic *On Liberty* while en route to his new post. Perhaps directly influenced by Mill, or possibly following the lead of Itagaki Taisuke, Kōno organized within the year a political society dedicated to promoting popular rights and representative government. The charter of the Sekiyōsha boldly proclaimed: "We have come together because government is for the people . . . and inherent rights of life and personal freedom, which are higher than the mountains and deeper than the sea, will endure forever on this earth."[67] Unlike the Risshisha, which had restricted membership to Tosa *shizoku*, the Sekiyōsha welcomed all persons who supported the society's goals, irrespective of "class, wealth or station." In addition to discussing current political issues, its members studied political science, economics, history, and even the natural sciences, relying for the most part on translations of European and American texts. At weekly meetings, which were open to the public, they discussed such classics of Western political thought as *On Liberty*, *The Spirit of the Laws*, *The History of English Civilization*, and *Social Contract*.

Four years after founding the Sekiyōsha, Kōno took a new position in Miharu district. There he established a second political society, the Sanshisha, and an academy, the Seidōkan. Before long, the Seidōkan graduated young men imbued with ideas of liberty, equality, and democracy who set up popular rights organizations in nearby villages, including one mountain village with a mere forty households.

The burgeoning political activity in rural areas that began in the late 1870s is one of the remarkable developments of the Meiji period. According to recent data, 303 societies sprang up in the six provinces around Tokyo, at least 120 in the northeastern region of the country, and approximately 200 in western and southwestern Japan.[68] To be sure, the political and social character of the societies varied considerably. Not all actively supported the popular rights movement or even considered politics to be their main activity; some restricted membership to men of similar social and economic status; and others were founded with the express purpose of enhancing the leaders' prestige. Nevertheless, most of the societies were influenced to some degree by the Popular Rights movement and supported the constitutional movement.

We have seen that *shizoku* popular rights leaders Itagaki Taisuke and Gotō Shōjirō saw representative government as a vehicle for regaining

67 Takahashi Tetsuo, *Fukushima jiyū minkenka retsuden* (Fukushima: Fukushima mimpōsha, 1967), p. 140. 68 Irokawa, *Jiyū minken*, p. 17.

influence in the national government. Although this was not their only motivation, their commitment to the concept of representative government was inextricably bound up with hopes of regaining their former positions as leaders of the Meiji government. This was not true, however, of the thousands of local notables who provided leadership and financial support for the constitutional phase of the Popular Rights movement. How, then, can we explain their commitment?

To some extent these men were reacting to political centralization, a process that reduced their local status and authority, especially after the government promulgated the so-called Three Laws on Local Government in 1878. The first of these invested the power to appoint prefectural governors in the Home Ministry and authorized prefectural governors to appoint district officials, thus giving the central government control over all but the village and town councils. The second law added a prefectural tax of up to 20 percent to the national land tax without granting taxpayers a say in how these revenues would be used. The third law provided what the more liberal-minded oligarchs hoped would be a first step toward institutionalizing limited popular participation in the governing process by establishing elected prefectural assemblies that had the right to discuss, but not initiate, legislation and to review the annual budget.

During the Tokugawa period the village headmen had performed many of the functions that now came to be carried out by the state bureaucracy. The erosion of their authority began in 1871 with the abolition of private fiefs, and by the latter half of the decade the extension of the powers of the state bureaucracy was becoming apparent. It is not surprising, then, that they were attracted to the doctrine of natural rights which accorded the propertied classes not only guarantees of private wealth but political participation as well. Moreover, natural rights justified both participation and the right to resist.[69]

However, neither the eclipse of traditional authority nor the desire to promote their economic interests accounts fully for the grass-roots support among local notables for the constitutional movement. We should not overlook the cultural dimension of the political ferment in the countryside that characterized this phase of the Popular Rights movement. As Irokawa Daikichi has argued, political activism at the village level expressed the desire of Japan's new citizens to transcend the narrow world of feudal culture.[70] Intellectually and socially, the Popular Rights movement opened up avenues of activity long denied

69 Bowen, *Rebellion*, pp. 303–13. 70 Irokawa, *Jiyū minken*, p. 49.

to commoners, a phenomenon that Irokawa's research on the community of Itsukaichi, a small market town located in the mountainous Nishitama district northwest of Tokyo, amply illustrates.

Early in 1880, the mayor of Itsukaichi and the heads of locally prominent families – the former mayor, the supervisor of the village school, the mayor of a nearby hamlet – founded the "Learning and Debating Society." According to the first article of the society's charter, its members pledged to "work together with indomitable spirit to develop liberty and improve society" and to relate to one another "as brothers of the same flesh and bone, with love and respect as if one big family."[71] Much like the Sekiyōsha and Sanshisha, politics began with self-education. Using translations of Western classics and secondary works, the members avidly absorbed the "new knowledge." In 1881, when the movement to draft a national constitution reached its climax, these mountain villagers, ostensibly the "ignorant and unlearned" whom the oligarchs declared "satisfied in their stupidity," eagerly debated the shape and substance of Japan's future constitution. A list of subjects discussed by the society included fifteen topics concerned with drafting a national constitution, nine with the legal system, and six with civil rights.[72] Several of the younger members of the society became accomplished political orators who campaigned actively on behalf of popular rights. One member, Chiba Takusaburō, produced a complete draft of a national constitution which, in terms of protection of citizens' rights, ranks high among the more than thirty extant draft constitutions.[73]

Intellectuals, most of whom were former samurai, played an instrumental role in publicizing natural rights theory and kindling enthusiasm for political reform. Nakamura Masanao and Fukuzawa Yukichi were pioneers of the Meiji "enlightenment" whose translations and essays first introduced Western culture and political institutions; younger, more radical thinkers like Ueki Emori, Nakae Chōmin, and Ōi Kentarō were ideologues as well as political activists.[74] But we should also note the contribution of many young intellectuals who dedicated themselves to the constitutional movement. Beginning in the late 1870s, scores of Tokyo journalists and amateur orators carried the

71 Irokawa Daikichi, *Kindai kokka no shuppatsu*, vol. 25 of *Nihon no rekishi* (Tokyo: Chūō kōronsha, 1966), p. 91.

72 Irokawa Daikichi, *Meiji no bunka* (Tokyo: Iwanami shoten, 1970), p. 105. Translation issued by Princeton University Press in 1985 as *The Culture of the Meiji Period*, ed. Marius B. Jansen. For a chart of organizations formed in villages near Tokyo, see p. 49.

73 Irokawa, *Meiji no bunka*, pp. 107–8.

74 Irokawa, *Kindai kokka*, pp. 86–90.

constitutional campaign directly to the people. Dressed dramatically in black capes and broad-brimmed hats, they popularized a new kind of politics – barnstorming.

Because of the comparatively high rates of literacy and urbanization at the start of the Meiji period, journalism provided a vocation for politically ambitious young men excluded from government service. Numa Morikazu and his colleagues in the Ōmeisha, an intellectual circle founded in 1873 to discuss Western legal institutions, exemplified this new type of urban intellectual. Numa, who had fought on the Tokugawa side during the Restoration wars, bought the *Tokyo–Yokohama Mainichi Shimbun* in 1879 and immediately used the paper as a forum for the constitutional movement, publishing twenty-seven editorials between November 1879 and January 1880 that advocated the early convening of a national assembly. At the same time, the Ōmei Society established a network of provincial branches that promoted discussion and debate of political issues. Some highly committed members toured villages and market towns; traveling by ricksha, horseback, and even on foot, they lectured at temples, schools, storehouses, and wayside shrines, wherever they could assemble a crowd. One young journalist delivered over twenty speeches during a two-month tour that took him as far north as Sado Island in the Japan Sea.[75]

With the support of hundreds of local political societies and countless dedicated individuals in villages and towns across the country, the constitutional movement generated a deluge of petitions. As we have seen, organizations affiliated with the Kokkai kisei dōmei had collected over 100,000 signatures by the spring of 1880, and although the government repeatedly refused to accept petitions, enthusiasm for the campaign showed no sign of abating. Even after the highly publicized failure of Kokkai kisei dōmei representatives Kataoka Kenkichi and Kōno Hironaka that April, leaders of provincial petition movements came streaming into Tokyo, if anything more determined to succeed. From Sagami came Amano Seiryū who arrived in Tokyo in June and vowed not to return home until the government received his countrymen's petition. Furuya Senzō of Yamanashi first sought an audience with Prince Iwakura and, when rebuffed, threatened to take his demands directly to the emperor during the next imperial tour, thus emulating the English nobles who had forced King John to sign the Magna Charta. And in an episode that symbolized both the remark-

75 Irokawa, *The Culture of the Meiji Period*, pp. 237–8.

able achievements of this phase of the Popular Rights movement and the limits of its power, Matsusawa Kyūraku persevered for fifty days in a futile effort to present petitions containing more than 25,000 signatures from his native Shinano.[76]

The constitutional campaign thus succeeded beyond all expectations in mobilizing popular support: sixty petitions and a quarter of a million signatures by the end of 1880, a mere year and six months after Sakurai Shizuka's seemingly naive appeal to his countrymen. Not surprisingly, this mass mobilization alarmed conservatives. In an often-quoted letter to Itō Hirobumi dated July 4, 1879, Yamagata Aritomo, chief of the army general staff, noted the growth of the Popular Rights movement and predicted, "Every day we wait the evil poison will spread more and more over the provinces, penetrate the minds of the young, and inevitably produce unfathomable evils."[77] In the same letter he voiced the fear that popular rights leaders hoped to overthrow the government when the time was right. Yamagata did not, of course, fear an armed rising. Until the mid-1880s the movement eschewed violence and at no point constituted a credible military threat, in marked contrast with the *shizoku* counterrevolution. Rather, what Yamagata and other conservatives feared was loss of control: The constitutional movement had given birth to new organizations, ideologies, and class alliances; it presented the ominous specter of the people acting not merely to protect parochial interest but also to demand a voice in determining the future of the nation. Consequently, conservative and pragmatic leaders favored concessions to preempt the goals of the mass movement while preserving the principal structures of oligarchic rule.

Until the mid-1870s the Meiji government had only local opposition movements with which to contend, but not a hostile public; no issue or party had transcended the various community, class, and status barriers to popular mobilization that were inherited from Tokugawa feudalism. But once opponents voiced demands for alternative institutions and the press joined the campaign, the oligarchs began to restrict free expression of opinion and citizens' rights to organize. The first target was the press. In 1875 and 1877 the government promulgated press and libel laws that were used to silence dissident journalists. As the Popular Rights movement gained momentum, the number of arrests increased, rising from approximately sixty in 1875 and 1876 to more than three hundred in 1880. Freedom of assembly was also

76 Irokawa, *Kindai kokka*, pp. 103–4. 77 Translation from Ike, *Beginnings*, p. 93.

restricted. The Ordinance on Public Meetings, published on April 5, 1880, while the first meeting of the newly formed Kokkai kisei dōmei was still in session, gave the police considerable authority to investigate and regulate the activities of political groups. All associations were required to submit membership lists and charters and to obtain permits before convening public meetings. Uniformed police attended all rallies and speeches and intervened if the speaker deviated from the approved topic or made statements "prejudicial to public tranquility." The law also denied soldiers, police, teachers, and even students the right to appear at political meetings.[78] Employed selectively but forcefully when the occasion demanded, the press and public meetings laws provided a legal framework for political repression. According to police records, 131 political meetings were disbanded in 1881 and 282 in 1882. Many more never took place because the police simply denied permits to assemble. In addition, editors and journalists critical of the government were fined or jailed, sometimes for seemingly modest proposals. For example, the editor of the *Azuma*, a Tokyo newspaper, was sent to jail for two years and fined ¥200 merely for voicing the opinion that the emperor, no less than other government officials, was a public servant.[79]

Nevertheless, the constitutional movement was ultimately defeated without resort to systematic repression. No such coercion was needed, for the oligarchs neatly defused the mass movement by conceding the very issue that had so aroused public enthusiasm. After extensive consultation among the leading ministers, consultations that revealed fundamental differences among them, Ōkuma Shigenobu, the only advocate of the early establishment of an English-style parliament and cabinet, was expelled from the government on October 12, 1881, at the very moment that the delegates to the semiannual meeting of the Kokkai kisei dōmei were debating proposals for convening a constituent assembly, and the government announced that the emperor would graciously grant a constitution and convene a national assembly before the end of the decade.[80]

Although much more than a tactical move to stem the tide of popular agitation, the imperial proclamation struck the Popular Rights movement at its most vulnerable point. From the beginning, liberal opponents of the oligarchy had steadfastly insisted on the harmonious

78 McLaren, *JGD*, pp. 495–9. 79 Ike, *Beginnings*, p. 90.

80 The controversy within the oligarchy over the constitution is described in detail in George Akita, *Foundations of Constitutional Government in Japan, 1868–1900* (Cambridge, Mass.: Harvard University Press, 1967), pp. 31–67.

relationship between the imperial and the popular will and staked their claim to legitimacy on the proposition that representative institutions would fulfill the aims of the imperial state by eliminating "despotic ministers" who stood between the emperor and the people, that is, barriers between ruler and ruled. Rhetorically committed to justifying liberal reform in the name of imperial sovereignty, advocates of popular rights were trapped when the oligarchs, speaking through the Meiji emperor, appropriated the issue of constitutional reform for the throne. Leaders of the Popular Rights movement could not continue agitation without disputing the imperial prerogative, even though it was apparent to all that in writing the imperial constitution, the oligarchs would be able to dictate the form and content of the new body politic. To reject this would have required a radical redefinition of liberal ideology and goals and a fundamental critique of the Meiji state. No leader, theorist, or faction subsequently demonstrated the capacity to reconstitute liberalism as a mass movement, and having failed to transform popular enthusiasm for representative government into institutions of independent political power, the liberals "won" a constitution while losing the war against oligarchic rule.

After October 1881, the Popular Rights movement splintered. There were at least four distinct developments: formation of national political parties, agitation for greater power in local and prefectural government, rise of an insurrectionist faction, and the emergence of a radical populist movement.[81] None enjoyed more than temporary success; each was suppressed or chose to disband well before the convening of the first elected national assembly.

The creation of a national political party to replace the Kokkai kisei dōmei came after the announcement of an imperial constitution in October 1881. Proposals for such an organization had been made the previous year, but disagreement between those who advocated building up local affiliates and those who wanted a strong metropolitan party had delayed implementation. The issue was first debated at the October 1881 plenary session of the Kokkai kisei dōmei, but no sooner had discussion begun than the delegates learned that the oligarchs had announced a specific date for promulgating an imperial constitution. In an atmosphere of urgency and confusion, the Tosa faction took control. Itagaki Taisuke was elected party president, and his allies and

81 Many historians consider the various conflicts between 1882 and 1885 as constituting a separate phase of the popular rights movement and label them collectively as "incidents of extremism" (*gekka jiken*). See Bowen, *Rebellion*, "Introduction."

Tosa followers filled the executive postions, virtually excluding the rural and commoner contingents.

Although the record of the Liberal Party (Jiyūtō) is mixed, on the whole it probably did more to hinder than to promote effective opposition to oligarchic rule. On the positive side, 149 local societies affiliated with it, thus creating for the first time a political party with elected leaders, a party platform, a permanent secretariat, and a national membership. In addition, it published a newspaper, set up a legal bureau, and provided at least some funding and advice to local movements. On the other hand, because the Tosa faction monopolized the top positions, factional rivalries intensified. Competing for public support with an eye to future elections, the Jiyūtō leaders put as much effort into attacking the Constitutional Progressive Party (Rikken Kaishintō), a rival liberal party headed by the Saga leader Ōkuma Shigenobu, as it did the government. Moreover, although he was undoubtedly a charismatic figure, Itagaki was at best an unsteady leader who often appeared to have been more interested in promoting his career than his party. He caused irreparable damage in 1882 when he allowed himself to be co-opted by the government for a second time after being persuaded by Gotō Shōjirō to embark on an extended tour of Western nations, one year after assuming the party presidency, apparently at government expense.[82] To make matters worse, he left Japan at a time when violent repression of the Fukushima Jiyūtō and a deepening agricultural recession created demands for direct action by the party rank and file. Leaderless, the Jiyūtō neither aided nor controlled radical groups acting in its name.

If the national Jiyūtō failed to define new goals, in some localities party leaders revived the mass movement by contesting the state bureaucracy's control of local government. The most effective local Jiyūtō leader was Kōno Hironaka, who, in the spring and summer of 1882, skillfully rallied liberal delegates to the Fukushima prefectural assembly. Kōno's campaign provoked a strong reaction, and eventual repression, at the hands of the governor, Mishima Michitsune, a loyal servant of the Home Ministry. What happened in Fukushima deserves our attention, for it illustrates both the strength of opposition movements supported by local elites and the limits to dissent that the state was prepared to tolerate.[83]

82 Gotō, *Jiyū minken*, p. 95. In fact, the money was provided by Mitsui interests at government request.

83 The conflict in Fukushima is given a different interpretation in Bowen, *Rebellion*, pp. 8–28.

When he was elected chairman of the Fukushima prefectural assembly in 1881, Kōno's first act was to introduce motions calling for universal male suffrage and the election of district magistrates and opposing recent increases in prefectural spending, especially for the governor's office and police. However, the issue that Kōno chose to dramatize was largely symbolic: the refusal of the governor to acknowledge the legitimacy of the popularly elected assembly's role as a forum for the expression of political opinion. Governor Mishima, a Satsuma samurai and former protégé of Ōkubo Toshimichi, ignored the assembly and failed to answer two assembly requests that he attend its discussion of the budget. Kōno called for a vote of no confidence with a speech that vividly expressed the tenor of the confrontation:

> This assembly was established to represent public opinion, and therefore public policy should be carried out in accord with its opinions. Let there be no mistaking that today's world is not the world of the past and that today's people are different from the people of former days. . . . Yet, [Governor Mishima] has not attended one session of the assembly; not only has he failed to take the will of the people into consideration, but he has shown his contempt for this precious public assembly.[84]

After Kōno's oration, the assembly voted to suspend debate until the governor appeared in person in the assembly chamber. Mishima, who had allegedly warned against "robbers, arsonists, and the Jiyūtō" when he took office, refused to back down. The battle lines were drawn.

Because the assembly lacked the legal authority to reject the budget or withhold appropriations, the vote to suspend debate amounted to a strong vote of censure and marked the beginning of an aggressive campaign by the Fukushima Jiyūtō to create a groundswell of popular support, comparable to the earlier petition campaign, that the oligarchs would not be able to ignore. In this they succeeded, for local Jiyūtō speakers were soon attracting large and enthusiastic crowds. Governor Mishima responded by turning to the police, who frequently refused to issue permits for political meetings and who intervened as soon as criticism of the government was voiced. What happened at a Jiyūtō rally in Ishikawa district in August was typical. Speaking to the topic "Who Is to Blame?" a local activist developed the theme that repressive government bred revolution. Arguing that English misrule had brought on the American independence movement and that tyrannical emperors and aristocrats in Russia had given rise to anarchism,

84 Gotō Yashushi, *Jiyū minken undō* (Osaka: Sōgensha, 1958), p. 88.

he then turned his attention to Japan: "Do not the police seize on a single word or phrase to throw the speaker in jail and disband the meeting?" he asked. At this the policeman on the podium stepped forward and declared the meeting a threat to public order. The speakers were ordered to step down, and the audience was dispersed.[85]

Concurrent with, but independent of, the campaign led by Kōno Hironaka, the Aizu Jiyūtō in western Fukushima organized local opposition to a major road construction project that Governor Mishima had assigned top priority. Residents of Aizu wanted the roads built; in fact, they had already approved additional taxes and corvée labor as part of an agreement on funding that had been negotiated with Mishima's representatives. But when it was discovered that the central government was paying considerably less than had been promised and that the residents would have no say in planning the route, the local Jiyūtō mounted a petition drive and tax boycott. Because the Aizu Jiyūtō was made up of the local notables and many party members were village mayors, it was able to mount large and effective protests, at least in the countryside.[86]

Backed by the Home Ministry, Governor Mishima ordered his subordinates to break the boycott. Two hundred and thirty policemen were sent to Aizu; homes were raided; property was seized; and leaders were harassed and arrested. Strong-arm tactics intimidated some of the party members, but they also aroused popular passions. Although the local Jiyūtō leadership tried to avoid violent confrontation, on a fateful day late in November a large crowd of villagers, urged on by young Jiyūtō activists who had recently arrived in Aizu, marched on the district jail in Kitakata where two leaders of the boycott were incarcerated. In the course of the demonstration, someone in the crowd, very possibly an agent provocateur, threw stones at the station, breaking several panes of glass. Immediately the police, swords drawn, charged and attacked the unarmed crowd, killing one demonstrator and wounding several others. Mishima, who was in Tokyo when the incident occurred, seized upon the incident as a pretext for legal action against the Fukushima Jiyūtō. He immediately sent a secret communiqué to his secretary which began: "The rioting of the scoundrels in Kitakata provides an excellent opportunity to arrest them all, bar none."[87] Within less than a week, one thousand Jiyūtō party members and sympathizers in Fukushima had been arrested; many were tortured; and some died while in

85 Takahashi, *Fukushima retsuden*, p. 47.
86 Shimoyama Saburō, "Fukushima jiken shōron," *Rekishigaku kenkyū*, no. 186 (May 1955): 5.
87 Takahashi Tetsuo, *Fukushima jiken* (Tokyo: San'ichi shobō, 1970), p. 187.

police custody. Most of them had never set foot in Aizu during the period of the protest.

In incidents that are collectively known as the "Fukushima incident," Jiyūtō-led resistance to Governor Mishima is usually considered the first of the so-called *gekka jiken,* violent incidents that marked the final stage of the Popular Rights movement. Yet in most respects, Jiyūtō activity in Fukushima shared more with the second phase of the Popular Rights movement, the constitutional movement, than with subsequent insurrections. As in the campaign for constitutional government, the majority of its leaders were of the local notable class, respectable and solid citizens who naturally inclined toward peaceful politics within the law. But despite such limited goals and peaceful tactics, the authorities had responded with violence, finally bringing the full weight of the judicial system to bear on the opposition.[88]

Nevertheless, the Fukushima incident was indeed a turning point in the Popular Rights movement, for the authoritarian face of the oligarchy had been revealed for all to see, causing a decline in support for the Jiyūtō among more cautious party members to whom commitment to representative government was not worth the risks of continued agitation. In this sense, the "incident" was both an end and a beginning. Mishima broke the power of a deeply entrenched local opposition movement, as he had allegedly been instructed to do upon taking office; and to young radicals, who continued the struggle against oligarchic rule, violence now appeared to be politically and morally justified.

In the last years of the Popular Rights movement, opposition to the Meiji oligarchy turned violent. It is essential, however, to distinguish between popular uprisings driven by acute economic distress, as in the Chichibu revolt of 1884, and the several insurrectionist plots of which the Kabasan incident is perhaps the best example. Whereas local leaders in Chichibu who had only recently joined the Jiyūtō organized thousands of destitute farmers around economic issues, the sixteen Kabasan rebels acted without popular support in an ill-conceived attempt to bring about revolution by assassination. Whereas the principal goal of the Chichibu uprising was debt relief, revenge and despair with conventional politics motivated the young Jiyūtō radicals of Kabasan. Hence it is the contrasts between Chichibu and Kabasan

88 Fifty-seven party members of the Fukushima Jiyūtō were charged with treason. Although six party members, including Kōno, had signed a "blood oath" to overthrow the oligarchy, there was no other evidence that any of them were actually plotting an insurrection.

that are of the greatest significance, for each movement possessed elements of revolutionary mobilization while it lacked other, essential ingredients.

For the majority of the Kabasan conspirators, the initial motive was to assassinate Mishima Michitsune and thereby avenge the brutal suppression of the Fukushima Jiyūtō. Twelve members of the Kabasan group were natives of Fukushima and had either been arrested in 1882 or witnessed the crackdown. Still, revenge was not their only motive, and the assassination of government ministers was conceived to be more than an act of terrorism. The Kabasan rebels proceeded on the assumption that the simultaneous assassination of high-ranking officials would cause the government to fall and set the stage for a revolutionary seizure of state power. Nor were they alone in thinking that direct action was the only road open to opponents of the authoritarian state. After 1882, a sizable group in the Jiyūtō headed by Ōi Kentarō had begun to advocate insurrection, a strategy that proved to be profoundly wrong but that reflected the despair of many of the most committed party members.[89] The constitutional movement and the mass movement it had spawned were dead; the Jiyūtō party secretariat was controlled by the ineffectual and compromising Itagaki; and the naked use of state power against the Fukushima Jiyūtō had demonstrated the perils, as well as the futility, of legal agitation. Thus, the Kabasan group was exceptional in its choice of tactics – plans to use homemade bombs to kill officials attending a public ceremony – but not in its frustration with conventional politics.

The particulars of the adventures and misadventures of the Kabasan conspiracy need not detain us, for they have been recorded elsewhere and illustrate only the many pitfalls that await an amateur band of political assassins.[90] The more significant failure of the Kabasan group was the scant attention that it (and most of the radical Jiyūtō) paid to organizing support among the people. To some extent, its failure to recruit the local population to the cause of revolution reflected practical limitations – primarily the need to maintain secrecy – that the group's choice of tactics imposed. Moreover, most of the conspirators were *shizoku* or sons of wealthy farmers and not natives of the locale in which they established their headquarters. But most of all, the band proved to be naive in its expectations, believing that it could raise an

89 Gotō Yasushi, "Meiji jūshichinen no gekka shojiken ni tsuite," in Horie Eichi and Tōyama Shigeki eds., *Jiyū minken ki no kenkyū: minken undō no gekka to kaitai* (Tokyo: Yūhiku, 1959), vol. 1, p. 208. 90 Bowen, *Rebellion*, pp. 31–49.

army of sufficient size to march on Tokyo simply by appealing to the rural poor, recruiting gangs of miners, and freeing convicts, all without prior political work to explain the purpose of the revolt. Completely cut off from reality, they never posed a serious threat to state power.[91]

The conspirators' lack of interest in organizing the people is all the more surprising in light of the desperate economic situation of many small farmers and the signs of incipient unrest. Beginning in 1882, a severe depression that lasted more than four years racked the countryside. The collapse of the rural economy had been precipitated by antiinflationary policies adopted at the recommendation of Finance Minister Matsukata Masayoshi in the fall of 1881 to curb inflation and promote capital accumulation and industrialization. Over the next four years the government withdrew 36 percent of the paper currency in circulation and increased excise taxes more than fivefold. Prefectural and local taxes also rose as the costs of public works and services were transferred to prefectural and local government. At the same time, the government reduced expenditures, in part by selling off to private concerns most of the industrial enterprises it had established and run as state industries.

In purely economic terms, Matsukata's policies must be judged a success. Nearly bankrupt in 1881, the government increased the ratio of reserves to currency in circulation from 8 percent to 37 percent by 1886; the nation's balance of trade swung from a deficit to surplus; and interest rates declined, all of which encouraged long-term investment in a manufacturing sector with growing capital requirements. On the other hand, what benefited industry hurt agriculture, particularly the small and marginal producers who produced cash crops and had experienced the gains of the previous inflation of prices. The immediate effect of the deflation was to depress commodity prices, thus reducing farm income. Rice prices fell from a post-Restoration high of ¥14.40 per *koku* in 1881 to ¥4.61 per *koku* in January 1884; raw silk and cocoons, the principal cash crop in many districts of eastern Japan, declined by one-half between 1882 and 1884. At the same time that the farmers' incomes were falling, taxes rose. There were new taxes to pay on consumer goods, but in addition, the real burden of the land tax increased as commodity prices declined. Paid in cash, the land tax consumed a far greater portion of total household

91 Most of the insurrections of the period were discovered by the police well before the conspirators could act.

income, rising from an average of 16 percent of the national harvest in 1877 to 33 percent in 1884.[92]

All farmers suffered to some extent as a consequence of the Matsukata deflation. However, small-scale producers of cash crops, and especially farmers who customarily relied on short-term debt, were hit the hardest. Caught between the government and the local moneylender, saddled with drastically reduced income but high fixed costs, such farmers struggled to stave off bankruptcy. Even moderately well-to-do farmers caught in the same predicament often had to mortgage their land. As the full effects of the depression took hold, bankruptcies soared, rising nationally from 33,845 households in 1883 to 108,050 in 1885.[93]

It is not surprising then that rural unrest was on the rise. Beginning in 1883, hardpressed farmers in eastern Japan began to agitate for debt relief, typically banding together to demand debt rescheduling or suspension of interest payments. These locally organized movements, self-styled "debtor parties" (*shakkintō*) and "poor people's parties" (*kommintō*), appeared most frequently in sericulture districts among small producers for whom debt management was as much part of the productive cycle as was nurturing silkworm larvae and harvesting cocoons. According to one survey, there were sixty-two incidents of collective action by debtors in 1884, the trough of the agricultural depression, with the greatest concentration in Kanagawa and Shizuoka. These efforts were not entirely unsuccessful, for there were several cases in which creditors rescheduled loans and reduced interest rates.[94]

For the most part, the Jiyūtō, whose rural membership consisted largely of local notables and wealthy farmers, kept aloof from the debtor movement; some party members, moneylenders, and wholesalers in the silk trade were themselves the targets of agitation. But in Hachiōji, a market town west of Tokyo, Ishizaka Kōrei, a local leader of the Jiyūtō who had himself fallen into debt, organized a community effort to mediate between debtors and local creditors with Jiyūtō con-

92 Irokawa Daikichi, *Kindai kokka,* pp. 345–6, who bases himself on the research of Niwa Kunio.

93 Ibid., p. 353. This is, however, an area of continuing controversy, its parameters outlined by Bowen's estimate of three million bankruptcies in the mid-1880s (*Rebellion,* p. 104) and a recent assertion that much of the increase in tenancy was for newly reclaimed land and that "real income per farm worker fell only 9.2 percent from 1879–1881 [inflationary years] to 1882–1884." Richard J. Smethurst. *Agricultural Development and Tenancy Disputes in Japan 1870–1940* (Princeton, N.J.: Princeton University Press, 1986), p. 60.

94 Irokawa Daikichi, "Kommintō to Jiyūtō," *Rekishigaku kenkyū,* no. 247 (November 1960): 1–30.

nections. Although Ishizaka achieved only moderate success, it is likely that events in Hachiōji stimulated the much more vigorous movement that developed to the north in Chichibu, a movement that culminated in a full-scale uprising a few months later.

In Chichibu, a mountainous sericulture district northwest of Tokyo, debt-related protests developed into armed resistance by local farmers whose three-thousand-strong "Poor People's Army" sacked municipal offices and attacked moneylenders and credit companies.[95] The rebellion far exceeded the previous popular uprisings of the Meiji period, in terms of organization, militancy, and ideological articulation if not in numbers of participants. The Chichibu rebellion raises a number of questions. Why was its mobilization so successful? How radical were its goals and ideology? What was its relationship to the Jiyūtō, nationally and locally? And what, finally, does the Chichibu revolt tell us about opposition to oligarchic rule at the end of the People's Rights movement?

Debt relief, the issue around which the people of Chichibu organized, spoke to their most pressing need. In the 1880s, 70 percent of all households in Chichibu raised silkworms, and the local economy was devastated by the sharp drop in silk prices after 1881.[96] However, in contrast with the debtors' movements which originated among the poorest farmers and lacked politically sophisticated leadership, the Chichibu movement was led by middle and small farmers who had only recently fallen on hard times. The three men who initiated the campaign for debt relief in Chichibu – Ochiai Toraichi, Sakamoto Sōsaku and Takagishi Zenkichi – represented the middle stratum of village society: literate but without much formal education, economically self-sufficient but certainly not wealthy, respected by their peers but lacking the prestige and influence of local notables. Whatever their prior interest and involvement in the Popular Rights movement might have been, the first we learn of their political activity is a petition delivered to the district magistrate in 1883 urging measures to regulate usury. The next spring, discouraged by the government's failure to act on the debt issue and impressed by speeches denouncing the government's economic policies made by Ōi Kentarō during a recent tour, they joined the Jiyūtō. Nevertheless, when they organized a mass movement around the debt issue in August, they did not turn to the Chichibu Jiyūtō for help. Instead, they approached hard-

95 Bowen, *Rebellion,* pp. 49–67.
96 Inoue Kōji, *Chichibu jiken* (Tokyo: Chūō kōronsha, 1968), p. 12.

pressed small farmers like themselves and made the village the unit of recruitment and mobilization. By September, they had mobilized a core of more than one hundred committed supporters. The Chichibu Kommintō (Poor People's Party) had been born.[97]

The Chichibu Kommintō decided on armed resistance only after the police and courts refused to do anything about the debt crisis and local creditors rejected conciliation. Its leaders had tried to postpone the revolt as long as possible, first, in the hope that continued agitation would produce tangible results and, second, to allow sufficient time for preparations. The head of the Kommintō, Tashiro Eisuke, and several of his lieutenants wanted at least one month to plan the uprising, arguing that success depended on simultaneous risings in neighboring provinces. However, they were forced to act prematurely because local farmers faced imminent foreclosures; by October Chichibu moneylenders had begun to call in their debts.[98] The final decision for revolt was made on October 25, and one week later the Kommintō army assembled to hear Tashiro read out the orders of battle.

The brief success of the rebel army and its subsequent defeat were described and analyzed by Roger Bowen.[99] What concerns us here is not the collapse of the rebel army but the political character of the rebellion. Consider its military organization. The formal command structure contained a clearly articulated hierarchy of staff positions descending from Tashiro, the commander in chief, to batallion leaders, establishing clear lines of authority needed to formulate and implement strategy. In addition, the goals of the revolt were clearly outlined and were supported by the rank and file, many of whom insisted on the rightness of their actions even after their arrest. At least some units followed orders and fought spiritedly, even when outnumbered and outgunned. These and other facts suggest a level of political consciousness greater than that found in Tokugawa peasant revolts or the rural protests of the early Meiji period.

On the other hand, the sophisticated conception of military organization evident in the formal command structure broke down once the Kommintō army took the field. On the third day of the revolt, when it was learned that the Imperial army was closing in, the batallion commanders disobeyed orders, creating such confusion that further attempts to coordinate operations ended. When Tashiro absconded the following day, the greater part of the army, which had grown to over five thousand men, melted away. As in traditional peasant revolts,

97 Ibid., pp. 41–43. 98 Ibid., p. 72. 99 Bowen, *Rebellion*, pp. 59–67.

participation was neither individual nor entirely voluntary; to a large extent it represented a collective decision made by each village. And if there is evidence that some of the rank and file understood their actions in explicitly political terms, there is also evidence that many used the traditional language of *yonaoshi* (world rectification) to "equalize wealth," "aid the poor," and create "the kingdom of peace and tranquility" to describe the purpose of the revolt. They also raised banners proclaiming Itagaki Taisuke, "lord of world rectification" and referred to the Jiyūtō as "poor people's gold." This is not to argue that the entire movement in Chichibu was predominantly traditional or millenarian, but there can be no doubt that outside the ranks of the leaders, pre-Meiji concepts of resistance to authority still informed political consciousness.[100] According to the transcript of Tashiro's interrogation, the purpose of the uprising was to force the government to protect farmers threatened with foreclosure, to control usury, and to reduce local taxes. Armed resistance was the means, but the strategy was to use force to compel the government to accept their demands. More immediate objectives included punitive attacks against unscrupulous moneylenders, raising funds for local relief by threatening the rich, and attacking courthouses to destroy debt vouchers, mortgage deeds, and tax records. For most of the local leaders, the goals were economic and limited in scope. This was not true, however, of Kikuchi Kambei and Ide Tamemichi, Jiyūtō activists from neighboring Nagano Prefecture who went to Chichibu late in October. They interjected a broader political vision with demands for reduction of the land tax and the immediate convening of a national assembly, on the one hand, and a rhetoric of revolution that had little to do with the popular movement, on the other. The distance between the radical faction, most of whom were from outside Chichibu, and the majority of the local Kommintō leadership was made clear at the first meeting between Tashiro and Kikuchi. Tashiro insisted that the principal objective was debt relief, and Kikuchi was so disappointed that he tried to persuade Ide to return home.[101]

Finally, the role of the Jiyūtō remained marginal. A number of the leaders of the Chichibu Kommintō had recently joined the Jiyūtō or, as in the case of Tashiro, were associated though not formally enrolled in the party. But the Jiyūtō group in the Kommintō was not at all representative of the party membership, either locally or nationally. They had joined the Jiyūtō in 1884 out of concern for the plight of

100 Moriyama Gunjirō, *Minshū hōki to matsuri* (Tokyo: Chikuma shobō, 1981), p. 113. See also Irokawa, *Culture of the Meiji Period*, pp. 159ff. 101 Inoue, *Chichibu jiken*, p. 73.

impoverished farmers at the hands of local moneylenders. In the course of the campaign to negotiate relief measures, they had come to see the role of the state as the guardian of private property and contracts. In other words, they drew the crucial connection between state power and economic structure, and this gave a political dimension to their uprising. But the majority of the Jiyūtō members in Chichibu came from the well-to-do local notable class and took no interest in the campaign for debt relief. The same pattern prevailed in the Sakyu district of Nagano, which bordered Chichibu to the west. When Kikuchi led a force of several rebels there, hoping to attract new recruits, the well-established Jiyūtō gave them no help at all. Neither did Ōi Kentarō, head of the radical Jiyūtō faction in Tokyo. Informed of the rising in advance, Ōi sent a messenger with instructions to cancel the revolt. Nationally, Jiyūtō leaders condemned both Kabasan and Chichibu in an effort to disassociate themselves from the violence that they felt discredited the party. In fact, meeting in Osaka just before the Chichibu rebellion, the party executives voted to disband, partly out of recognition that they could not control radical groups acting in the party's name.[102]

With the voluntary dissolution of the Jiyūtō and the suppression of the Chichibu rebellion, the Popular Rights movement ended. Although Jiyūtō radicals plotted several more insurrections, each was discovered, and the conspirators were rounded up before they were put to the test.[103] What did the liberal movement accomplish?

Very little. The decade of agitation and ferment that began with the memorial of the Aikokukōtō in 1874 ended without achieving the institutional reforms needed to establish a democratic polity. It is true that the government, as it had promised, delivered a constitution in 1889 that provided the framework for limited representation at the national level. But the constitution written by the oligarchs so circumscribed the power of the elected lower house that it was another twenty years before the political parties gained a share of ministerial power, and it was 1918 before a parliamentarian became prime minister. Hence politics in the first half-century of modernization, the period in which the basic pattern of institutional and ideological articulation took shape, was bureaucratic and authoritarian. In most respects the

102 Irokawa, *Kindai kokka*, p. 241.

103 The final episode involved plans to send armed forces to Korea to aid the progressive faction in that country to seize power, thereby setting the stage for revolution in Japan. Marius B. Jansen, "Oi Kentarō: Radicalism and Chauvinism," *Far Eastern Quarterly* 11 (May 1952): 305–16.

society created by the Meiji oligarchy was "modern," being capitalistic, meritocratic, and scientific, but also politically and socially repressive and increasingly chauvinistic and militaristic. In the light of Japan's difficult task as an Asian nation industrializing in the predatory world of Western imperialism, it is impossible to predict how modernization might have differed under more liberal political leadership.[104] What we do know is that the liberals were excluded from power at the time when there was the greatest opportunity for progressive change.

Among the factors limiting the effectiveness of the People's Rights movement were factionalism, weak and compromising leadership, and a generally united oligarchy that did not hesitate to use the police and courts to harass and intimidate its opponents. But perhaps the fundamental weakness of Meiji liberalism was its acceptance of the imperial institution as the fountain of all legitimate political authority. Not only liberal polemics against the oligarchs but every constitution made public during the Popular Rights movement placed the imperial institution at the center of the new polity and stipulated joint rule by the emperor and the people.

The reliance of popular rights leaders on the Meiji emperor as a legitimizing institution signified an ideological commitment and not just a political stretegy aimed at swaying public opinion. Although it was opportunistic as well, in a more basic sense the linkage of the imperial with the popular will in the rhetoric of the Popular Rights movement points out the all-too-real confusion on the part of the first generation of Japanese liberals about the relationship between imperial and democratic institutions and demonstrates the limiting historical conditions that they faced. The emperor was the one political force that transcended all the particularistic social divisions of rank, class, domain, and family inherited from centuries of feudalism. Needing an emotionally compelling symbol of progressive political relationships, popular rights thinkers and activists wholeheartedly accepted the Meiji emperor. But though they were free to lay claim to the imperial will, they had no control over the institution to which they hitched their star. For the Meiji emperor, as well as being a potent symbol of the modern era, was also a political actor controlled by the oligarchs. As such, he could be used with devastating effect against any group that appealed uncritically to his authority.

104 The political parties that emerged in the Taishō period were scarcely less chauvinistic than most other groups in Japanese society and overall more jingoistic than the bureaucracy.

CONCLUSION

The leaders of the Meiji Restoration never surrendered power during their lifetimes, and despite attacks from both progressive and reactionary political forces, they stuck to their agenda of rapid, top-down transformation of political, social, and economic institutions. To understand why the leaders prevailed, we need to consider the social character of the opposition forces, their interests, and the choices the oligarchs made. Put simply, they made tactical concessions that reduced the friction between the emerging middle class and the state but crushed movements by socially marginal classes.

Confronted with protests against the land tax and the campaign for constitutional government, movements that mobilized propertied and educated segments of the population, the oligarchs offered concessions addressing the long-term class interests of these groups. By reducing the land tax in 1877, subsequently shifting the tax burden from property to consumption, and writing a constitution that gave substantial fiscal and legislative power to the elected lower house, the oligarchs deflected demands for more progressive reforms without either surrendering power or permanently alienating the future middle class. Despite relatively heavy property taxes and exclusion from the government, the wealthy farmers, landlords, entrepreneurs, and the commercial and educated classes benefited enormously from the progressive reforms of Meiji – especially reforms that brought citizen equality, meritocracy, protection of private property, and promotion of capitalist economic growth.

Early in this chapter we observed that historians in the West tend to credit traditional values such as consensus and loyalty to the emperor with minimizing "dysfunctional" conflict in Meiji, whereas most Japanese historians emphasize the repressive role of the state. But at least in the case of liberal opposition movements, it is interests rather than values that are salient. The propertied and educated had a sufficient material stake in the emerging social order to keep them from launching a truly radical attack on the government. Their class interests dictated compromise rather than unrestrained confrontation; they faced selective, and not massive, repression by the state.

However, the classes marginalized by the Meiji reforms, groups that were losing social power as a result of modernization, faced an entirely different situation. The traditional warrior and small-scale subsistence farmer did not fit into the new order, and the government sacrificed their social needs quite ruthlessly to speed national integration and capital accumulation. Victims of the particular development strategies pursued by the Meiji government, these groups suffered severe and irreversible decline in socioeconomic status. They had every reason to revolt, but why did their rebellion fail?

Historically, the ability of governments to repress rebellion has been profoundly influenced by interaction with world political and economic systems.[105] Japan in the mid-nineteenth century was no exception. In the decade preceding the Meiji Restoration, military and economic pressures of Western imperialism hastened the collapse of the Tokugawa bakufu. Commodore Matthew C. Perry's warships undermined the legitimacy of the shogun and created a sense of national crisis within the ruling class. Faced with a possible loss of national independence, the bakufu was forced to authorize a military mobilization that strained its own resources and strengthened the hostile daimyo. The commercial treaties imposed on the bakufu by the Western powers disrupted financial and commodity markets. Rampant inflation, food shortages, hoarding, and rice riots further weakened Tokugawa authority. In the end, only a few of the hereditary vassals of the Tokugawa house were willing to fight on its behalf. Overall, the victory of the *tōbaku* (overthrow the bakufu) movement was due less to its own strength than to the crippling effects of Western imperialism on the traditional bases of Tokugawa strength. In the absence of the acute foreign crisis, the *tōbaku* forces, which were numerically small, internally divided, and ideologically diverse, could not have seized power in 1868 without first achieving a much higher level of mobilization.

Conversely, in considering the defeat of opposition movements in early Meiji, we should not overlook the fact that the oligarchs were not subjected to new pressures from the imperialist powers. The commercial treaties imposed specific constraints on economic policy and reduced state revenues, and extraterritoriality continued to be a cause of national humiliation. But during the critical first decade of political and social reform, when tension between the government and the former samurai class was the greatest, the Western powers did not make new demands for diplomatic, trade, or territorial concessions. There is no doubt that the relaxation of external pressure enabled the government to push ahead with modernization. Fighting a major war in the 1870s would have strained the government's resources while strengthening the exponents of reaction both inside and outside the

105 Theda Skocpol, *States and Social Revolutions* (Cambridge, England: Cambridge University Press, 1979), pp. 23–4.

oligarchy; a prolonged conflict would have necessitated mobilizing the *shizoku*. Once the traditional warrior class had been rearmed, it is unlikely that the government could have eliminated its stipends and class privileges. And without these reforms, the basis of the alliance between the oligarchy and wealthy commoners and progressive *shizoku* – meritocracy, lower property taxes, and the 1889 constitution – would have vanished.

The second contextual factor that aided the government was the sequential, rather than simultaneous, rise of opposition forces. The oligarchs faced challenges from both reactionary and progressive movements, but they did not have to confront both at the same time. Although the *shizoku* revolts overlapped with protests against the land tax, the constitutional movement reached its apogee well after the danger of *shizoku* rebellion had passed. Moreover, the liberal phase of the Popular Rights movement coincided with a period of general prosperity. From the defeat of the Satsuma Rebellion to the Matsukata deflation, good weather, the strong export demand for silk, expansive monetary policies, and inflation that reduced the farmers' real taxes created unprecedented prosperity in the countryside – conditions more favorable to reformist politics than to radical movements. Finally, when the Matsukata deflation brought severe hardship to the villages in the 1880s, the constitutional movement was already in full retreat. And because the principal demand of the rural poor was debt relief, the Jiyūtō ignored them. Leaderless except in Chichibu, poor farmers did not mobilize effectively.

Without a conjuncture of external and internally destabilizing forces, revolts by *shizoku* and poor farmers could not possibly succeed so long as they remained localized movements. Mass mobilization along class lines was a precondition for success, yet in the end only a minority of *shizoku* and impoverished farmers took up arms against the state.

The very limited scale of antigovernment mobilization, despite the substantial decline in socioeconomic wellbeing nationwide, is the salient factor in the defeat of armed opposition to the Meiji oligarchy. Unlike the groups that rallied around the issues of property taxes and representative government, declassed *shizoku* and subsistence farmers had gained little and lost a great deal as a result of Meiji modernization. They had ample cause to take up arms, but comparatively few did.

There is very little evidence to support the claim that loyalty to the emperor, one of the traditional values assumed to have reduced political conflict in Meiji, had a decisive impact on the political behavior of ex-samurai who were faced with the dilemma between acquiescence in loss of status and social redundancy or revolt in defense of traditional privilege. As we have seen, the *shizoku* rebels of the 1870s had once been at the forefront of the Restoration movement, and there is no reason to believe that they were any less patriotic or that they regarded the imperial institution with less reverence than did the samurai who served the oligarchy. On the contrary, had they not already demonstrated a greater degree of personal commitment than had most of their peers?

If loyalty to the emperor was not the decisive factor inhibiting *shizoku* rebellion, then what was?

Shizoku in the 1870s lacked the organizational resources to mobilize around class interests because Meiji reforms had crippled traditional samurai structures of collective action. For nearly three centuries the feudal *kashindan* (daimyo retainer band) had defined the political world of the samurai. Living within pyramidal, rigid status hierarchies, samurai were subject to the absolute authority of daimyo and fief elders; stratified by hereditary rank within the domain, they were segregated from the samurai of other domains because of affiliation with a single military house. At least until the emergence of the activist *shishi* bands in response to the foreign crisis in the *bakumatsu* period, the *kashindan* stood as the only legitimate forum for political action. Consequently, when the government ordered the abolition of private fiefs in 1871 and disbanded the *kashindan,* it deprived the middle and low-ranking samurai – the strata least adequately compensated for the loss of traditional income and privilege – of familiar and authorized organizations for collective action. If they were to resist, they would first need to create new ideological and organizational structures. The vast majority were not able to do that.

Viewed from this perspective, it is not surprising that disaffected veterans of the *tōbaku* movement and not, for instance, Tokugawa loyalists led the *shizoku* revolts in the early Meiji period. Unlike their more conservative peers, they had already participated in voluntaristic political associations which to some degree transcended ascriptive status. Having once rebelled against established political authority, they could more easily authorize their own actions in terms of higher principles, even when this entailed breaking the emperor's laws. They did not, however, foresee the need to go beyond the organizations of the *tōbaku* movement, and they never developed class-based structures for political action. As we have seen, they continued to rely on local associations of like-minded "men of spirit," and these proved inadequate against the newly centralized state.

Meiji reforms also undercut the social basis of traditional village mobilization. As seen in village protests against the Meiji land tax, sustained opposition depended on the leadership of headmen and local notables. Although by no means entirely contingent on shared economic interests, the tradition of village officials leading protests against oppressive taxation was integrally bound up with the corporate features of the feudal tax system. But the Meiji land tax eliminated the village as a fiscal unit; landholding was fully privatized, and the payment of taxes was made an individual responsibility. Under these conditions, the impending bankruptcy of small farmers unable to pay the land tax became a class issue and ceased to be a matter of collective village concern. Moreover, the modernization of the legal system and security apparatus strengthened the position of the landlords and moneylenders. Unlike the bakufu and daimyo, the Meiji state provided policing at the village level, laws that protected private property, and courts to enforce them – all of which reduced local constraints on individual acquisition.

The sharp and permanent rise in tenancy during the agricultural depression of 1882–6 stands out as the most decisive change in rural relations in the early Meiji period. Deprived of the thin margin of protection that village solidarity had once provided, impoverished farmers suffered massive loss of land as a direct consequence of monetary and fiscal policies enacted by the oligarchy to spur capital accumulation and investment in industry. But only in Chichibu did they take up arms.

The conditions that made rebellion possible in Chichibu suggest the nature of the obstacles that existed elsewhere. In contrast with the situation in most areas, some, though not all, members of the local Jiyūtō took up the cause of indebtedness and foreclosures, thereby providing leadership. Second, the social structure favored collective action by the poor, inasmuch as a majority of farmers were threatened with bankruptcy. Nearly 70 percent of Chichibu farm household heads were small landowners who reared silkworms as a cash crop. In contrast with the cotton and rice export regions where subsistence farmers had already lost their land and become tenant farmers, most peasants in Chichibu were still struggling to keep their status as marginal cash-crop farmers. Third, as recently as 1866, under similar conditions of economic hardship and indebtedness among small-scale producers, the peasants of Chichibu had carried out massive attacks against moneylenders, local rice and silk dealers, and village officials in the name of "world rectification" (*yonaoshi*).[106]

In Chichibu, all the ingredients needed to pursue collective action were present: local leadership, a mass base, and familiar structures for peasant mobilization. However, whereas *yonaoshi*-type mobilization allowed the poor to carry out retribution against local propertied classes, it could not be sustained for a long period of time and had no chance of toppling the central government. The uprising dramatized the plight of impoverished farmers, but it did nothing to change the actual conditions of their lives.

It is part of the lore of Western historiography of the Meiji Restoration that in Japan, tradition aided rather than obstructed modernization. Although there is some truth to this interpretation, like many theories, it obscures even as it enlightens our understanding of historical process. What this analysis of the failure of the Meiji opposition movements suggests is that the Meiji reforms destroyed traditional structures of collective action that, if they had remained in place, would have permitted far broader mobilization against the programs of the Meiji government.

106 See Vlastos, *Peasant Protests*.

CHAPTER 5

JAPAN'S DRIVE TO GREAT-POWER STATUS

THE FOREIGN POLICY OF A MODERN STATE

Nothing is more striking, in tracing Meiji Japan's foreign affairs, than the fact that the Meiji period coincided with the emergence of several "modern states." The half-century before the outbreak of World War I in 1914 witnessed political, economic, social, and intellectual developments in the West that coalesced into the development of national entities, outlines of which have remained to this day. England, France, Germany, Italy, and other European countries, as well as the United States, evolved as centralized and integrated mass societies that, for want of a better term, have been called modern states. Although no two modern states were exactly alike, they were generally characterized by centralization of state authority, on the one hand, and mass incorporation into the economy and polity, on the other. These developments had, of course, been preceded by the democratic and the industrial revolutions of the late eighteenth and the early nineteenth century, but it was in most instances only after the 1860s that these earlier, and ongoing, revolutions conspired with other trends to create conditions for unified state systems.

The twin phenomenon of centralization and mass incorporation may be illustrated by the United States, the country that held the greatest fascination for the Japanese during the two decades after Perry. The America of Perry's days was not yet a full-fledged modern state. It was a country with serious cleavages between regions and economic interests. Although shared mythologies of the American Revolution generated a sense of common heritage, what a later generation would call a "civil religion," and although a sense of nationhood was buttressed by economic opportunity (a theme that Alexis de Tocqueville stressed in the 1830s), there also grew an apparently insoluble dispute about the nature of the American state. Those following Andrew Jackson, who believed in the integrity of national unity as expressed by the government in Washington, were increasingly on the defensive in the face of "nullifiers" like John C. Calhoun, who argued that the very essence of the nation lay in a compact among units to form a larger entity so that any of them retained the freedom to secede from the entity when the latter seemed to infringe on its rights. When the first Japanese embassy, led by Shimmi Masaoki, visited the United States in 1860, they were being unwitting witnesses to a drama that preceded the dissolution of the union.

The situation was vastly different when the second embassy, this time dispatched by the fledgling Meiji state and headed by Iwakura Tomomi, reached the United States in 1871. The four-year-long Civil War had settled the question about the inviolability of national unity. The country was to be governed as one political unit under a federal government with powers to emancipate and enfranchise slaves, regulate internal commerce, and use troops for maintaining domestic order. "Rebel states" in the South would never again attempt to create their separate sovereignty; instead they would try to promote their welfare within the larger national framework. The national government was now more centralized than before the Civil War, with civil reforms recruiting bureaucrats whose loyalty was to the new order. The armed forces, too, were increasingly bureaucratized. Although in the immediate postbellum years both the army and the navy dwindled in size, the nucleus of modern armed power remained, and its leaders were committed to the rationalization of organization, ordnance, and command.

The centralization of political authority reflected and confirmed economic integration. The United States grew as a huge national market, its agricultural sector producing all that its citizens needed, and much more. Railroads crisscrossed every region, and the newly developed technology of refrigeration and canning enabled farm and dairy products to travel thousands of miles to reach the consumer. Inevitably, problems arose in arbitrary railway tariff charges, unsanitary conditions of meats, or falling prices of wheat due to overproduction, and in every instance the federal government was viewed as an arbiter and regulator of conflicting interests. The government's most crucial contribution to the national economy, however, lay in its tariff policy. Protectionism provided a setting in which industrialization could grow apace. Capital for industrialization came from largely European, particularly British, sources, rather than from domestic savings, but the late nineteenth century also created a class of fabulously rich American capitalists who, by controlling the railways and expanding factories, were so influential in linking segments of the national economy that the government felt obliged, in 1890, to enact the first antitrust measures. But they did little to stem the trend toward the creation of a national economic order.

Mass incorporation into the national economy and polity was an integral part of this phenomenon. In the United States, it is true, the people had enjoyed greater freedom and opportunity than in most other countries since the late eighteenth century. Still, the situation after the Civil War was unique in that on the one hand, the federal government as well as the political parties were committed to the idea of national economic development through industrial, transportation, and financial development, whereas on the other hand, rapid economic change created significant social dislocations severely affecting the lower strata of society who often had recourse to organized political action. Both phenomena tended to deepen the government's involvement in the people's economic and social affairs – what Morton Keller has termed "the affairs of state" – while at the same time developing a pervasive sense of the people's common identity as workers, consumers, and often victims of forces beyond their control. In all this process a mass society was being created, a society that was at once more heterogeneous racially and socially, and more integrated politically, than earlier. Whether this was a desirable phenomenon for the health and growth of America was a question hotly debated by its leaders. Some urged a return to a less complicated era characterized by homogeneous local communities, and others sought to forge a new unity on the basis of cooperation among different interest groups under the benevolent leadership of the state. Still others advocated a class struggle as the only way to improve the living conditions of the masses. These alternatives pointed to a central question of the modern state: how to preserve order amid change. Given the rapid technological development and economic change, the state authority had to devise means for preventing unmanageable upheavals, but a politically conscious populace would not be satisfied with a stale stability that gave them no feeling of participation in public affairs and opportunities.

Thus both the state authority and the masses were gaining power. Whether one would grow at the expense of the other was never satisfactorily resolved, but on the whole it may be said that various mechanisms were devised to prevent either development and to maintain a balance between state and society. One such mechanism was party politics, and another was organized interest groups. These institutions mediated between governmental leadership and bureaucracy, on the one hand, and mass interests and aspirations, on the other. Also important were the intellectuals, professionals, social workers, and educators who served as intermediaries among the different groups, and between them and the government. They were the experts capable of understanding – so it was thought – the forces of modern transformation. They would work to make the process of modernization more beneficial and less painful to the society at large; they would provide technical expertise for public administrators to cope with complex issues of the industrial age; and they would put brakes on both governmental power and popular power lest they should get out of hand and undermine social unity. Usually called reformers or liberals, these were the individuals who were the country's leaders without being part of the state, and who spoke for the masses without being totally identified with them. Thus functionally they were against state dictatorships, mass revolutions, and class struggles. Rather, they were reformists trying to accommodate forces of change within manageable frameworks. Their task was not an easy one, for they had to chart a middle course between revolution and reaction and between authoritarianism and anarchy.

Such, in rough outline, were the forces that were shaping American society after the Civil War. Although the existence and abolition of slavery made the country unique, in most other instances the experience was similar to those elsewhere in the West. The European countries, too, had their domestic strife and civil wars before they emerged as centralized states with civilian and armed bureaucracies, national markets, and mass politics and culture. When the Japanese awoke to the importance of turning to the West, then, they were presented with precisely those features that made them modern states. Of course, they may not have been aware that this was a rather recent development, a stage in Western history. But they were naturally more interested in the present than in the past, and they could not have chosen a more suitable moment for transforming their own country. They had models everywhere they looked, and it required no unusual imagination for them to pattern their national development after these models. They did not pick just one model, but several, and so they borrowed certain institutions from Britain, some from Germany and France, and still others from the United States. Such selectivity is not surprising in view of the fact that Western nations, too, were avidly copying one another with a view to transforming themselves into powerful modern entities.

The emergence of modern states inevitably had serious repercussions on international affairs. First, a modern state by definition had greater military resources at its command. Its armed forces were better organized and more effectively mobilized than earlier because of the state's centralized system of bureaucracy and taxation. The armed forces represented the state, both internally to maintain law and order (against "public enemies" such as dissidents, subversives, and sometimes even strikers) and to demonstrate national power abroad. Military organization, ordnance, and intelligence were improved, and vast strides were made in building faster ships, better fortifications, and more efficient systems of communication. Because these developments were taking place simultaneously in most countries, it was not surprising that they should have intensified, rather than contributed to diminishing, a sense of insecurity in each country, which would now be confronted with potential adversaries with larger ships and better-equipped soldiers. Under the circumstances, the idea of national defense expanded. Basic to the new definition was a global perspective. All regions of the world were perceived to be interlinked because of technological improvements and increased armament, and for a nation to maintain secure defenses it was considered imperative to adopt a global strategy. As Alfred Thayer Mahan noted in the 1890s, "Defense means not merely defense of our territory, but defense of our just national interests, whatever they be and wherever they are." Echoing such a view, an American army officer wrote in 1892, "Now we have interests abroad which are endangered by threats of aggression far from our own borders."[1] The broadened concept of defense was a characteristic feature of the late nineteenth century and reflected the emergence of centralized states. It compelled strategic reformulation and produced certain ideas that remained influential through World War I. They included the quantitative enlargement and qualitative improvement of armed forces, the acquisition of bases and coaling stations, and the development of a geopolitical outlook that might call for a combination of "land powers" against "sea powers," as Mahan advocated, or for the establishment of an economically viable regional bloc such as "Mitteleuropa," an idea developed by some German economists and military thinkers.[2]

Equally important were military alliances. As ultimately exemplified by Britain's decision to terminate its "splendid isolation," the capitals of Europe became aware at this time that no one country

1 Graham Cosmas, *An Army for Empire: The United States Army in the Spanish-American War* (Columbus: University of Missouri Press, 1971), pp. 35–7.

2 David E. Kaiser, *Economic Diplomacy and the Origins of the Second World War* (Princeton, N.J.: Princeton University Press, 1980), p. 5.

would be able to maintain its security in a world of expanding armament and improving technology. It would be necessary to form alliances and ententes to pool several countries' resources and labor power against contingencies. At the outset, when an alliance was concluded between Germany and Austria-Hungary in 1879, few could have foreseen that this presaged a rigid structure of alliances that led ultimately to war. At that time, this and other similar undertakings appeared to be temporary expediencies designed to provide their signatories with a sense of security; they would be replaced by other alliances as conditions changed. However, within less than thirty years after 1879, there had emerged two groups of powers into which the major European countries had become divided: the Triple Alliance of Germany, Austria-Hungary, and Italy, on the one hand, and the Triple Entente of Britain, France, and Russia, on the other. They vied with one another for more efficient armed forces, and within each group its member states exchanged strategic and mobilization plans. Peace was maintained precariously in the form of a balance of power between the two camps. But it could give way to conflict, and when it did, it was likely to involve all these countries and even more.

Strategic implications, however, were not the only by-product of the emergence of modern states. Also crucial was the fact that each state was committed to rapid economic development, particularly overseas trade and domestic industrialization. Sometimes called *neomercantilism*, this commitment was different from seventeenth-century mercantilism in that it stressed the growth of national economic units as producers and as markets in the global economic system. The state encouraged the expansion of worldwide trade and investment activities, while at the same time facilitating the growth of domestic industry. Western nations were economically linked to one another by a gold standard that made national currencies convertible into gold and other currencies. But the states remained economic units, and governments fostered the creation of national marketplaces by establishing transportation networks, encouraging cooperation between capital and labor, and protecting domestic industry and agriculture against foreign competition. All these activities could be carried out more efficiently than formerly now that each government had built up a system of administration by career bureaucrats. Their task was to ensure the stability of the gold standard and the success of industrialization. These were linked to foreign affairs in that they sustained the new modern states, providing them with revenue for further armament expenditures. Increased armaments, in turn, were seen as a means of protecting the country's trade routes and overseas possessions that were linked to the domestic economy.

This last phenomenon, that is, the incorporation of overseas possessions and spheres of influence into the domestic economic and strategic system, was then and has since been termed *imperialism*. Although the term has been so broadened as to include almost any type of domination by one country over another – even by a noncapitalist or underdeveloped state over another – it also connoted something specific, a development that coincided with the emergence of centralized industrial states.[3] Although not all such states undertook imperialist policies, the nations that did were invariably "powers" that were going through the process of political centralization and economic modernization. This was because they had enough economic, military, and administrative resources to dominate the less powerful and less developed areas of the world. Their bankers, industrialists, and merchants sought to maximize their profits through finding and enlarging overseas markets and through obtaining cheap raw materials and foodstuffs in the tropical regions for consumption at home by the laboring population. Although these activities had been going on since the inception of the Industrial Revolution in the eighteenth century, at the end of the nineteenth century their endeavors were more readily supported, and often encouraged, by the state. Its bureaucratic and military apparatus could be used to seek overseas markets as well as bases; they provided the labor power necessary to protect rights and prerogatives obtained; and both economic and military activities enhanced the state's prestige and power. Somehow it was believed that all successful modern powers must expand overseas. Much of this expansion, of course, deviated little from more traditional forms of expansion such as emigration to the American continent or trade with other advanced countries. However, there was also great concern with incorporating less developed parts of the globe into modern state systems. These "peripheral" areas would constitute the fringes of the modern states geographically and politically; they would never be fully integrated into the polity. But they would serve as dependable markets, as *raisons d'être* for large armed establishments and bureaucracies and as symbols of status and power in international affairs.

This last was very important, particularly with regard to the masses in the metropolises whose tax contributions as well as votes were necessary for an imperialist program. Their support could be obtained by

3 Various interpretations of imperialism are aptly summed up by Wolfgang Mommsen, *Theories of Imperialism*, Engl. ed. (New York: Random House, 1980).

painting a picture of an expanding empire as an invigorating and noble enterprise in the service not only of the state but also of civilization and humanity. Because the empire now contained tropical regions and populations, it could be presented as a duty – even a "burden" in Rudyard Kipling's famous construction – incumbent upon more advanced and civilized peoples to provide the former with order and purpose. If metropolitan voters and taxpayers were not in a missionary mood, then they could be told that the new possessions gave them added opportunities to better themselves. If they did not fare well at home, they could always go to these areas where they would be treated as superior beings and would be guaranteed protection by their government. Their nationalism, which was daily being cultivated through news of international rivalries as well as promoted by domestic policies of centralization, could be counted on to support acts that resulted in additions of more territory under the country's control. Some political parties took advantage of this expansionist sentiment by identifying themselves with imperialism in order to obtain a mass following. In a sense they mediated between government and people. By channeling mass emotions away from domestic issues, which, as George Bernard Shaw noted, could lead to revolution, and deflecting them to the support of imperialism, the parties ensured domestic order at the expense of international stability.[4] But this phenomenon – sometimes referred to as *social imperialism* – could go much beyond obtaining mass satisfaction with the polity. An emotionally aroused public opinion could be transformed into irresponsible jingoisms not easily controllable even by the government. If that should happen, foreign policy issues would seriously undermine domestic order. The modern state, in this way, was built on a precarious balance between obtaining mass support for military strengthening and overseas expansion and avoiding mass extremism that could unleash far more emotional and irrational forces than could be accommodated in the political apparatus.

THE MEIJI POLITY AND SOCIETY

This brief sketch helps put Meiji Japanese foreign affairs in context and perspective. It is important to recall that Japan, too, was transforming itself as a modern state. Its foreign relations were an aspect as well as a product of that process. Other chapters in this volume treat the domestic developments at greater length, so it should be sufficient

4 On social imperialism, see Bernard Semmel, *Imperialism and Social Reform: English Social Imperial Thought, 1895–1914* (London: Allen & Unwin, 1960).

here to note that between 1868 and 1912 – the forty-five years of the Meiji emperor's rule – Japan came to acquire almost all of the ingredients of a modern state that other countries were also in the process of obtaining. First, internal administrative unity replaced the cumbersome Tokugawa system. The new Tokyo government quickly established a bureaucratic apparatus so that within a few years after 1868 it boasted of a multitude of ministries of Finance, Home Affairs, Foreign Affairs, and others for which "enlightened" elites were recruited. These elites were mostly former samurai who had been active in bakufu and *han* affairs in the years before the Restoration, and many of them had spent several years studying in the West. They were technical experts whose loyalty was to the new regime under the nominal head of the emperor. The latter symbolized the fact that the country was now administratively and politically centralized, a system in which professional bureaucrats would play a pivotal role. Their work was sustained and protected by the newly created armed forces that, too, represented central authority against latent localism. The suppression of the Satsuma Rebellion of 1877 marked a successful alliance of Japan's new bureaucrats and armed forces, some recruited from peasant families, against the remnants of the old order.

Administrative centralization was accompanied by the development of a national economy. Even before 1868, of course, the country had been unified as a national market through commerce, uniform currencies, and domestic travel. But the Meiji government was intent on providing national leadership for economic development so that the country as a whole would "increase production and create industry," as one of the slogans put it. This was essentially an administrative task, involving tax reforms so as to obtain revenue from the agricultural sector and to turn it over for industrialization. The government took steps to identify and protect merchants and industrialists, to establish model factories and quality inspection stations, and to instill in the people the idea that "enriching the country" was just as important a goal as was "strengthening its defense."

Mass incorporation into the new polity, in the meanwhile, grew quickly. This took various forms, ranging from a comprehensive system of population registers to universal military conscription. The idea was to create an administratively effective system so that the government would be able to reach out to the entire population as citizens of the state. Their services were needed not only as potential soldiers and loyal subjects but ultimately as the backbone of the modern Japanese nation. An educated, enlightened citizenry was considered an essential part of the entity. Hence there was an early emphasis on education, both at the schools and in various political and professional activities. The people had to be politically conscious and economically developed if they were to support the new arrangements as citizens, producers, and taxpayers. This process of mass incorporation, of course, was destined to give rise to social movements that were not all supportive of the state. Although the awakening of political consciousness was a vital part of the formation of the modern state, it could develop into a force of protest against specific governmental decisions, general thrusts of national policy, or even the Meiji state itself. These forces, broadly termed the "Freedom and People's Rights" movement, made their appearance during the 1870s, evidence that Japan was already acquiring yet another characteristic of a modern state. For mass movements were a necessary component of a society that was undergoing political and economic centralization. Although such movements could, and often did, present obstacles in the way of centralization, functionally there could be no centralized modern society without politically conscious citizens.

The two could be related in a number of ways. The twentieth century has produced such extreme examples as the totalitarian mass societies in Nazi Germany and Stalinist Russia, or the "mass-line" politics in Maoist China. They all linked the masses with the state through centralized indoctrination, party dictatorship, and mass meetings. Few institutions stood between the state and the people. In the late nineteenth century, however, almost all modernizing states retained family, church, business, community, and other institutions that mediated between them. They functioned as checks on state power, on the one hand, and as agents of modernization, on the other, in the sense that through them the people would be socialized, educated, and developed into citizenry. Most important, there were political parties that spoke for both the state and the people. They provided personnel for the government and also represented the diverse interests and viewpoints of the people.

Meiji Japan fitted into this pattern. Already by the 1870s numerous political parties, study groups, and community organizations had come into being, superimposed on traditional family and religious institutions. Their growth was ensured by the government's policy of encouraging education, social mobility, economic development, and political consciousness. Both those who benefited from such developments and those who felt left out found it easy to organize. Early political parties were an amalgam of divergent interests and viewpoints, some urging the state to do more for modernization and others opposing the process as too swift and confusing. Even the latter, however, lent their hands to the modernization process in that they contributed to political organizing efforts and to arousing mass interest in national affairs. After all, they had no recourse for seeking amends other than through organizing themselves and demonstrating their causes in accordance with the various grievance procedures that were being set up. In the end, the bulk of the "premodern" dissidents found themselves joining existing political parties or being co-opted into working for the state.

It does not mean, of course, that Japan as a modern state did not have special characteristics of its own. All nations are unique. But uniqueness generally lies in historical diversity. Although Japanese history made the country different, the same was true of other countries. Moreover, some peculiar features of Meiji Japan should probably be considered within the framework of its development as a modern state, that is, as minor variations on a common theme. Among such variations two stood out in the Meiji era: the emperor system and the military's "right of supreme command." Although most modern states at that time were monarchies, the Japanese case was unique in that the imperial institution was consciously used to create a centralized bureaucratic system. By identifying the new arrangements as rule by the sacred emperor, an aura of sanctity was accorded to them. Japan's armed forces and bureaucrats would be "the emperor's soldiers and officials," making them perhaps less vulnerable to partisan attacks than might have been the case in other societies with shorter periods of dynastic history. By combining a newly created bureaucracy, civilian and military, with the prestige of a fifteen-hundred-year-old institution, the Meiji leaders succeeded in giving modernization almost instant legitimacy. Second, they early perceived the need to separate military administration from strategic affairs, and in 1878 they established a general staff independent of the Ministry of War. The former would control strategic planning, tactical decisions, and military intelligence. These, comprising matters pertinent to "the right of supreme command," would enable the general staff to report directly to the emperor, thus sustaining its separate status from civilian bureaucracies. The system was learned from Prussia, but it grew into an extremely important aspect of the Japanese state, because the "independence" of the supreme command was combined with the imperial institution. Already by 1879, army leaders such as Saigō Tsugumichi and Ōyama Iwao were arguing that as the civilian and constitutional government was expected to expand, it would be desirable to maintain the separate existence of the military.[5]

It is these characteristics that have led some historians to define the Meiji state as "emperor absolutism." Presumably such a definition makes sense in stressing the pivotal roles played by the emperor and the military. Evidently the two were under much less restraint than in other modern states, perhaps with the exception of czarist Russia. These features, however, do not alter the fact that Japan was emerging as a modern state in the late nineteenth century. The imperial institution and the military right of supreme command represented the centralizing forces, the first prerequisite for such a state. Whether these institutions made Japan an "absolutist" state cannot be discussed in the abstract. To the extent that their appearance coincided with that of the civilian bureaucracy and popular movements, it may be said that all were aspects of modern transformation. To the degree that these latter weakened relative to the power of the emperor and the military, Japan became less "democratic" and more totalitarian. The key question was whether there developed a mutually reinforcing relationship between state and society so that both the central government and the people benefited from the new arrangements.

Japanese foreign relations become significant in such a context. How Japan's emergence as a modern state determined its foreign relations; how the latter in turn affected the nature of the modern Japanese state and how Japanese society's unique features resulted in peculiar foreign policy decisions are among the most interesting questions that arise. Unfortunately, there are few systematic treatments of the subject, although the Foreign Ministry has been scrupulous about publishing its documentary compilations.[6] Most writings are little more than conventional narratives of diplomatic relations, as illustrated by the multivolume *Nihon gaikō shi* (History of Japanese diplomacy) by Kajima Morinosuke.[7] These volumes, some of which have been translated into English, are simplistic compendia of official documents, with little analysis. Where interpretation is attempted, it is almost invariably in the framework of justifying Japan's actions. Less parochial but similarly oriented to chronological treatment are the few other general histories of Meiji foreign relations that have been pub-

5 Yamanaka Einosuke, *Nihon kindai kokka no keisei to kanryōsei* (Tokyo: Kōbundō, 1974), pp. 64–8, 70.

6 Gaimushō, *Nihon gaikō bunsho*. Over 151 volumes, reaching the year 1926 in 1986.

7 Morinosuke Kajima, *The Diplomacy of Japan, 1894–1922*, 3 vols. (Tokyo: Kajima Institute of International Peace, 1976–80); in Japanese, Kajima heiwa kenkyūjo, *Nihon gaikō shi*, 34 vols. (Tokyo: Kajima kenkyūjo shuppankai, 1970–73 and *Nihon gaikō shi, bekkan*, 4 vols. (1971–4).

lished, such as Hanabusa Nagamichi's *Meiji gaikō shi* (History of Meiji diplomacy) and Shinobu Seizaburō's *Nihon gaikō shi* (History of Japanese diplomacy).[8] This last contains systematic essays by Marxist-oriented historians and provides the best survey to date of Meiji foreign affairs. There are also numerous monographs that describe in laborious detail various diplomatic incidents and negotiations of the Meiji era, most of which, however, are conventional diplomatic history in that they document intergovernmental relations, with little attention paid to the interplay between them and domestic developments. Many of them focus on a few individuals so that the foreign affairs as presented are little more than a sum total of what they said and did.

One looks in vain for studies that transcend a parochial, nationalistic treatment, or antiquarian diplomatic history. At this stage of scholarship, the most plausible approach would seem to be a comparative one in which Japanese foreign affairs are comprehended in comparison with those of other modern states. Such a study would be useful not only to students of Japanese history but also to modern international history. Unfortunately, these latter have all but ignored Japan or manifested only the most superficial knowledge of its history and politics. Note, for instance, that virtually all historians who, for the past thirty years, have been engaged in fierce and productive debate on the nature of modern imperialism have had little to say about Japanese imperialism. Wolfgang Mommsen's *Theories of Imperialism* (English edition, 1980), though a splendid synthesis of the key interpretations that have been offered by students of modern imperialism, does not once mention Japan. There is thus a regrettable gap between these two groups of specialists. It is in part to fill this gap that the following sections have been written.[9]

CONSOLIDATION OF DOMESTIC AND FOREIGN AFFAIRS, 1868–1880

The awareness that domestic and external affairs were intimately linked was, of course, always present during the Tokugawa era. After all, the Edo regime built its administrative and legal system on the basis of curtailing and controlling all foreign contact. The assumption, from the time of Tokugawa Ieyasu, had been that such contact would

8 Hanabusa Nagamichi, *Meiji gaikō shi* (Tokyo: Shibundō, 1960), and Shinobu Seizaburō, ed., *Nihon gaikō shi: 1853–1972*, 2 vols. (Tokyo: Mainichi shimbunsha, 1974).

9 This gap will be more difficult to justify since the appearance of Ramon H. Myers and Mark R. Peattie, eds., *The Japanese Colonial Empire, 1895–1945* (Princeton, N.J.: Princeton University Press, 1984).

be detrimental to domestic order. This was ultimately because international affairs were seen as disorderly, confusing, and constantly shifting, in which countries vied with one another for power and material gains. Obviously, international disorder could not be allowed to intrude on domestic order. Toward the end of the eighteenth century, the shogunate allowed a few individuals to have access to the Westerners in Nagasaki, but the intention was to use this contact to strengthen the regime. The policy eventually backfired, as various domains, too, came to appreciate the value of Western arms, artifacts, and ideas as a means for their own strengthening and for bringing about a change in the country's political system.

Given this background, it is not surprising that from the beginning the Meiji regime should have sought to establish control over foreign affairs as an essential prerequisite for consolidating its power at home. In March 1868, the imperial government in Kyoto (eleven months before it moved to Tokyo as the new capital) issued a proclamation calling on the people to cooperate with its foreign policy. "Domestic conditions are unstable," it said, but "external dealings are extremely important." In such a situation, the new regime's stability appeared to depend on the willingness of various factions to deal with foreigners only through the government, and on the readiness of the foreigners to cooperate in this process. Such were, the proclamation said, the "trends of the times" (*jisei*).[10] This was a delicate process, but on the whole the new leaders succeeded in preventing foreign affairs from exacerbating domestic tensions and in using external issues to stabilize internal order. In this sense, the story of Japan during the 1860s and 1870s is comparable to that of Prussia in the same period, in which external and internal affairs likewise developed in a symbiotic fashion. The situation was different in the neighboring country of China, in which a brief period of "restoration" after the turmoil of the Taiping Rebellion – a restoration that was supported by the Western powers – was followed by a sustained period of antiforeign attacks, decentralization of political authority, and mass disaffection, a situation that proved to be fertile ground for further foreign encroachment.

Japan's relative success in the years after 1868 was due fundamentally to the recognition of the intimate link between domestic and foreign affairs that the new leaders shared. They thus took foreign relations with the utmost seriousness lest they render ineffective their

10 Shinobu Seizaburō, ed., *Nihon gaikō shi* (Tokyo: Mainichi shimbunsha, 1974), vol. 1, p. 74; Inō Tentarō, *Nihon gaikō shisō shi ronkō* (Tokyo: Komine shoten, 1965), vol. 1, pp. 42–3.

effort to establish a new domestic order. A few examples will illustrate how this was done.

First, antiforeign attacks were banned and, when they did take place, were severely dealt with. The new regime knew all too well how indiscriminate assaults on foreigners could undermine its claim as the government of the country; similar attacks had fatally wounded the Tokugawa shogunate's standing in the international sphere. Foreign complications would serve only to keep the country in turmoil, which in turn would invite further diplomatic incidents. To deal with these dangers, the government had to improve its system of law enforcement and legal procedure. It also engaged in an extensive propaganda campaign to inform the populace that antiforeign attacks were against "the laws of the world." The country was now going to develop in accordance with these laws, and therefore its people should not act on the basis of "old, stained habits." By accepting the laws of the universe, Japan would be able to "assert its prestige throughout the world."[11] The people were exhorted to join this task. It was a brilliant strategy, combining the prohibition of antiforeignism with the vision of a glorious future, both calculated to consolidate the government's authority and prestige. Apparently, within a few years after 1868 virtually all segments of the population and all factions among the former samurai accepted the new orientation, so that antiforeign incidents visibly abated.

The issue of antiforeign assaults was closely connected to that of legal reforms in the country, looking eventually to the abolition of extraterritoriality. To the extent that the Meiji government successfully stamped out antiforeign outbursts, the country would be safe for foreign residents. Foreigners would no longer have to be confined to restricted areas to protect them from violence. They would be free to travel and live in the interior. All this would assume that the Japanese people would treat overseas visitors with deference. At the same time, such a situation would make obsolete the special system of legal protection that had been granted to foreigners in the form of consular jurisdiction. There would no longer be much justification for its existence, and foreigners would have to be asked to obey Japanese laws like anybody else. If extraterritoriality were abolished, it would be a sign that foreigners were perfectly safe in Japan and that the country had a system of laws that they could accept. In both cases, the government would be credited with having transformed Japan into a modern legal state. Its prestige, both internally and externally, would be enhanced.

11 Shinobu, *Nihon gaikō shi*, vol. 1, p. 74; Inau, *Nihon gaikō shisō shi*, vol. 1, pp. 64–5.

Already in April 1869 Iwakura Tomomi noted the need for treaty revision, as the presence of foreign troops in the country and the foreigners' extraterritorial rights were a violation of Japanese independence.[12] Few would have disputed the view, and in 1871, when Iwakura led a large mission to the United States and Europe, the emissaries were entrusted with the task of initiating preliminary discussions of treaty revision. They were not to undertake formal negotiation, for the Meiji leaders felt that the country's internal reforms had not yet progressed to the point that it could boast a completely modernized system of laws. As the government's instruction to the ambassadors pointed out, "nations must possess equal rights" in their treaty relationships, but Japan had been deprived of such rights because of "the defects of its traditional custom and Oriental political institutions." These deficiencies, however, were now being overcome, and a new legal system was being established. It would take a few more years to complete the task by drastically revising civil, criminal, tax, trade, and other laws. The mission was in part intended for an extensive observation of Western legal institutions and political systems so that the "political institutions of the most enlightened and powerful nations" could be introduced to the Japanese people.[13] In Kume Kunitake's *Bei–Ō kairan jikki* (*True Account of Observations of America and Europe*), one sees a massive documentation of the embassy's observations, ranging from scenery and architecture to the politics, economy, and history of the Western countries.[14] It is not surprising that one of the things that struck the visitors most was the way in which governments and people appeared to be struggling for common goals such as national strengthening and well-being. They carried away the strong impression that a modern nation must have not only a strong central government but also an enlightened and motivated populace. Because this was the very theme of the emerging states in the West, the trip could not have taken place at a more opportune moment. Particularly pertinent was the German example, as the Japanese visit coincided with the establishment of the newly unified nation and Prince Otto Bismarck frankly explained to the Japanese the need for realism and hard work if they hoped to succeed in their own task of nation building.

After the embassy's return, legal reforms proceeded apace, and in 1880 the government promulgated new criminal laws. But treaty revi-

12 Shinobu, *Nihon gaikō shi*, vol. 1, p. 78. 13 Ibid., p. 85.

14 Marlene Mayo, "The Western Education of Kume Kunitake 1871–76," *Monumenta Nipponica* 28 (1973): 3–67.

sion could not be easily achieved. On the one hand, foreigners sought to hold onto their privileges and reminded the Japanese that their modern reforms were still not complete; they would need to revise further their civil, tax, and commercial laws. Domestic travail, as evidenced by Saigō Takamori's resignation from the government in 1873 and his open rebellion four years later, was not calculated to give confidence to foreigners regarding Japan's political stability. Although negotiation for revision was not interrupted by the rebellion of 1877, the foreign governments were unwilling to concede that their nationals could subject themselves to Japanese jurisdiction. Tokyo's leaders sought to mollify them by offering to appoint foreign judges in Japanese courts in cases involving foreign residents, but even such concessions produced no immediate response by the powers.[15]

Equally important, the government's seeming lack of success and willingness to consider concessions such as the appointment of foreign judges aroused the resentment of the politically active segments of the population that strengthened in proportion to the delay in the treaty revision negotiations. To the extent that one may speak of "public opinion" or "mass politics" in Japan during the 1870s, the treaty question played a major part in their development. A vocal minority from the beginning was opposed to "mixed residence," that is, the opening of the interior for foreign residence, business, and property ownership. Although opinion was divided on this and other specific issues, newspapers and nascent political organizations – Aikoku kōtō (Public Party of Patriots) was organized in 1874 – were adept in taking advantage of the treaty question to demand more "freedom and people's rights." They insisted that the best way to put an end to the foreigners' extraterritorial privileges was to mobilize and organize popular opinion by convening a national assembly. The establishment of such an assembly, which was an institution in almost all Western states, would not only demonstrate that Japan was now as modern a country as theirs but would also be effective in presenting a massive national sentiment in favor of treaty revision. Foreigners would thus be persuaded to relinquish their special privileges and accord to Japan the status of an equal, sovereign nation.

Thus ironically, mass integration into the polity was being achieved because of the government's alleged failure to have the powers recognize the country as an independent, modern state. The only solution to the dilemma, according to government leaders, was to push for

15 The best concise summary of treaty revision negotiations remains Inoue Kiyoshi, *Jōyaku kaisei* (Tokyo: Iwanami shoten, 1955).

further legal and political reforms, so that foreigners would have no excuse for treating the country as semicivilized, while at the same time making certain that during the 1870s movements for popular rights and for treaty revision were aspects of the same drive for the nationalization of the Japanese polity.[16]

In the meantime, the government became interested in regaining tariff autonomy. All existing treaties stipulated that duties imposed on foreign imports were to be determined by agreement between Japan and other governments. This "treaty tariff" system was viewed by the Japanese government and public as an infringement on sovereignty, just as consular jurisdiction was. It deprived the country of much needed revenue as it undertook economic modernization. Public finance was in a chronically critical situation, in which taxes had to be raised. The people, too, were quick to establish a connection between their heavy tax burden and the absence of tariff autonomy. As Foreign Minister Terashima Munenori pointed out in 1876, such a sentiment could revive antiforeign hysteria. In order to "satisfy public sentiment, maintain law and order, and expand foreign trade," it was imperative to "regain our national rights" by seeking the restoration of tariff autonomy.[17] Between 1876 and 1879 Terashima concentrated on this issue, rather than extraterritoriality, as the first priority in treaty revision negotiation. He achieved modest successes when the United States, Russia, Italy, and several others indicated their willingness to restore tariff autonomy to Japan, but Britain, France, and Germany stood adamant, and the efforts bore no immediate result. Although the Western countries' trade with Japan was minuscule at this time, amounting in most instances to less than 1 percent of their total volume of trade, they all viewed export trade as an important ingredient of national economic growth. Treaty tariffs provided an effective means for maintaining their "informal empires" overseas. Some powers, notably the United States, took the position that trade would expand even after Japan regained tariff autonomy; in fact, the friendly relationship that would result from it could be calculated to tie the two countries closer together economically. Moreover, the United States under the Republican administrations was practicing a highly protectionist trade policy, causing Japanese officials like Itō Hirobumi to call for a protectionist policy of their own as beneficial to the country.[18]

16 Shinobu, *Nihon gaikō shi,* vol. 1, p. 112; Sakeda Masatoshi, *Kindai Nihon ni okeru taigaikō undō no kenkyū* (Tokyo: Tokyo daigaku shuppankai, 1978), p. 7.

17 Shinobu, *Nihon gaikō shi,* vol. 1, p. 108.

18 Shimomura Fujio, *Meiji shonen jōyaku kaisei shi no kenkyū* (Tokyo: Yoshikawa Kóbunkan, 1962), p. 80.

Although protectionism was practiced by few other countries at that time, all believed that industrialization and extensive trade went hand in hand. Ultimately, then, the question of tariff autonomy hinged on the readiness of the Western nations to permit an economically modernizing Japan to enter their system of international relations. As of the 1870s, few of them were.

Treaty revision graphically illustrated the close links between domestic political developments and foreign affairs. No less important in this context were the territorial questions. Modern history has shown that few issues arouse as intense a popular passion as territorial issues do, and few are regarded as a more telling index of a state's ability to govern or of a government's claim to legitimacy. A modern state is defined as a territorial entity in which center and periphery are united in a conception of national unity and defense. It is no accident that during the second half of the nineteenth century the geographical boundaries of such countries as the United States, Italy, Germany, and the Low Countries became more clearly defined and that where there were ambiguities, as was the case in Alsace and Lorraine and most notably in the Balkans, in which Russia, Austria-Hungary, and Turkey had conflicting claims, there was always a strong likelihood of armed hostilities. Nationalistic sentiment could easily be mobilized through government propaganda and the press whenever it was felt that a country's justifiable territorial claim was being violated; on the other hand, the government would be held accountable for ensuring territorial integrity and security so that its authority would be seriously undermined when it gave the impression of succumbing to external pressures on a territorial question.

Meiji Japan was no exception. The new leaders assumed as a matter of course that one of their first tasks would be to establish clearly definable national boundaries. This could have been a relatively easy undertaking, compared with the complex situation in Europe where historical, ethnic, and religious diversities never quite corresponded to distinct geographical boundaries. Japan was characterized by no such complexity, and during the Tokugawa period its domain had been confined to the four major islands. Beyond them, however, were regions of ambiguous definition that had not been incorporated into another power's domain. For this reason, the Japanese were eager to establish clear demarcations for these areas. Such incorporation would not only define the limits of the new Japanese state to come under the jurisdiction of the central government; it would also enable the latter to plan for national defense and development. The populace, in the meantime, would have a new conception of the nation so that they would be under the protection of the new government anywhere within the new boundaries.

Reflecting such perceptions, the Meiji government early showed an interest in establishing a clear boundary to the north of Hokkaido. There lay the large island of Sakhalin and the chain of smaller islands, the Kurils, that arched the northwestern Pacific from Hokkaido to Kamchatka. In the mid-nineteenth century both these territories were sparsely populated by Russians and Japanese. The latter were a minority, mostly fishermen, but they would have to be protected if indeed they were living in Japanese territory. The perpetuation of mixed residence, in which the two nationals lived together in ambiguous status, appeared undesirable. Japan could have drawn a line close to Hokkaido so that Japanese living in Sakhalin and the Kurils would be considered beyond the protection of the government, or else they would be told to return to Japan proper. (This has been the situation since 1945.) But this was an option that the Tokyo government found hard to accept. It would imply a retreat and damage the new regime's domestic and external prestige. It would bring Russia that much closer to Japan proper. Russian ships had temporarily seized the island of Tsushima (lying between Kyushu and Korea) in 1861, causing a near panic among Japanese in that part of the country. Similar incidents could recur if Russia gained Sakhalin and the Kurils. On the other hand, there was little compelling reason that those territories should belong to Japan. Territorial enlargement would complicate the question of administration and defense; it could give rise to further problems with Russia, as it would bring Japan closer to Russia's territory in Siberia and the Maritime Provinces; and it was not at all clear whether the government and the people of Japan were prepared to divert their resources to the economic development of Sakhalin and the Kurils when they had just begun a project for settling and developing Hokkaido.

In the end, Tokyo's response showed the government's receptivity to domestic pressures. In 1874 it decided to evacuate Japanese residents from Sakhalin, intimating a decision to concede the whole island to the Russians. At the same time, Japan insisted on its claim to the whole of the Kuril island chain. This was for reasons of prestige; it would placate domestic opposition unhappy about the Sakhalin retreat and also demonstrate to the other powers that Japan would make concessions only on a quid pro quo basis. All this would add to the sense of national unity and clarify the limits of state administration. It was symbolic of the concern with national unity that the government should have turned to Enomoto Takeaki, one of the staunchest supporters of the late shogunate against the new regime, who had established an ill-fated republic in Hokkaido before being captured and imprisoned and who had been released from prison only in 1872, to go to St. Petersburg to negotiate a settlement of the territorial question. In 1875 Enomoto successfully concluded a treaty along the lines of his instructions, resulting in an "exchange" of Sakhalin for the Kurils. Henceforth Russia was to control the entire island of Sakhalin but was to cede all of the Kurils to Japan. The treaty was popular, as it was the first significant settlement with a Western power in which Japan had been treated like an equal and had not been forced to make humiliating concessions.[19]

Somewhat more clear-cut was the disposition of the Ryūkyū kingdom, consisting of the island of Okinawa and its vicinity. Standing almost equidistant from Kyushu, Korea, and Taiwan, the islands had been governed as part of Satsuma *han*, but their rulers had also sent tributary missions to the Chinese court under the Ch'ing dynasty. Ethnically and culturally, the people of Ryūkyū were distinct from, though related to, both the Chinese and the Japanese, although their language was closer to Japanese. The question that the Meiji government faced was whether the island population should now be incorporated into the Japanese state, extending to them the jurisdiction and protection of the central authority. From the beginning there was little hestitation to answer the question in the affirmative, the national government placing the kingdom of Ryūkyū under the jurisdiction of Kagoshima Prefecture (formerly Satsuma *han*) in 1871. It was resolved that because the Tokugawa regime had, indirectly through Satsuma, ruled over the kingdom, the Tokyo government should do likewise but also go a step further and turn it into an administrative district of the country. This entailed extending the national government's protection to the Ryūkyū population, a matter that suddenly surfaced as a grave national issue when in 1871 some fifty-odd island fishermen who had been shipwrecked and drifted to Taiwan were massacred by aborigines.

The incident was a test of the Meiji regime's ability to affirm its leadership of a modern state. If those fishermen, Ryūkyū subjects, were to be considered Japanese citizens, it would be incumbent upon the government to seek satisfaction for their tragedy from the Chinese government, which had control over Taiwan, a province of China. If

19 On the Sakhalin–Kurils "exchange" treaty, see John J. Stephan, *The Kuril Islands: The Russo-Japanese Frontier in the Pacific* (New York: Oxford University Press, 1975).

they were not viewed as Japanese citizens, Japan's claim to the Ryūkyūs would, of course, be destroyed. This was something the leaders could not concede, especially in view of an aroused domestic opinion. Both within and without the government, voices called for strong action to avenge the damages done to Japanese citizens and to "punish" the "uncivilized" people of Taiwan who had dared to assault Japanese subjects. The vocabulary was similar to what Westerners had used in retaliating against Japanese attacks on their nationals. (Commodore Perry, in fact, had dealt severely with Okinawan authorities when one of his sailors was killed by local residents.) Inaction in the face of such an assault would be taken as a sign of weakness, as evidence that Japan was not yet as strong a state as America and the European countries.

Presumably, satisfaction could have been obtained from the Ch'ing government, but the latter was unwilling to discuss the issue on the grounds that the massacre had been caused by "uncivilized people," beyond the reach of Chinese "politics and religion."[20] Such an argument, of course, revealed the Chinese authorities' lack of understanding of the responsibilities of a modern state – which is not surprising in that they were similarly irresolute and insensitive when a far more serious incident arose closer to home, the massacre of French missionaries in Tientsin, in the same year, 1871. (Several years afterwards, Chinese officials resorted to Japanese and Western language in their efforts to hold the United States government responsible for the killing of Chinese immigrants in western states.) For two years after 1872, when the incident became known, Japanese and Chinese officials engaged in inconclusive talks over the incident, but in the end the former decided to act unilaterally by sending a punitive expedition to Taiwan. This was fundamentally in response to domestic pressures. These years saw a series of critical clashes and confrontations among the country's political leaders, the most dramatic of which was the 1873 dispute on the Korean question, resulting in the resignation from the government of several influential men. In such a situation, those who remained in power – Ōkubo Toshimichi, Ōkuma Shigenobu, and others – felt they needed an issue that would dissipate some of the dissidents' unhappiness, coalesce national opinion, and reaffirm the regime's prestige. An expedition to Taiwan was chosen as a viable solution. It was officially approved at a cabinet meeting of February 6, 1874, and an expeditionary force of 3,000 was organized under Saigō

20 Shinobu, *Nihon gaikō shi,* vol. 1, p. 90.

Tsugumichi. They landed in Taiwan on May 22, and after incurring some 573 casualties, all but 12 of which were due to tropical diseases, they established control over the areas inhabited by the aborigines.

The fact that the Taiwan expedition came more than two years after the massacre took place indicates that it was less a reactive move than a deliberate response to domestic needs. This explains why the Japanese government informed foreign governments of the impending expedition at the very last moment and did not even bother to tell China about it until after the expedition had taken place.[21] From the Japanese point of view, the important thing was to carry out the expedition to placate domestic opposition and, by having the Chinese recognize its legitimacy, to assert control over the people of Ryūkyū as Japanese citizens. After some protracted postexpedition negotiations in Peking, in which Ōkubo himself took part, the Ch'ing court acquiesced in recognizing the "justice" of the expedition, in return for Japan's evacuation of Taiwan. Because the seizure of that island was never an original Japanese aim, this was accomplished without arousing domestic resentment. It was enough that the Japanese had acted like the other powers in protecting its nationals by a show of force.

The Chinese-Japanese agreement on the settlement of the Ryūkyū massacre was a blow to China's prestige, especially in view of the 1871 treaty between the two countries that had established normal diplomatic relations between them and granted mutual extraterritoriality. The treaty also included a provision for mutual assistance and mediation in case one of the signatories entered a dispute with a third power. But the Taiwan expedition threatened to undermine the framework of friendly relations that such provisions implied. The Japanese were aware that their policy of incorporating the Ryūkyūs into their national boundaries – which was to be effected in 1879 – would create tensions with China. But they reasoned that as a modern state, Japan could no longer acquiesce in an anomalous situation in which the island people were not fully integrated into the nation. Moreover, if these people were to be considered Japanese subjects and protected by Japanese arms, it would become necessary to assume responsibility for the defense of the islands. Japan might have to build a naval base there to station a fleet and also to cope with a potential internal turmoil – the Okinawan king did not conceal his displeasure at the abolition of his own kingdom – through military means. All these measures would be tantamount to extending Japanese control into a region close to

21 Ibid., p. 94.

Taiwan and the Chinese mainland. It is not surprising, under the circumstances, that Chinese officials should have become increasingly alarmed over the situation and that during the second half of the 1870s a sense of acute crisis should have developed between the two countries. That in turn would confront the Japanese with the need for strengthening their military and for defining their strategic priorities. Though little was done in those areas at this time, it should be noted that Japan was following the pattern of other states in that the delimitation of territorial boundaries went hand in hand with a redefinition of security needs, resulting in calls for increased armament and long-range war plans. The transformation of China in Japanese perception in the 1870s, from a friendly neighbor of equal status to a potential adversary, is a good illustration of the way in which a modern state stressed power considerations in its external affairs.

Power in a modern state, however, meant more than armament and war plans. It also developed in combination with economic and social forces at home. For the state to have an effective foreign policy, it was vital to mobilize domestic resources to the full. We have seen this in connection with treaty revision. Equally significant for the 1870s was the developing crisis with Korea. Nowhere were the links between domestic and foreign affairs more graphically demonstrated, and nowhere were the promise as well as the frustrations of modernization more tellingly revealed, than in the tangle of events and decisions that dotted Japanese-Korean relations after the Meiji Restoration. Meiji leaders early recognized the clear links between the Korean question and the establishment of domestic order. As Kido Takayoshi wrote in 1869, a vigorous assertion of policy toward Korea "would instantly change Japan's outmoded customs, set its objectives abroad, promote its industry and technology, and eliminate jealousy and recrimination among its people."[22] Behind such bombast lay historical factors that had defined a tortuous pattern of relationship between the two countries. The Japanese liked to talk of "restoring" an ancient relationship between the two countries now that they had effected their own internal "restoration." The Tokugawa regime had dealt with the Korean kingdom through the lord of Tsushima, and the Koreans had viewed such connections as distinctly inferior to their tributary relationship with China. Perpetuation of the

22 Key-Hiuk Kim, *The Last Phase of the East Asian World Order: Korea, Japan, and the Chinese Empire, 1860–1882* (Berkeley and Los Angeles: University of California Press, 1980), p. 125. Kido reversed his position after taking part in the Iwakura mission to the West and also opposed the Taiwan expeditions.

existing arrangements would imply that Japanese-Korean relations were still comprehended within the traditional world order defined by China. If Japan were to "restore" domestic arrangements to eradicate feudalism and if part of that undertaking involved the establishment of a new framework of foreign affairs, then it followed that Japanese-Korean relations, too, must be placed on a new footing. The matter was complicated, however, because it was never clear how that footing was to be defined and because division on this question threatened the very domestic stability in Japan that was the basic objective of the Meiji leaders.

Kido's assertion just cited revealed a widely shared view that a strong stand toward Korea would be a good way to unify domestic opinion and consolidate the base of the new leadership in Japan. But ironically, the Korean issue almost destroyed the nascent Meiji government. There is not enough space here to chronicle the fascinating story of internal strife in Japan during the 1870s which brought about the defeat of *sei-Kan ron* (the movement for a Korean expedition). As one Japanese historian has pointed out, even Saigō Takamori, usually identified with that movement, was initially opposed to the use of force.[23] He wanted to use diplomacy, such as the dispatch of a high-level embassy to Seoul headed by himself, to solve the impasse in Korea, in which the Yi dynasty refused to accede to Japanese demands for a new diplomatic relationship. But his political opponents, such as Kido, Iwakura, and Ōkubo, feared that a successful consummation of the project could enhance Saigō's prestige, thus undermining their own power. Because they were dedicated to consolidating the Meiji state, they had to oppose Saigō's plans. Frustrated, he in turn came to call for a more militant policy in Korea so as to embarrass the Kido–Iwakura faction. The conflict ultimately led to the Satsuma uprising of 1877. In all these developments, Korea was but a context in which domestic rivalries were played out.

It was obvious that the government had to achieve some diplomatic success quickly. Its passivity would be contrasted not only with the growing tide of *sei-Kan ron* but also with Saigō's advocacy of a diplomatic solution. What the Kido–Iwakura leadership carried out was close to what Saigō had advocated: the dispatch of a high-level mission to Korea to seek to establish diplomatic relations between the two countries. The government also hoped to silence advocates of forceful measures by dispatching three gunboats to Korean waters in 1875.

23 Shinobu, *Nihon gaikō shi*, vol. 1, p. 92.

When one of them was fired on at Kanghwa Bay, it retaliated by bombarding some coastal batteries. Thus provided with a pretext for sending an emissary, Tokyo dispatched an embassy headed by Kuroda Kiyotaka in January 1876. Fully conscious of the parallel between his own and the Perry expedition, Kuroda was accompanied by three warships and succeeded in concluding a treaty with the Korean kingdom roughly similar to the treaties that Japan had been forced to negotiate during the 1850s. The Korean treaty stipulated that the kingdom was "an independent nation," thereby putting an end to its tributary relationship with the Chinese empire. The opening of three ports for Japanese trade was provided for, as was Japanese consular jurisdiction in Korea. Compared with the Japanese-Chinese treaty of 1871, this was clearly one that established an unequal relationship between Japan and another country.

It would be wrong to conclude, however, that the 1876 treaty with Korea was the product of a premeditated plan for expansion and that it was the first step for Japan's continental imperialism. It was more a case of the Japanese leaders' eagerness for a diplomatic success in order to consolidate their power at home. In this they achieved their goal. The treaty was hailed as a sign that Japan was now in a position to enjoy some of the same rights in another country that Westerners had gained in Japan. It was the first nation to have opened up Korea to foreign intercourse. The resulting prestige enhanced the power of the Meiji leadership, although this very success led dissidents under Saigō to stage the unsuccessful Satsuma Rebellion of 1877.

The story of Japanese foreign affairs between 1868 and 1880, then, should primarily be seen as subsidiary to domestic developments. The consolidation of centralized power at home and the incorporation of larger segments of the population into the new polity had first to be achieved, and external issues had to be put in that context. This is hardly different from other countries, in particular Germany and the United States, which, too, were just then emerging as modern states. Of course, compared with theirs, the Japanese economy was far less industrialized, and its trade was still largely controlled by foreign merchants enjoying treaty privileges. It was hardly surprising that a key goal of the Japanese state should have been to seek revision of the treaties. At the same time, the Meiji leaders shared the views of their Western counterparts that national power must be defined broadly, in terms of the people's productivity, education, and discipline, as well as an efficient system of administration. They understood that a modern state must have clearly defined geographical boundaries as well as a sense of nationhood on the part of the people living within them. Although threatened with periodic internal turmoil, the Japanese state was on a firmer footing at the end than at the beginning of the 1870s, in many ways the crucial decade in modern international history. The result was that after 1880, when the tides of change in the world moved faster, Japan was in a position to understand, identify with, and use them for its further strengthening.

DOMESTIC POLITICS AND OVERSEAS EXPANSION, 1880–1895

After the 1880s European international relations entered a phase of colonial expansion and imperialist rivalries. Although neither colonialism nor power politics was a new phenomenon and although during the preceding decade Britain and Russia had signaled the opening of the Near Eastern question by clashing in Afghanistan and Turkey, it was in the 1880s that the tempo quickened, with France, Britain, Germany, and other states avidly extending their power to areas hitherto either loosely tied to European powers or lying beyond their control. In 1881 France established a protectorate over Tunis; in 1882 Britain occupied Egypt; in 1883 Germany began its colonial activities in Southwest Africa; during 1884–5 France and Britain extended their respective sways to Indochina and Burma; and in 1889 Germany, Britain, and the United States divided up the Samoan kingdom into three segments for their tripartite condominium. By the mid-1890s most of the Middle East, Africa, Asia, and the Pacific had fallen under the domination of one or another of the Western powers. China, Japan, and Korea were among the few noncolonized states in 1880, but by 1895 China and Korea had lost part of their sovereignty, thanks largely to Japanese expansionism.

Such a brief listing makes the conclusion inescapable that Japan joined the ranks of imperialist states and began behaving like them overseas. No amount of apologetic writing alters the fact that between 1880 and 1895 Japan did establish colonial enclaves and spheres of dominance over Korea, Taiwan, and parts of China. It is surprising, however, how little effort writers have made to fit Japanese expansionism into the general history of late-nineteenth-century imperialism and to fit the Japanese case into theories of imperialism. Most European writings on imperialism concentrate on Britain, France, and Germany. American historians, on their part, have written volumes about the emergence of the United States as an imperialist in the late 1890s but have on the whole tended to treat the phenomenon in isolation, separate from European and Japanese imperialism. Russian scholars, quite predictably, do write a great deal about czarist imperialism. They have also published far more about Japanese imperialism than have historians of other European countries; perhaps this reflects the fact that the rivalry between Russia and Japan was a key feature of the age of imperialism in East Asia. However, virtually all Soviet writings on the subject are presented in Marxist-Leninist formulations, and they are as susceptible to criticism as are similar accounts of British, French, or German imperialism. If anything, Leninist concepts are much more difficult to apply to less developed economies such as Russia and Japan at the turn of the century than to Britain and other countries. Despite this, Japanese writings on imperialism have also tended to be largely couched in Marxist-Leninist terms. The result is that when Japanese imperialism is fitted into the general history of modern imperialism, it is usually little more than a mechanistic exercise in applying rigid theories to the country. This has taken the form of locating the emergence of capitalism, the bourgeoisie, monopoly interests, and the like, as they are credited with having brought about late-nineteenth-century and early-twentieth-century imperialism. As with Marxist interpretations of European imperialism, however, it has been difficult to establish a correspondence between economic developments and specific instances of overseas expansion.

Neo-Marxists such as Andre G. Frank and Harry Magdoff have presented less rigid and more usable generalizations, although few of them have worked specifically on Japan.[24] It is their contention that regardless of the different rates of capital accumulation or levels of industrialization, the Western nations had, by the late nineteenth century, linked themselves to other parts of the world, turning the latter into their "satellites." These "satellites" provided raw materials, markets, and infrastructures, thereby making themselves dependent on the metropolitan economies. The result, according to this argument, was the perpetual underdevelopment of non-Western countries, which was in a symbiotic relationship with the development of the West. These writers term this total structure of dependency *imperialism.* Japan, obviously, is one exception to this pattern of Western domination, a fact that Frank has explained rather tautologically, saying that it escaped the dependency status by not becoming a satellite of the

24 A. G. Frank, *Latin America: Underdevelopment or Revolution* (New York: Monthly Review Press, 1970); Harry Magdoff, *The Age of Imperialism: The Economics of U.S. Foreign Policy* (New York: Monthly Review Press, 1969).

West. At least such a framework is useful, as it takes into account that despite its relative underdevelopment, Japan in the 1880s was not incorporated into a global economic system as a satellite of an advanced capitalist nation. On the contrary, as this chapter has emphasized, the country was on its way to becoming a centralized mass society, that is, a modern state. The country's basic political and bureaucratic framework had been established; the leadership had just survived a serious challenge to its authority; and the ground was being laid for the promulgation of a constitution and the convening of a national assembly, the Imperial Diet. More important than such institutional provisions was the fact that the populace had been educated and politicized. Often they had grown more politicized than the leaders had bargained for; the movement for "freedom and people's rights" throughout the 1870s had indicated that segments of the population were well educated, versed in political theory, and intent on resisting the growth of state authority. But those who held power recognized the importance of a politically alert opinion, and they had tried to channel it in the direction of national cohesiveness. The result, at the beginning of the 1880s, was that the politically essential preconditions for turning Japan into a modern state had been sufficiently fulfilled.

These basic achievements meant that in the 1880s, when the European powers stepped up their tempo of imperialist domination, the Japanese state, with a centralized bureaucracy and aroused public opinion, was in a far better position to understand and respond to these developments than were the other countries of Asia, the Middle East, or Africa. Japan's own imperialism must be understood in that context. In other words, its foreign dealings were now backed up by a stronger, more centralized government and were affected by domestic opinion and interest groups with greater self-assertiveness than before. Power, summing up armed forces, public opinion, and economic resources, could be better mobilized, just as it was being mobilized by other advanced countries. To the extent that the disparity between stronger and weaker power areas throughout the globe provided the setting for imperialist pressures, as David Landes has noted, it followed that Japan would represent the former and hence develop as an imperialist.[25]

In some such fashion, the Japanese began their story of overseas expansion, which culminated in the establishment of control over vast

25 David Landes, "Some Thoughts on the Nature of Economic Imperialism," *Journal of Economic History* 21 (1961): 496–512.

areas of Asia within thirty years. It should be pointed out, however, that expansion was always considered in the context of the growth of the modern Japanese nation and that as such it took many forms, not just formal colonial domination. The latter was not an end in itself, a premeditated goal for its own sake, but an aspect of Japan's development in a world environment defined by the major powers.

Basic to such a conception was a view of international affairs that the Japanese had begun to develop through their contact with Western countries and peoples during the 1870s and that was confirmed by the latters' overseas expansionism in the new decade. That view was expressed in such phrases as "war without warfare," "economic warfare," or "the struggle for survival," all expressions common in Japanese utterances at this time. That the international arena was controlled by the powerful, industrializing nations of the West was already clearly recognized. Added to this was the idea that those powers were constantly struggling with one another for greater national strength, not necessarily through war but through other means as well. There were, in fact, few, if any, armed hostilities among Western powers at that time. But this did not mean that they were not preparing for such conflict or that they were not constantly trying to augment their power. Even more important, not simply armies and navies but the total resources of a given country seemed to be committed to these goals. The people in these countries, the Japanese found, were energetic, vigorous, and aggressive, sharing with their leaders a sense of devotion to power, prestige, and wealth. They were, in short, engaged in a "war without warfare" or, as it came to be called in the 1890s, a "peacetime war." That the Japanese should do likewise was taken for granted by virtually all who spoke or wrote on the matter, although, as elsewhere, they differed among themselves as to the means for achieving the same ends. They were unanimous in believing that vigorous foreign policies and enterprises were a sign of internal health and power. Conversely, overseas activities by Japanese would rebound to the benefit of the home country. This was the theme of "expansion" broadly defined, a theme that came to be repeated with almost monotonous regularity in the 1880s and the subsequent decades. This was also imperialism, but it would be best to reserve that term for expansion into less powerful and less developed areas, such as Korea and China. There the Japanese came into contact with other imperialists and engaged in imperialist rivalries. But it should not be forgotten that there were other kinds of activities, such as emigration to Hawaii and trade with the West, that were equally important.

Japanese-Korean relations during the 1880s reflected a sense of power and urgency not visible earlier. As befitting a leadership that had survived a serious domestic challenge to its authority, the Meiji government in the late 1870s and early 1880s launched a program for extending its political and economic control over the peninsular kingdom. Export trade to Korea expanded phenomenally, not only bringing Japanese goods (matches, copper, and so on) there, but also shipping Western commodities from Japan to Korea (only 11.5 percent of total Japanese exports to Korea in 1882 consisted of goods made in Japan). Korea's rice and soybeans were imported into Japan in growing volume, Japan almost always purchasing 90 percent of all Korean exports. In 1881 a military advisory group was dispatched from Japan to start working on a modernized army for Korea.[26] These moves were obviously connected with the perceived needs of the Japanese state. Economic control over Korea was considered both desirable and feasible. Both the revenue from the export trade and the grains imported from the peninsula were considered important to Japan's industrialization, and the supervision of Korean military affairs ensured that nothing would happen to disrupt these emerging economic ties. It is unlikely that much thought was given at this time to imperialist rivalries in Asia in general, although the Japanese were quite aware of Russian expansionism in the north and its French and British counterpart in the south. Rather, it appears that it was considered desirable to use the opportunities provided by the nearby kingdom for the enhancement of Japanese power, economic and political.

This objective was supported by the populace. If anything, politically active segments of the population – the antigovernment press, dissident leaders who gathered around Ōkuma Shigenobu and created a minor crisis in 1881, and various political organizations – became even more interested in Korean affairs than the government was. Political movements evolved around the domestic issues of constitutional government and the convening of a national Diet, but the dissidents and popular rights activists often called on the nation to turn their attention overseas and promote reforms in China and Korea. Many of them felt frustrated in their challenge to the domestic leadership and believed that the best strategy was to arouse popular opinion about the government's alleged passivity toward Korea. Some were convinced that reforms in Japan would follow those in Korea. Others went further and advocated an alliance of Japanese and Korean reform-

26 Hattori Shisō, *Kindai Nihon gaikō shi* (Tokyo: Kawade shobō, 1954), p. 105.

ers so as to enlighten and civilize their countries. Tarui Tōkichi expressed such opinions in his famous *Dai–Tō gappō ron* (Unification of great Asia), written in 1885, calling on the two countries to unite to become a strong Asian power. (Fukuzawa Yukichi's even more famous *Datsu–A ron* – On leaving Asia – was also published that year and sought to refute Tarui's argument by asserting that it would be impossible to unite with a more backward country like Korea.)

In this way, both government and populace came to incorporate Korean issues into their own respective visions of national power and domestic arrangements. Expansionism was domestic politics by extension. It soon became apparent, however, that events in Korea itself were equally crucial to determining the course of Japanese expansionism. In a way similar to the circumstances in the "peripheral areas" that created and strengthened European imperialism in Africa and the Middle East, events in Korea played a key role in affecting the specific course that Japan was to take. In 1882, followers of the Taewongun, the de facto ruler of Korea between 1864 and 1873 who had been forced into retirement by the supporters of Queen Min for his extreme antiforeign policies, staged a coup against the Min and their alleged Japanese allies. The insurgents killed the Japanese officers in charge of training the new army and attacked the legation in Seoul. Minister Hanabusa Yoshitomo and his aides barely escaped and returned to Nagasaki on board a British ship. The Taewongun was restored to power, only to be forcibly taken to China by Chinese troops that were dispatched to Seoul to prevent further disorder.[27]

The Japanese might have decided to disengage themselves from the Korean peninsula then and there. Such a decision would have spared them from becoming involved in complex Korean politics and, even more important, with China. It might also have compelled them to turn their attention elsewhere, such as Sakhalin or Taiwan. However, the leaders in Tokyo considered inaction an admission of failure and were unanimous that something had to be done. Nongovernmental opinion also called for a quick response; it would surely seize upon government inaction as a failure of leadership. Tokyo's approach to the crisis was twofold. On the one hand, it would eschew hasty military action against the Korean government, as it would exacerbate the tensions already mounting between Japan and China. Instead, Japan would try to conclude an agreement with the Korean court to prevent a recurrence of similar outbursts. At the same time, the Japanese

27 Kim, *Last Phase*, pp. 316–25.

would make plans for a possible military engagement with Korea and, possibly, with China. The first approach led to the conclusion of an agreement in August 1882, stipulating that the Korean government would send a mission of apology to Japan, indemnify for the loss and damages to Japanese lives, and agree to the stationing of Japanese troops to guard the legation in Seoul. The second stipulation brought about a plan for strengthening armaments in preparation for a possible war with China over the Korean question. Particularly urgent appeared to be naval construction, in which Japan was believed to lag far behind China's naval building program. It would be necessary, Iwakura noted, to construct larger and faster ships. Because the Meiji regime eschewed large-scale foreign borrowing, funds for this had to come from domestic resources, that is, increased taxes. Popular opposition to them could be mitigated by a rhetoric of national defense and an image of China as a potential adversary. The press and political organizations generally cooperated by accepting such rhetoric. As many historians have pointed out, from around this time, patriotism and national assertiveness came to characterize popular movements in Japan. Opinion leaders such as Fukuzawa Yukichi, as well as most political parties, supported the government's stand in Korea and the military-strengthening programs as a way to enhance national prestige and obtain recognition by the powers that Japan was one of them.[28]

The growth of such patriotic sentiment deserves examination, for it came to provide a domestic context for Japanese foreign policy. Patriotism in the sense of particularistic ethnocentrism had, of course, existed throughout Japanese history, fostered by geographical isolation, relative racial homogeneity, and cultural self-consciousness. It had manifested itself in an extreme form when bands of samurai attacked and cut down the foreigners who came to Japan in the 1850s. Thirty years later, however, this indigenous sentiment had been reinforced by deepening contact with other countries, East and West, and had also become more organized. It found its expression in the press, political movements, and educational institutions. As such, it was little different from the patriotism and "jingoism" in the West, which were also aspects of its modern transformation. It may be, however, that in Japan traditional ethnocentrism had developed into modern patriotism without a substantial metamorphosis, whereas in the West, nationalism had intervened in the process. Nationalism as it grew after the late eighteenth century was not simply an exclusive, particularistic

28 Shinobu, *Nihon gaikō shi*, vol. 1, pp. 124–6.

sentiment. In its inception, it had been part of the democratic revolution, in which national identity was sought less in a country's ethnic and historical uniqueness than in the belief that it embodied certain universal values such as freedom and human rights. That sentiment never completely disappeared from the emotive vocabulary of the modern states in the late nineteenth century, and in fact the tension between it and more romantic, particularistic emotions, extolling the greatness of a country for its culture and soil, provided a theme in the self-perceptions of modern peoples. In Japan, too, there were currents of thought that stressed the universality of goals of modernization. Industrialization, constitutionalism, popular enlightenment, and similar objectives were viewed as universally valid, and it was thought that Japan would be considered a more self-respecting nation in proportion as it approximated these goals. But except for a small number of writers and activists, these objectives did not easily provide a vision for a more ideal international order. In the West, nationalism could often be transformed into internationalism because a nation could envision a world order that embodied some of the universalistic principles that it exemplified itself. Serious and sustained efforts in this direction were made by the Japanese only after World War I. In the late nineteenth century, universalistic objectives were usually viewed as a means for particularistic ends, for the strengthening and enrichment of the country. Or else they would provide the vocabulary for an activist policy in Korea or China in the name of Asia's "awakening," a geographical particularism.[29] It is not surprising, then, that movements for popular rights or constitutionalism could easily turn into patriotic moves or that the leaders of those movements would more often than not find themselves impelled to take a lead in chauvinistic adventures overseas.

Such considerations help one understand the growing support during the 1880s for the use of force against Korea or China. It was not, as is so often alleged by historians, that the Japanese felt superior to their Asian neighbors and resorted to military action; rather, they couched their belligerence in some universalistic vocabulary. They decided to prepare for possible armed hostilities with Korea and China for reasons that had to do more with the consolidation of the modern Japanese state than with any ideology. But they found it convenient to justify their action by stressing the need for Japan to emulate the West and "leave Asia," in Fukuzawa's famous words of 1885. Here patriotic assertiveness was combined with the language of universalism (that is,

29 Sakeda, *Kindai Nihon*, pp. 63–5.

Westernization). It was obvious that the former was a more potent force than the latter was. It was because of this that patriotism could be a double-edged instrument, for it would be boundless and might arouse national expectations that could not be fulfilled. Subsequent history showed that quite often the government had to restrain popular patriotism in carrying out its foreign policy. Here too, one sees an instance in which mass incorporation into the polity was a fundamental feature of the foreign relations of a modern state.

All these factors contributed to the development of Japanese relations with Korea and China after 1882. The struggle for power in Korea between the followers of the Taewongun and Queen Min was now joined by that between the "independence faction" and the "conservatives," the former seeking Japan's support and the latter China's. An attempted coup by the "independence" group, openly assisted by Japanese minister Takezoe Shin'ichirō and his hundred-man legation guard, was executed at the end of 1884, resulting in the brief establishment of a pro-Japanese government under the reigning king, dedicated to the "independence" of Korea from Chinese suzerainty. However, this proved short-lived, as "conservative" Korean officials requested the help of Chinese forces that had been stationed in Korea. Two thousand troops marched to the palace and surrounded it. The coup collapsed, and an angry Korean mob retaliated by killing ten Japanese officers and thirty other Japanese residents in Seoul. Some leaders of the "independence" faction, including Kim Ok-kyun, fled to Japan. The result was a further exacerbation of Chinese-Japanese relations.[30]

The situation tested the Japanese government's ability to maintain domestic control, for national opinion was aroused by news of the humiliation, and pressures mounted for punitive action against China. The use of force was called for in the popular press in order to occupy Seoul, protect Japanese lives, and, if necessary, diminish and eliminate Chinese influence in Korea. Those steps would enhance Japanese power and honor, it was asserted, and unite further the leaders and the people of the country. The Tokyo government was well aware of the need to respond to those pressures, but it considered the further use of force premature. Reinforcement of Japanese troops and ships would surely provoke countermeasures by the Chinese, and a situation would be created in which the two countries would find it difficult to avoid an open clash. Because Japan had just begun a program for an arma-

30 See Hilary Conroy, *The Japanese Seizure of Korea: 1868–1910* (Philadelphia: University of Pennsylvania Press, 1960) for an excellent treatment of the 1884 incident.

ment buildup, its military leaders were virtually unanimous in counseling caution, at least for the time being. A premature war with no assurance of victory would not only devastate the national economy but would also cause the government's leadership to be questioned and lead to domestic turmoil. Civilian officials, too, were inclined to take a less belligerent stand in view of the fact that Foreign Minister Inoue Kaoru was in the middle of serious negotiations for treaty revision. A foreign war would certainly complicate those negotiations. At the same time, it was considered dangerous to national prestige and domestic stability to acquiesce in China's military presence in Korea, a symbol of humiliation for Japan. The most plausible solution, then, had to be an agreement with the Chinese for a mutual reduction and evacuation of forces in Korea. With this as the key objective, Itō Hirobumi went to Tientsin to confer with Li Hung-chang, the Chinese negotiator. The 1885 Li–Itō convention was, in terms of the objective, a success. The two governments agreed to withdraw their troops from Korea; furthermore, they pledged to give each other prior notice should it become necessary once again to send armed forces to the peninsular kingdom.[31]

The agreement, however, could not silence Japanese domestic opinion, which had been aroused by the rhetoric of national power and patriotism. Disappointed by what they took to be the government's passivity, advocates of stronger action in Korea or toward China continued their agitation, often in clandestine meetings and secret plots for creating disturbances in the neighboring countries. They often employed the rhetoric of Asianism to present their arguments. The idea was that it was incumbent upon the Japanese to take the lead for the salvation of all Asia, in particular Korea and China. They should be willing to go to these countries, engage in efforts to eliminate corrupt and weak regimes, reform their institutions, and urge their people to join together to stop avaricious European nations.[32] The emergence of Asianism in the mid-1880s marked the beginning of an interesting phenomenon in Japan's modern relations with the neighboring countries: the activities of individual Japanese, without official backing, in Korea, China, and other countries whose behavior could often be an embarrassment but at times useful to the government in Tokyo. They

31 See Bonnie B. Oh, "Sino-Japanese Rivalry in Korea, 1876–1885," in Akira Iriye, ed., *The Chinese and the Japanese: Essays in Political and Cultural Interactions* (Princeton, N.J.: Princeton University Press, 1980).

32 On Asianism, one must still go back to the pioneering study by Marius B. Jansen, *The Japanese and Sun Yat-sen* (Cambridge, Mass.: Harvard University Press, 1954).

were, in essence, little different from Western missionaries, explorers, and filibusters who roamed all over the world; they had no explicit official sanction for their acts but could turn to their home governments for protection when necessary. But the Japanese case was notable because of its close connections with the internal politics of all countries, including Japan. Frequently, those Japanese – many of them were called *shishi* (heroes) – started out in opposition to the government and sought to influence domestic politics in their own country by bold acts in Korea or China. These acts were usually of a conspiratorial nature; they would contact antigovernmental factions and individuals in Korea or China and plot to undermine, if not overthrow, the existing regimes. If successful, their endeavors would be rewarded by changes in Japan's domestic politics. In this sense, they were a potential threat to internal political authority. On occasion, however, their activities might be useful for extending Japanese power on the continent, just as missionaries provided an opportunity for Western nations to obtain and extend their rights abroad. Japanese activists, in contrast with Western missionaries, were, at the same time, driven by the ideology of Asianism, and this made their support awkward for Tokyo's officials, particularly during the 1880s when they were trying to Westernize legal and commercial institutions so as to obtain their goal of treaty revision. In this sense, Asianism functioned as the antithesis of the official dedication to Westernization. Those who felt revulsion toward the fad of Western clothes, manners, dancing, and the like found in the Asianist ideology an alternative that could give them a vocabulary with which to assault the government.

For all these reasons, continental issues became bound up with domestic developments in the years after 1885. Political movements at home tended to challenge public authority and threatened to nullify the efforts of the government and military to obtain treaty revision and maintain calm on the Korean peninsula while strengthening the armed forces. It would be wrong to say, however, that this rift menaced the foundation of the modern Japanese state. On the contrary, it could be argued that all these popular movements were indications of an aroused national sentiment and that regardless of their Asianist opposition to the government's Westernizing programs, they revealed a heightened sense of patriotism that, combined with stronger arms, could eventually be put to use in foreign wars. In that sense, there was no fundamental contradiction between public and private activities; they might differ on means, and they might represent their acts in contrasting rhetorical frameworks, but they both were solidifying the basis of the Japanese state as it staged its first imperialist ventures.

Moreover, it is worth noting that the use of force in Korea and armament expansion were not the sum total of the efforts that went into the consolidation of the Japanese state. Treaty revision negotiations went on throughout these years, as did the domestic reforms that led to the promulgation of the constitution in 1889 and the convening of the Diet in 1890. Efforts were being steadily made to regain control over Japanese trade from foreign merchants, to improve the quality of products for export, and to reduce imports by encouraging domestic industrialization in textiles and other light manufactures. These efforts were considered just as important to national wealth and strength as military activities. In fact, some writers and officials believed that it was in the nonmilitary spheres that the struggle for power among nations was being waged and must be won. This harked back to an earlier emphasis on "enriching the nation," but the situation was more urgent in the 1880s because the Western powers were visibly growing in economic strength and expanding rapidly all over the globe. It would not be enough, under the circumstances, for Japan to seek to maintain a balance of power on the Korean peninsula. Such an aim paled in significance beside the far larger goal of mobilizing the resources of the whole country for economic growth and expansion. This, too, was an important part of the story in the period before the Sino-Japanese War.

It was from the 1880s onwards that foreign trade established itself as a serious objective of the Meiji state. The fiscal retrenchment policy of Finance Minister Matsukata Masayoshi, in office between 1881 and 1892, had the effect of reducing government expenditures, encouraging private industry, discouraging foreign imports, and making Japanese commodities more competitive in overseas markets. Between 1880 and 1885, total Japanese exports increased from ¥28.4 million to ¥36.7 million. Still an insignificant volume (world trade during the decade of the 1880s amounted to over £3 billion), it nevertheless marked a significant trend. Exports from Japan to Korea, for instance, increased by over 90 percent between the mid-1880s and the early 1890s, of which commodities made in Japan increased by 160 percent from ¥511,000 to ¥1.313 million.[33] These consisted of cotton yarn, piece goods, and other manufactured items, products of industrialization. Regardless of political and military issues, there was little ques-

33 Hattori, *Kindai Nihon*, p. 107.

tion that here was a fundamental development in Japanese capitalism that was finding a ready market nearby.

Equally important was the beginning of Japanese emigration overseas. It was more an idea than an achievement, but already during the 1880s, writers were stressing the need for resettling the country's surplus population so that they would contribute to the nation's wealth and strength. In one of the earliest treatises on the subject, Mutō Sanji, a businessman, wrote in 1887 that Japan's lower, laboring classes should be resettled in large numbers overseas, particularly in Hawaii and the west coast of the United States. It would not only give them better opportunities to earn a livelihood but would also contribute to enriching the nation through their remittances home.[34] At the time, it is true, there were fewer than five thousand Japanese in Hawaii, and only a little over one thousand in California and other western states.[35] But these figures were roughly equal to the number of Japanese in Korea and China. Whereas those in the neighboring countries were engaged in commercial, educational, and, frequently, political and military activities, quite often under the supervision of the Japanese authorities, Japanese who crossed the Pacific were predominantly agricultural and manual workers. To men like Mutō, these were far more productive pursuits and far more beneficial in the long run for the country, for the rich climate and soil of Hawaii and America, as well as the high cost of white labor, ensured that Japanese would have no trouble obtaining employment and contributing to the economic growth of the host territories. Even more important, they would become better known to Americans and other Westerners through their overseas immigration, settlement, and hard work. That in turn should redound to enhance the country's prestige.

It is interesting to note that the theme of augmenting national power by engaging in "peaceful warfare" throughout the world never disappeared in the 1890s, despite the continuing tensions with China that ultimately led to war in 1894. If anything, treaty revision, trade expansion, and emigration were pursued with even greater vigor than earlier. As during the 1880s, this reflected the Japanese leaders' perception of both domestic needs and the further growth of the West's economic and military power. On the domestic front, the convening of the first session of the Diet under the new constitution, taking place in

34 Akira Iriye, *Pacific Estrangement: Japanese and American Expansion, 1897–1911* (Cambridge, Mass.: Harvard University Press, 1972), p. 23.
35 *Nichi-Bei bunka kōshō shi: Ijū hen* (Tokyo: Yōyōsha, 1955), pp. 50, 382.

November 1890, established a basic framework for political action. The first election gave the voters – albeit with a restricted franchise, enabling only 1.1 percent of the population to vote – an opportunity to experiment with a Western system of political choice. Political parties now geared their activities toward gaining influence in parliamentary politics; they sometimes supported, and at other times collaborated with, men in power in order to gain their influence. The unenfranchised, of course, would seek to organize themselves and agitate for their rights, but here too, the framework was largely defined by the new parliamentary system. Henceforth it would be the political parties that would mediate between government and people, as was the case in most Western nations.

If domestic developments were gradually falling into place, continued Western power and influence defined Japanese perceptions of external affairs. What particularly attracted their attention was the fact that the Western powers that had steadily extended their spheres of action, incorporating ever-wider regions of the world into their domains, now appeared to be bent on massive undertakings in Asia and the Pacific. Having established control over Burma, Indochina, and the Maritime Provinces, they seemed to be pushing for the interior of China as well as Korea, as exemplified by the launching of the construction of the Trans-Siberian Railway in 1891 and the various powers' attempts to gain influential positions in Korean politics by providing the kingdom with financial and military advisers. In the West, moreover, voices began to be heard, stressing that the future of world politics would be decided in Asia and the Pacific. Alfred Thayer Mahan, Henry Norman, Charles Pearson, and others started writing alarmist tracts, urging their readers to pay close attention to this region for its geopolitical and economic significance. Having penetrated Africa and the Middle East, it now seemed incumbent upon the Western powers to extend their influence to Asia and the Pacific. The region was of strategic significance because of its landmass and the wide ocean; it contained a majority of humankind; and it was rich in natural resources. Rivalries among the powers were likely to be increasingly played out and determined in this area.[36] Such activities and views were well known to the Japanese, heightening a sense of urgency that they too must act more energetically, both in the passive sense of avoiding victimization by the more aggressive West and also in the sense of extending their own power in order to join the ranks of the

36 Iriye, *Pacific Estrangement*, pp. 19–20.

great powers. As Inagaki Manjirō, who had studied with Robert Seeley at Cambridge University, asserted in *Tōhōsaku* (Eastern policy, 1891), a work comparable to the English historian's expansionist writings, Japan must understand its geopolitical requirements and strive to strengthen itself economically and militarily. The two went hand in hand, but the most urgent need was for further economic growth through commerce and industrialization. This would be a momentous task but a crucial one, for the center of world politics was shifting to Asia and the Pacific. The powers that emerged victorious in the competition in that part of the world were destined to be the leaders in the coming century.[37] Few would have disagreed, and similar ideas made their appearance throughout the first half of the 1890s. That this was no idle talk can be seen in specific instances of economic strengthening. For example, 1893 marked the year when domestically manufactured cotton yarn surpassed imports for the first time since the 1860s. Although imported cotton products still surpassed exports, the gap was steadily narrowing, thanks to phenomenal increases in the export of cotton yarn to Korea and China.[38] Equally significant, overseas expansion through emigration, colonization, and even outright seizures of some tropical islands came to be vigorously advocated in the early 1890s. It was around then that the term *hatten* (expansion) took on the connotation of establishing Japanese communities and enclaves throughout the globe as a source as well as a symbol of national power. As writer after writer noted, only a vigorous, expansionist people, willing to take risks and fight against obstacles in strange countries, deserved to be powerful. Like Westerners, the Japanese must go abroad, work hard, and bring as many areas of the world as possible under Japanese influence. Because the country was far from prepared militarily to push for such expansion and because Western nations, too, appeared to be enlarging their domains through peaceful means such as commerce and emigration, Japan should do likewise. It should particularly look to regions that were relatively sparsely populated but richly endowed with natural resources. Many writers thus pointed to the importance of the South Seas. Expansion in the south, they asserted, recalling the memories of Japanese activities in the Philippines, Siam, and elsewhere in the sixteenth century, would prove to be the answer not only to Japan's population problem but also to its quest for great-power status. There were others, however, who continued to believe that Hawaii and the American continent would prove to be

37 Ibid., pp. 35–6.
38 Sumiya Mikio, *Dai Nihon teikoku no shiren* (Tokyo: Chūō kōronsha, 1965), pp. 66–7.

even more advantageous. Already in 1892 there were 4,500 Japanese in America; in 1893, there were 22,000 Japanese in Hawaii. They were viewed as a spearhead of much larger waves of emigration across the Pacific. In order to assist in such activities and to find other suitable areas for "colonization through peaceful methods," a colonization society was organized in 1893 by some of the leading publicists and politicians of the time.[39] Summing up this rising expansionist sentiment, Tokutomi Iichirō (Sohō) declared on the eve of the Sino-Japanese War, "Certainly our future history will be a history of the establishment by the Japanese of new Japans everywhere in the world."[40]

The crisis in Korea that culminated in the Chinese war in 1894 should be put in the context of this expansionist sentiment. Extending Japanese power and influence on the continent of Asia was part of a larger vision, such as Tokutomi's. Only by developing itself through expansion, it was believed, would the Japanese nation be able to emerge as a power in the world arena and to cope with the expanding powers of the West. At the same time, expansionism would provide a new national objective for the Japanese people. Instead of being preoccupied with internal squabbles and domestic concerns, they would be driven by a vision of boundless opportunities overseas. "Overseas settlement," as the manifesto of the colonization society put it, "is a vital aspect of the national policy, adopted at the Meiji Restoration, of elevating our spirit, broadening our vista, introducing new knowledge, and reforming people's minds." Having just had their first national election for the convening of the Diet, it was as if the Japanese people were now being exhorted to concern themselves with grandiose schemes for overseas expansion, not just with internal political matters. In this fashion, overseas expansionism could serve as a device for turning national opinion outward. Whether consciously or unconsciously, the country's literary and educational leaders, too, delighted in stressing patriotic themes and exhorting readers and students to consider Japan's unique history and traditional beauty as well as its modernizing achievements. The focusing on these themes, however, did not mean the fostering of a neoisolationist mentality. Rather, they were cited as evidence of the strengths and virtues of the Japanese nation on the threshold of overseas expansion. They would give confidence to the people as they sought to pursue activities abroad. It is true that some thinkers took strong exception to patriotism as a basis for expansion. They were more interested in individual liberty, human

39 Iriye, *Pacific Estrangement*, pp. 40–1. 40 Ibid., p. 44.

rights, and other Western values. In some instances the conflict between the two was unbridgeable. In most cases, however, it would appear that the Japanese managed to embrace patriotic themes while holding onto a more universalistic rhetoric. After all, that was what they thought they observed in Western countries. Whether complacent or uneasy about the juxtaposition of such visions, the Japanese found themselves defining their personal and national objectives in an environment of deepening contact with the outside world.[41]

Given this background, the war with China from 1894 to 1895 was viewed with equanimity and often enthusiasm by most Japanese. It seemed to fit into their policies, economic programs, and expansionist mentality. The occasion for war was provided by a rebellion (led by the Tonghaks, a banned organization) in Korea, impelling the court in Seoul to seek Chinese assistance in putting it down. Over two thousand Chinese soldiers landed at the western port of Asan. The situation threatened to test the Chinese-Japanese agreement of 1885, according to which the two countries were to coordinate their action in case they decided to reintroduce forces into Korea. As it turned out, the Korean authorities were able to suppress the rebels even while the Chinese forces were confined to Asan. But the Japanese government decided to seize this opportunity to reduce Chinese power and extend Japanese influence in the peninsula. Such a decision implied war, and the Japanese leaders were well aware of it. In fact, such men as Foreign Minister Mutsu Munemitsu and other cabinet members welcomed the opportunity, for military action could be presented to the populace and the Diet as a necessary step for obtaining more rights in Korea and otherwise expanding Japanese influence on the continent of Asia. They correctly judged that they would obtain national support. The Diet, which had caused trouble to the cabinet on budgetary issues, quickly fell into line, and the press was similarly compliant. Japan's armed forces, too, were judged to be ready. Since the 1880s they had been steadily augmented. Moreover, it had been considered most likely that they would first be used in Korea. This was because of the view, which Yamagata Aritomo had expressed openly at the first session of the Diet in 1890, that national independence hinged on the defense of the country's "lines of interest." Every country, he asserted, must protect its boundaries by defending these lines. Such views were similar to strategic conceptions being developed in the West and expressed the eagerness of the Japanese to identify with the

41 Irokawa Daikichi, *Kindai kokka no shuppatsu* (Tokyo: Chūō kōronsha, 1966), pp. 464–78.

advanced Western countries by accepting their formulations of national defense. And it was clear in Yamagata's speech, as well as in more secret military plans being worked out in the early 1890s, that these "lines of interest" primarily meant the Korean peninsula. If Japan were to consider Korea of immediate relevance to the national defense, it followed that its military spending and war plans would have to be geared to at least maintaining the status quo in the peninsula through a balance of power between Japan and China. But such an objective might lead to armed clashes with China, and thus preparations had been made for a hypothetical war with that country.

Here again, Japanese behavior fitted into the general pattern of the modern Western states which, too, were engaged in making elaborate war plans and armament programs as means for augmenting national power. What is particularly notable about the Japanese case is that it was the first non-Western state that was now joining the ranks of the militarily strong, imperialistic powers. It is significant that on July 16, 1894, Japan finally achieved its goal of concluding a new treaty with Britain, providing for the abolition of extraterritoriality in five years in return for the opening up of the country for "mixed residence." Unlike earlier treaty drafts, the Japanese-British treaty contained no provision for an interim appointment of foreign judges in cases involving foreigners. The successful consummation of this agreement, after close to thirty years' efforts, symbolized the growing status of Japan as a modern state and the willingness of the West to recognize it as such. The Japanese people, whose views were now channeled through the political parties and expressed in often-acrimonious debate in the Diet, were not united in welcoming the prospect of foreigners residing in the interior of the country, but they nevertheless took the signing of the new treaty as evidence that Japan was emerging as a major power, now in a better position than before to assert itself in the world arena, in particular in the developing crisis with China.

War was declared against China only sixteen days after the signing of the British treaty. Actually, the first shot was fired on July 25, when the Japanese fleet off the west coast of Korea attacked Chinese warships; four days later, Japanese troops that had been dispatched to Korea engaged Chinese forces in Asan. By then Japan's objective in Korea was no longer the maintenance of a balance between Japan and China, but the ejection of Chinese influence from the peninsula. This goal could be achieved by destroying Chinese land forces in Korea and ships in the Yellow Sea, which was accomplished with relative ease by September. After October, the Japanese expanded their spheres of action, invading the Liaotung peninsula, later Weihaiwei in Shantung Province, and engaging in a sea battle with China's Peiyang fleet. By March 1895, Japanese forces had occupied Lushun (Port Arthur), Talien (Dairen), and Weihaiwei and had destroyed most of the Chinese fleet. The Chinese government saw no alternative but to seek to end the war. On March 18 it approached the United States minister in Peking to obtain America's good offices as a mediator.

The war was enormously popular. The political parties vied with one another in expressing their support and voting funds for military supplies and manpower. They, as well as the press, considered the conflict eminently justifiable in view of Korea's need for reform and China's alleged refusal to promote it. Japan, as the most modernized nation in Asia, had the obligation, it was asserted, to come to the aid of its weaker neighbor and to punish the Chinese who had not awakened to the importance of cooperating with the Japanese to spread civilization in Asia. All such rhetoric reflected Japan's self-perception that the nation was now behaving as a modern power, one prerequisite for it being a willingness to extend national horizons to assume responsibility for the peace and stability of nearby areas. Perhaps one of the most notable statements about the war was made by Tokutomi Sohō when he asserted, two days before the opening of hostilities, "I do not advocate war just for the sake of it. I am not advocating plundering of other lands. But I insist on war with China in order to transform Japan, hitherto a contracting nation, into an expansive nation."[42] By waging war, Japan would establish a beachhead in Asia and be recognized as an expanding nation, a symbol of its great-power status. Self-consciousness about overseas expansion emerged as the most significant product of the Chinese war. The few thousands that had already gone abroad, to Asia, Hawaii, and North America, would now be joined by hundreds of thousands, just as the expanding countries of the West had been sending overseas waves of merchants, settlers, and adventurers. The Japanese would dedicate themselves to the task of expansion, for only by doing so would they be counted among the world's great nations. In short, they would join them as an imperialist nation.

IMPERIALISM AND MILITARISM, 1895–1912

Imperialism, as we noted, characterized part of the external behavior of modern states in the late nineteenth and early twentieth centuries.

42 Iriye, *Pacific Estrangement*, p. 44.

It expressed the energies, orientations, and interests of a modern state at that particular period, but not necessarily of modern capitalism at a certain stage of development. Obviously, Japanese capitalism and industrialization were just getting under way when war with China came, and it would be impossible to treat them as sources for Japanese imperialism in the way that one might treat the subject for more mature capitalist countries. Industrial and finance capitalism, rather, should be viewed as one ingredient in a modern state, but not always the most predominant factor. It was the state that undertook the overseas expansion. And the key to this phenomenon was the coalescence of domestic forces toward both the creation of centralized authority and the generation of mass society. Imperialism affirmed and further strengthened these trends. Japan was no exception. It undertook military action in Korea and sought to entrench its power on the continent of Asia because it was politically and militarily equipped to do so and because national opinion firmly supported such action. The war and its aftermath, in turn, strengthened the centralizing tendencies of the polity, contributed to industrialization, and militarized society. As in other modern nations, however, these developments in turn created new divisions and tensions among segments of the population. Although external expansion never ceased to be a driving objective of both state and society, this did not prevent a rift between the two about the mode of expansion and about the ways in which the benefits of expansion might be distributed. Like Europeans and Americans, the Japanese began to recognize the burden as well as the glory of empire; although all partook of the latter, the burden was unevenly shared, giving rise, at least in the minds of some, to questions about the inequities of the modern Japanese empire. The years after the Sino-Japanese War, then, may be seen as a period in which imperialism came to occupy a central position in the politics, economy, and culture of the Japanese state and in which tensions as well as convergence characterized national opinion.

Victories on land and sea caused Japanese politicians, publicists, and citizens to dream of empire, just as a war three years later would drive the American people in the same way. Empire connoted prestige and power and also fitted into the vision of implanting Japanese interests and influence extensively abroad. But specific questions had to be raised about the immediate goals of expansion. Expulsion of Chinese power from Korea – the so-called independence of Korea – no longer satisfied the expansionist urge. Both government and people assumed, after all the victories, that the nation deserved more. The army thought a foothold in the Liaotung peninsula indispensable for defending the now enlarged concept of national defense; the navy looked southward to Taiwan; the political parties insisted that Japan should aim at obtaining these and more, including some provinces in China proper; and the country's press generally took the view that the war was but an opening chapter in Japan's new status as an empire.[43] The final terms of peace that the Japanese delegation, headed by Itō, presented to Li Hung-chang at Shimonoseki in April 1895 reflected such optimism and ambitions. China was to recognize that Korea was an independent state, cede the Liaotung peninsula and Taiwan to Japan, pay Japan an indemnity of 200 million taels (about ¥300 million) in seven years, open up four treaty ports, grant Japan most-favored-nation status as well as the right to navigate the Yangtze River, and give the Japanese the right to engage in manufacturing in China.

These terms, which the Chinese had no choice but to accept, albeit reluctantly and after prolonged negotiations, represented the view, as Itō told Li, that a "victor is of course entitled to claim any place he likes" for territorial cession and that if the Chinese refused them, Japan would continue the war and claim even more.[44] Fundamentally, Japan's peace terms expressed the country's perceived requirements as a major power. The securing of the "lines of interest," overseas territorial acquisitions, equal status with the Western powers in China, economic rights on the continent, and an indemnity payment to enable Japan to continue with its industrialization program – these were considered to be indispensable to the nation if it were to make good its pretensions as a power. Domestically, too, these cessions would appeal to the people's expansive sentiment, unite opinion and stifle opposition, and justify additional military expenditures. The war and the resulting peace, publicists never tired of asserting, established Japan's reputation as a great power, and the Japanese would gain the respect that they had coveted so long from Europeans and Americans.

Subsequent developments showed that the Japanese did gain such a reputation and respect but that these did not end their problems. If anything, they created complications in Japan's external affairs, which in turn deepened cleavages at home. As was the case in the West, imperialism, considered a prerequisite for modern states, threatened to undermine domestic order by generating expectations that could not always be fulfilled, by increasing governmental expenditures that had to be financed through taxation, by strengthening the bureaucracy

43 Ibid., p. 46; Sumiya, *Dai Nihon*, p. 36.
44 Morinosuke Kajima, *The Diplomacy of Japan, 1894–1922* (Tokyo: Kajima Institute of International Peace, 1976), vol. 1, pp. 235–41.

and the armed forces in defense of empire, and, most fundamentally, by creating new issues of national and personal identity. In Europe these problems and tensions provided an environment in which the modern imperialist states dealt with their external and internal affairs and which ultimately produced a calamitous war among them. At the same time, serious efforts were made to prevent war through such means as armament reduction, arbitration treaties, pacifism, various types of internationalist organizations, and the fostering of economic interdependence. This last was considered particularly crucial if international affairs were to reduce tension in the world and within each society. Although economic interdependence would not develop as the guiding concept of capitalist international relations until after the World War, it began to be presented as an alternative to imperialism at the turn of the century. According to its theorists, such as John A. Hobson, Andrew Carnegie, Norman Angell, and others, imperialism was not a necessary condition or an inevitable phase of modern capitalism; it was, rather, a perversion. Modern states, they insisted, could maintain amicable relations externally and stable order domestically by engaging in peaceful pursuits of business activities. Other analysts disagreed, asserting that modern capitalism inevitably led to imperialism and that imperialism produced war abroad and class tensions at home, both leading to revolutionary upheavals until noncapitalist, nonimperialistic societies emerged to ensure world peace.

These and other kinds of debate on the nature of modern capitalism and imperialism were taken seriously by the Japanese, now that they, too, had joined the ranks of imperialists. They would participate in the drama of imperialist politics and contribute to the debate. Like Westerners, they had to consider how domestic stability could be preserved while they undertook overseas expansion and whether such expansion would lead to increased international tensions and war or to greater harmony and interdependence among nations.

There was no easy answer. Immediately after signing the Shimonoseki treaty, Japan's confidence and optimism were jolted when Russia, France, and Germany presented their "friendly counsel" that Japan retrocede the just-obtained Liaotung peninsula to China. The tripartite intervention expressed the powers' alarm at the quick tempo of Japanese expansionism and their determination to preserve as much of China as possible for their own exploitation. There was little unusual about such maneuvers, but the intervention made an indelible impression on Japanese minds that imperialist politics was ruthless and kept nations in a perpetual state of potential conflict. This was a confirmation of earlier views about the ambitiousness of the West, but it showed the Japanese that their achievement of great-power status had not changed the situation. All that happened was that Japan was now in a position to play the same game. Thus instead of giving up their dream of Asian empire, they took this incident as a merely temporary setback, determined that once opportunity presented itself, they would regain the foothold. In this sense their imperialism led to further imperialism and, because war would be inevitable in the process, armament and militarization. Likewise, there was also trouble in the other territorial acquisition, Taiwan. Although no power disputed its transfer to Japan, the Chinese and native Taiwanese on the island put up a fierce struggle against its incorporation into the Japanese empire without their consent. Hoping that the tripartite intervention in Manchuria could be extended to Taiwan, they resisted the Japanese army of occupation, numbering 60,000 troops. In the end the uprising was suppressed, but only after causing 4,600 deaths among the Japanese through fighting and tropical diseases.[45] Still, few Japanese thought they should give up the island as unworthy of the effort. Huge expenditures to suppress the uprising could be justified only by maintaining it under colonial rule. Further expenses would be forthcoming to establish a system of administration for law and order, education, and the health of the island's population.

Nor did Korea's alleged independence end all the problems on the peninsula. "Independence" amounted, in Japan's conception, to replacing Chinese with Japanese influence, and steps were taken to "reform" the Korean government and military administration by introducing to the country the kinds of measures that Meiji Japan itself had undertaken in the late 1860s. These measures provoked Korean resistance, and many, including the Taewongun and Queen Min, sought to undermine Japan's influence by turning to foreign powers, particularly Russia, the very country that the Japanese blamed for initiating the tripartite intervention in Manchuria. In October 1895, Japanese authorities in Seoul staged a coup to eliminate supporters of Queen Min and pro-Russian forces. The attempt ended up in the murder of the queen but not much else, and it produced fierce anti-Japanese agitation throughout Korea. Russian influence increased further. Thus, even Korean "independence," the initial aim of Japanese policy that had led to the war with China, could no longer be taken for granted.

45 On the Taiwanese resistance movement, see Hsü Shih-k'ai, *Nihon tōchika no Taiwan* (Tokyo: Tōkyō daigaku shuppankai, 1972); and Hung Chao-t'ang, *Taiwan minshukoku no kenkyū* (Tokyo: Tōkyō daigaku shuppankai, 1970).

Yet despite all these frustrations, the Japanese were determined to push ahead with their imperialism, rather than abandoning it as too frustrating and hopelessly complicated. The Diet obligingly passed one military expansion bill after another, budgetary allocations for armed forces increasing from ¥24 million before the war to ¥73 million in 1896 and ¥110 million in 1897. The political parties supported these increases as a matter of course, for they all accepted imperialism as a necessary and desirable attribute of the Japanese state. If Westerners seemed interested in pushing the Japanese out of Manchuria and if the Chinese, Taiwanese, and Koreans appeared hostile to their schemes, they would respond by affirming, rather than retreating from, their imperialism. Again, this was the standard response of the imperialist powers at that time. The costs were enormous, but it was generally believed that in domestic political terms, the cost of retreat and retrenchment would be even more devastating. Moreover, if the advanced capitalist countries of the West were holding onto their imperial and colonial domains despite their obvious expense, it seemed even more imperative for Japan to do likewise, for otherwise the Western powers would further extend their control and grow even more powerful. It would then be too late, and far too expensive, to undertake Japan's own expansion. Such appeared to be the case when, starting in 1897, the European nations obtained bases, leaseholds, and concessions in China, so that within a year the whole of China had been divided into their spheres of influence. Although it was far from clear what specifically Japan would gain by acting likewise and although Japanese capital for building railways and developing mines in China was meager, Tokyo did not hesitate to join the scramble for concessions, successfully inducing the Chinese to consider Fukien Province, opposite Taiwan, Japan's sphere of influence where the Japanese would have prior rights.

There was general approval of such acts in part because they took place simultaneously with industrialization which, in turn, was considered one of the keys to modern states. Industrial production, primarily of cotton and silk textiles but also including iron and steel, grew rapidly after the Sino-Japanese War, more than doubling in volume between 1895 and 1900. Some of this would have taken place even if the war and the resulting colonization had not taken place. But part of the industrial revolution was undoubtably linked to these external affairs. For instance, cotton textile exports, surpassing imports for the first time in 1897, were tremendously aided by the opening of more treaty ports in China as a consequence of the war and by an optimism prevailing among industrialists at the time in investing capital in machinery. The iron and steel industry, for its part, was a clear response to the needs of the armed forces. The Yawata Iron Works, created by an act of the Diet in 1895, was a typical example. It began producing iron by 1901, the first successful development in heavy industry in Japan. Likewise, the shipbuilding industry was given impetus by naval construction, the government subsidizing shipyards to construct merchant ships to be used in the expanding opportunities of Korea and China.[46]

Imperialism, then, coincided with rapid industrialization, confirming the prevailing view that all these, as well as great-power status, were part of a single historical development. The Japanese state, it appeared, was now a bona fide member of the community of modern, industrial, great powers. The *Asahi* newspaper echoed this view when it asserted that imperialism was an expression of basic national energy made manifest through the organization of the state. Just as other countries had their dissenters from such a perception, however, in Japan too there existed currents of thought that questioned this equation's alleged inevitability. One strain, comparable to some of the antiimperialist views in the West, was the theme of peaceful expansion, as opposed to militarism and imperialism. Perhaps the most influential writer in this vein at the turn of the century was Kōtoku Shūsui, who published *Nijū seiki no kaibutsu teikokushugi* (Imperialism, the monster of the twentieth century) in 1901. In it he castigated patriotism, militarism, and imperialism as a waste of national resources that brought nothing but suffering to the people. He was not, he wrote, opposed to peaceful economic expansion through trade, production, and the spread of civilization. Another influential writer, Ukita Kazutami, did not condemn imperialism so harshly, arguing that the nation had no choice but to practice it if it were to maintain its independence and participate actively in world politics and civilization. At the same time, however, Ukita echoed Kōtoku's stress on peaceful expansion, asserting that "peaceful, economic, and commercial" expansion in Asia, the Pacific Ocean, and the Western Hemisphere was as crucial to the national well-being as was more frankly militaristic control over Korea and Taiwan.[47] Both writers, and numerous others who shared their views, assumed it would be possible to engage in less militaristic, more peaceful overseas expansion. They did not consider imperialism inevitable, but at the same time they took it

46 Sumiya, *Dai Nihon*, pp. 61–75. 47 Iriye, *Pacific Estrangement*, pp. 78–80.

for granted that the country would continue to industrialize, expand its trade, and raise the people's level of education and well-being by means of peaceful activities overseas. They were echoing the strain of thinking in the West that eventually created an outlook known as liberal internationalism.

Although this strain identified itself with comparable developments in the West, another strand of dissent took a more particularistic, Asianist stand. Asianism, as noted earlier, had tended to be sporadically mouthed by those who were impatient with the government's foreign policy. After 1895 the situation changed, with the Japanese having established themselves above other Asian peoples. This imperialism, however, did not altogether stifle Asianist activities. If anything, it encouraged the growth of Pan-Asianist ideology and organized movements for a number of reasons. First, there was a psychological need to justify Japan's seizure of Taiwan or establishment of spheres of influence in China, not merely as something the nation had to do to emulate Western imperialists or to defend its "lines of interest," but also as a way to awaken and reform Asians by providing them with law and order and introducing them to the benefits of modern civilization. Japan had an obligation to do so as the only modernized country of Asia. Even though Japan had now joined the ranks of the great powers, some felt that it remained, and should remain, an Asian power, as Asia was where Japan lay geographically and historically. Japan, therefore, had a special mission to perform in this region. This type of thinking produced a cultural and philosophical Pan-Asianism best exemplified by Okakura Tenshin who asserted in 1902 that "Asia is one." All countries and peoples east of the Suez seemed to be united in certain fundamental principles, as opposed to those in the West. This view could be used to rationalize the idea that the aim of Japanese imperialism was to reunite all of Asia against Western imperialism. Although no such sweeping view would be advocated until the 1930s, the concept of Asian uniqueness was sufficiently influential for it to give rise to a number of movements and organizations. Among the most powerful was the Tōa Dōbun Shoin (East Asian common cultural association), founded by Konoe Atsumaro in 1898 and dedicated to the cooperation of the Chinese and Japanese. The two peoples, Konoe asserted, were destined to work together for the regeneration of Asia. There were, in addition, many smaller organizations and societies with similar objectives. They were carryovers from the earlier activities by the *shishi*, but they now found their spheres of action much enlarged and better protected because of the expansion of Japanese control over the continent. Some of them, like Miyazaki Torazō, were interested in assisting Chinese revolutionaries, whereas others helped the constitutionalists like Liang Ch'i-ch'ao. There were many underground networks of personal ties between Chinese and Japanese, all imbued with the idea that the two peoples shared a common destiny. In all such movements, it was an article of faith that Japan must not be satisfied with great-power status but must do something to give meaning to its national existence.[48]

Japanese foreign affairs after the turn of the century, then, may be examined in terms of these various developments. Imperialism defined the basic framework, and it had a history of its own, but interlocked with it were other themes such as peaceful expansion and Pan-Asianism which, too, affected official policy and popular perceptions. All these, moreover, must be seen against the background of domestic political and economic developments. The Meiji state was, by 1900, over thirty years old, and few thought it possible to challenge its legitimacy. The only direct threat came in 1910, when Kōtoku, now an anarchist after having spent a few years in the United States, plotted to assassinate the emperor.[49] But the state was too powerful to be destroyed by isolated violence. More important was the way in which state authority would be restrained by the maturing of the political parties and the growing self-assertiveness of the Diet. Moreover, as Japanese capitalism continued to make strides, giving rise to financial combines (zaibatsu) at one level and to the socialist movement at another, it remained to be seen whether the modern Japanese state would be able to accommodate these economic and social developments and what new definition of domestic order and stability might emerge. Japanese imperialism both affected and was affected by the outcome of such questioning.

The diplomacy of imperialism, that is, the interrelationship among the powers, fully incorporated Japan, and Japanese action in Asia played a crucial role in its evolution after the turn of the century. Nothing better illustrates this than the signing of the Anglo-Japanese alliance in 1902. A product of careful deliberations and cumbersome negotiations which historians have minutely described,[50] the alliance finally recognized Japan's status as a major power. In 1900–1, Japan

48 Marius B. Jansen, *Japan and China: From War to Peace, 1894–1972* (Chicago: Rand McNally, 1975), pp. 137–8, 162–4; and Miyazaki Tōten, *My Thirty-Three Years' Dream*, trans. Etō Shinkichi and Marius B. Jansen (Princeton, N.J.: Princeton University Press, 1982).

49 See F. G. Notehelfer, *Kōtoku Shūsui: Portrait of a Japanese Radical* (Cambridge, England: Cambridge University Press, 1971).

50 Ian Nish, *The Anglo-Japanese Alliance: The Diplomacy of Two Island Empires 1894–1907* (London: Athlone, 1966).

participated in the international expedition to China to fight against the Boxers and in the subsequent conference with the Ch'ing authorities to restore order. Whether one interprets the Boxer uprising as a manifestation of Chinese nationalism or of more traditional antiforeignism, there is little doubt that Japan played a role as a protector of Western interests in China, dispatching as many as ten thousand soldiers, about the same number as the troops sent by all the Western powers combined. The Japanese were rewarded by being invited to the peace conference, the first time that Japan attended an international conference as a full-fledged member. After 1901 Japan became one of the "Boxer protocol powers," with the right to station troops in the Peking–Tientsin region. Its newly won status made the country a factor in power politics among nations, with Britain willing to allot Japan a role as its principal partner in Asia, and Russia sought to counter the trend by entrenching itself in Manchuria. But the impact of the Anglo-Japanese alliance was not confined to Asia. Although the subsequent chain reaction was but dimly foreseen in 1902, it is possible to link it to the great war of 1914. For the alliance had the effect of forcing France closer to Britain, as the French, allied with Russia after 1894, feared an involvement with the British on account of the Japanese-Russian rivalry in Asia. The British-French entente of 1904, mutually recognizing their spheres of influence in Egypt and Morocco, was a harbinger of further strengthened ties between the two powers that eventually came to include strategic coordination against Germany. Russia, in the meantime, moved steadily closer to Britain, forming its own entente with the latter in 1907 over colonial questions. Because the world war of 1914 pitted the entente powers (Britain, France, and Russia) against Germany and its allies (Austria and Italy), its origins, as far as the power-political aspect was concerned, went back to the formation of the Anglo-Japanese alliance which, in turn, was a response to the rise of Japan as an imperialist power.

There is little doubt that the Japanese welcomed the British alliance as an added confirmation of their status in the world. But the alliance was by no means the only alternative open to them. Some of their leaders, such as Itō, favored a Russian alliance to settle the dispute over Korea. Because it had been Russian influence that had been ascendant in Korea after 1895, and Russia that had seized the Liaotung peninsula in 1898, they argued that only through some understanding with that power would Japan be able to attain its objective, which was defined in a cabinet decision of 1903 as the "securing of national defense through the protection of Korean independence."

What Japan sought was the powers' recognition of its special interests in Korea and, as a longer-range goal, elsewhere in China. The Russians' recognition of Japan's special interests would have been just as acceptable as a British alliance, but in the end Tokyo's officials judged that more would be gained through the latter option. What is striking was the assumption by the Japanese that this sort of imperialist collusion and understanding was the best means for protecting their rights. They were confident that the major powers would seriously consider a Japanese alliance. They were not disappointed, and after 1902 imperialist Japan established itself as a key factor in world politics.

In that situation, it might have been possible to arrive at some understanding with Russia so that the latter would recognize Japan's special position in Korea, in return for Japanese acquiescence to Russian interests in Manchuria. An "exchange" of Manchuria for Korea would have been in accordance with the imperialist practices of the day. Despite protracted negotiations between the two countries, however, Tokyo and St. Petersburg were unable to come to terms, thus convincing the Japanese that their position in Korea would be vulnerable so long as Russian influence remained predominant in southern Manchuria. Even so, it might have been possible to continue talks in the hope that domestic conditions in Russia, China, or Korea or the international situation might change in such a way as to induce the Russians to loosen their grip on Manchuria. Certainly, there was no optimism that a war with Russia could be won or that Japan was economically prepared to finance it.

The decision for war, made by the cabinet in early February 1904, can be understood only in the domestic context. The Russian presence in Manchuria was reported in sensational fashion by the press and helped create the impression that the czarist regime would persist in its intransigence unless Japan showed its determination to use force. Political parties, publicists, and intellectuals organized prowar movements and put pressure on the government. Their argument was that the struggle between the two powers in Korea would not end until one of them retreated; because it was unthinkable for Japan to do so, it must be prepared to use force to reduce Russian power. As seven Tokyo Imperial University professors asserted in a memorial that they presented to Prime Minister Katsura Tarō in June 1903, "a fundamental settlement" of the Manchurian problem was needed if Japan were to secure its position in Korea. They were supported by middle-echelon officials in the Foreign Ministry and the service ministries, who were convinced that Japan should strike before it was too late.

Their argument could easily have been countered on practical and theoretical grounds, but it is suggestive that the only organized movement against the war was carried out by some socialists, several of Christian persuasion: men like Kōtoku Shūsui, Sakai Toshihiko, and Uchimura Kanzō. Socialism in a country that was just beginning to industrialize could not boast the authority and history that its counterpart in Europe did, but it nevertheless suggested an alternative to the definition of the modern state as an imperialist that was taken for granted by the supporters of an assertive policy toward Russia. Japanese socialists called for arms reduction and racial equality and condemned chauvinism and war as serving only the interests of the aristocracy and the military but not the welfare of the people. Although recognizing that the majority of the people appeared to be clamoring for war, the socialists, who published their views in their organ, *Heimin shimbun* (People's daily), opposed it as unjust and wasteful of resources. In a famous editorial written shortly after the declaration of war, they appealed to the Russian people to join forces with the Japanese to condemn the two governments' imperialistic ambitions that had led to war. "Patriotism and militarism are our common foes," the editorial asserted, expressing a clearly alternative view of modern states and interstate relations.

The enormous clamor for war revealed that such ideas were not widespread in Japan at that time. Patriotism, militarism, and imperialism were accepted as necessary conditions for the existence of the nation. If successfully waged, war would further enhance Japan's prestige and standing among the community of great powers. And even if unsuccessful, as many leaders feared, the war would have shown that the Japanese would fight for their "self-defense" and "rights" rather than meekly submit to Russian pressure and reduce themselves to the status of a second-rate nation. It was such a sentiment rather than specific gains that drove Japan's leaders and people to war with mighty Russia.[51] This, of course, does not make the Russo-Japanese War any less imperialistic. It was quintessentially an imperialistic war, fought between two powers over issues outside their national boundaries, at the expense of the Koreans and Chinese who had no say in the matter. But it was not a product of economic interests in any immediate sense. Japan was so poor financially that it had to borrow over ¥100 million in London and New York, an amount that accounted for more than

51 The best recent treatment of war jingoism prior to the Russo-Japanese War is in Sakeda, *Kindai Nihon*, chap. 4. The most authoritative account of the coming of war is by Ian Nish, *The Origins of the Russo-Japanese War* (London: Longman Group, 1985).

one-third of the total cost of the war, whereas Russia relied on the financial markets of Paris. Japanese trade with Korea was extensive, to be sure, but that alone was not the cause of the difficulties with Russia. Japan's economic interests in Manchuria were not negligible, but they hardly comprised a substantial portion of the country's total trade. There was as yet no significant investment overseas. The war was not produced by economic pressures but by the sentiment inside and outside the government that it was the only alternative if the country were to remain a viable entity as a modern power.[52]

At first it appeared as if this judgment were a correct one. Not only did the country's armed forces achieve impressive military victories, but it also succeeded in raising loans abroad. Its prestige rose as never before, and the people once again showed unity and cooperation in executing the war. Patriotism, militarism, and imperialism were reaffirmed, and they in turn contributed to strengthening the Japanese state. At the peace conference in Portsmouth, New Hampshire, the Japanese gained the southern half of Sakhalin as well as most of the rights that the Russians had enjoyed in southern Manchuria, including the ports of Dalny (Dairen) and Port Arthur and the branch of the Chinese-Eastern Railway between Changchun and Dairen. Moreover, before the end of the war Japan took the unilateral step in Korea to turn it into a protectorate. Not one outside power protested this or the peace settlement. Having consolidated its hold on Korea, extended its sway over south Manchuria, acquired the southern half of Sakhalin, and destroyed the Russian fleet, Japan had, by late 1905, emerged undisputably as a major power, even the key power in Asia. That was the moment of glory the Japanese had dreamed of since the humiliating days half a century earlier.

The glory, however, did not end the quest for great-power status abroad and social order at home that would be commensurate with each other. If anything, a new search began almost instantaneously after the end of the war, a search that in many ways would continue for several more decades. It was symbolic of the uncertain situation that the signing of the Portsmouth treaty should have been the occasion not for jubilation and thanksgiving but for mob attacks on police stations and official residences in Tokyo. The public, whose expectations had been raised by military successes and whose patriotic fervor had added fuel to insular arrogance, expressed their anger at what they viewed as meager fruits of victory. They thought they deserved more than was

52 For a discussion of the economic aspect of the war, see Shimomura Fujio, "Nichi-Ro sensō no seikaku," *Kokusai seiji* 3 (1957): 137–52.

obtained at the peace conference and blamed this on the government and the United States, who had mediated between the two combatants. It was as if domestic order was unraveling at the very moment when it should have been solidified.[53] The state of confusion at the moment of glory was well described by the novelist Tokutomi Roka, who had initially joined his countrymen in calling for a punitive war against Russia but later, before the end of the conflict, turned to pacifism. In a memorable essay written soon afterwards, Roka asserted that Japan's "joining the great powers" had done little to ensure its security or economic interests. These were still dependent on the armed forces, alliances with other powers, and colonial products. Moreover, Japanese victory had aroused the fears of other nations which would try to cope with the new development by augmenting their own military forces. There was also a danger of racial antagonism. Because Japan was the only nonwhite power, its victory might embolden colored races throughout the world and, by the same token, antagonize the white peoples. This would surely lead to a racial conflict. All these problems indicated, he wrote, that the victory over Russia was a hollow one; it was a victory filled with "melancholy." The only solution, according to him, was to end Japan's reliance on military force and to transform the country into one devoted to peace and justice.[54]

Few accepted Roka's pacifism and idealism, but many shared his diagnosis. It is one of the ironies of modern Japanese diplomatic history that at the very moment when the country had gained recognition as a formidable power, its sense of isolation, insecurity, and lack of direction were also enhanced. As Itō wrote in 1907, Japan had never been so isolated in the world.[55] Although in 1905 the British alliance had been renewed and in 1907 a new entente was signed with Russia for maintaining the postwar status quo in Asia, the country was faced with many other problems. The United States, the country that in the late 1890s had expanded into Asia and the Pacific simultaneously with Japan, now posed a challenge because of its naval expansion, its opposition to exclusive rights and interests in Manchuria, and, above all, its hostility toward Japanese immigrants. The immigration crisis arose as a result of the influx of Japanese into California after the turn of the century and particularly after the Russo-Japanese War. In Japanese perception the immigrants were to have been the spearhead of an expanding nation, a bridge between the two countries. But the Ameri-

53 See Shumpei Okamoto, *The Japanese Oligarchy and the Russo-Japanese War* (New York: Columbia University Press, 1970).

54 Akira Iriye, *Nihon no gaikō* (Tokyo: Chūō kōronsha, 1966), pp. 4–5.

55 Ibid., pp. 9–10.

cans rejected such expansionism and began talking of war on racial grounds. Britain, Japan's ally, sided with the United States on this issue. In the meantime, the Koreans, Chinese, and other Asians grew increasingly resentful of Japanese imperialism. Although some of them openly expressed their pleasure at Japan's defeating a Western power, they soon came to view Japanese imperialism as no less evil than the West's. If anything, the sense of injustice was all the greater as they viewed the Japanese as Asians who dared to copy Westerners in subjugating fellow Asians. A nationwide boycott of Japanese goods in China in 1908 and the assassination of Itō Hirobumi by a Korean nationalist in 1909 clearly revealed the kind of trouble that the Japanese now faced in Asia. If they were not accepted in America and were opposed in Asia, where and how could they expand?

That Japan should continue to be an expanding nation was taken for granted by virtually all publicists. Even Tokutomi Roka supported it, but in his case expansion was to be primarily a moral movement, in which Japan took the lead in spreading "justice in the four seas." His brother, Sohō, wrote that Japan's mission lay in promoting the harmony of the white and yellow races as a way to leading mankind to a world of humanism. Less abstract were those like Ozaki Yukio and Kayahara Kazan who exhorted their readers to "venture out to all parts of the world" as emigrants and settlers.[56] Then there were others who thought the time was opportune for undertaking a massive expansion of trade. "Just as England tremendously expanded its foreign trade after the victory over Napoleon," wrote Kaneko Kentarō, who had raised loans in the United States during the war, "so can Japan be expected to take advantage of the new situation to increase trade and promote national strength."[57] Finally, the official policy of "postwar management" referred to extending Japanese influence in Korea and Manchuria politically and economically. As much as ¥200 million was provided as initial capital for the operation of the South Manchuria Railway and its feeder lines. With the railway as the artery in southern Manchuria, private business entered the scene and invested in coal mines, soybean exports, and the importation of textiles. In Korea, in the meantime, Japanese advisers instituted monetary and police reforms; efforts were made to settle Japanese farmers by having crown lands distributed to them; and large numbers of poor merchants and

56 Iriye, *Pacific Estrangement*, p. 100; and Akiya Iriye, "Kayahara Kazan and Japanese Cosmopolitanism," in A. M. Craig and D. H. Shively, eds., *Personality in Japanese History* (Berkeley and Los Angeles: University of California Press, 1970), pp. 373–98.

57 Iriye, *Pacific Estrangement*, p. 128.

laborers from Japan sought quick riches by attaching themselves to the colonial establishment.

The more the Japanese expanded, and the more they talked of further expansion, the greater appeared to be the obstacles in the way. Diplomatic complications, naval rivalries, and racial disputes mounted. These were inevitable by-products of expansionism, but few were willing to question the premise that expansion was vital to the country's development as a modern state. Although the government tried in vain to cope with the mounting crises overseas, it also directed its attention to the domestic base of imperialism. It strengthened martial laws to cope with internal disorder, modernized its armed forces, and extended compulsory education from four to six years, with an emphasis on ethics.[58] But the people were now more politically and socially aroused than before the war, and they were less willing to accept what was given them. Constitutionalism and industrialization, which had earlier provided a focus for national energies, were no longer sufficient as objectives. It was not modernization but the future of a modern society that concerned the public. Patriotism, which had defined its mission as the making of a great power, proved incapable of providing new aims, wrote Ishikawa Takuboku, the poet.[59] Prime Minister Katsura shared the sense of crisis and sought to cope with the situation by having the emperor issue a new rescript in 1908, calling on the people to cooperate with one another, avoid waste, and work hard. This was a stale program, hardly enough to provide a vision of ideal domestic order.

Publicists fared little better. They all accepted the need for solidifying a domestic basis for overseas expansion and exhorted the people to continue to develop commerce and industry. But these were ineffectual ideas in the face of social unrest. Some leaders tried to define the nation's domestic goals by talking of the importance of "creating a new Japanese people," as the Social Education Association, organized in 1906, proclaimed. The new people were to be "a great cosmopolitan people" oriented toward peace and humanism. By molding themselves into such a people, they would contribute to both internal and international peace. The association typified these postwar concerns by stressing education and social harmony as means for avoiding a serious crisis in Japan's domestic and foreign affairs. These were to be made symbiotic so that domestic order would approximate, as well as contribute to, international order. As Takada Sanae, a famous economist and a founder of the association, remarked, the Japanese must cultivate "a

58 The best recent treatment of postwar state control is by Ōe Shinobu, *Nichi-Ro sensō no gunjishiteki kenkyū* (Tokyo: Iwanami shoten, 1976). 59 Sumiya, *Dai Nihon*, p. 344.

talent for engaging in worldwide activities through harmonizing international and national tendencies."[60] This was a plausible argument, anticipating the internationalism of the 1920s. But it had little specific to offer for coping with domestic problems. Education, designed to make the Japanese more cosmopolitan and tolerant, was about the only specific program that Takada and others like him could propose. Even then, there was no assurance that a more educated populace might not begin to question the basic premises of the Japanese state or that the intellectuals might not turn inward, aloof from the mundane concerns of society. In the meantime, cosmopolitanism was not yet effective enough to enable the nation to understand, let alone cope with, the issues of racial prejudice in the West or of antiimperialist movements in Asia – the twin challenge that was to baffle the Japanese for many more decades.

The Meiji era ended in uncertainty, in both its external relations and its internal affairs. The last years of the Meiji emperor (1910–12) saw the formal annexation of Korea as a colony, another renewal of the British alliance, and the signing of commercial treaties with the United States and Britain, providing for Japan's tariff autonomy for the first time. These were achievements in line with the country's great-power status. The period also coincided with revolutionary movements within China, culminating in the overthrow of the Manchu dynasty in 1912, and nationalistic upheavals in the Balkans that threatened the stability of empires in Europe and the Middle East. Unbeknownst to all but a handful of the most prescient, the great powers were fast sliding into a state of confrontation from which there could be no escape but war. All that the Western states, and Japan, had accomplished in the preceding half-century would go up in smoke in a fierce struggle for no other cause than power, prestige, and patriotism. The Great War was a failure of the modern states to define a viable world order, and it also demonstrated how fiercely and blindly the central authorities and the people in these states would concentrate their resources in order to destroy one another.

Japan was spared much of this destruction. Instead, it even took advantage of the European conflict to extend its hold on the Asian continent. By so doing, it ran headlong into antiimperialism in China and Korea, a clear manifestation of mass nationalism that became the basis for their own eventual emergence as modern states. In the meantime, the Japanese people began to question the national objectives

60 Iriye, *Pacific Estrangement*, p. 127.

and domestic arrangements that had been defined for them as part of the nation's growth as a modern state. They stressed other themes and looked for an alternative order at home. In so doing, they created a cleavage in their midst, between those oriented toward change and those entrenched in the existing order. The struggle did not end until after another major war.

Japan's drive to great-power status during the Meiji era, then, was one device by which the nation's leaders sought to establish a connection between domestic and external relations. Political and economic change at home, and the assertion of power and influence abroad, reinforced each other so that within forty-odd years after the Meiji Restoration, the nation was a modern state and an imperialist power. Like other countries, the Japanese accepted the two as interdependent, as two sides of the same coin. Only a small number questioned the equation, and the majority of Japan's leaders and public opinion assumed that all viable modern states were also imperialist. It would be left to a future generation to recognize that this was not necessarily so and that the nation need not be militaristic or imperialistic in order to undertake domestic modernization.

BIBLIOGRAPHY

Akita, George. *Foundations of Constitutional Government in Modern Japan: 1868–1900*. Cambridge, Mass.: Harvard University Press, 1967.

Amino Yoshihiko. *Muen, kugai, raku*. Tokyo: Heibonsha, 1978. 網野善彦, 無縁苦界・楽, 平凡社

Aoki Kōji. *Meiji nōmin sōjō no nenjiteki kenkyū*. Tokyo: Shinseisha, 1967. 青木虹二, 明治農民騒擾の年次的研究, 新生社

Aoki Kōji. *Hyakushō ikki sōgō nempyō*. Tokyo: San'ichi shobō, 1971. 青木虹二, 百姓一揆総合年表, 三一書房

Aoki Michio. *Tempō sōdōki*. Tokyo: Sanseidō, 1979. 青木美智男, 天保騒動記, 三省堂

Arakawa Hidetoshi, "Kinsei no kikin" *Rekishi kōron* 8 (1976): 32–49 荒川秀俊, 近世の飢饉, 歴史公論

Araki Seishi. *Shimpūren jikki*. Tokyo: Daiichi shuppan kyōai, 1971. 荒木精之, 神風連実記, 第一出版協会

Arima Seiho. *Takashima Shūhan*. Tokyo: Yoshikawa kōbunkan, 1958. 有馬成甫, 高島秋帆, 吉川弘文館

Akimoto Masao. *Chiso kaisei to nōmin tōsō*. Tokyo: Shinseisha, 1968. 有元正雄, 地租改正と農民闘争, 新生社

Asao Naohiro. "Shōgun seiji no kenryoku kōzō." In *Iwanami kōza Nihon rekishi*. 岩波講座日本歴史 Vol. 10 (*kinsei* 2), 1975. 朝尾直弘, 将軍政治の権力構造

Asao, Naohiro, with Marius B. Jansen. "Shogun and Tennō." In John W. Hall et al., eds. *Japan Before Tokugawa*. Princeton, N.J.: Princeton University Press, 1980.

Bakhtin, M. M. *The Dialectic Imagination*, Trans. and ed. Michael Holquist and Caryl Emerson. Austin: University of Texas Press, 1982.

Banno, Masataka. *China and the West: 1858–1861, the Origins of the Tsungli Yamen*. Cambridge, Mass.: Harvard University Press, 1964.

Beasley, W. G. *Great Britain and the Opening of Japan 1834–1858*. London: Luzac, 1951.

Beasley, W. G. *Select Documents on Japanese Foreign Policy 1853–1868*. London: Oxford University Press, 1955.

Beasley, W. G. *The Meiji Restoration*. Stanford, Calif.: Stanford University Press, 1972.

Bitō Masahide. "Mito no tokushitsu." In Imai Usaburō, Seya Yoshihiko, and Bitō Masahide, eds. *Mitogaku*. Vol. 53 of *Nihon shisō taikei*. Tokyo: Iwanami shoten, 1973. 尾藤正英, 水戸の特質, 今井宇三郎, 瀬谷義彦, 尾藤正英編, 水戸学, 日本思想大系, 岩波書店

Bitō Masahide. "Sonnō-jōi shisō." *Iwanami kōza Nihon rekishi*. Vol. 13 (*kinsei* 5), 1977. 尾藤正英, 尊王攘夷思想

Bitō Masahide. "Bushi and the Meiji Restoration." *Acta Asiatica* 49 (1985): 78–96.

Blacker, Carmen. "Millenarian Aspects of the New Religions." In Shively, ed. *Tradition and Modernization in Japanese Culture*.

Bolitho, Harold. *Treasures Among Men: The Fudai Daimyo in Tokugawa Japan*. New Haven, Conn.: Yale University Press, 1974.

Bowen, Roger W. *Rebellion and Democracy in Meiji Japan*. Berkeley and Los Angeles: University of California Press, 1980.

Buyō Inshi. "Seji kemmonroku." In *Nihon shomin seikatsu shiryō shūsei*. Vol. 8. Tokyo: Misuzu shobō, 1969. 武陽隠士, 世事見聞録, 日本庶民生活史料集成, みすず書房

Catoriadis, Corneilus. *L'Institution imaginaire de la société*. Paris, Seuil. 1975.

Conroy, Hilary. *The Japanese Seizure of Korea: 1868–1910*. Philadelphia: University of Pennsylvania Press, 1960.

Cosmas, Graham. *An Army for Empire: The United States Army in the Spanish-American War*. Columbus, Mo.: University of Missouri Press, 1971.

Craig, Albert M. *Chōshū in the Meiji Restoration*. Cambridge, Mass.: Harvard University Press, 1961.

Craig, Albert M. "The Restoration Movement in Chōshū." In Hall and Jansen, eds. *Studies in the Institutional History of Early Modern Japan*.

Craig, Albert M. "The Central Government." In Jansen and Rozman, eds. *Japan in Transition*.

Craig, Albert M., and Donald Shively, eds. *Personality in Japanese History*. Berkeley and Los Angleles: University of California Press, 1970.

Duus, Peter. "Whig History, Japanese Style: The Min'yūsha Historians and the Meiji Restoration." *Journal of Asian Studies* 33 (May 1974): 415–36.

Ericson, Mark David. "The Tokugawa *Bakufu* and Leon Roches." Ph.D. diss., University of Hawaii, 1978.

Etō, Shinkichi, and Marius B. Jansen, trans. *My Thirty-Three Years' Dream: The Autobiography of Miyazaki Tōten*. Princeton, N.J.: Princeton University Press, 1982.

Frank, A. G. *Latin America: Underdevelopment or Revolution*. New York, Monthly Review Press, 1970.

Frost, Peter. *The Bakumatsu Currency Crisis*. Harvard East Asian monographs, no. 36. Cambridge, Mass.: Harvard University Press, 1970.

Fujikawa Yū. *Nihon shippei shi*. Tokyo: Heibonsha, 1969. 富士川游, 日本疾病史, 平凡社

Fujitani Toshio. "*Okagemairi*" *to* "*eejanaika*." Tokyo: Iwanami shoten shinsho edition, 1968. 藤谷俊雄,「おかげまいり」と「ええじゃないか」, 岩波書店

Fukushima Masao. *Chiso kaisei*. Tokyo: Yoshikawa kōbunkan, 1968. 福島正夫, 地租改正, 吉川弘文館

Furushima Toshio. "Bakufu zaisei shūnyū no dōkō to nōmin shūdatsu no kakki." In Furushima, ed. *Nihon keizaishi taikei*, vol. 6, 1973. 古島敏雄, "幕府財政収入の動向と農民収奪の画期", 日本経済史大系

Furushima Toshio, ed. *Nihon keizaishi taikei*. 6 vols. Tokyo: Tokyo daigaku shuppankai, 1973. 古島敏雄編, 日本経済史大系, 東京大学出版会

Gaimushō, ed. *Nihon gaikō bunsho*. Over 151 vols., reaching the year 1926 in 1986. 外務省編, 日本外交文書

Gluck, Carol. "The People in History: Recent Trends in Japanese Historiography." *Journal of Asian Studies* 38 (November 1978): 25–50.

Gluck, Carol. *Japan's Modern Myths: Ideology in the Late Meiji Period*. Princeton, N.J.: Princeton University Press, 1985.

Gotō Yasushi, *Jiyū minken undō*. Osaka. Sōgensha, 1958. 後藤靖, 自由民権運動

Gotō Yasushi. "Meiji jūshichinen no gekka shojiken ni tsuite." In Horie Eichi and Tōyama Shigeki, eds. *Jiyū minken ki no kenkyū: minken undō no gekka to kaitai*. Vol. 2. Tokyo: Yūhikaku, 1959. 後藤靖, 明治十七年の激化諸事件に付いて, 堀江英一, 遠山茂樹編, 自由民権期の研究：民権運動の激化と解体, 有斐閣

Gotō Yasushi. "Chiso kaisei hantai ikki." *Ritsumeikan keizai gaku* 9 (April 1960): 109–52. 後藤靖, 地租改正反対一揆, 立命館経済学

Gotō Yasushi. *Shizoku hanran no kenkyū*. Tokyo: Aoki shoten, 1967. 後藤靖, 士族反乱の研究, 青木書店

Gotō Yasushi. *Jiyū minken: Meiji no kakumei to hankakumei*. Tokyo: Chūō kōronsha, 1972. 後藤靖, 自由民権：明治の革命と反革命, 中央公論社

Hackett, Roger F. *Yamagata Aritomo in the Rise of Modern Japan: 1838–1922*. Cambridge, Mass.: Harvard University Press, 1971.

Haga Noboru, "Bakumatsu henkakuki ni okeru kokugakusha no undō to ronri." In Haga Noboru and Matsumoto Sannosuke, eds. *Nihon shisō taikei*. Vol. 51, *Kokugaku undō no shisō*. Tokyo: Iwanami shoten, 1971. 芳賀登, 幕末変革期における国学者の運動と論理, 芳賀登・松本三之介編, 国学運動の思想, 日本思想大系, 岩波書店

Haga Noboru. "Edo no bunka." In Hayashiya, ed. *Kasei bunka no kenkyū*. 芳賀登, 江戸の文化, 林屋編, 化政文化の研究

Hall, John W. "Changing Conceptions of the Modernization of Japan." In Jansen, ed. *Changing Japanese Attitudes Toward Modernization*.

Hall, John W. *Tanuma Okitsugu (1719–1788): Forerunner of Modern Japan*. Cambridge, Mass.: Harvard University Press, 1955.

Hall, John W., and Marius B. Jansen, eds. *Studies in the Institutional History of Early Modern Japan*. Princeton, N.J.: Princeton University Press, 1968.

Hanabusa Nagamichi. *Meiji gaikō shi*. Tokyo: Shibundō, 1960. 英修道, 明治外交史, 至文堂

Hanley, Susan B., and Kozo Yamamura. *Economic and Demographic Change in*

Preindustrial Japan, 1600–1868. Princeton, N.J.: Princeton University Press, 1977.

Hardacre, Helen. *Kurozumikyō and the New Religions of Japan*. Princeton, N.J.: Princeton University Press, 1986.

Harootunian, H. D. "Ideology As Conflict." In Tetsuo Najita and J. Victor Koschmann, eds. *Conflict in Modern Japanese History*. Princeton, N.J.: Princeton University Press, 1982.

Harootunian, H. D. *Things Seen and Unseen: Discourse and Ideology in Tokugawa Nativism*. Chicago: University of Chicago Press, 1988.

Harootunian, H. D. *Toward Restoration*. Berkeley and Los Angeles: University of California Press, 1970.

Hattori Shisō. *Kindai Nihon gaikō shi*. Tokyo: Kawade shobō, 1954. 服部之総, 近代日本外交史, 河出書房

Hauser, William B. *Economic Institutional Change in Tokugawa Japan: Osaka and the Kinai Cotton Trade*. Cambridge, England: Cambridge University Press, 1974.

Hayashiya Tatsusaburō, ed. *Kasei bunka no kenkyū*. Tokyo: Iwanami shoten, 1976. 林屋辰三郎編, 化政文化の研究, 岩波書店

Hayashiya Tatsusaburō, ed. *Bakumatsu bunka no kenkyū*. Tokyo: Iwanami shoten, 1978. 林屋辰三郎編, 幕末文化の研究, 岩波書店

Hibbett, Howard. *The Floating World in Japanese Fiction*. London: Oxford University Press, 1959.

Hiraishi Naoaki. "Kaiho Seiryō no shisōzō." *Shisō* 677 (November 1980): 46–68. 平石直昭, 海保青陵の思想像, 思想

Hirata Atsutane zenshū kankōkai, eds. *Shinshū Hirata Atsutane zenshū*. 15 vols. Tokyo: Meicho shuppan, 1976–80. 平田篤胤全集刊行会編, 新修平田篤胤全集, 名著出版

Hirosue Tamotsu, ed. *Origuchi Shinobu shū*. Tokyo: Chikuma shobō, 1975. 広末保編, 折口信夫集, 筑摩書房

Hōseishi gakkai, eds. *Tokugawa kinreikō*. 11 vols. Tokyo: Sōbunsha, 1958–61. 法制史学会編, 徳川禁令考, 創文社

Hoston, Germain A. *Marxism and the Crisis of Development in Prewar Japan*. Princeton, N.J.: Princeton University Press, 1986.

Hsü Shih-k'ai. *Nihon tōchika no Taiwan*. Tokyo: Tokyo daigaku shuppankai, 1972. 許世楷, 日本統治下の台湾, 東京大学出版会

Hsu, Immanuel C. Y. *China's Entrance into the Family of Nations: The Diplomatic Phase, 1858–1880*. Cambridge, Mass.: Harvard University Press, 1968.

Huber, Thomas M. *The Revolutionary Origins of Modern Japan*. Stanford, Calif.: Stanford University Press, 1981.

Huffman, James L. *Fukuchi Gen'ichirō*. Honolulu: University of Hawaii Press, 1979.

Hung Chao-t'ang. *Taiwan minshukoku no kenkyū*. Tokyo: Tokyo daigaku shuppankai, 1970. 黄昭堂, 台湾民主国の研究, 東京大学出版会

Ike, Nobutaka. *The Beginnings of Political Democracy in Japan*. Baltimore: Johns Hopkins University Press, 1950.

Ikeda Yoshimasa. "Bakufu shohan no dōyō to kaikaku." In *Iwanami kōza Nihon rekishi*. Vol. 13 (*kinsei* 5), 1977. 池田荀正, 幕府諸藩の動揺と改革

Imaizumi Takujiro, comp. *Essa sōsho*. 19 vols. Sanjō: Yashima shuppan, 1932–. 今泉鐸次郎編, 越佐叢書, 三条：野島出版

Inoue Kiyoshi. *Jōyaku kaisei*. Tokyo: Iwanami shoten, 1955. 井上清, 条約改正, 岩波書店

Inoue Kiyoshi. *Nihon gendaishi*. Tokyo: Tokyo daigaku shuppankai, 1967. 井上清, 日本現代史, 東京大学出版会

Inoue Kōji. *Chichibu jiken*. Tokyo: Chūō kōronsha, 1968. 井上幸治, 秩父事件, 中央公論社

Inui Hiromi and Inoue Katsuo. "Chōshū han to Mito han." In *Iwanami kōza Nihon rekishi*. Vol. 12 (*kinsei* 4), 1976. 乾宏巳, 井上勝生, 長州藩と水戸藩

Iriye Akira. *Nihon no gaikō*. Tokyo: Chūō kōronsha, 1966. 入江昭, 日本の外交, 中央公論社

Iriye, Akira. "Kayahara Kazan and Japanese Cosmopolitanism." In Albert Craig and Donald Shively, eds., *Personality in Japanese History*. Berkeley and Los Angeles: University of California Press, 1970.

Iriye, Akira. *Pacific Estrangement: Japanese and American Expansion, 1897–1911*. Cambridge, Mass.: Harvard University Press, 1972.

Irokawa Daikichi. "Konmintō to Jiyūtō." *Rekishigaku kenkyū* 247 (November 1960): 1–30. 色川大吉, 困民党と自由党, 歴史学研究

Irokawa Daikichi. *Kindai kokka no shuppatsu*. Vol. 25 of *Nihon no rekishi*. Tokyo: Chūō kōronsha, 1966. 色川大吉, 近代国家の出発, 中央公論社

Irokawa Daikichi. *Meiji no bunka*. Tokyo: Iwanami shoten, 1970. 色川大吉, 明治の文化, 岩波書店

Irokawa, Daikichi. *The Culture of the Meiji Period*. Princeton, N.J.: Princeton University Press, 1985.

Ishii Takashi. *Bakumatsu bōekishi no kenkyū*. Tokyo: Nihon hyōronsha, 1944. 石井孝, 幕末貿易史の研究, 日本評論社

Ishii Takashi. *Gakusetsu hihan: Meiji ishin ron*. Tokyo: Yoshikawa kōbunkan, 1968. 石井孝, 学説批判：明治維新論, 吉川弘文館

Ishikawa Jun. *Watanabe Kazan*. Tokyo: Chikuma shobō, 1964. 石川淳, 渡辺崋山, 筑摩書房

Itō Shirō. *Suzuki Masayuki no kenkyū*. Tokyo: Aoki shoten, 1972. 伊藤至郎, 鈴木雅之の研究, 青木書店

Jameson, Frederic. *Marxism and Form*. Princeton, N.J.: Princeton University Press, 1971.

Jansen, Marius B. "Oi Kentarō: Radicalism and Chauvinism." *Far Eastern Quarterly* 11 (May 1952): 305–16.

Jansen, Marius B. *The Japanese and Sun Yat-sen*. Cambridge, Mass.: Harvard University Press, 1954.

Jansen, Marius B. *Sakamoto Ryōma and the Meiji Restoration*. Princeton, N.J.:

Princeton University Press, 1961.

Jansen, Marius B., ed. *Changing Japanese Attitudes Toward Modernization*. Princeton, N.J.: Princeton University Press, 1965.

Jansen, Marius B. "Tosa During the Last Century of Tokugawa Rule." In Hall and Jansen, eds. *Studies in the Institutional History of Early Modern Japan*. Princeton, N.J.: Princeton University Press, 1968.

Jansen, Marius B. *Japan and China: From War to Peace, 1894–1972*. Chicago: Rand McNally, 1975.

Jansen, Marius B. "Japanese Imperialism: Late Meiji Perspectives." In Ramon H. Myers and Mark R. Peattie, eds. *The Japanese Colonial Empire, 1895–1945*. Princeton, N.J.: Princeton University Press, 1984.

Jansen, Marius B. "Rangaku and Westernization." *Modern Asian Studies* 18 (October 1984): 541–53.

Jansen, Marius B., and Gilbert Rozman, eds. *Japan in Transition: From Tokugawa to Meiji*. Princeton, N.J.: Princeton University Press, 1986.

Kaiser, David E. *Economic Diplomacy and the Origins of the Second World War*. Princeton, N.J.: Princeton University Press, 1980.

Kajima Morinosuke. *Nihon gaikō shi*. 34 vols. Kajima heiwa kenkyūjo. Tokyo: Kajima kenkyūjo shuppankai, 1970–3. 鹿島守之助, 日本外交史, 鹿島平和研究所

Kajima, Morinosuke. *The Diplomacy of Japan*, 1894–1922. 3 vols. Tokyo: Kajima Institute of International Peace, 1976–80.

Kano Masanao. *Shihonshugi keiseiki no chitsujo ishiki*. Tokyo: Chikuma shobō, 1969. 鹿野政直, 資本主義形成期の秩序意識, 筑摩書房

Kawaji Toshiakira. *Shimane no susami*. Tokyo: Heibonsha, 1973. 川路聖謨, 島根のすさみ, 平凡社

Keene, Donald. *The Japanese Discovery of Europe, 1720–1820*. Stanford, Calif.: Stanford University Press, 1969.

Kim, Key-Hiuk. *The Last Phase of the East Asian World Order: Korea, Japan, and the Chinese Empire, 1860–1882*. Berkeley and Los Angeles: University of California Press, 1980.

Kitajima Masamoto. *Bakuhansei no kumon*. Vol. 18 of *Nihon no rekishi*. Tokyo: Chūō kōronsha, 1967. 北島正元, 幕藩制の苦悶, 日本の歴史, 中央公論社

Kitajima Masamoto. *Mizuno Tadakuni*. Tokyo: Yoshikawa kōbunkan, 1969. 北島正元, 水野忠邦, 吉川弘文館

Kiyooka, Eiichi, trans. *The Autobiography of Fukuzawa Yukichi*. Tokyo: Hokuseidō Press, 1948.

Kodama Kōta, ed. *Ninomiya Sontoku*. Vol. 26 of *Nihon no meicho*. Tokyo: Chūō kōronsha, 1970. 児玉幸多編, 二宮尊徳, 日本の名著, 中央公論社

Koga-shi shi hensan iinkai, ed. *Koga-shi shi: shiryō kinseihen (hansei)*. Koga, 1979. 古河市史編纂委員会編, 古河市史, 史料近世編 (藩政), 古河

Konishi Shigenao. *Hirose Tansō*. Tokyo: Bunkyō shoin, 1943. 小西重直, 広瀬淡窓, 文教書院

Koschmann, J. Victor. "Discourse in Action: Representational Politics in the

Late Tokugawa Period." Ph.D diss., University of Chicago, 1980.

Koschmann, J. Victor. *The Mito Ideology: Discourse, Reform, and Insurrection in late Tokugawa Japan, 1790–1864*. Berkeley and Los Angeles: University of California Press, 1987.

Kuroita Katsumi, ed. *Zoku Tokugawa jikki*. In *Kokushi taikei*. Vol. 49. Tokyo: Yoshikawa kōbunkan, 1966. 黒板勝美編, 続徳川実記, 国史大系, 吉川弘文館

Landes, David. "Some Thoughts on the Nature of Economic Imperialism." *Journal of Economic History* 21 (1961).

LeFort, Claude. *Les Formes de l'histoire: Essais d'anthropologie politique*. Paris, Gallimard, 1978.

McLaren, Walter W., ed. "Japanese Government documents, 1867–1889." *Transactions of the Asiatic Society of Japan* 42 (1914): pt. 1.

McMaster, John. "The Japanese Gold Rush of 1859." *Journal of Asian Studies* 19 (May 1960): 273–88.

Maeda Ichirō, ed. *Kōza Nihon bunkashi*. Vol. 6. Tokyo: San'ichi shobō, 1963. 前田一良編, 講座日本文化史, 三一書房

Magdoff, Harry. *The Age of Imperialism: The Economics of U.S. Foreign Policy*. New York, Monthly Review Press, 1969.

Maruyama Masao. *Nihon seiji shisōshi kenkyū*. Tokyo: Tokyo daigaku shuppankai, 1953. 丸山真男, 日本政治思想史研究, 東京大学出版会

Maruyama Masao. "Chūsei to hangyaku." In *Kindai Nihon shisōshi kōza*. 8 vols. Tokyo: Chikuma shobō, 1960. 丸山真男, 忠誠と反逆, 近代日本思想史講座, 筑摩書房

Maruyama, Masao. *Studies in the Intellectual History of Tokugawa Japan*. Translated by Mikiso Hane. Princeton, N.J.: Princeton University Press, 1974.

Masumi Junnosuke. *Nihon seitō shi ron*. 7 vols. Tokyo: Tokyo daigaku shuppankai, 1965–80. 升味準之輔, 日本政党史論, 東京大学出版会

Matsumoto Sannosuke. *Kokugaku seiji shisō no kenkyū*. Tokyo: Yūhikaku, 1957. 松本三之介, 国学政治思想の研究, 有斐閣

Matsumoto Sannosuke. *Tennōsei kokka to seiji shisō*. Tokyo: Miraisha, 1969. 松本三之介, 天皇制国家と政治思想, 未来社

Matsuzaki Kōdō. *Kōdō nichireki*. In Tōyō bunko series. 6 vols. Tokyo: Heibonsha, 1970–83. 松崎慊堂, 慊堂日暦, 東洋文庫, 平凡社

Mayer, Arno J. *Dynamics of Counter Revolution in Europe, 1870–1956*. New York, Harper & Row, 1971.

Mayo, Marlene. "The Western Education of Kume Kunitake 1871–1876." *Monumenta Nipponica* 28 (1973): 3–68.

Medzini, Meron. *French Policy in Japan During the Closing Years of the Tokugawa Regime*. Cambridge, Mass.: Harvard University Press, 1971.

Mito-han shiryō. 5 vols. Tokyo: Yoshikawa kōbunkan, 1970. 水戸藩史料, 吉川弘文館

Miyagi-chō shi, shiryōhen. Sendai: Miyagi-ken Miyagi-chō, 1967. 宮城町史, 史料編, 仙台, 宮城県宮城町

Miyamoto Chū. *Sakuma Shōzan*. Tokyo: Iwanami shoten, 1932. 宮本仲, 佐久間

象山, 岩波書店

Miyamoto Mataji, ed. *Han shakai no kenkyū*. Kyoto: Mineruva shobō, 1972. 宮本又次編, 藩社会の研究, ミネルヴァ書房

Miyao Sadao. "Minka yōjutsu." In *Kinsei jikata keizai shiryō*. Vol. 5. Tokyo: Yoshikawa kōbunkan, 1954. 宮負定雄, 民家要術, 近世地方経済史料, 吉川弘文館

Miyata Noboru. "Nōson no fukkō undō to minshū shūkyō no tenkai." In *Iwanami kōza Nihon rekishi*. Vol. 13 (*kinsei* 5), 1977. 宮田登, 農村の復興運動と民衆宗教の展開

Mizuno Tadashi. *Edo shōsetsu ronsō*. Tokyo: Chūō kōronsha, 1974. 水野稔, 江戸小説論叢, 中央公論社

Mommsen, Wolfgang. *Theories of Imperialism*. New York: Random House, 1980.

Moriyama Gunjirō. *Minshū hōki to matsuri*. Tokyo: chikuma shobō, 1981. 森山軍治郎, 民衆蜂起と祭り, 筑摩書房

Morris, Ivan. *The Nobility of Failure: Tragic Heroes in the History of Japan*. New York: Holt, Rinehart and Winston, 1975.

Mounsey, August H. *The Satsuma Rebellion*. London: Murray, 1879. Reprinted by University Publications of America, Washington, D.C., 1979.

Murakami Shigeyoshi. *Kinsei minshū shūkyō no kenkyū*. Tokyo: Hōzōkan, 1977. 村上重良, 近世民衆宗教の研究, 法蔵館

Murakami Shigeyoshi and Yasumaru Yoshio, eds. *Nihon shisō taikei*. Vol. 67, *Minshū shūkyō to shisō*. Tokyo: Iwanami shoten, 1971. 村上重良, 安丸良夫編, 民衆宗教と思想, 日本思想大系, 岩波書店

Muromatsu Iwao, ed. *Hirata Atsutane zenshū*. 15 vols. Tokyo: Ichidō, Hirata gakkai, 1911–18. 室松岩雄編, 平田篤胤全集, 一致堂, 平田学会

Mutobe Yoshika. "Ken-yūjun kōron." In Nakajima Hiromitsu, ed. *Shintō sōsho*. Vol. 3. October 1897. 亡人部是香, 顯幽順考論, 中島博光編, 神道叢書

Nagahara Keiji. *Rekishigaku josetsu*. Tokyo: Tokyo daigaku shuppankai, 1978. 永原慶二, 歴史学叙説, 東京大学出版会

Nagahara Keiji. "Zenkindai no tennō." *Rekishigaku kenkyū* 467 (April 1979): 37–34. 永原慶二, "前近代の天皇", 歴史学研究

Nagai Hideo. *Jiyū minken*, Vol. 25 of *Nihon no rekishi*. Tokyo: Shōgakkan, 1976. 永井英夫, 自由民権, 日本の歴史, 小学館

Nagai Shōzō, ed., Nichi-bei bunka kōshō shi: Ijū hen. Tokyo. Yōyōsha, 1955. 永井松三, 日米文化交渉史, 移住編, 洋々社

Naitō Chisō. *Tokugawa jūgodaishi*. 6 vols. Tokyo: Shin jimbutsu ōraisha, 1969. 内藤耻叟, 徳川十五代史, 新人物往来社

Najita Tetsuo. "Ōshio Heihachirō (1793–1837)." In Craig and Shively, eds. *Personality in Japanese History*.

Najita Tetsuo. "Structure and Content in Tokugawa Thinking." Unpublished manuscript.

Nakajima Ichisaburō. *Hirose Tansō no kenkyū*. Tokyo: Dai-ichi shuppan kyōkai, 1943. 中島市三郎, 広瀬淡窓の研究, 第一出版協会

Nakamura Tetsu. "Kaikokugo no bōeki to sekai shijō." In *Iwanami kōza Nihon rekishi*. Vol. 13 (*kinsei* 5), 1977. 中村哲, 開国後の貿易と世界市場

Nakamura Yukihiko. *Gesakuron*. Tokyo: Kadokawa, 1966. 中村幸彦, 戯作論, 角川書店

Nakamura Yukihiko and Nishiyama Matsunosuke, eds. *Bunka ryōran*. Vol. 8 of *Nihon bungaku no rekishi*. Tokyo: Kadokawa, 1967. 中村幸彦, 西山松之助編, 文化繚乱, 日本文学の歴史, 角川書店

Nakamura, James. *Agricultural Production and the Economic Development of Japan 1873–1922*. Princeton, N.J.: Princeton University Press, 1966.

Naramoto Tatsuya. *Nihon kinsei no shisō to bunka*. Tokyo: Iwanami shoten, 1978. 奈良本辰也, 日本近世の思想と文化, 岩波書店

Nish, Ian. *The Anglo-Japanese Alliance: The diplomacy of Two Island Empires 1894–1907*. London: Athlone, 1966.

Nish, Ian. *The Origins of the Russo-Japanese War*. London: Longman Group, 1985.

Niwa Kunio. "Chiso kaisei to chitsuroku shobun." In *Iwanami kōza Nihon rekishi*. Vol. 15 (*kindai* 2), 1963. 丹羽邦男, 地租改正と秩禄処分

Niwa Kunio. "Chiso kaisei." In Nihon rekishi gakkai, ed. *Nihonshi no mondai ten*. Tokyo: Yoshikawa kōbunkan, 1965. 丹羽邦男, 地租改正, 日本歴史学会編, 日本史の問題点

Nomura Denshirō, ed. *Ōkuni Takamasa zenshū*. 7 vols. Tokyo: Yukōsha, 1937–9. 野村傳四郎編, 大國隆正全集, 有光社

Norman, E. H. *Japan's Emergence As a Modern State: Political and Economic Problems of the Meiji Period*. New York: Institute of Pacific Relations, 1940 and later printings.

Notehelfer, F. G. *Kōtoku Shūsui: Portrait of a Japanese Radical*. Cambridge, England: Cambridge University Press, 1971.

Notehelfer, F. G. *American Samurai: Captain L. L. Janes and Japan*. Princeton, N.J.: Princeton University Press, 1985.

Numata, Jiro. "Shigeno Yasutsugu and the Modern Tokyo Tradition of historical Writing." In Beasley and Pulleybank, eds. *Historians of China and Japan*.

Numata Jirō, et al. *Yōgaku (I)*. In *Nihon shisō taikei*. Vol. 64. Tokyo: Iwanami stoten, 1976. 沼田次郎等編, 洋学 (上), 日本思想大系, 岩波書店

Ōba Osamu. *Edo jidai ni okeru Chūgoku bunka juyō no kenkyū*. Tokyo: Dōhōsha, 1984. 大庭修, 江戸時代における中国文化受容の研究, 同朋社

Ōe Shinobu. *Nichi-Ro sensō no gunjishiteki kenkyū*. Tokyo: Iwanami shoten, 1976. 大江志乃夫, 日露戦争の軍事史的研究, 岩波書店

Ōguchi Yūjirō. "Tempō-ki no seikaku." In *Iwanami kōza Nihon rekishi*. Vol. 12 (*kinsei* 4), 1976. 大口勇次郎, 天保期の性格

Oh, Bonnie B. "Sino-Japanese Rivalry in Korea, 1876–1885." In Iriye, ed. *The Chinese and the Japanese: Essays in Political and Cultural interactions*.

Okamoto Ryōichi. "Tempō kaikaku." In *Iwanami kōza Nihon rekishi*. Vol. 13 (*kinsei* 5), 1963. 岡本良一, 天保改革

Okamoto, Shumpei. *The Japanese Oligarchy and the Russo-Japanese War*. New

York: Columbia University Press, 1970.

Ōkubo Toshiaki, ed. *Meiji ishin to Kyūshū*. Tokyo: Heibonsha, 1968. 大久保利謙, 明治維新と九州, 平凡社

Ono Masao. "Kaikoku." In *Iwanami kōza Nihon rekishi*. Vol. 13 (*kinsei* 5), 1977. 小野正雄, 開国

Onodera Toshiya. " 'Zannen san' kō: Bakumatsu Kinai no ichi minshū undō o megutte." *Chiiki shi kenkyū* 2 (June 1972): 47–67. 小野寺逸也, "残念さん" 考：幕末畿内の一民衆運動を巡って, 地域史研究

Osaka-shi sanjikai, ed. *Osaka-shi shi*. 7 vols. Osaka: Osaka shiyakusho, 1911–15. 大阪市参事会編, 大阪市史, 大阪市役所

Rekishigaku kenkyūkai, eds. *Meiji ishinshi kenkyū kōza*. 7 vols. Tokyo: Heibonsha, 1968. 歴史学研究会編, 明治維新史研究講座, 平凡社

Sagara Tōru, ed. *Hirata Atsutane*. Vol. 24 of *Nihon no meicho*. Tokyo: Chūō kōronsha, 1972. 相良亨編, 平田篤胤, 日本の名著, 中央公論社

Saitō Gesshin. *Bukō nempyō*. 2 vols. Tokyo: Heibonsha, 1968. 斉藤月岑, 武江年表, 平凡社

Saitō Shōichi. *Ōyama-chō shi*. Tsuruoka: Ōyama-chō shi kankō iinkai, 1969. 斎藤正一, 大山町史, 鶴岡：大山町史刊行委員会

Sakai, Robert. "Feudal Society and Modern Leadership in Satsuma han." *Journal of Asian Studies* 16 (May 1957): 367–76.

Sakata Yoshio. *Meiji ishin shi*. Tokyo: Miraisha, 1960. 坂田吉雄, 明治維新史, 未来社

Sakata, Yoshio, and John W. Hall. "The Motivation of Political Leadership in the Meiji Restoration." *Journal of Asian Studies* 16 (November 1956): 31–50.

Sakeda Masatoshi. *Kindai Nihon ni okeru taigai kō undō no kenkyū*. Tokyo: Tokyo daigaku shuppankai, 1978. 酒田正敏, 近代日本における対外硬運動の研究, 東京大学出版会

Sasaki Junnosuke. "Bakumatsu no shakai jōsei to yonaoshi." In *Iwanami kōza Nihon rekishi*. Vol. 13 (*kinsei* 5), 1977. 佐々木潤之介, 幕末の社会情勢と世直し

Satō Shōsuke. *Yōgakushi no kenkyū*. Tokyo: Chūō kōronsha, 1980. 佐藤昌介, 洋学史の研究, 中央公論社

Satō Shōsuke et al. *Watanabe Kazan / Takano Chōei / Sakuma Shōzan / Yokoi Shōnan / Hashimoto Sanai*. In *Nihon shisō taikei*. Vol. 55. Tokyo: Iwanami shoten, 1977. 佐藤昌介等, 渡辺華山, 高野長英, 佐久間象山, 横井小楠, 橋本左内, 日本思想大系, 岩波書店

Scheiner, Irwin. "Benevolent Lords and Honorable Peasants." In Najita and Scheiner, eds. *Japanese Thought in the Tokugawa Period*.

Semmel, Bernard. *Imperialism and Social Reform: English Social Imperial Thought, 1895–1914*. London. England: Allen & Unwin, 1960.

Seto Mikio. "Minshū no shūkyō ishiki to henkaku no enerugii." In Maruyama Teruo, ed. *Henkakuki no shūkyō*. Tokyo: Gendai jaanarizumu shuppankai, 1972. 瀬戸美喜雄, 民衆の宗教意識と変革のエネルギー, 丸山照雄編, 変革期の宗教, 現代ジャーナリズム出版会

Shiba Kōkan. *Shumparō hikki*. In *Nihon zuihitsu hikki*. Vol. 1. Tokyo: Yoshikawa kōbunkan, 1936. 司馬江漢, 春波樓筆記, 日本随筆筆記, 吉川弘文館

Shibahara Takuji. "Hanbaku shoseiryoku no seikaku." In *Iwanami kōza Nihon rekishi*. Vol. 14, *Kindai* 1. Tokyo: Iwanami shoten, 1962. 芝原拓自, 反幕諸勢力の性格, 岩波講座日本歴史

Shimomura Fujio. "Nichi-Ro sensō no seikaku." *Kokusai seiji* 3 (1957): 137–52. 下村富士男, 日露戦争の性格, 国際政治

Shimomura Fujio. *Meiji shonen jōyaku kaisei shi no kenkyū*. Tokyo: Yoshikawa kōbunkan, 1962 (1957): 137–52. 下村富士男, 明治初年条約改正史の研究, 吉川弘文館

Shimoyama Saburō. "Fukushima jiken shōron." *Rekishigaku kenkyū*. 186 (August 1955): 1–13. 下山三郎, 福島事件小論, 歴史学研究

Shinano Kyōikukai, ed. *Shōzan zenshū*. 5 vols. Nagano: Shinano Mainichi shimbunsha, 1934–5. 信濃教育会編, 象山全集, 長野：信濃毎日新聞社

Shinobu Seizaburō, ed. *Nihon gaikō shi: 1853–1972*. 2 vols. Tokyo: Mainichi shimbunsha, 1974. 信夫清三郎編, 日本外交史, 1853–1972, 毎日新聞社

Skocpol, Theda. *States and Social Revolutions*. Cambridge. England: Cambridge University Press, 1979.

Shōji Kichinosuke. *Tōhoku shohan hyakushō ikki no kenkyū: shiryō shūsei*. Tokyo: Ochanomizu shobō, 1969. 庄司吉之助, 東北諸藩百姓一揆の研究：史料集成, 御茶の水書房

Shōji Kichinosuke. *Yonaoshi ikki no kenkyū*. Tokyo: Azekura shobō, 1970. 庄司吉之助, 世直し一揆の研究, 校倉書房

Smethhurst, Richard J. *Agricultural Development and Tenancy Disputes in Japan, 1870–1940*. Princeton, N.J.: Princeton University Press, 1986.

Smith, Thomas C. *The Agrarian Origins of Modern Japan*. Stanford, Calif.: Stanford University Press, 1959.

Smith, Thomas C. "Ōkura Nagatsune and the Technologists." In Craig and Shively, eds. *Personality in Japanese History*.

Sonoda Hiyoshi. *Etō Shimpei to Saga no ran*. Tokyo: Shin jinbutsu ōraisha, 1978. 園田日吉, 江藤新平と佐賀の乱, 新人物往来社

Stephan, John J. *The Kuril Islands: The Russo-Japanese Frontier in the Pacific*. New York: Oxford University Press, 1975.

Sugi Hitoshi. "Kaseiki no shakai to bunka." In Aoki Michio and Yamada Tadao, eds. *Tempōki no seiji to shakai*. Vol. 6 of *Kōza Nihon kinseishi*. Tokyo: Yūhikaku, 1981. 杉仁, "化政期の社会と文化," 青木美智男, 山田忠雄編, 天保期の政治と社会 (講座日本近世史 6), 有斐閣

Sugimoto, Yoshio. "Structural Sources of Popular Revolts and the Tōbaku Movement at the Time of the Meiji Restoration." *Journal of Asian Studies*. 34 (August 1975): 875–89.

Sugiura Mimpei. *Ishin zenya no bungaku*. Tokyo: Iwanami shoten, 1967. 杉浦明平, 維新前夜の文学, 岩波書店

Sugiura Mimpei. *Kirishitan, rangaku shū*. Vol. 16 of *Nihon no shisō*. Tokyo: Chikuma shobō, 1970. 杉浦明平, キリシタン／蘭学集, 日本の思想, 筑摩書房

Sumiya Mikio. *Dai Nihon teikoku no shiren*. Vol. 22 of *Nihon no rekishi*, Tokyo: Chūō kōronsha, 1965. 隅谷三喜男, 大日本帝国の試煉, 日本の歴史, 中央公論社

Suzuki Shigetane. *Engishiki norito kōgi*. Tokyo: Kokusho kankōkai, 1978. 鈴木重胤, 延喜式祝詞講義, 国書刊行会

Tahara Tsuguo et al., eds. *Hirata Atsutane, Ban Nobutomo, Okuni Takamasa*. Vol. 50 of *Nihon shisō taikei*. Tokyo: Iwanami shoten, 1973. 田原嗣郎等編, 平田篤胤, 伴信友, 大國隆正, 日本思想大系, 岩波書店

Takagi Shunsuke. *Eejanaika*. Tokyo: Kyōikusha rekishi shinsho, 1979. 高木俊輔, ええじゃないか, 教育社歴史新書

Takahashi Tetsuo. *Fukushima jiken*. Tokyo: San'ichi Shobō, 1970. 高橋哲夫, 福島事件, 三一書房

Takahashi Tetsuo. *Fukushima jiyū minkenka retsuden*. Fukushima: Fukushima mimpōsha, 1967. 高橋哲夫, 福島自由民権家列伝, 福島：福島民報社

Takasu Yoshijirō, ed. *Mitogaku taikei*. 10 vols. Tokyo: Mitogaku taikei kankōkai, 1941. 高須芳次郎編, 水戸学大系, 水戸学大系刊行会

Tamamuro Taijō. *Seinan sensō*. Tokyo: Shibundo, 1958. 圭室諦成, 西南戦争, 至文堂

Tanaka Akira. *Meiji ishin*. Vol. 24 of *Nihon no rekishi*. Tokyo: Shōgakkan, 1976. 田中彰, 明治維新, 日本の歴史, 小学館

Tokuda Kōjun, ed. *Shiryō Utsunomiya han shi*. Tokyo: Kashiwa shobō, 1971. 徳田浩淳, 史料宇都宮藩史, 柏書房

Totman, Conrad. "Political Reconciliation in the Tokugawa Bakufu: Abe Masahiro and Tokugawa Nariaki, 1844–1852." In Craig and Shively, eds. *Personality in Japanese History*.

Totman, Conrad. "Fudai Daimyo and the Collapse of the Tokugawa Bakufu." *Journal of Asian Studies* 34 (May 1975): 581–91.

Totman, Conrad. *The Collapse of the Tokugawa Bakufu, 1862–1868*. Honolulu: University of Hawaii Press, 1980.

Tottori-han shi. 7 vols. Tottori: Tottori kenritsu toshokan, 1971. 鳥取藩史, 鳥取：鳥取県立図書館

Tōyama Shigeki. *Meiji ishin*. Tokyo: Iwanami shoten, 1951. 遠山茂樹, 明治維新, 岩波書店

Tsuda Hideo. "Tempō kaikaku no keizaishiteki igi." In Furushima, ed. *Nihon keizaishi taikei*. Vol. 4, 1965. 津田秀夫, 天保改革の経済史的意義, 古島敏雄編, 日本経済史大系, 東京大学出版会

Tsuji Tatsuya. "Tokugawa Nariaki to Mizuno Tadakuni." *Jimbutsu sōsho furoku*, no. 154. Tokyo: Yoshikawa kōbunkan. 辻達也, 徳川斉昭と水野忠邦, 人物叢書付録, 吉川弘文館

Uete Michiari. *Nihon kindai shisō no keisei*. Tokyo: Iwanami shoten, 1974. 植手通有, 日本近世思想の形成, 岩波書店

Umegaki, Michio. "From Domain to Prefecture." In Jansen and Rozman, eds. *Japan in Transition*.

Umegaki, Michio. *After the Restoration: The Beginnings of Japan's Modern*

State. New York: New York University Press, 1988.

Vlastos, Stephen. *Peasant Protests and Uprisings in Tokugawa Japan*. Berkeley and Los Angeles: University of California Press, 1986.

Wakabayashi, Bob Tadashi. *Anti-Foreign Thought and Western Learning in Early Modern Japan*. Cambridge, Mass.: Harvard University Press, 1985.

Walthall, Anne. "Narratives of Peasant Uprisings in Japan." *Journal of Japanese Studies* 42 (May 1983): 571–87.

Watanabe Shūjirō. *Abe Masahiro jiseki*. 2 vols. Tokyo, 1910. 渡辺修二郎, 阿部正弘事蹟

Webb, Hershel. *The Japanese Imperial Institution in the Tokugawa Period*. New York: Columbia University Press, 1968.

Westney, D. Eleanor. *Imitation and Innovation: The Transfer of Western Organizational Patterns to Meiji Japan*. Cambridge: Harvard University Press, 1987.

Wilson, George. "The Bakumatsu Intellectual in Action: Hashimoto Sanai and the Political Crisis of 1858." In Craig and Shively, eds. *Personality in Japanese History*.

Yamamura, Kozo. *A Study of Samurai Income and Entrepreneurship: Quantitative Analyses of Economic and Social Aspects of the Samurai in Tokugawa and Meiji Japan*. Cambridge, Mass.: Harvard University Press, 1974.

Yamamura Kozo. "The Meiji Land Tax Reform and Its Effects." In Jansen and Rozman, eds. *Japan in Transition*.

Yamanaka Einosuke. *Nihon kindai kokka no keisei to kanryōsei*. Tokyo: Kōbundō, 1974. 山中永之佑, 日本近代国家の形成と官僚制, 弘文堂

Yamanaka Hisao. "Bakumatsu hansei kaikaku no hikaku hanseishiteki kenkyū." *Chihōshi kenkyū*. 14 (1954): 47–56. 山中壽夫, 幕末藩政改革の比較藩政史的研究, 地方史研究

Yamazaki Masashige, ed. *Yokoi Shōnan ikō*. Meiji Shoin, 1942. 山崎正董編, 横井小楠遺稿, 明治書院

Yasuba, Yasukichi. "Anatomy of the Debate on Japanese Capitalism." *Journal of Japanese Studies* 2 (Autumn 1975): 63–82.

Yasumaru Yoshio. *Nihon kindaika to minshū shisō*. Tokyo: Aoki shoten, 1974. 安丸良夫, 日本近代化と民衆思想, 青木書店

Yates, Charles L. "Restoration and Rebellion in Satsuma: The Life of Saigō Takamori (1827–1877)." Ph.D. diss., Princeton University, 1987.

Yokoyama Toshio. *Hyakushō ikki to gimin denshō*. Tokyo: Kyōikusha rekishi shinsho, 1977. 横山十四男, 百姓一揆と義民伝承, 教育社歴史新書

GLOSSARY-INDEX